# THE SACRED BOOKS OF THE HINDUS

TRANSLATED BY VARIOUS SANSKRIT SCHOLARS

# THE DAILY PRACTICE OF THE HINDUS

# THE SACRED BOOKS OF THE HINDUS

OTHER TITLES AVAILABLE FROM THIS SERIES

The Upanisads

Yajnavalkaya Smriti, in 2 Parts

The Chhandogya Upanisad, 2 volumes

Patanjali's Yoga Sutras

The Vedantasutras of Bhadrayana, 2 volumes

The Vaisesika Sutras of Kanada

The Narada Sutras

Sandilya Sutras

The Nyaya Sutras of Gotama

The Gheranda Samhita

The Purva Mimamsa Sutras.of Jaimini

The Samkhya Philosophy, 2 volumes

The Brihajjatakam of Varaha Mihira

The Sukraniti

The Brihadaranyaka Upanisad, 2 volumes

The Siva Samhita

The Positive Background of Hindu Sociology, 2 volumes

The Matsya Purana, 2 volumes

The Svetasvatara Upanisad

Devata. The Hindu Gods

The Daily Practice of the Hindus

Introduction to the Yoga Philosophy

Studies in the First Six Upanisads

Sri Narada Pancharatram

The Bhakti-Ratnavali

The Srimad Devi Bhagawatam, 2 volumes

The Adhyatma Ramayana

The Aitareya Brahmanam, 2 volumes

The set is also available seperately

**THE DAILY PRACTICE OF THE HINDUS**

**THIS VOLUME IS A PART OF THE SERIES**

**THE SACRED BOOKS OF THE HINDUS**

INDIVIDUAL VOLUMES BEING RELEASED ON DEMAND FROM THE READERS


First published by COSMO 2008

ISBN 81-307-0536-2

***Published by***
COSMO PUBLICATIONS
*for*
GENESIS PUBLISHING PVT. LTD.
24-B, Ansari Road, Darya Ganj,
New Delhi-110 002,
INDIA

***Printed and bound in India***

# THE SACRED BOOKS OF THE HINDUS

TRANSLATED BY VARIOUS SANSKRIT SCHOLARS

EDITED BY

MAJOR B. D. BASU, I.M.S. (RETIRED)

# THE DAILY PRACTICE OF THE HINDUS

CONTAINING THE MORNING AND MIDDAY DUTIE:

By

SRISA CHANDRA VASU

Cosmo Publications

2008 New Delhi

# FOREWORD.

In this book both the Vaidikî and Tântrikî Sandhyâs are given. All twice-born persons are entitled to the first; while the Tântrikî is meant for all mankind, without distinction of caste, race or creed. The Yajur Vedi Sandhyâ is based upon the text published by Pandit Devi Datt Joshi. It is an excellent hand-book. A chapter on the Sandhyâ of the Ṛig-Vedins as well as one on the Tântrikî Sandhyâ is added.

In the present edition, the Midday Duties, namely, the worship of Viṣṇu, Shiva, &c., is also given, as well as the Five Great Sacrifices. The book is more than double the size of the last edition.

I have consulted, in giving commentary on the Vedic mantras, the edition of the Ânandâśrama series also.

The translation of the Vedic mantras is, in many cases, my own and, in some instances, taken from Griffith, MaxMûller, Whitney, and Peterson.

My sons-in-law, Babu Nandalal Sinha, M.A., B.L., and Professor Lalit Mohan Kar, Kavyatirtha, M.A., B.L., have greatly assisted me in revising this edition for the press.

S. C. V.

# CONTENTS.

Page.

## CHAPTER XII.

### *Pûjâ of Nârâyaṇa.*



## CHAPTER XIII.

### *Śiva Pûjâ.*

Page.

## CHAPTER IX.

### *Midday duties.*



## APPENDIX.

# THE DAILY PRACTICE OF THE HINDUS.

## CHAPTER I.

A HINDU generally belongs to one of the five divisions of the Hindu Religion. He is either a Śaiva or a Vaiṣṇava or a worshipper of Gaṇapati or of Śakti or of Sûrya. Besides this, he belongs to a particular Veda. The daily practice and Sandhyâ systems, therefore, are not uniform in all parts of India. As a type we give the following, as current in Bengal, among the Sâma-Vedi Brâhmaṇas and as in the Upper India among the Yajur-Vedis.

One day and night consists of 24 hours. It is divided into eight parts, each consisting of three hours, called Yâma or Prahara. Half of this is called Yâmârdha or one hour and a half, which is the unit of calculation. The whole day and night is thus divided into 16 Yâmârdhas. The daily practice of a Hindu is shown in the following table :—

I. *Morning duties* :—

16th Yâmârdha. 4-30 A. M. to 6 A. M.

(*a*) Awakening, (*b*) Necessary washings and ablutions, (*c*) Sipping water or Âchamana, (*d*) Cleansing the teeth, (*e*) Bathing and Tarpaṇa, (*f*) Sandhyâ and Meditation.

II. *Forenoon duties* :—

1st Yâmârdha. 6 A. M. to 7-30 A. M. Worship of the special Deity, Guru, &c.

2nd. 7-30 A. M. to 9 A. M. Study of sacred works (Vedas).

3rd. 9 A. M. to 10-30 A. M. Working for the family maintenance.

III. *Noontide duties* :—

4th. 10-30 A. M. to 12 noon.

(*a*) Bath, (*b*) Tarpaṇa, (*c*) Sandhyâ, (*d*) Suryopasthâna, (*e*) Brahma yajña, (*f*) Devapujâs, as Gaṇeśa, Śiva, Viṣṇu pujâ, &c.

5th. 12 to 1-30 P. M.

(1) Five great sacrifices :

(*a*) To Bhutas, (*b*) To Pitṛis, (*c*) To Devas, (*d*) To Brahma, (*e*) To men.

(2) Taking food.

IV. *Afternoon duties* :—

6th. 1-30 P. M. to 3 P.M. and 7th. 3 P. M. to 4-30 P.M. } Study of secular literature, Itihâsa, Purâṇas, &c.

V. *Evening duties* :—

8th. 4-30 P. M. to 6 P. M.

(*a*) Seeing friends, (*b*) Evening Sandhyâ.

VI. *Night duties* :—

9th and 10th. 6 P. M. to 9 P. M.

(*a*) Duties omitted or left unperformed during the day.

(*b*) Form and direction of bed.

(*c*) Conversation, &c., with wife, children, &c.

11th to 15th. 9 P. M. to 4-30 A. M. Sleep.

The above will show the scope of the subject on which this book is written. It is not possible to fully treat all these within the compass of a single small treatise. We shall, therefore, describe the Sandhyâ and the Tarpaṇa duties in detail, while briefly touching on the other points.

Moreover, under our present circumstances, it is not possible for the majority of our people, to carry out these duties, in the order laid down above. Formerly, daily work for an hour and a half was sufficient for the acquisition of enough wealth, for the maintenance of one's family. The wants were few, the mode of living was simple, and the struggle for existence was not so keen. Now-a-days a person has to work between 10 A. M. and 4 P. M. generally to obtain his livelihood. So that the duties of the 4th to the 7th Yâmârdhas cannot be now performed at their proper time. Those duties, if performed at all, must be done either in the morning or in the evening.

Though all these duties cannot now be performed in their due order daily, yet it is good to know something of them, first, to keep alive the ideal, and secondly, to perform them strictly on those days when business is not done. On Sundays and holidays observed in schools, colleges and public offices, every good Hindu has an opportunity of performing his daily duties, as laid down by the ancient sages; and can thus keep alive the old type, in readiness for the coming of better conditions of life, when the whole world will again learn that the object of human life is not to waste it in a feverish anxiety and race after physical objects and comforts, but to use it in developing the mental, moral and spiritual powers latent in man.

These daily practices will also keep alive in him the memory that he is not only a physical being owing duties to his family, kinsmen, guests, and out-casts as well as to beasts and birds, but that he is a spiritual being as well, owing duties to the various grades of spiritual entities—Pitṛis, Devas, &c., and, while teaching him the laws of health and good living, it will cultivate his moral nature by developing love, kindness, and charity, together with a firm reliance on the God in him.

**On awakening he should recite :—**

ब्रह्मा मुरारिस्त्रिपुरान्तकारी
भानुः शशी भूमिसुतो बुधश्च ।
गुरुश्च शुक्रः शनिराहुकेतू
कुर्वन्तु सर्वे मम सुप्रभातम् ॥

*Transliteration* :—Brahmâ, Murâri, Tripurânta-kârî,
Bhânuḥ, Śasî, Bhûmi-suto, Budhaś cha,
Guruś cha Śukraḥ, Śanî, Râhu-Ketû,
Kurvantu sarve mama suprabhâtam.

"Let Brahmâ, Viṣṇu (the foe of Mura), Śiva (the slayer of Tripura), the Sun, Moon, Mars, Mercury, Jupiter, Venus, Saturn, the ascending and the descending Nodes, let all (the Celestials) make the morning auspicious for me."

On awakening from sleep, but before leaving his bed, the first thing that he should do is to pay homage to the great God of his system and the Planetary Spirits working out His will in connection with it. This is done by reciting the first śloka, which shows us the Great God in His three-fold aspect of Brahmâ, the Creator, Viṣṇu, the Preserver, and Śiva, the Regenerator, and His minor manifestations, in the nine Planetary Logoi who control and guide the evolution of each planet, namely, Bhânu, the Moon, Mars, Mercury, Jupiter, Venus, Saturn, Râhu (Uranus?) and Ketu (Neptune?). Bhânu ordinarily means the Sun, but may it really not refer to the planet nearest to the sun, the planet Vulcan? So also the Moon may refer to the Earth, as according to the mystic teaching the latter is the child of the first. Râhu and Ketu in exoteric writings mean the two nodes of the moon, the passage of the earth and the moon through which causes the Solar and the Lunar eclipses. These, however, cannot be strictly called "Planets," as they are mathematical points rather than physical bodies. May it not be that they are used either as blinds or that they refer to Uranus and Neptune? The story of the genesis of these planets shows that they might originally have referred to the planets, Uranus and Neptune. When nectar came out from the churning of the cosmic ocean, the Devas began to drink it. An Asura, being disguised as a Deva, was found drinking it too. The immortal fluid had not reached below his throat, when his head was cut off by the Chakra of Viṣṇu. The effect of the Amṛita was such that the Asura's head and trunk became immortal planets—and, though the Asura did not become a Deva or a "shining one," like other planets (for Uranus and Neptune are not visible to the ordinary sight), yet it became immortal in its own way. Hence Uranus and Neptune, though planets, are still outside our system of evolution, and their bodies are that of an Asura, "the elder son of Parjâpati," *i.e.*, these belong to a former Kalpa and not to the present Śveta-Varâha-Kalpa.

The great beings who control these are meant here by these names, and not the physical visible planets--though the physical planets need not be ignored, for each planet is the physical vesture of its ruler, as our physical body is the nucleus of all our higher bodies—Prâṇamaya, Manomaya, &c. And as our physical body is surrounded and interpenetrated, layer after layer, by these subtle bodies, forming the human aura which extends in the case of advanced souls to several miles away from the physical bodies, in the form of a sphere, so the subtle bodies of these Planetary Angels (Logoi) extend in radiation and form spheres intersecting each other, and interpenetrating to some extent one the other, while the sphere of the great God, the Parama-Iśvara, is a sphere interpenetrated by none, but penetrating all, embracing all, including all, ruling all and controlling all. And therefore He is called Akhandamandalâkâra—the unbroken sphere—the only sphere which influences all, but is influenced by none. On the other hand, the influences of the spheres of the Planetary Angels are varied in intensity, or otherwise, according to the aspects or the positions which, from time to time, they occupy with regard to each other.

**Then remember the Teacher :—**

प्रातः शिरसि शुक्लाब्जे द्विनेत्रं द्विभुजं गुरुम् ।
प्रसन्नवदनं शान्तं स्मरेत्तन्नामपूर्वकम् ॥

*Transliteration* :—Prâtaḥ śirasi śuklâbje, Dvi-netram dvi-bhujam Gurum,
Prasanna-vadanam śântam, smaret tan-nâma-pûrvakam.

*Word meaning* :—Prâtaḥ, in the morning ; śirasi, in the head ; śuklâbje, in the white-lotus ; dvi-netram, two-eyed ; dvi-bhujam, two-handed ; Gurum, the Guru ; Prasanna, benignant ; vadanam, face ; śântam, full of peace ; smaret, let him remember ; tad, his ; nâma, name ; pûrvakam, preceded by (*i.e.*, first uttering).

"In the morning let him remember his Guru, uttering his name and thinking him as in the white lotus of his head, having two eyes, and two hands, with benignant countenance, full of peace."

**Let him then salute the Teacher reciting :—**

ओं नमोऽस्तु गुरवे तस्मै इष्टदेवस्वरूपिणे ।
यस्य वाक्यामृतं हन्ति विषं संसारसंज्ञकम् ॥

*Transliteration* :—Om Namostu, Gurave tasmai, Iṣṭa deva—svarûpiṇe,
Yasya Vâkyâmṛitam hanti, viṣam samsâra—samjñakam.

*Word meaning* :—Om, aum ; namaḥ, salutation ; astu, let there be ; Gurave, to the Guru ; tasmai, to him ; iṣṭa, worshipped (tutelary) ;—deva, God ;—svarûpiṇe, having the form or essential nature ; yasya, whose ; vâkya, speech ; amṛitam, nectar ; hanti, destroys ; viṣam, poison ; samsâra, transmigratory existence ; samjñakam, called.

"Salutation to that Guru who is Iṣṭa Deva incarnate, the nectar of whose speech destroys the poison called Samsâra."

Next to the great God in his threefold aspect, and His Emanations, the Planetary Spirits or Logoi, there is no higher object of veneration and homage to man, than his Gurudeva, the Man-God living in the eternal and for ever.

**Then let him think:-**

अहं देवो न चान्योऽस्मि ब्रह्मैवाहं न शोकभाक् ।

सच्चिदानन्दरूपोऽहं नित्यमुक्तस्वभाववान् ॥

*Transliteration:*—Aham devo na chânyo'smi, Brahmaivâham na śokabhâk,

Sach-chid-ânanda-rûpo'ham, nitya-mukta-svabhâvavân.

*Word meaning:*—Aham, I; devah, a deity; na, not; cha, and; anyaḥ, another; asmi (I) am; Brahma, Brahman; eva, verily, even; aham, I; na, not; śoka-bhâk, sorrow-part, partaking of sorrow; sat, being; chit, intelligence; ânanda, bliss; rûpa, form; aham, I; nitya, always; mukta, free; svabhâva-vân, having the nature.

"I am Divine and not anything else. I am, indeed, Brahman, above all sorrows; my form is existence, intelligence and bliss; and eternally free is my nature."

Next after his God and his Guru, the Hindu reminds himself, on awakening, as to the true nature of his own self and its Eternal Destiny. He reminds himself that his true real self is neither this man of clay: of blood, bones and flesh; nor this man of passion: of love and hatred, attraction and repulsion; nor this man of intellect, analysing and synthesising. But he, the humble devotee, is in essence one with his Guru and one with his God—Eternal Monad "developing his powers in Time and Space." Therefore he repeats to himself the above śloka.

It is necessary in this age of sordid interests and low ideals, that the divine origin of man should be asserted in the strongest language possible, that he may be made to look upon himself as the reflected image of God, the Eternal, the All-knowing, the All-joy. Unless the man realises the greatness of his own Eternal Self, he will not leave the pettinesses and littlenesses caused by the upâdhis with which in his ignorance he identifies himself.

On awakening, therefore, the Hindu remembers and reminds himself of these Three Great Truths, the God with His Cosmic Agents, the Guru with his tender compassion, and the Self with his progressive destiny.

But this last fact is sometimes liable to misapprehension; and so, he should express his humility and weakness in the following verses.

**Let him repeat:-**

लोकेश चैतन्यमयाधिदेव श्रीकान्त विष्णो भवदाज्ञयैव ।

प्रातः समुत्थाय तव प्रियार्थं संसारयात्रामनुवर्त्तयिष्ये ॥

जानामि धर्मं न च मे प्रवृत्तिः जानाम्यधर्मं न च मे निवृत्तिः ।
त्वया हृषीकेश हृदि स्थितेन यथा नियुक्तोऽस्मि तथा करोमि ॥

*Transliteration* : —Lokeśa, Chaitanya-mayâdhideva,
Śrikânta, Viṣno, bhavadâjñayaiva,
Prâtaḥ Ṣamutthâya tava priyârtham
Saṃsâra yâtrâm anuvarttayiṣye.
Jânâmi dharmam na cha me pravṛittiḥ,
Jânâmyadharmam na cha me nivrittiḥ,
Tvayâ Hṛiṣikeśa hṛidi sthitena,
Yathâ niyukto'smi tathâ karômi.

"Oh Lord of the Universe! Oh All-Consciousness! Presiding Deity of all! Lord of Fortune! Oh Viṣṇu! at Thy bidding, and to please Thee alone, I (rise this morning and) enter upon the discharge of my worldly duties."

"I know what is Dharma (righteousness), yet I feel no attraction for it; I know what is not Dharma, yet I do not have any repulsion for it. Oh Lord of the senses! Oh Thou, seated in the heart! (may) I do Thy commands as ordered by Thee (in my conscience)."

And so the fourth thing that a Hindu must remember on awakening, is his lower, struggling, sinning self. It is only now and then that the flashes from his Higher True Self illumine his intellect. It may be lives before the Guru is reached, and æons before the God is found, but the ugly fact that stares him in the face, every hour and minute of his life, is his weak, wavering, sinning self. Therefore, lest the glory of his future destiny may turn his head, make him forgetful of his present limitations (as, unfortunately, is the case with some misguided persons), the Hindu recalls the fourth truth regarding his own present unworthiness and feebleness in the foregoing verses. Compare St. Paul's "The good which I would, I do not; but the evil which I would not, that I do."

Having thus reminded himself of his God, his Guru, his Higher Self, and his personal Self, the Hindu should dedicate all his actions that he is going to perform during the day to his Higher Being, and do all actions, not for the sake of his personal self, but because it is his duty to do so, because the duty of the faithful servant is to please his master; and hence he recites the above verses daily.

Having recited these mantras and making a mental programme of his day's work, he leaves the bed and touches the earth with his right foot uttering:—

"ॐ प्रियदत्तायै भुवे नमः"

Aum! priyadattâyai Bhuve namaḥ.

"Oh Earth, the giver of all that is good to us, I bow before Thee."

## CHAPTER II.

*The Guru and the Guru Stotra.*

This word Guru is sometimes very vaguely employed both in Sanskrit and English to designate every kind of teacher. But, strictly speaking, the word should be exclusively applied to the highest spiritual teachers of humanity, while the words Âchârya and Upâdhyâya may be reserved for indicating secular and semi-secular teachers. The Guru, therefore, to whom the Hindu ought really to render his homage, is the particular liberated soul, Jivanmukta—the person who has united his Lower to the Higher Self—who, though on the threshold of Nirvâṇa, voluntarily renounces that privilege, in order to remain behind, to serve his less-advanced brothers, and who would not enter the place of peace, so long as a single soul of his Kalpa remains to be served. These glorious Beings—the Gurus—the Flowers of humanity—the Directors of human evolution and Saviours of mankind—are those whom Indian wisdom has named *Jivanmuktas*—free souls—*Mahâtmâs*—Great souls. They belong to no particular nationality or country, to no particular creed or sect. The consciousness of humanity has borne unanimous testimony to the existence of these Great Ones; for They have in all ages and climes been the guides and guardians of mankind, and have ever drawn devoted, sincere, selfless aspirants to their presence. Thus a Persian poet sings of them :—

گروهے عملدار و عزلت نشین ✻ قدم هاے خاکي دم آتشین
سلاطین عزلت گدایان حی ✻ منازل شناسان گم کرده پی
بسر وقت شان خلق کی ره برند ✻ که چون آب حیوان به ظلمت درانند
جو پروانه آتش بخود در زنند ✻ نه چون کرم پیله بخود در تنند
به یك ناله کوهے ز جابر کنند ✻ به یك ناله ملکے بهم بر زنند
چو باد انند پنهان و چالاك پو ✻ چو سنگ آنند خاموش و تسبیح گو
شب و روز در بحر سودا و سوز ✻ ندانند ز آشفتگي شب ز روز
چنان فتنه بر حسن صورت نگار ✻ که با حسن صورت ندارند کار

"There is a class of men who are men of practice and deed and who dwell in seclusion. Monarchs in seclusion, apparent beggars in life, knowers of the goal of life, but they appear as if they had lost their way. How can mankind find out their existence, when they are as hidden as the fabulous waters of life. Like the self-sacrificing moth, they burn themselves in the fire of love, they are not like the selfish caterpillar that smothers itself in its own cocoon. They have a body of dust but breath of fire, with one shout they uproot a mountain from its base, with one wail they overturn a whole kingdom. Like wind they are invisible, but swift of motion, like stone they are silent, but always in devotion. Night and day, so immersed are they in the ocean of love and divine ecstacy, that they do not know the night from the day. So enchanted are they with the beauty of the Creator of the external appearances, that they have nothing to do with the beauty of appearance."

Such are the only Gurus of the Hindus—nay, of all humanity. It is to such a Guru that the Hindu addresses his *stotra*, when he says :—

अखण्डमण्डलाकारं व्याप्तं येन चराचरम् ।
तत् पदं दर्शितं येन तस्मै श्रीगुरवे नमः ॥ १ ॥
अज्ञानतिमिरान्धस्य ज्ञानाञ्जनशलाकया ।
चक्षुरुन्मीलितं येन तस्मै श्रीगुरवे नमः ॥ २ ॥
गुरुर्ब्रह्मा गुरुर्विष्णुर्गुरुर्देवो महेश्वरः ।
गुरुरेव परं ब्रह्म तस्मै श्रीगुरवे नमः ॥ ३ ॥
स्थावरं जङ्गमं व्याप्तं यत् किञ्चित् सचराचरम् ।
तत्पदं दर्शितं येन तस्मै श्रीगुरवे नमः ॥ ४ ॥
चिन्मयं व्यापितं सर्वं त्रैलोक्यं सचराचरम् ।
तत् पदं दर्शितं येन तस्मै श्रीगुरवे नमः ॥ ५ ॥
सर्वश्रुतिशिरोरत्नविराजितपदाम्बुजः ।
वेदान्ताम्बुजसूर्यो यो तस्मै श्रीगुरवे नमः ॥ ६ ॥
चैतन्यो शाश्वतो शान्तो व्योमातीतो निरञ्जनः ।
बिन्दुनादकलातीतो तस्मै श्रीगुरवे नमः ॥ ७ ॥
ज्ञानशक्तिसमारूढस्तत्त्वमालाविभूषितः ।
भुक्तिमुक्तिप्रदाता च तस्मै श्रीगुरवे नमः ॥ ८ ॥
अनेकजन्मसंप्राप्तकर्मबन्धविदाहिने ।
आत्मज्ञानप्रदानेन तस्मै श्रीगुरवे नमः ॥ ९ ॥
शोषणं भवसिन्धोश्च ज्ञापनं सारसम्पदः ।
गुरोः पादोदकं सम्यक् तस्मै श्रीगुरवे नमः ॥ १० ॥
न गुरोरधिकं तत्त्वं न गुरोरधिकं तपः ।
तत्त्वज्ञानात् परं नास्ति तस्मै श्रीगुरवे नमः ॥ ११ ॥
मन्नाथः श्रीजगन्नाथो मद्गुरुः श्रीजगद्गुरुः ।
मदात्मा सर्वभूतात्मा तस्मै श्रीगुरवे नमः ॥ १२ ॥
गुरुरादिरनादिश्च गुरुः परमदैवतम् ।
गुरोः परतरं नास्ति तस्मै श्रीगुरवे नमः ॥ १३ ॥

त्वमेव माता च पिता त्वमेव, त्वमेव बन्धुश्च सखा त्वमेव ।
त्वमेव विद्या द्रविणं त्वमेव, त्वमेव सर्वं मम देवदेव ॥ १४ ॥

*Transliteration* :—Akhaṇḍa maṇḍalâkâram, Vyâptam yena charâcharam,
Tat padam darśitam yena, Tasmai śrigurave namaḥ.

*Word meaning* :—Akhaṇḍa, unbroken; maṇḍala, sphere; âkâram, form; Vyâptam, is pervaded; Yena, by whom; Charâcharam, universe of the moving and the non-moving beings; Tatpadam, that supreme being; Darśitam, has been shown; Yena, by whom; Tasmai, to that; Śrigurave, glorious Guru; namaḥ, salutations.

1. "Salutations to that glorious Guru who has shown to me that Supreme Being, who in the form of a sphere of unbroken glory pervades this universe of the moving and non-moving beings."

*Transliteration* :—Ajñâna timirândhasya, Jñânâñjana śalâkayâ,
Chakṣurunmîlitam yena, Tasmai śrigurave namaḥ.

*Word meaning* :—Ajñâna, ignorance; Timira, (by) the darkness; Andhasya, blinded; Jñâna, wisdom; Añjana, collyrium; Śalâkayâ, stick; Chakṣu, eye; Unmîlitam, opened; Yena, by whom.

2. "Salutations to that glorious Guru who, when my sight was blinded by the darkness of ignorance, restored to it the light of knowledge and truth."

*Transliteration* :—Gurur Brahmâ gurur Viṣṇur, Gurur devo Maheśvaraḥ,
Gurur eva param Brahmâ, Tasmai &c., &c., &c.

*Word meaning* :—Guruḥ, the Master; Brahmâ, (is) Brahmâ; Guruḥ, the Master; Viṣṇuḥ, (is) Viṣṇu; Guruḥ, the Master; Devaḥ, (is) the God; Maheśvaraḥ, Śiva; the great Lord; Guruḥ, the Master; Eva, even; Param, (is) Supreme; Brahma, Brahman.

3. "Salutations to the glorious Guru; for Guru is Brahmâ, He is Viṣṇu, and even the Lord Mahâdeva is He: nay, the Guru is even the Supreme Brahman Itself."

*Transliteration* :—Sthâvaram jaṅgamam vyâptam, Yat kiñchit sacharâcharam,
Tatpadam darśitam yena, Tasmai, &c.

*Word meaning* :—Sthâvaram, fixed; Jaṅgamam, moving; Vyâptam, pervaded; Yat, what; Kiñchit, soever; Sacharâcharam, with moveable or immoveable; Tat, that; Padam, state; Darśitam, was shown; Yena, by whom.

4. "Salutations to that glorious Guru who has revealed to me that Highest State which pervades all that is fixed or moving, all that exists, whether animate or inanimate."

*Transliteration* :—Chinmayam Vyâpitam sarvam, Trailokyam sacharâcharam,
Tatpadam darśitam yena, Tasmai, &c.

*Word meaning* :—Chinmayam, pure Intelligence ; Vyâpitam, is pervaded ; Sarvam, all ; Trailokyam, the three worlds ; Sacharâcharam, moveable and immoveable ; Tat, that ; Padam, state ; Darśitam, was shown ; Yena, by whom.

5. "Salutations to the glorious Guru who has shown me that Supreme All-Intelligence that pervades the three Lokas (physical, astral and mental) with all that moves and stays therein."

*Transliteration* :—Sarva śruti śiroratna, Virâjita padâmbujah,
Vedântâmbuja sûryo yo, Tasmai, &c., &c.

*Word meaning* : —Sarva, all ; Śrutiḥ, revelation ; Śiroratnaḥ, crest-jewel ; Virâjitah, are decorated ; Padâmbujaḥ, lotus of feet ; Vedânta-âmbuja, the lotus of Vedânta ; Sûryaḥ, sun ; Yah, who.

6. "Salutations to the glorious Guru whose lotus feet are bedecked with the crest-jewels of all Revelations, and who is the sun that makes the bud of Vedânta to blossom."

*Transliteration* :—Chaitanyaḥ śâśvataḥ śânto, Vyomâtîto nirañjanaḥ,
Vindu nâda kalâtîto, Tasmai, &c.

*Word meaning* :—Chaitanyaḥ, intelligence ; Śâśvataḥ, eternal ; Śântaḥ, calm ; Vyomâtîtaḥ, above space or vyoma ; nirañjanaḥ, untouched by pollution ; Vindu, point, or nirvânic plane ; nâda, sound ; Kalâtîtaḥ, above kalâ, or plane of mahâ-nirvâna.

7. "Salutations to the glorious Guru who is Intelligence Itself, the Eternal, the Calm above space, untouched by pollution, and above the Vindu (mental ?), Nâda (Arûpa), and Kalâ (Nirvâṇa ?)."

*Transliteration* :—Jñânaśakti samârûḍha, Tattva mâlâ vibhûṣitaḥ,
Bhukti mukti pradâtâ cha, Tasmai, &c.

*Word meaning* :—Jñâna, wisdom, intelligence ; Śakti, power ; Samârudhaḥ, riding, controlling ; Tattva, truth ; Mâlâ, garland ; Vibhûṣitaḥ, adorned ; Bhukti, worldly prosperity ; Mukti, salvation ; pradâtâ, giver ; Cha, and.

8. "Salutations to the glorious Guru who controls the Jñâna Śakti, who is adorned with the garland of Tattvas and from whom proceed both worldly and spiritual welfare."

*Transliteration* :—Anekajanmasamprâpta, Karmabandhavidâhine,
Âtmajñânapradânena, Tasmai, &c.

*Word meaning* :—Aneka, more than one, many ; Janma, birth ; Samprâpta, accumulated ; Karma, work, karma ; bandha, bond ; Vidâhine, to the burner ; to him who burns up ; Âtma-jñâna, Self-knowledge ; pradânena, by giving.

9. "Salutations to the glorious Guru who, by giving the knowledge of the Self, burns up the bonds of the accumulated Karmas of many a birth."

*Transliteration* :—Śoṣanam bhava sindhoś cha, Jñâpanam sâra sampadaḥ.
Guroḥ pâdo'dakam samyak, Tasmai, &c.

*Word meaning* :—Śoṣanam, drying up ; Bhava, world ; Sindhoḥ, of the ocean ; Cha, and ; Jñâpanam, revealing ; Sâra, essential, real ; Sampadah, beatitude ; Guroḥ, of the Master ; Pâda, foot ; Udakam, water ; Samyak, completely.

10. "Salutations to the glorious Guru, the water sanctified by the touch of whose feet dries up the ocean of unreal existence, and reveals the real beatitude."

*Transliteration* :—Na guror adhikam tattvam, Na guror adhikam tapaḥ,
Tattvajñânât param nâsti, Tasmai, &c.

*Word meaning* :—Na, not ; Guroḥ, than the guru ; Adhikam, greater ; Tapah, penance ; Tattva-jñânât, than the knowledge of truth ; Param, highest ; Nâsti, there is not.

11. "There is no Tattva higher than the Guru, there is no Tapas higher than the Guru, there is nothing higher than Tattvajñâna : Salutations therefore to that glorious Guru."

*Transliteration* :—Mannâthah Śrî Jagan Nâtho, Madguruḥ Śrî Jagad-Guruḥ,
Madâtmâ sarvabhutâtmâ, Tasmai, &c.

*Word meaning* :—Man, my ; nâthaḥ, lord ; Śrî, Blessed ; Jagat, world ; Nâthaḥ, lord ; Mad guruḥ, My guru ; Śrî jagad-guru, is the blessed Teacher of the world ; Mad-âtmâ, my Self ; Sarva, all ; Bhutâtmâ, all creatures' Self.

12. "My Lord is the Lord of the universe, my Guru is the Guru of the universe, my Self is the Self of all creatures : Salutations to that glorious Guru."

*Transliteration* :—Gurur-Âdir anâdiś cha, Guruḥ paramadaivatam,
Guroh parataram nâsti, Tasmai, &c.

*Word meaning* :—Guruḥ, the Master ; Âdiḥ, the beginning ; Anâdiḥ, without beginning, end ; Parama, highest ; Daivatam, divinity ; Parataram, higher ; nâsti, there is not.

13. "The Guru is the beginning, the Guru is the end, and even eternity is He ; the Guru is the highest divinity : Salutations, therefore, to that glorious Guru."

*Transliteration* :—Tvam eva mâtâ cha pitâ tvam eva,
Tvam eva bandhuś cha sakhâ tvam eva,
Tvam eva vidyâ draviṇam tvam eva,
Tvam eva sarvam mama deva-deva.

*Word meaning* :—Tvam, thou ; Eva, even ; Mâtâ, mother ; Pitâ, father ; Bandhuḥ, friend, kinsman ; Vidyâ, learning ; Draviṇam, riches ; Sarva, everything ; Mama, my ; Deva-deva, O God of gods.

14. Thou art verily my mother, Thou art the father, indeed, my friend also art Thou and companion as well. Thou, indeed, art my learning, and possessions, too, art Thou, Thou art my all in all, O Lord, Thou art the God of gods.

## CHAPTER III.

### ON BATHING.

Then he should attend to the call of nature. If he lives in a village, he should go to a distance of 100 bows (200 yards) from the site, into a field in the south-west direction, and if he lives in a city, he should go to a distance four times the above, *i.e.*, 800 yards, and answer the nature's call, with his sacred thread resting on his ear or thrown in the form of a garland behind his back.

"Let him not eject urine or fæces in the high-way, nor on ashes, nor where kine are grazing."

"Nor on the tilled ground, nor in water, nor on wood raised for burning, nor, *unless he be in great need*, on a mountain, nor on the ruins of a temple, nor at any time on the nest of white ants."

"Nor in ditches with living creatures in them, nor walking, nor standing, nor *on the bank of a river*, nor on the summit of a mountain."

"Nor let him ever eject them looking at the wind, or at fire, or at a priest, or at the sun, or at water, or at cattle."

"But let him void his excrements, having covered the earth with wood, potsherds, dry leaves and grass, or the like, carefully suppressing his utterance, wrapping up his breast and his head."

"By day let him void them with his face to the north, by night with his face to the south; at the sunrise and at sunset, in the same manner as by day."

"In the shade or in darkness, whether by day or by night, let a Brâhmana ease nature with his face turned as he pleases; and in places where he fears injury to life from wild beasts or from reptiles."

"Of him, who should urine against fire, against the sun or against a twice-born man, the wind, all that is sacred would perish."—MANU.

Thus, after answering the nature's call he should wash his body. "Oily exudation, seminal fluids, blood, dandruff, urine, fæces, ear-wax, nailparings, phlegm, tear, concretions on the eyes, and sweat, are the twelve impurities of the human frame." Of these, the first six are purified by earth and water, and the remaining six by mere water. But he should avoid the mud of the following places:—

The earth thrown by wild ants, the earth thrown up by rats or mice, the earth taken from under the water, the earth which has been partly used by another for purificatory purposes, the earth fit for plastering the house, the earth having insects in it, and the earth thrown up by the plough. Any other clay may be used for purificatory purposes.

"By the man, who desires purity, one piece of earth, together with water, must be used for the conduit of urine, three for that of the fæces; so ten for one hand, that is, the left; seven for both."

"Such is the purification of married men; that of the students must be double; that of the hermits, triple; and that of the men wholly recluse, quadruple."

—MANU V, 136-137.

The above system can easily be followed even now-a-days in villages, but it is somewhat impossible in cities. According to our present mode of living, every house has got its privy, and so the necessity of going out has been avoided. Whether it is a change for the better or worse, it is doubtful. The old system had many advantages of its own, which the new cannot claim. It taught men to be more energetic, and gave them exercise in the morning, whether they liked it or not. It, moreover, made our houses neat and clean, and the necessity of setting apart a portion of it for the accumulation of filth was not required, nor was there any necessity then for costly systems of sanitation and drainage. Nor under the old system, did society compel a class of men to a degraded form of livelihood. In fact, if we ponder over the advantages of the old system, we shall find that its disadvantages are comparatively few, while its good points are many.

### Achaman.

Let him wash his hands and feet. Sitting by facing east, the feet should be washed first, beginning with the left foot: and then the right foot. After the feet, the hands should be washed. Then the śikhâ or the tuft of hair on the crown of the head should be tied.

*The Śikhâ.*—The śikhâ should be tied by reciting the Gâyatri, to be described later on. A Śûdra should recite the following mantra:—

ओं ब्रह्मवाक्यसहस्रेण शिववाक्यशतेन च ।

विष्णोर्नाम सहस्रेण शिखाग्रन्थिं करोम्यहम् ॥

*Transliteration*:—Om Brahma vâkya sahasreṇa, Śiva vâkya śatena cha.

Viṣṇor nâma sahasreṇa, Śikhâ granthim karomyaham.

*Translation*:—With the thousand names of Brahmâ and hundred names of Śiva, with the thousand names of Viṣṇu, I tie the tuft.

After purifying himself, he should perform Âchamana by sipping the water.

**Recite the following Mantra:—**

ॐ तद्विष्णोः परमं पदं सदा पश्यन्ति सूरयः ।

दिवीव चक्षुराततम् ॥

*Transliteration*:—Tad Viṣṇoḥ paramam padam sadâ paśyanti sûrayaḥ; Diviva chakṣur âtatam.

*Word meaning*:—*Tad*, That. The well-known padam taught in all scriptures, namely, svarga or heaven.

*Viṣṇoḥ*, of Viṣṇu, the all-pervading God. *Paramam*, the highest, the loftiest. *Padam*, place, *i.e.*, Svarga. *Sadâ*, always. *Paśyanti*, see, through scriptural vision. *Sûrayaḥ*, the learned, the wise, the princes and patrons of sacrifice. *Divi*, in the sky. *Iva*, as if, like. *Chakṣuḥ*, the eye. *Âtatam*, spread out, laid.

"Om, That Viṣṇu's seat supreme, the strong Ones ever see (Distinctly.) As roams the eye in sky (with unobstructed gaze)."

—Rig. I, 22. 20.

The *method* of performing Âchamana is thus laid down by Yâjñavalkya :—

"He is to sit facing the north or the east, with his hands between the knees, in a clean spot. A twice-born is daily to sip the water of Brahmatirtha. The beginning of the great finger (thumb) is the Brahmatîrtha. Water should be thrice drunk, the lips should be twice rubbed, the nose, ears and the eyes should be touched with water. The water should be in the natural pure state, free from foam and bubbles.

"The Brâhmaṇa becomes pure by the water reaching the heart, the Kṣatriya, the throat, and the Vaiśya, the palate. Women and Śûdras become pure, directly the waters once reach the tongue and the lips, respectively."

This Âchamana ceremony is considered to have an important and mysterious function in the life of a Hindu. It is *the* purification *par excellence.* It is to be performed after every act in which there might be the slightest suspicion of impurity. Relative as is the human nature, a man is sure to perform, in the course of the day, some acts which must be impure. However holy he may be, he must at least attend to the calls of nature and become physically impure. He must, therefore, constantly counterbalance the evil effect of one set of acts by the purificatory properties of another set of acts. Âchamana is one of the latter. It is to be performed at the beginning of every good work. Minute details as to the mode of its performance are to be found in the Śâstras. The full act consists (1) in the thrice sipping of water ; (2) then in rubbing the mouth with the portion of the palm nearest to the thumb, twice ; once from the right to the left and then from the left to the right ; (3) then in touching the mouth with the three middle fingers joined ; (4) then to touch the nostrils with the thumb and the index finger ; (5) then to touch the holes of the eyes and ears by the thumb and the ring finger ; (6) then to touch the navel with the little finger ; (7) then to touch the heart with the palm of the hand ; (8) then to touch the head with all the fingers ; (9) and the arms with the end of the fingers ; thus cleansing all the holes of the body.

The method of sipping the water is also peculiar. Water sufficient to immerse a pea should be taken in the hollow of the palm, and sipped from the root of the thumb.

The various portions of the palm have different names with regard to using it in different ceremonies ; and the portion of the palm nearest to the root of the thumb is called Brahmatîrtha ; that of the root of the little finger is called Prajâpatitîrtha ; the portion near to the root of the index finger is called Pitṛi-tîrtha ; and the ends of the fingers are called the Devatîrtha. Brahmatîrtha is used in Âchamana, the Pitṛi-tîrtha is used in giving oblation of water to the Pitṛis, and so on.

This division of the palm into four parts may have arisen from the following considerations. The four quarters of the heaven are sacred to the four classes of deities. East is sacred to the Devas, North to the Riṣis or Prajâpatis, West to the Asurâs and the South to the Pitṛis. If facing east, one places his right hand flat on the ground with the palm upwards, then the tips of the fingers will point towards east, the Prajâpati-tîrtha will be towards north, the Pitṛi-tîrtha will point towards south and the Brahma towards the west. The same fact is also recalled by the various positions of the sacred thread. The ordinary form of wearing it is on the left shoulder (upavîti); if it is worn on the right shoulder, it is called Prâchîna-viti; if worn round the neck like a garland, it is Nivîti.

The mantra used in Âchamana is one of the grandest Riks of the Vedas. It re-calls at once the Highest Being and the Highest State—the Supreme Viṣṇu and His Highest Heaven. The wise see Him and His glorious Land of Joy-Eternal, not dimly and darkly as through a fog, not in the partial glimpse of the ecstatic saint and Sadhu, but with the unclouded vision of the Seer, like as the Eye fixed in the midheaven would see the whole earth spread underneath it, without the least hinderance—the loftiest peaks cannot obstruct its piercing gaze—all will be spread out beneath him on a flat surface. So do the wise see the Heaven and its Lord The very idea which this mantra recalls would purify all ordinary impurities.

Then let him cleanse his teeth with a twig of one of the trees named hereafter, or with some dentifrice. The twigs of the following trees may be used:—Date palm, *Kadamba*, *Karancha*, Banyan, Tamarind, Bamboo, Mango, *Nim*, Apâmârga, Bel, Âkanda and fig tree.

While cutting the twig from the tree or using it,—

**Recite the following:—**

आयुर्बलं यशोवर्चः प्रजाः पशुवसूनि च ।

ब्रह्म प्रज्ञाञ्च मेधाञ्च त्वं नो देहि वनस्पते ॥

*Trasliteration*:—Âyur balam yaśo varchaḥ,
Prajâḥ paśu vasûni cha,
Brahma-prajñâñ cha medhâñcha,
Tvam no dehi vanaspate.

*Word meaning*:—Âyus, long life; Balam, strength; Yaśas, fame; Varchas, lustre; Prajâḥ, progeny; Paśu, cattle; Vasûni, wealth; Cha, and; Brahma, Brahman; Prajñâṃ, wisdom; Medhâṃ, intelligence; Tvam, thou; Naḥ, to us; Vanaspate, O Lord of Forest (or Lord of all desirable things); Dehi, give.

"Oh forest Lord! give thou to us long life and strength and fame, with Brahma, lustre, sons, cattle and riches too. Give us, O Lord supreme! Wisdom, Divine and Intellingence."

A true Hindu would not heedlessly injure the slightest object that has life. A tree is as much a manifestation of the Divine Wisdom and Power as the man himself, and the Devas engaged in the building up of a flower, love their handiwork with as much fond regard as the artist, who paints its picture, loves the semblance. The man, who, through thoughtlessness or ignorance, injures these divine works, incurs the anger and the ill-will of these elemental workers. Therefore, a Hindu in plucking a flower or cutting a twig, prays to the Supreme and asks the permission of the industrious ones who have made it. By the very fact that he recognises their labour and appreciates their actions, he propitiates these Sylvan Devas and gets their goodwill and blessing.

The length of the twig varies with the caste and the sex of the person. A Brâhmaṇa should use a twig of 12 fingers long (9 inches), the Kṣatriya, 9 fingers long (about 7 inches), the Vaiśya, 8 fingers long (6 inches), the Śûdra, 6 fingers long (4½ inches), and all women 4 fingers long (three inches).

The teeth should be rubbed gently; in no case should blood come out.

The teeth should not be rubbed on the following days:—(1) Śrâddha days, (2) Birth day, (3) Marriage day, (4) when there is indigestion, (5) Fasting days and (6) Pârvaṇa days. The parvas are the 14th, the 9th days of the moon, the new-moon and the full-moon days, and the Saṅkrânti day (the last day of the solar month, when the sun passes from one house to another). So also the 1st, 6th and 8th days.

On these days he should wash the mouth with mouthfuls of water, twelve times.

When using a dentrifice, use only the ring finger or the thumb, or any other finger as convenient.

Let him then perform the early morning bath, and after that Sandhyâ.

The morning bath should therefore be *brief*. Moreover, if a person is not in a good state of health, he need not have this bath: but may content himself with the mid-day bath. Every house-holder is required to bathe twice, and an ascetic thrice (morning, mid-day and evening).

"A Brâhmaṇa house-holder should bathe at two *Sandhyâs* (the time between two praharas or fourth part of the day); but the ascetic should do so at all the three Sandhyâs."

In a hot country like India, these baths are absolutely necessary for cleanliness and health. The early morning bath is done before the sun rises, when the eastern sky is tinged with the dim rays of the rising sun.

After bath, one should put on his forehead the *tilaka* of clay, sacrificial ashes or sandal paste; the clay of the bed of the Ganges or of the Gomati is preferable to other earths. The form of the *tilakas* varies with the caste of the person. The Brâhmaṇa has Urddhva-puṇḍra, *i.e.*, puṇḍra stretching upwards, the Kṣatriya has triple puṇḍra, the Vaiśya has semilunar, and the Śûdra, the circular.

Persons in ill health may not pour water on their head, but wash the other portions of their body: or they may rub their skin with a wet towel.

The morning bath, from its very nature, must be quickly and briefly done. Oil should not be used.

It would be convenient, however, to describe a few of the details of a regular bath, as done at mid-day, for some of them apply to the morning baths also. The bath should be made in current water, as far as possible, standing towards the direction from which there is the flow, the head should be immersed thrice. If at home, then he should turn his face towards the East.

Substitutes of the bath are as follows :—

"Mantra or by repetition of sacred hymns. Bhauma or with tilaka of sacred clay, Âgneya or with sacrificial ashes, Vâyavya or in the wind that comes mixed with the dust raised by cows, Divya, in the rain, Vâruṇa in the water of rivers, &c., without mantras, and, lastly, Mânasa or mental, done by intently thinking over Viṣṇu, are the seven well-known baths."

If a person for some unavoidable reason is unable to perform the proper bath, then he may substitute any one of the above seven. For the majority of the readers of this book, the mid-day bath with water is impossible, as they might be in their place of business at the time. They can, however, with least difficulty, think at the time intently on Viṣṇu and thus perform the mental bath, or they may repeat in their minds the three Mârjana Mantras and thus have the satisfaction of having done their duty. The three Mârjana Mantras are आपोहिष्ठा, &c. Rig. Veda X. 9, 1 to 3.; and mantras IV, V, and VI. They are given further down in the chapter on Sandhyâ. All the *five* mantras, beginning with शन्नो आपो, may be used also.

When going to bathe, he should carry the clay for rubbing on the body, the *tila* for *tarpaṇa* and the grass for purifying water. He should have Darbha grass in his hands, make a square on the water with a side six feet long. He should then repeat the Saṅkalpa or the process of drawing in all his wandering outgoing energies, and focussing them on a particular object—in this case the maguetising of water for th e purposes of Bath.

**The Sankalpa mantra is**

ओं विष्णुरोम् तत् सद् अद्य अमुके मासि, अमुके पक्षे, अमुके तिथौ अमुक गोत्रः श्री अमुक देव शर्मा श्रीविष्णुप्रीतिकामः प्रातःस्नानमहं करिष्ये.।

*Transliteration* :—Om! Viṣṇur; Om tat sat, adya——mâsi;——pakṣe,——tithau,——gotrah, Srî——deva śarmâ (or varmâ, if a Kṣattriya), Śrî Viṣṇu prîtikâmaḥ, prâtasnânam aham, Kariṣye.

"Om Viṣṇu; Om Tat Sat; to-day in the month of———, in the bright/dark fortnight; in the——day of the moon, I———, Deva Śarmâ, of——— Gotra, am going to have a morning bath in order to please Śri Viṣṇu."

And repeat over it the mantra ओं नामे नारायणाय Om, Namo Nârâyaṇâya. Then he should *invoke* the seven Celestial streams from the solar orb.—

ॐ गङ्गे च यमुने चैव गोदावरि सरस्वति ।

नर्म्मदे सिन्धु कावेरि जलेऽस्मिन् सन्निधिं कुरु ॥

*Transliteration* :—Om Gaṅge cha Yamune chaiva,
Godâvari Sarasvati,
Narmade Sindhu Kâveri,
Jale'smin sannidhim kuru.

*Word-meaning.*—*Cha*, and; *Jale*, in water; *Asmin*, in this; *Sannidhim*, presence, abode; *Kuru*, make ye.

3

"O ye Ganges, Yamuna, Godâvari, Sarasvati, Narmadâ, Sindhu and Kâveri, make your abode in this water."

Then he should address the following to the Ganges with joined palms, seven times :—

ॐ विष्णुपादप्रसूतासि विष्णवी विष्णुपूजिता ।
पाहि नस्त्वेनसस्तस्मादाजन्ममरणान्तिकात् ॥ १ ॥
तिस्रः कोट्यर्द्धकोटी च तीर्थानां वायुरब्रवीत् ।
दिवि भुव्यन्तरिक्षे च तानि ते सन्ति जाह्नवि ॥ २ ॥
नन्दिनीत्येव ते नाम देवेषु नलिनीति ।
वृन्दा पृथ्वी च सुभगा विश्वकाया शिवा सिता ॥ ३ ॥
विद्याधरी सुप्रसन्ना तथा लोकप्रसादिनी ।
क्षमा च जाह्नवी चैतन्या शान्ता शान्तिप्रदायिनी ॥ ४ ॥
एतानि पुण्यनामानि स्नानकाले प्रकीर्त्तयेत् ।
भवेत् सन्निहिता अत्र गङ्गा त्रिपथगामिनी ॥ ५ ॥

Om Viṣṇu-pâda prasûtâsi, Vaiṣṇavî Viṣṇu-pûjitâ ;
Pâhi nas tvenasas tasmâd, Âjanma-maraṇântikât. (1).
Tisra-koṭy ardha-kotî cha, Tîrthânâm Vâyurabravît ;
Divi bhuvyantarikṣe cha, Tâni Te santi Jâhnavi. (2).
Nandinî'tyeva te nâma Deveṣu Nalini'ti cha,
Vrindâ Prithvî cha Subhagâ, Viśvakâyâ Śivâ Sitâ. (3).
Vidyâdharî Suprasannâ, Tathâ Loka-prasâdinî,
Kṣamâ cha Jâhṇavî Chaitanyâ Śântâ Śânti-pradâyinî. (4).
Etâni punya nâmâni Snâna-kâle prakîrtayet,
Bhavet sannihitâ atra Gaṅgâ Tripatha-gâmini. (5).

(1) From Viṣṇu's holy foot-step born, thou Viṣṇu force, by Viṣṇu honoured,
Protect us mother! wash our sins, that we commit from birth till death.

(2) In heaven, firmament, and earth are Thirty-five millions of holy places ;
Thus Vâyu teacheth us, but all in Thee, O mother, are comprised.

(3) In Deva-world thou art named Nandini, and Nalini is thy name too.
Vrindâ, Prithvi, Subhagâ, or Viswakâyâ, Śivâ, Sitâ,

(4) Vidyâdhari, Suprasannâ, thou art Lokaprasâdinî.

And Kṣemâ, Merciful is thy name, Jâhnavi and Śântâ and Śânti-pradâyinî great consoler Giver of consolation and Jâhnavi.

(5) When these her holy names are all recited at the time of bath, then there the mystic Gangâ comes, who flows in Heaven, sky and earth.

The setting apart of a particular portion of the water of a river shows the scientific nature of the process. A man is endowed with but a limited energy, he can only influence a limited sphere. In order, therefore, not to waste his energy on too wide an area, the Hindu, before he bathes, fixes a limit : and it is within that, that he intends to exercise his spiritual power. The ordinary water is vitalized and spiritual energy imparted to it, by the process of magnetization with the repetition of the above mantras. The difference between mere अवगाहन or bath and स्नान or regular bath, consists in this. One is, as it were, immersion in water. It produces mere physical effect. The other is bathing in water vitalized by the bather with the sacred mantras, and produces, in addition, spiritual results.

If he bathes in the Ganges, he should repeat *also* the following, after the above :—

ओं विष्णुपादार्घ्यसंभूते गंगे त्रिपथगामिनि ।
धर्म्मद्रवीति विख्याते पापं मे हर जाह्नवि ॥
श्रद्धया भक्तिसम्पन्ने श्रीमातर्देवि जाह्नवि ।
अमृतेनाम्बुना देवि भागीरथि पुनीहि माम् ॥

" O born from Viṣṇu's sacred foot, Gangâ that flows in triple path.

Thou O ! Holy current called, remove my sins ; O Jâhnavi.

O mother ! Goddess Jâhnavi ! with thy immortal waters make me all pure, thy loving devotee, Divine Bhâgîrathi."

Then repeating seven times the mantra ॐ नमो नारायण he should pour water three times on his head with joined hands.

Then he should rub the clay on his body with the following mantras :—

ओं अश्वकान्ते रथक्रान्ते विष्णुक्रान्ते वसुन्धरे ।
मृत्तिके हर मे पापं यन्मया दुष्कृतं कृतम् ॥
उद्धृतासि वराहेण कृष्णेन शतबाहुना ।
नमस्ते सर्वभूतानां प्रभवारिणि सुव्रते ॥
आरुह्य मम गात्राणि सर्वपापं प्रमोचय ॥

" By horses trod, by chariots charged, O Earth ! by Viṣṇu's step-encased,

Remove my sins, O Mrittikâ, whatever ill deeds I may have done,
From primeval Ocean wast uplifted by Kriṣṇa, hundred-armed Boar.
Salutations to thee, the producer of all creatures and of good deeds,
Pervade all my body, free me from all sin " (Taittiriya Âraṇyaka, X. 1. 1.)

Some use, instead of clay, the gram powder or powder of some of the pulses. Most of these are very good substitutes for soap. The latter is costly and not so useful from the medical point of view as clay or powder.

Oil may be used at mid-day bath. It should not be used on the sacred days on which teeth-rubbing is also forbidden. The body should be dried with a separate cloth, and not with that which is worn. The worn wet cloth should not be squeezed to get rid of its water, so long as the Tarpana is not finished. He should not bathe in a tank belonging to a private person.

No sacred functions like Japa, Homa, &c., can be performed without bath.

The Snâna or bath is of three kinds: नित्यं Nitya (daily); नैमित्तिकं (occasional, which is to be performed in addition to the Nitya, on particular occasions only, such as when there is an eclipse, &c.); काम्य (with desire of fruit—such as on pilgrimage, &c.)

This mantra has another version, to be found in the Taittirîya Âraṇyaka, X. 1. 1., as given below :—

अश्वक्रान्ते रथक्रान्ते विष्णुक्रान्ते वसुन्धरा ।

शिरसा धारिता देवि रक्षस्व माम् पदे पदे ॥

*Transliteration* :—Aśvakrânte rathakrânte Viṣṇukrânte Vasundharâ, Śirasâ dhâritâ devi rakṣasva mâm pade pade.

*Word-meaning* :—अश्वक्रान्ते, O earth ! trod by horses. The ground which is trod by the horses, in order to sanctify it, is called asva-krântâ land. In certain ceremonies, it is laid down that the earth must be trampled well by the hoofs of the horses, in order to sanctify it for religious purposes, विष्णुक्रान्ते O earth ! charged by chariots for the purpose of sanctifying it. O earth ! by Viṣṇu trod. In His Avatâra as Trivikrama, the Lord trod the earth. Thus the earth has triple sanctification, वसुन्धरा; The holder of wealth, शिरसा, on the head, धारिता, held or placed, देवि, Shining one, मां, me, who is about to bathe in this water, रक्षस्व, protect, पदे पदे, at every step.

*Translation* :—O earth ! Thou art sanctified by the treading of the War-horses and chariots, and the Lord Himself hath made thee holy by His walking on Thee in one of His Down-comings ! Thou art holder of wealth, I hold Thee on my head. Protect Thou me from all dangers at every step.

*Note* :—This apparently is addressed to earth before entering into the water of the river. It is a prayer for protection from the dangers lurking in the river-bed. In Tantras, the names Asvo-krântâ, and Viṣṇu krântâ and Ratha-krânta are applied to various divisions of India.

उद्धृतासि वराहेण कृष्णेन शतबाहुना ।

भूमिर्धरणी लोकधारिणी ॥

*Transliteration*: —Uddhṛitâsi varâhena Kriṣṇena śatbâhunâ, Bhumirdharaṇî lokadhâriṇî.

*Word-meaning* :—उद्धृता, raised up, असि, thou-art, वराहेण, by the Boar, कृष्णेन, by the black, शतबाहुना, by the hundred-handed, भूमिः, as earth, धेनुः, as cow, giver of all desires, धरणी, upholder of all crops, लोकधारिणी, upholder of all living creatures.

*Translation* :—Thou art further sacred, as thou hast been raised from the Deep by the Lord when He appeared as the black colored Boar having hundred arms. Thou art Bhûmi, thou the upholder of all crops and of all creatures.

मृत्तिके हन मे पापं यन्मया दुष्कृतं कृतम् ।
त्वया हतेन पापेन जीवामि शरदः शतम् ॥

*Transliteration*:—Mṛittike hara me pâpaṃ yanmayâ duṣkṛitam kritam, Tvayâ hatena pâpena jivâmi śaradaḥ śataṃ.

*Word meaning*:—मृत्तिके, O clay ! हन, destroy ; मे पापं, my sins ; यत् मया, what by me ; दुष्कृतं कृतम्, bad deeds done ; त्वया हतेन, by thee destroyed; पापेन, sins ; जीवामि, I may live ; शरदः शतम्, autumns hundred.

*Translation* :—O earth ! destroy my sins ! whatever evil deeds I may have done. Thou destroying my sins, I shall live a hundred years.

---

## CHAPTER IV.

### *Tarpana*, or the Peace-Offering.

Tarpaṇa is of two kinds—Principal and Subsidiary. The first is ordained for all twice-born snatakas : and for widows. The subsidiary tarpaṇa, however, is a *part* of bathing as taught in the Brahmâṇḍa Purâṇa. It is thus a Nitya duty for all. Its non-performance is sinful. It should be performed with wet cloth while standing in water after the bath, taking the water in the palm of both hands together as a cup.

After having bathed and put on the caste mark (tilaka) on the forehead, let him perform Tarpaṇa of the Devas, the Riṣis and the Pitṛis.

" Let the pure twice-born having bathed perform daily, in their due order, the offering of oblations to the Devas, Risis and the Pitṛis."

According to some, he, whose father is alive, need not perform tarpaṇa.

The Tarpaṇa, like Snâna (Sacred bath) of which it forms an integral part, is also of two kinds, one an abbreviated and the other the full form. Like Snána, it is also of three kinds, *nitya*, *naimittika* and *kámya*.

With practice it becomes very simple. After bathing and while standing in water, handfuls of water are offered to one's ancestors—Divine, Spiritual and Human. The method of Tarpaṇa is thus laid down in Padma Purâṇa :—

" Let him first offer water to Brahmâ, then to Viṣṇu, then to Rudra, then to Prajâpati."

"The Devas, the Yakṣas, as well as the Nâgas, the Gandharvas, the Apsaras, the Asuras, the Crooked and the Creeping ones, and those of beautiful wings, so also the trees, the beasts and the birds, the Holders of knowledge, the Holders of water, those who walk in space, the creatures that are without food, those who are addicted to sin and irreligion, for the satisfaction of all those, this water is offered by me":—with the recitation of the above mantra let him pour out one handful of water. All this is to be done wearing the sacred thread in the ordinary way, on the left shoulder and facing *east*.

"Then he should turn *north*, wear the thread round the neck, and offer water to the sons of Manu, to the sons of Riṣis and to the Riṣis—Sanaka, Sananda, and Sanatana the third, Kapila, Asuri, Boḍhu, and Pañchaśikhâ—let all get satisfaction by this water offering."

"Then turning *east*, and with upavîti, he should offer water to Marîchi, Atri, Aṅgiras, Pulastya, Pulaha and Kratu, Prachetas, Vasiṣṭha, Bhṛigu and Nârada. All Devas and Riṣis should be offered barley and water."

"Then having put the sacred thread on the right shoulder, and placing the left knee on the ground, let him offer water to Agniswâttas, Saumyas, Haviṣmantas, Uṣmapas, Sukâlinas, Barhiṣadas, and Âjyâpas. Let him also, with devotion, offer water to his own immediate ancestors with sandal and *tila*."

The Principal Tarpaṇa—called also Pitṛi yajña one of the five great Sacrifices—is performed at mid-day : after the second or mid-day bath. If a person is unable to perform the mid-day bath, then he should not perform this second (or Principal) Tarpaṇa, the first Tarpana done in the morning after the morning bath would suffice, for that is considered as equivalent to Pitṛi yajña.

If through some cause, such as illness, &c., one cannot take the morning and mid-day bath, then he should perform the main tarpaṇa after finishing the mid-day sandhyâ (inclusive of its subsidiary sandhyâṅga tarpaṇa).

One should perform tarpaṇa with rain-water.

If he performs tarpaṇa outside the river, he should mix sesamum with water, except on Sundays, Fridays, Dvâdaśî, Saptami, Saṅkrânti and birth tithi.

The full method of Tarpaṇa is laid down below :—

1. Let him face the *south* and with the sacred thread on his right shoulder (*Prâchînâvîti*) and with joined palms *invoke* the Tîrthas :—

ओं कुरुक्षेत्रं गयागङ्गा प्रभासः पुष्कराणि च ।

तीर्थान्येतानि पुण्यानि तर्पणकाले भवन्त्विह ॥

*Transliteration.*—Om ! Kurukṣetra Gayâ Gaṅgâ. Prabhâsa Puṣkarâṇi cha, Tîrthâny etâni puṇyâni, Tarpaṇakâle bhavantu iha.

*Word-meaning.*—Om ! Kurukṣetra—the field of the Kurus ; Gayâ, Gaya ; Gaṅgâ, the Ganges ; Prabhâsa Puṣkara, the Prabhâsa and the Puṣkara ; cha, and ; tîrthâni, the sacred waters or places of pilgrimage ; puṇyâni, the holy ; tarpaṇa-kâle, at the time of offering tarpaṇa ; bhavantu, let them become ; iha, here.

*Translation.*—"Om ! Let the sacred Tîrthas of Kurukṣetra, Gayâ, Gangâ, Prabhâsa, of Puṣkara, be present here at the time of Tarpaṇa."

2. *To the Four* (*Quaternary*). Then he should turn to the *east*,

with the sacred thread on the left shoulder (upavîti), and recite the following mantras :—

ओं ब्रह्मा तृप्यताम्, Om! Brahmâ tripyatâm,—(Om! may Brahmâ be satisfied) and offer one handful of water by Deva-tîrtha.

ओं विष्णुस्तृप्यताम्, Om Viṣṇus tripyatâm,—(Om! may Viṣṇu be satisfied) and offer one handful of water by Deva-tîrtha.

ओं रुद्रस्तृप्यताम्,—Om Rudras tripyatâm,—(Om! may Rudra be satisfied) and offer one handful of water by Deva-tîrtha.

ओं प्रजापतिस्तृप्यताम्, —Om Prajâpatis tripyatâm,—(Om! may Prajâpati be satisfied) and offer one handful of water by Deva-tîrtha.

2a. *To all jîvas.* Then take a handful of water and say :—

ओं देवा यक्षास्तथा नागा गन्धर्वाप्सरसोऽसुराः ।,

क्रूराः सर्पाः सुपर्णाश्च तरवोजम्भगाः खगाः ।

विद्याधरा जलाधारास्तथैवाकाशगामिनः ।

निराहाराश्च ये जीवाः पापेऽधर्म्मे रताश्च ये ।

तेषामाप्यायनायैतद्दीयते सलिलं मया ॥

*Transliteration.*—Om. Devâ yakṣâs tathâ nâgâ, Gandharvâ-psaraso' surâḥ, Krûrâḥ sarpâ suparnâś cha, Taravo jambhagâḥ Khagâḥ,

Vidyâdharâ jalâdhârâs, Tathaivâkâśagâminaḥ, Nirâhârâś cha ye jivâḥ, Pâpe dharme, ratâś cha ye, Teṣâm âpyâyanâyaitad, Dîyate salilam mayâ.

*Translation.*—" Om! the Devas, the Yakṣas, as well as the Nâgâs, the Gandharvas, the Apsaras, the Asuras, the crooked and the creeping ones and those of beautiful wings, so also the trees, the beasts, the holders of knowledge, the holders of water, those who walk in space—the creatures that are without food, those who are addicted to sin and irreligion—for the satisfaction of all these, this water is offered by me," *and pour down the said water by the Devatîrtha.*

3. *To Sages.* Then turn to the *north*, with the sacred thread round the neck (*nâvîti*), and give two handfuls of water, by the Prajâpati tîrtha, reciting the following mantras :—

ओं सनकश्च सनन्दश्च, तृतीयश्च सनातनः ।

कपिलश्चासुरिश्चैव, वोढुः पञ्चशिखस्तथा ॥

सर्वे ते तृप्तिमायान्तु, मद्दत्तेनाम्बुना सदा ॥

*Transliteration.*—Om! Sanakaś cha Sanandaś cha, Tritîyaś cha Sanâtanaḥ. Kapilaś cha Âsuriś chaiva, Boḍhuḥ, Pañchaśikhâs tathâ ; Sarve te triptim âyantu, Mad datten âmbunâ sadâ.

*Translation.*—" Om! Sanaka, Sananda and Sanâtana the third, Kapila and Âsuri, Boḍhu and Panchaśikhâ as well—let all get satisfaction by water offered by me."

4. *To Ṛiṣis and Prajâpatis.* Then turn to the *east*, with the sacred thread on the left shoulder (*upavîti*) and say :—

ओं मरीचिस्तृप्यताम्,—Om! Marichis tripyatâm (Om! may Marîchi be satisfied) and offer one handful of water by the Deva tîrtha.

ओं अत्रिस्तृप्यताम्,—(Om! may Atri......&c.) and offer, &c.

ओं अङ्गिरास्तृप्यताम्,—(Om! may Aṅgirâ be satisfied), &c.

ओं पुलस्त्यस्तृप्यताम्,—(Om! may Pulastya be satisfied), &c.

ओं पुलहस्तृप्यताम्,—(Om! may Pulaha be satisfied), &c.

ओं क्रतुस्तृप्यताम्,—(Om! Kratu), &c.

ओं प्रचेतास्तृप्यताम्,—(Om! Prachetâ), &c.

ओं वशिष्ठस्तृप्यताम्,—(Om! Vaśiṣtha), &c.

ओं भृगुस्तृप्यताम्,—(Om! Bhṛigu), &c.

ओं नारदस्तृप्यताम्,—(Om! Nârada), &c.

ओं देवास्तृप्यन्ताम्,—(Om! Devas), &c.

ओं ब्रह्मर्षयस्तृप्यन्ताम्,—(Om! Brahmarṣis), &c.

5. To *Pitṛis.* Then turn to the *south* with the sacred thread on the right shoulder (*Prâchînâ-vîti*) and say

ओं अग्निष्वात्ताः पितरस्तृप्यन्तामेतदुदकं तेभ्यः स्व

*Transliteration* :—Om agniṣ vâttâḥ p...ras tripyantâm, etad udakam tebhyaḥ svadhâ.

*Translation* :—Om! may the Agniṣvâttâ Pitṛis be satisfied, this water is poured for them, *Svadhâ!*

And offer each three handfuls of water by the Pitṛitîrtha.

ओं सौम्याः पितरस्तृप्यन्तामेतदुदकं तेभ्यः स्वधा,

(Om! may Saumya pitṛs be satisfied)—&c., &c.

ओं हविष्मन्तः पितरस्तृप्यन्तामेतदुदकं तेभ्यः स्वधा,

Om! Haviṣmanta, &c.

ओं ऊष्मपाः पितरस्तृप्यन्तामेतदुदकं तेभ्यः स्वधा,

Om! Uṣmapâs, &c.

ओं शौकालिनः पितरस्तृप्यन्तामेतदुदकं तेभ्यः स्वधा,

Om! Śaukalinas, &c.

ओं बर्हिषदः पितरस्तृप्यन्तामेतदुदकं तेभ्यः स्वधा,

Om! Barhiṣadas, &c.

ओं आज्यपाः पितरस्तृप्यन्तामेतदुदकं तेभ्यः स्वधा,

Om! Âjyapâs, &c.

6. *Yama tarpana.* Then let him offer *three* handfuls of water to the fourteen Yamas, saying :—

ओं यमाय धर्म्मराजाय मृत्यवे चान्तकाय च,
वैवस्वताय कालाय सर्वभूतक्षयाय च,
औदुम्बराय दध्नाय नीलाय परमेष्ठिने,
वृकोदराय चित्राय चित्रगुप्ताय वै नमः ॥

*Transliteration* :—Om ! Yamâya Dharmarâjâya,
Mrityave Chântakâya cha,
Vaivasvatâya, Kâlâya, Sarva-bhûta-Kṣayâya oha,
Auḍumbarâya Dadhnâya, Nilâya Parameṣṭhine,
Vrikodarâya Chitrâya, Chitraguptâya vai namaḥ.

*Translation* :—" Om ! To Yama, to Dharmaraja, to Mṛityu, to Antaka, to Vaivasvata, to Kâla, to Śarvabhûta-Kṣaya, to Auḍumbara, to Dadhna, to Nila, to Parameṣṭhi, to Vṛikodara, to Chitra, and to Chitragupta salutations be, salutations be."

7. *Invocation of ancestors.* Then, with joined palms, he should invoke his family ancestors saying :—

ओं आगच्छन्तु मे पितरः इमम् गृह्णन्त्वपोञ्जलिम्,

*Transliteration* :—Om, âgachchhantu me pitaraḥ, imam gṛihṇantva-poñjalim.

*Translation* :—" Om ! may my ancestors come hither and accept this water oblation."

(*a*) *Paternal ancestors.* Then take a handful of water with *tila* (sesamum) in it, and offer it to the ancestors, saying :—

विष्णुरोम् !   ...गोत्रः पिता..................

देवशर्म्मा तृप्यताम् एतत् सतिलगंगोदकं तस्मै स्वधा ॥

Viṣṇur Om !......gotraḥ, pitâ....... deva śarmâ (varmâ, if a Kṣatriya and Gupta if a Vaiśya) tripyatâṃ, etat satila gaṅgodakaṃ tasmai svadhâ.

Offer *three* such *anjalis* (handfuls) with the above mantra to each. So on with the other ancestors in this order :—Grandfather (pitâmaha) great-grandfather, maternal grandfather, mother's grandfather, mother's great-grandfather, as given below :—

Grandfather विष्णुरोम्......गोत्रः पितामह......देव शर्म्मा तृप्यताम् एतत्, &c., &c. three handfuls.

Great-grandfather विष्णुरोम्........ गोत्रः प्रपितामह......देवशर्म्मा, &c., &c. three handfuls.

Mother's father विष्णुरोम् गोत्रः मातामह......देवशर्म्मा, &c., &c., &c., three handfuls.

Mother's grandfather विष्णुरोम्........गोत्रः प्रमातामह......देवशर्म्मा, &c., &c., three handfuls.

Mother's great-grandfather विष्णुरोम्.. ...गोत्रः वृद्धप्रमातामह......देवशर्म्मा, &c., &c., three handfuls.

Mother विष्णुरोम्......गोत्रा माता...... देवी तृप्यताम् एतत् सतिलगंगोदकं तस्यै स्वधा, three handfuls.

Grandmother पितामही, &c., three handfuls.

Great-grandmother, प्रपितामही &c., three handfuls.

7. (*b*) After offering three handfuls to these six male ancestors and

three female ancestors, let him offer *One* handful to each maternal female ancestor.

Mother's mother मातामही, &c. One handful.
Mother's grandmother, प्रमातामही &c. Do.
Mother's great-grandmother, वृद्धप्रमातामही, &c. Do.

*One handful* should also be offered to other male and female ancestors, such as uncles, aunts, brothers, sisters, &c.

8. *To sufferers in hell.* Then let him recite the following and pour *three* handfuls of water :—

ओं नरकेषु समस्तेषु यातनासु च ये स्थिताः ।
तेषामाप्यायनायैतद् दीयते सलिलं मया ॥

*Transliteration* :—Om ! Narakeṣu samasteṣu yâtanâsu cha ye sthitâḥ, Teṣâm âpyâyanâyaitad, Diyate salilam mayâ.

*Translation*:—Om ! In hell's dark horrors or in torments thrown,
Where'er they may be, may waters poured by me,
Assuage their sufferings and their pains allay.

9. *To all ancestors.* Then let him recite the following and pour three handfuls :—

ओं ये बान्धवाबान्धवा वा येऽन्यजन्मनि बान्धवाः ।
ते तृप्तिमखिलां यान्तु ये चास्मत्तोयकांक्षिणः ॥

*Transliteration* :—Om ! ye bândhavâ, a bândhavâ vâ, Ye anye janmani bândhavâḥ, Te triptim akhilâm yântu, Ye châsmat toya Kankṣiṇaḥ.

*Translation* :—" Om ! let those who are my kinsmen, friends,
In times gone-by or present life or foes on earth,
Get satisfaction and unending peace,
Yea all who look for waters from my hands."

10. *To the whole creation.* Then let him pour three *añjalis*, reciting the following mantras :—

ओं आब्रह्मभुवना लोका देवर्षिमुनिमानवाः ।
तृप्यन्तु पितरः सर्वे मातृमातामहादयः ॥
अतीतकुलकोटीनाम् सप्तद्वीपनिवासिनाम् ।
मया दत्तेन तोयेन तृप्यन्तु भुवनत्रयम् ॥

*Transliteration* :—Om ! Â Brahma bhuvanâlokâ,
Devarṣi muni mânavâḥ,
Tripyantu pitaraḥ sarve, mâtṛi mâtâ mahâdayaḥ,
Atîta kula koṭinâm, sapta dvîpa nivâsinâm,
Mayâ dattena toyena, tripyantu bhuvana trayam.

*Translation* :—From Brahma's brilliant realm to densest gloom of

Let Devas, Riṣis, men and Munis all,
Be pleased ; and Fathers, Mothers, mother's fathers too.

Let kinsmen of my myriad births, and those,
Who dwell in seven sea-girt isles and regions three,
Get satisfaction from these waters poured by me.
Then let him offer three more oblations, saying :—

ओं आब्रह्मस्तम्बपर्यन्तं जगत् तृप्यतु ॥

*Transliteration* :—Om ! Â Brahmas stamba paryantam Jagat tripyatu.

*Translation* :—Om ! Let the whole universe from Brahmâ down to the humblest tuft of grass be satisfied.

11. *To childless dead* : Then let him squeeze out a little water from his wearing under-cloth (Dhoti) and offer a handful of it, saying :—

ओं ये चास्माकं कुले जाता अपुत्रा गोत्रिणो मृताः ।
ते तृप्यन्तु मया दत्तं वस्त्रनिष्पीड़नोदकम ॥

*Transliteration* :—Om ! Ye châsmâkam kulejâtâ, Aputrâ gotriṇo mṛitâḥ,

Te tripyantu mayâ dattam Vastra niṣpîḍanodakam.

*Translation* :—Om ! Let those who in our clan were born and sonless died,

Or died too soon ere Gotra rites could be performed,

Be satisfied. To them I give these waters from my garments squeezed.

After this, and not so long till this, he should squeeze out all water from his *dhoti* to dry it.

12. Then let him salute with bowed head, reciting :—

ओं पिता स्वर्गः पिता धर्म्मः पिता हि परमं तपः ।
पितरि प्रीतिमापन्ने प्रीयन्ते सर्वदेवताः ॥

*Transliteration* :—Om ! Pitâ svargaḥ pitâ dharmaḥ, pitâhi paramam tapaḥ

Pitari prîtim âpanne prîyante sarva devatâḥ.

*Translation* :—Om ! Father is heaven, father is Dharma, and Tapas is father too,

When Father satisfaction gets, then Devas all are satisfied.

13. Then let him repeat ten times the mantra ओं विष्णु : Om Viṣnu, in order to remedy accidental defects in the performance of the above ceremony.

14. Then let him finish by reciting :—

ओं अज्ञानाद् यदि वा मोहात् प्रच्यवेताध्वरेषु यत् ।
स्मरणादेव तद्विष्णोः सम्पूर्णः स्यादिति श्रुतिः ॥
ओं प्रीयतां पुण्डरीकाक्षः सर्वयज्ञेश्वरोहरिः ।
तस्मिन्स्तुष्टे जगत्तुष्टं प्रीणिते प्रीणितं जगत् ॥

*Transliteration* :—Om ! ajñânâd yadi vâ mohât Prachyavetâdhvareṣu yat ; Smaraṇâd eva tad Viṣṇoḥ, Sampûrṇaḥ syâd iti śrutiḥ,

Om ! Prîyatâm Puṇḍarikâkṣaḥ Sarva yajñeśvaro Hariḥ, Tasminstuṣṭe jagat tuṣṭam, Prîṇite prîṇitam jagat.

*Translation* :—Om ! Through ignorance or want of heed,

In sacrifice defects occur ;

They all, however, perfection reach,

Through Viṣṇu's name, so Śrutis teach.

Om ! Be pleased, O lotus-eyed Lord,

Hari ! that rules all holy rites,

Him gratified, creation smiles,

When He is pleased, the worlds feel glad.

15. Then offer the fruit to God saying :—

मया यदिदं कर्म्म कृतं तत् सर्वं भगवति विष्णौ समर्पितम् ॥

*Transliteration* :—Mayâ yad idam karma kritam tat sarvam Bhagavati Viṣṇau samarpitam.

*Translation* :—" The fruit of all this ceremony done by me, I offer to the Adorable Viṣṇu all."

(a) *Bhiṣma Tarpaṇa.* Some add Bhiṣma Tarpaṇa in their daily practice. They recite the following mantras after Yama Tarpaṇa :—

वैयाघ्रपद्यगोत्राय सांकृतिप्रवराय च ।

अपुत्राय ददाम्येतद् सलिलं भीष्मवर्म्मणे ॥

*Transliteration* :—Vaiyâghrapadya gotrâya Sâṅkṛiti pravarâya cha,

Aputrâya dadâmy etad salilam Bhishma Varmaṇe.

*Translation* :—To sonless Bhiṣma, spotless soul, Of Vaiyâghrapadya's famous clan, And of the House of Sânkriti, With love these waters thee I give.

Then salute Bhiṣma with the following praṇâma :—

भीष्मः शान्तनवो वीरः सत्यवादी जितेन्द्रियः ।

आभिरद्भिरवाप्नोतु पुत्रपौत्रोचितां क्रियाम् ॥

*Transliteration* :—Bhîṣma Śântanavo vîraḥ, satyavâdî jitendriyaḥ

Âbhir adbhir avâpnotu purtra-pautrochitâm kriyâm.

*Translation* :—O Bhîṣma, Truthful, chaste and wise,

Śântanu's son, of heroic heart, May thou, by waters hereby poured,

Get satisfaction such as those,

The Fathers get from sons, grandsons.

# CHAPTER V.

## GÂYATRÎ.

॥ ओम् भूर्भुवः स्वः तत्सवितुर्वरेण्यं भर्गो देवस्य धीमहि-
धियो यो नः प्रचोदयात्

Rig Veda III. 62. 10.

Pada : तत् । सवितुः । वरेण्यम् । भर्गः । देवस्य । धीमहि । धियः । यः । नः । प्रचोदयात् ॥

Sáyana यः = सविता देवः, नः = अस्माकं । धियः = कर्माणि धर्मादि विषया वा बुद्धीः प्रचोदयात् = प्रेरयेत् । तत् = तस्य । देवस्य = द्योतमानस्य । सवितुः = जगत् स्रष्टुः । वरेण्यं = संभजनीयं। भर्गः = तेजः । धीमहि = ध्यायेम॥

*English meaning* :—यः = who ; नः = our ; धियः = Buddhi or Intellects ; प्रचोदयात् = incites or moves or directs ; तत् = of that, His ; देवस्य = of the shining one ; सवितुः = of the Creator ; वरेण्यं = adorable ; भर्गः = light ; धीमहि = We meditate.

1. We meditate upon the adorable light of that Shining Creator, who incites our Buddhi.

*N.B.*—This famous Mantra is almost impossible to be translated. It should be meditated upon. The unfoldment (prachodana) of the Buddhi Principle (Dhi) is facilitated by it. The method of meditation consists in affirming "योऽहं सोऽसौ योऽसौ सोऽहम्" = "What I am that He is, what He is that I am.

2. *Another meaning* :—तत् may qualify भर्गः "We meditate on *that* adorable light of the Deva Savitâ which ( यः = यत् ) incites our Buddhi."

3. *Another meaning* :—"We meditate on the adorable luminous orb (bharga) of that Divine Sun who directs all over Activities."

4. *Another meaning* :—"We 'obtain (dhîmahi = dhârayâmaḥ) desirable food (bharga = annam) (through the grace) of that Deva Savitâ who directs our intelligence," *i.e.*, we become the receptacle of all food, &c.

According to Srî Sankarâchârya this Mâhâ-Mantra reveals the Supreme Self, who is all power, all-revealer, and who is the Self of all. The Gâyatrî with the Praṇava and its *seven* Vyâhritis, and the Śiras is the essence of all the Vedas. This Gâyatrî should be meditated upon in *Prâṇâyâma* with *all* its seven Vyâhritis and the Śiras. The same Gâyatrî, with the Praṇava and the *three* Vyâhritis, and ending in Praṇava is to be meditated upon in *Japa*. The Pure Gâyatrî denotes the unity of Brahma and Pratyagâtman. The phrase "dhiyo yo nah prachodayât"—"may He unfold our Buddhi"—declares the Pratyagâtman, who is the Inner Witness of all, and who is the Illuminator of the antaḥkaraṇa or Buddhis of all. The declaration that He directs our Buddhis shows Him to be the Supreme Brahman, one with the Self in All. Therefore Savitâ refers to the Supreme Brahman. The Mantra, therefore, should be explained thus.

तत् = That, *viz.*, the self-evident, the subjective (Pratyabhûta) Para-Brahma. सवितुः = the substratum of all illusions of duality, of the whole cosmos, and the cause of its creation, preservation and destruction. वरेण्यं = adorable or the chosen of all; the form of intense Bliss. भर्गः = *Consumer* of all faults of Avidyâ, the sole and only object of knowledge. देवस्य = The illuminer or revealer of all, the one indivisible, un-consciousness. धीमहि = We meditate, in this wise:--This "I" of mine which is the percipient of all objects presented to it by the senses, Manas and Buddhi, is in its essence the Brahman, all-consciousness, self-luminous, devoid of all imperfections, the supreme bliss. The unity between the All-perceiving Pratyagâtman, the subjective Self, and Brahman is a unity of identity. Thus this Gâyatrî declares the Brahman as the Self of all.

गायत्र्यर्थमाह योगियाज्ञवल्क्यः ॥

देवस्य सवितुर्वर्चो भर्गमन्तर्गतं विभुम् ।
ब्रह्मवादिन एवाहुर्वरेण्यञ्चास्य धीमहि ॥ १ ॥
चिन्तयामो वयं भर्ग धियो यो नः प्रचोदयात् ।
धर्मार्थकाममोक्षेषु बुद्धिवृत्तीः पुनः पुनः ॥ २ ॥
बुद्धेश्चोदयिता यस्तु चिदात्मा पुरुषो विराट् ।
वरेण्यं वरणीयञ्च जन्मसंसारभीरुभिः ॥ ३ ॥
आदित्यान्तर्गतं यच्च भर्गाख्यं तन्मुमुक्षुभिः ।
जन्ममृत्युविनाशाय दुःखस्य त्रितयस्य च ॥ ४ ॥
ध्यानेन पुरुषो यश्च द्रष्टव्यः सूर्यमण्डले ।
मन्त्रार्थमपि चैवायं ज्ञापयत्येवमेव हि ॥ ५ ॥

*Gâyatrî as explained by Yogi-Yajñavalkya.*

The parent of all beings produced all states of existence, for he generates and preserves all creatures: therefore is he called the generator. Because he shines and sports, because he loves and irradiates, therefore is he called resplendent or divine, and is praised by all deities. We meditate on the light, which, existing in our minds, continually governs our intellects in the pursuit of virtue, wealth, love and beatitude. Because the being who shines with seven rays, assuming the form of time and of fire, matures productions, is resplendent, illumines all, and finally destroys the universe, therefore he, who naturally shines with seven rays, is called light or the effulgent power. The first syllable denotes that he illumines worlds; the second consonant implies that he colours all creatures; the last syllable signifies that he moves without ceasing. From his cherishing all, he is called the irradiating preserver.

NOTES.

*Gâyatrî.*—This famous verse occurs in the Rigveda III. 62. 10., and this is also found in the Yajurveda III. 35., and in the Sâmaveda also. We give its translation according to the various orientalists:—

*MaxMüller.*—'We meditate on that adorable light of the divine Savitṛi who should rouse our thoughts' (Br. Up. VI. 3. 6).

In another place he translates it thus :—Tat Savitur vareṇyam, *i.e.*, 'this of Savitṛi, to be chosen.' Bhargo devasya dhîmahi, *i.e.*, 'the splendour of the god we meditate on.' Dhiyo yo naḥ prachodayât, *i.e.*, 'who should stir up our thoughts.'

*Roer.*—Let us reflect on the Adorable Light of Savitar who quickens our understanding.

*Griffith*—May we attain that excellent glory of Savitar the God : so may he stimulate our prayers.

*Jones.*—Let us adore the supremacy of that divine Sun who illuminates all, from whom all proceed, to whom all must return, whom we invoke to direct our understandings aright in our progress towards His holy seat.

*Madhva.*—On the Great God, the Progenitor, the much adored Light, do we meditate on, who sends forth our intellects.

*Eggeling.*—May we obtain the glorious light of the divine Savitṛi, who, we trust, may inspire our prayers.

Maitrâyaṇa-Brâhmaṇa Upaniṣad explains it thus :—

This (the sun) is Prajâpati's all-supporting body, for in it this all is hid (by the light of the sun) ; and in this all it (the light) is hid. Therefore this is worshipped.

(The Savitṛi begins :) Tat Savitur vareṇyam, *i.e.*, 'this of Savitṛi, to be chosen.' Here the Âditya (sun) is Savitṛi, and the same is to be chosen by the love (r) of Self, thus say the Brahma-teachers.

(Then follows the next foot in the Savitṛi) : Bhargo devasya dhîmahi, *i.e.*, 'the splendour of the god we meditate on.' Here the god is Savitṛi, and therefore he who is called his splendour, him I meditate on, thus say the Brahma-teachers.

(Then follows the last foot) : Dhiyo yo naḥ prachodayât, *i.e.*, 'who should stir up our thoughts.' Here the dhiyaḥ are thoughts, and he should stir these up for us, thus say the Brahma-teachers.

(He now explains the word bhargas). Now he who is called bhargas is he who is placed in yonder Âditya (sun), or he who is the pupil in the eye. And he is so called, because his going (gati) is by rays (bhâbhiḥ) ; or because he parches (bharjayati) and makes the world to shrivel up. Rudra is called Bhargas, thus say the Brahma-teachers. Or bha means that he lights up these worlds ; ra, that he delights these beings ; ga, that these creatures go to him and come from him ; therefore being a bha-ra-go, he is called Bhargas. (VI. 7).

*Colebrooke.* 1.—Let us meditate on the Adorable Light of the Divine Ruler (Savitṛi) : May it guide our intellects.

2. Om ! Earth (Bhûḥ) ! Sky (Bhuvaḥ) ! Heaven (Svaḥ) ! Middle Region (Mahaḥ) ! Place of births (Janaḥ) ! Mansion of the blessed (Tapaḥ) ! Abode of Truth (Satyam) ! We meditate on that Adorable Light of the resplendent generator, which governs our intellect ; which is water, lustre, savour, immortal faculty of thought, Brahmâ, earth, sky, and heaven.

*Commentary.*—That effulgent power which governs our intellects is the primitive element of water, the lustre of gems and other glittering substances, the savour of trees and herbs, the thinking soul of living beings : it is the creator, preserver, and destroyer ; the sun, and every other deity, and all which moves, or which is fixed in the three worlds, named, earth, sky and heaven. The supreme Brahmâ, so manifested, illumines the seven worlds ; may he unite my soul to his own radiance : (that is, to his own soul, which resides effulgent in the seventh world, or mansion of truth). On another occasion, the concluding prayer, which is the Gâyatrî of Brahmâ, is omitted, and the names of the three lower worlds only are premised. Thus recited, the Gâyatri, properly so called, bears the following import : "On that effulgent Power, which is Brahmâ himself, and is called the light of the radiant Sun, do I meditate, governed by the mysterious light which resides within me for the purpose of thought ; that very light is the earth, the subtile ether, and all which exists within the created sphere ; it is the three-fold world, containing all which is fixed or moveable : it exists internally in my heart, externally in the orb of the Sun ; being one and the same with that effulgent Power, I myself am an irradiated manifestation of the supreme Brahmâ."

Earth ! Sky ! Heaven ! Let us meditate on (these and on) the most excellent light and power of that generous, sportive, and resplendent Sun, (praying that) it may guide our intellects.

*Muir.*—We have received that excellent glory of the divine Savitṛi; may he stimulate our understandings (or hymns, or rites.)

*Benfey.*—May we receive the glorious brightness of this, the generator, of the god who shall prosper our works

*Râma Mohan Roy.*—We meditate on that Supreme Spirit of the splendid Sun who directs our understandings.

*A note by Sir William Jones*:—What this Sun and Light are to this visible world, that are the *Supreme good* and *truth*, to the intellectual and invisible universe; and, as our corporeal eyes have a distinct perception of objects enlightened by the Sun, thus our souls acquire certain knowledge, by meditating on the light of truth, which emanates from the Being of beings: that is the light by which alone our minds can be directed in the path to beatitude.

---

## CHAPTER VI.

### SANDHYÂ.

*The etymology of Sandhyâ explained.*—The prayer of the Hindus is called Sandhyâ. It is a compound term, made up of two words, "Sam" and "Dhyâ;" meaning "perfect" or "complete" (sam), meditation or concentration (dhyâ). Therefore, the prayer of the Hindus principally consists of meditation on the attributes of God and of His creation—the world and man. It is less of petitionary in its characteristics than of meditative.

*The time.*—The time for this meditation or Sandhyâ is declared also by this term itself. In this sense the word "Sandhyâ," is derived from the word "Sandhi" or "Union," that is, the time (of forty-eight minutes or a Muhûrta) between the night and day, *viz.*, the morning and evening twilights. The time of union between the fore-noon and the after-noon, *viz.*, the mid-day is also called Sandhyâ. The morning Sandhyâ should be commenced before the sun rises, and finished with the rising of the sun. The evening Sandhyâ should be commenced before the sun begins to set, and finished with the complete setting of that luminary and the rising of the stars.

The *full* time for these twilight meditations thus consist of forty-eight minutes in the morning and forty-eight minutes in the evening, during the periods of the day, before the man enters upon his worldly duties in the morning, and after he has finished all those duties in the afternoon.

But God is not only to be remembered at those times only when one is separate from all worldly concerns, but in the very heart of all these transactions. Therefore, at *noon*, also meditation should be performed for that time is also Sandhyâ time. Under the present economical conditions of the world, it is not possible for Hindus, who are in service or business, to perform their mid-day Sandhyâ in full detail. But they can withdraw their mind for a few minutes, wherever they may be, whether in their offices, shops, exchanges, trains, etc., and fix it on God with a short prayer.

*Gâyatrî.*—The main or the central point of Sandhyâ consists in the prayer called "Gâyatrî." It is a sacred mantra or hymn consisting of the following syllables in the original Saṃskṛit:—

*Gâyatrî.*—Tat-sa-vi-tuḥ, va-re-ny-aṃ, Bhar-go, De-va-sya, dhî-ma-hi. Dhi-yo, Yo, naḥ, pra-cho-da-yât. Om.

*Mahâ Vyâhritis*:—Om Bhûḥ, Bhuvaḥ, Svaḥ.

The first five syllables are called Mahâ Vyâhritis or the Great exclamations, or the Words of Power, by utterance of which God created the three worlds—physical (Bhûḥ), emotional (Bhuvaḥ), and mental (Svaḥ.) Besides the *three* Mahâ-Vyâhritis—Bhûḥ, Bhuvaḥ and Svaḥ, there are four other Vyâhritis employed in Prâṇâyâma only. But they are simply called Vyâhritis and not Mahâ-Vyâhritis. The remaining twenty-four syllables, which form ten words, is called Gâyatrî, *par excellence*, or the prayer (gâya) that saves (tri), or the Lord who saves. Many explanations are given of this most ancient hymn, and we give one of them here; several others have already been given in the last chapter.

(1) *O Supreme Brahman* (*Om, consisting of three letters, A, U, M, meaning Creator, Preserver, and Regenerator*), *Thou art the Creator of all beings* (*Bhûḥ*), *their Sustainer* (*Bhuvaḥ*), *and their Final Goal* (*Svaḥ*).

*I meditate* (*dhîmahi*) *on the Adorable* (*Vareṇyam*), *Blissful* (*Bhargah*) (*form of God*), *the Conscience* (*Savituḥ, the Inciter, the Inner Compeller*). *May He stimulate* (*Prachodayât*) *all our* (*Naḥ*) *faculties* (*dhiyaḥ*.)

Thus the prayer of the Hindus may be summed up in these words:—

O God, who art the Creator, Preserver, and Regenerator (of the three worlds, physical, emotional, and mental), we meditate on that adorable, blissful form of Thine, which is in our heart as Conscience. May Thou illumine all our faculties.

*Japa*.—The method of prayer consists in reciting the above mantra *ten*, or *twenty-eight*, or *hundred and eight* times.

This is the absolutely necessary portion of a Hindu prayer, and this silent muttering is called Japa. Constantly uttering this Mantra, and meditating on God, and praying to Him to illumine his intellect, will, in the long run, bring about a state of mind which will be pure from all grosser elements. Every one, who calls himself a Hindu, however busy he may be, should utter this prayer, if not in Saṃskrit, then in his own mother tongue, at the three stated times.

A full Sandhyâ, however, consists of several parts, and their arrangements and order differ according to the school to which a Hindu belongs. Some of these elements of Sandhyâ are devotional, others hygienic, physiological, emotional, intellectual, and intuitional. We give them in their order as found among the Ṛigvedins whose Sandhyâ is most rich in Vedic mantras, and may stand, therefore, as a prototype for all other Sandhyâs.

(1) *Prâṇâyâma*. After bathing, to purify the external physical body, and sipping of water (Âchamana), the inner organs, or the circulatory systems should be regulated and purified by Prâṇâyâma, or breathing exercise. It mainly consists in slowly drawing in the air through the right nostril, then closing both the nostrils, and retaining the air for the space of a minute, and lastly, by expelling the air slowly through the right nostril. To regulate the time of this in-drawing, retention, and expulsion of air, the above Gâyatri mantra is recited with certain additions, which raises the total number of syllables to sixty. And as one syllable may take one second to pronounce it, the period of retention would be

one minute, and so also the periods of in-drawing and expulsion. The Gâyatrî thus modified for Prâṇâyâma, or breathing exercise, consists of the following syllables :—

*Vyâhṛitis.*—Om Bhûḥ, Om Bhu-vaḥ, Om Svaḥ, Om Ma-haḥ, Om Ja-naḥ, Om Ta-paḥ, Om Sa-ty-am.

The seven Vyâhritis Bhuḥ Bhuvaḥ, &c., mean as follows :—

Bhûḥ = सन्मात्रम्. The Mere *Being*. Sat.

Bhuvaḥ = The All-Intelligence, because he illumines or manifests (bhâvayati = prakâśayati) all. *Becoming*. Chit.

Svaḥ = The All-*Bliss*. It comes from su-vriyate, *i.e.*, सुष्ठु सर्वैः व्रियमाण सुखस्वरूपम् ॥ Perfection. Ânanda.

Mahaḥ = The All-mighty, the adored of all (mahîyate-pûjyate).

Janaḥ = The All-cause, because It produces (Janayati) all.

Tapaḥ = All-Energy or All-Light or Tejas.

Satyam = All-True = सर्वबाध-रहितं

Thus the seven Vyâhritis denote the seven attributes of the Deity—Pure Being, All-knowledge, Supreme-Bliss, the Almighty, the Great Cause, the Luminous and the true.

*Gâyatrî.*—Om. Tat Sa-vi-tur Va-re-ṇy-am Bhar-go De-va-sya dhî-ma-hi ; dhi-yo yo naḥ pra-cho-da-yât.

*Śiras.*—Om. Âp-o jyo-tî ra-so-'mri-tam Brah-ma Bhûr Bhu-vas Svar Om.

The meaning of the Śiras is this.

आपः = All-pervading, which reaches (âpnoti) all.

ज्योतिः = All-light. The manifester.

रसः = The All-essence : because surpasseth all.

अमृतं = Immortal, above the Saṁsâra.

The whole means "I am that Brahman, which is designated by the word Aum, whose essence is Existence, Intelligence and Bliss, which is eternally Free, and who is All-pervading, All illumining and the Supreme above all."

The object of this breathing exercise is primarily, to purify the blood, to expand the lungs and the chest, and thus to give a tone to all internal organs of the body, and secondarily, to sanctify the whole body and to make it a temple of God, by meditating that He dwells in His creative aspect in the digestive organs at navel, or solar plexus, in His preservative aspect in the heart, or the circulatory system, and in His regenerative or bliss-giving aspect in the brain, or nervous system.

The meaning of the Prâṇâyâma Mantra is the same as that of Gâyatrî, as above given, the additional words denote some additional attributes of God as ruler of the seven worlds (physical, emotional, intellectual, intuitional, creative, volitional, and the eternal). The Śiras explains the attributes of God as all-pervading, luminous, all love, and the immortal and the absolute. The full Prâṇâyâma mantra, therefore, means :—

O God, Thou art the Creator, Preserver, Regenerator, the most

Adorable, the Life, the Energy, and the Eternal (Ruler of) the seven worlds—physical, emotional, intellectual, intuitional, creative, volitional, and the eternal.

We meditate on that adorable, blissful form of Thine, which is in our heart as Conscience. May thou illumine all our faculties.

I acknowledge Brahman to be All-pervading (Âpas), All-intelligence (Jyoti), All-happiness (Rasa), and Immortality (Amṛitam). He is Bhûḥ (the All-support), Bhuvaḥ (the All-nourisher), and Svaḥ (the All-approachable).

Thus this breathing exercise, which forms the second stage in the Sandhyâ of the Hindus, the first stage being bathing, purifies the inner body of man, and quietens the mind, and fits it for meditation.

A full Prâṇâyâma consists of the triple process of drawing-in, restraining, and expelling of the air. *Three* such Prâṇâyâmas should be performed in every Sandhyâ.

It will be observed that before reciting the mantras, certain words are mentally repeated showing who is the Seer or the Ṛiṣi, or Revealer of that mantra. In other words, *First*, who is the person, who being inspired first uttered the mantra. *Secondly*, who is the Devatâ, or the object of meditation, or invocation, or address in that mantra, and *thirdly*, what is the particular metre, rhythm, or key in which that mantra should be recited, and *fourthly*, what is the particular object sought to be accomplished by that Mantra.

In the case of Prâṇâyâma, the syllable OM, has for its Seer the sage Brahmâ himself, for its deity the aspect of God in the physical world called Agni, and for its metre or key Gâyatrî. It is to be employed in the beginning of all sacred rites. In the case of the seven Vyâhṛitis the revealer is the sage Prajâpati, and the divinities of the seven planes are, (1) Agni (ether) of *Bhuḥ* or the physical plane, (2) Vâyu of *Bhuvaḥ* or the emotional plane, (3) Âditya of *Svar* or the intellectual plane, (4) Brihaspati, or the Lord of Voice, or of the Word, is Divinity of *Mahar* or the intuitional plane, (5) Varuna of *Jana* or the creative plane, (6) Indra of *Tapas* or the plane of Will and Power, (7) and the All-God or Viśvedevâ of *Satyam* or the plane of the Truth or Eternity. These seven Vyâhṛitis are employed to accomplish Prâṇâyâma, as well as Prâyaśchitta or repentance.

These seven Vyâhṛitis are to be chanted in the seven keys of the musical octave, or in the seven well-known metres of the Veda known as Gâyatrî, Uṣṇik etc.

Similarly, of the mantra Gâyatrî, the Revealer is the sage Viśvâmitra, the deity invoked is the God in the aspect of Savitâ, or Conscience, the metre is Gâyatrî, or the first key of the octave, and the object to be accomplished by it is the regulation of breath and the atonement of all sins.

Similarly of the Śiras the Revealer is the sage Prajâpati, the aspects of Divinity invoked by it are Brahmâ, Agni, Vâyu, and Sûrya, *viz.*, Brahmâ presides over the Âpas or the Water or the All-pervading aspect of God ; Agni presides over the All-intelligence or Light aspect of God ; Vâyu presides over the All-loving (or sweetness or Rasa) aspect of God, and Sûrya presides over the Immortal or Amrita aspect of God. Its metre is Anuṣṭup. And it also is employed to accomplish Prâṇâyâma and is a prayer for forgiveness also.

Note here the function ascribed to Vâyu, *viz.*, as expressing the Rasa or the Love-aspect of God, and it is for this reason that Madhva, the Founder of the Theistic School, calls Vâyu the Beloved Son of God, the Lover of man, the Mediator between God and man. Because Vâyu represents the love-aspect of God.

Thus in reciting every Vedic Mantra, one must know these four things:—(1) Who is the Revealer or Ṛiṣi of that Mantra. It is a simple act of gratitude to remember His name. (2) Who is the particular Devatâ or the aspect of God referred to in that Mantra. (3) What is the particular key or the metre in which that mantra is to be chanted. (4) What is the particular object of the ritual in or for which that mantra is to be employed.

(2) *Morning Âchamana by Mantra, or simply Mantra-Âchamana.*

As Snâna, or bathing, purifies the physical body, and Prâṇâyâma, or breathing exercise, purifies the emotional, or the animal body, so this Mantra-Âchamana, purifies the mental body. It is to be distinguished from the ordinary Âchamana or sipping of water, the mantra of which is 'Tat Viṣṇoh paramam padam &c.' The Mantra for the purificatory ceremony of the mental body resolves when analysed, into a prayer to God to forgive all the sins of the person praying, and to burn up all his evil deeds. Man, according to Hindu Philosophy, is clothed in five sheaths or vestures, called respectively (1) Annamaya-koṣa, or the sheath of food or the physical body, (2) Prâṇamaya-koṣa, or the sheath of vital breaths, or the animal body, or the emotional sheath, the seat of desires which a man has in common with all animals, in other words, the vital functions, (3) the Manomaya-koṣa, or the sheath of mind, or the mental body, or the rational soul, or the body that distinguishes man from the lower animals (4) Vijñanamaya-koṣa or Intuitional body and (5) Anandamaya-koṣa or Bliss-body. It is with the mental body that a man performs sacrifices in order to go to heaven ; and it is with the mental body that a man plans mischiefs to rob others of their possessions and to appropriate them himself. So this mental body is a double-faced animal, one face turned towards heaven and the other towards earth, one Divine and the other Satanic. The deity presiding over this mental body is called Manyu, a word which may be translated as 'spirit of Love as well as the spirit of wrath.' In its first sense, Manyu is identified with God in His beneficent aspect, and in the second sense, it is identified with Wrath, the Spirit of Destruction or Indignation. Thus in the Ṛigveda X. 83 and 84, we find hymns addressed to Manyu, where He is the Spirit of Wrath, or warlike ardour, which makes men kill each other and pray for victory. Thus Manyu is addressed :—

(1) He who hath reverenced thee, Manyu, destructive bolt, breeds for himself forthwith all conquering energy. Ârya and Dâsa will we conquer with thine aid, with thee the Conqueror, with conquest-sped.

(2) Manyu was Indra, yea, the God was Manyu, Manyu was Hotar, Varuṇa, Jâtavedas.
The tribes of human lineage worship Manyu. Accordant with thy fervour, Manyu, guard us.

(3) Come hither, Manyu, mightier than the mighty, chase with thy fervour for ally, our foemen.

Slayer of foes, of Vṛitra, and of Dasyu, bring thou to us all kinds of wealth and treasure.

That Manyu is the type of man in his present state of evolution, half beast and half God, we find from another hymn (Atharva Veda, Bk. XI, hymn 8) which in 34 verses describes the creation of man and the various Devas (spirits) that entered into the body of man. A few extracts from that hymn will make this clear :—

(1) When Manyu brought his consort home forth from Saṅkalpa's dwelling place,
Who were the wooers of the bride, who was the chief who courted her ?
(2) Fervor and Action were the two, in depths of the great billowy sea :
These were the wooers of the bride ; Brahmâ the chief who courted her.
(3) Ten Gods before the Gods were born together in the ancient time.
Whoso may know them face to face may now pronounce the mighty word.
(7) He may account himself well versed in ancient time who knows by name,
*The earth that was before this earth*, which only wisest sages know.

After describing the creation of the body of man and its fashioning by Tvaṣṭâ, the hymn goes on to describe how various Devas entered into the body and made man what he is.

(18) When Tvaṣṭar, Tvaṣṭar's loftier Sire, had bored it out and hollowed it, (the body).

Gods made the mortal their abode, and entered and possessed the man.
(19) Sleep, specially. Sloth, Nirṛiti, and deities whose name is Sin,
Baldness, old age, and hoary hairs within the body found their way.
(20) Theft, evil doing, and deceit, truth, sacrifice, exalted fame,
Strength, princely power, and energy entered the body as a home.
(21) Prosperity and poverty, kindnesses and malignities,
Hunger and thirst of every kind entered the body as a home.
(22) Reproaches, freedom from reproach, all blamable, all blameless deeds,
Bounty, belief, and unbelief, entered the body as a home.
(23) All knowledge and all ignorance, each other thing that one may learn,
Entered the body, prayer, and hymns, and songs, and sacrificial texts.
(24) Enjoyments, pleasures, and delights, gladness, and rapturous ecstasies,
Laughter and merriment and dance entered the body as a home.
(25) Discourse and conversation, and the shrill-resounding cries of woe,
All entered in, the motives and the purposes combined therewith.
(26) Inbreath and outbreath, ear and eye, decay and freedom from decay,
Breath upward and diffused, voice, mind, these quickly with the body move.
(27) All earnest wishes, all commands, directions, and admonishments,
Reflections, all deliberate plans entered the body as a home.
(28) They laid in the abhorrent frame those waters hidden, bright, and thick,
Which in the bowels spring from blood, from mourning or from hasty toil.
(29) Fuel they turned to bone, and then they set light waters in the frame,
The molten butter they made seed : then the Gods entered into man.
(30) All waters, all the Deities, Virâj with Brahmâ at her side :
Brahmâ into the body passed : Prajâpati is Lord thereof.
(31) The Sun and Wind formed, separate, the eye and vital breath of man.
His other person have the Gods bestowed on Agni as a gift.
(32) Therefore, whoever knoweth man regardeth him as Brahmâ's self : For all the Deities abide in him as cattle in their pen.

This long quotation will show what was the real function of Manyu. Manyu is God in His aspect of terribleness or wrath. Manyu is man in his aspect of irresoluteness, stumbling and rising, and rising and stumbling. The Mantra-Âchamana is, therefore, the prayer of the sinning man to the God within whose wrath he has incurred, asking Him to forgive his sins, the sins of commission as well as of omission. Mantra-Âchamana, therefore, is the means by which the impurities of the mind, caused by sin, are washed away. This washing away of sins is symbolically represented by the sipping of water. The water is conceived as carrying away all his sins, and as being poured into the great Reservoir, the great Purifier, the God called the Sun, the God called the Agni. It is remorse and repentance which are the chief means of purifying the mental body or Manomaya Koşa.

God is called Manyu or Wrath, because He is not only Merciful, but is the Punisher of the wicked also. Manyu, therefore, is an aspect of God and is the same as Ṛudra. When applied to MAN, it means the immortal human principle and it is this *manyu*, that distinguishes *man* from all lower creations, who have no immortal soul. Thus in the Śatapatha Brâhmaṇa, IX. 1. 1, 6 we find :

"When Prajâpati had become disjointed, the deities departed from him. Only one god did not leave him, to wit, Manyu (wrath); extended he remained within. He (Prajâpati) cried, and the tears of him that fell down settled on Manyu. He became the hundred-headed, thousand-eyed, hundred-quivered Rudra. And the other drops that fell down, spread over these worlds in countless numbers, by thousands; and inasmuch as they originated from crying (rud), they were called Rudras (roarers)."

But is it not a blasphemy to say that God has Manyu or wrath or anger and that the Rudra or the terrible is one aspect of God ? Not at all. There are certain acts at which God Himself may be rightly indignant. Thus to quote Oliver Lodge,

"Nevertheless, I am sure that what may without irreverence be humanly spoken of as fierce Wrath against sin, and even against a certain class of sinner, is a Divine attribute." He gives several illustrations of this: "There are many grades of sin; and anyone may know the kind of sin which excites the anger of God, by bethinking him of the kind which arouses his own best and most righteous anger. I can imagine that the infernal proceedings of Nero and of the Holy Inquisition were repugnant and nauseating to the Universe to a degree which was almost unbearable. The fierce indignation that would blaze out if one were maliciously to torture a child or an animal in view of an ordinary man or woman, would surely be a spark of the Divine wrath; and we have been told that a millstone round the neck of a child-abuser is too light a penalty."

So righteous indignation at certain acts of degraded humanity, such as, ingratitude or insulting an innocent woman, etc., are illustrations. Thus war may be justified when it is undertaken to defend a cause which is righteous, to remedy an evil at which not only the blood of men would boil, but at which the wrath of the Rudra would blaze forth. Therefore, this prayer to Manyu is perfectly appropriate for Man.

## MÂRJANA.

(3) *Mârjana.* This ceremony is also a part of purification of the mental body. It consists in sprinkling of water with Kuśa blades on one's body and on the ground, reciting certain Vedic mantras. The Ṛigvedins pronounce about eleven mantras, nine of which are taken from the Rigveda, while one is taken from the Atharva Veda, and another from the Yajur Veda. These mantras are more in the nature of prayer or petitions addressed to God in His aspect of Âpas or Waters or the All-pervader. It shows that man by his repentance and remorse feels himself at one with his God, and so entitled to ask favours from Him. It also contains prayer for the purification of the mental body.

(4) *Aghamarṣaṇa.* As Âchamana was a confession of sin, and Mârjana, a prayer for the purification of sin, Aghamarṣaṇa may be considered to be an active act of the man to destroy the very seed of sin from his soul, and to expel this sin (personified as a man, or rather a demon) from his body. This is done by rising in meditation to the very beginning of creation, when there existed God and God alone Who is Ritam or the Eternal Moral Law, and Who is Satyam or Eternal Law of Nature. Repeating certain Vedic Mantras, he strongly imagines that the Person of Sin goes out of his body, and that he is now perfectly pure and that his bodies, physical, emotional, and mental, are now attuned with the Infinite, and that he is ready to approach God and address Him face to face.

(5 and 6) *The Arghya of Sûrya and Prayer to Him.* The meaning of offering Arghya to Sûrya is to show respect to Him as one does when a high personage honors one's home with a visit, and the prayer to Sûrya naturally follows after *arghya* offering and consists of six Vedic Mantras taken from Rigveda I. 115. They describe the physical Sun, in their external literal meaning, but they are really addressed to the Divine Sun, the Great Supreme. These verses are songs of praise and glorify the mighty Deity.

The following extract is taken from Colebrooke to explain these three connected ceremonies, that of Aghamarṣaṇa, Sûrya Arghya, and Suryopasthâna (Miscellaneous Essays Vol. I. p. 140 *et seq.*)

'The Supreme Being alone existed: afterwards there was universal darkness: next, the watery ocean was produced by the diffusion of verdure: then did the Creator, Lord of the universe, rise out of the ocean, and successively framed the sun and moon, which govern day and night, whence proceeds the revolution of years; and after them He framed heaven and earth, the space between, and the celestial region.' [The term Ritam and Satyam with which the text begins, both signify "truth;" but are here explained as denoting the Supreme Brahma on the authority of a text quoted from the Veda (Taitt. Up.) " Brahm, is truth, the one immutable being, He is truth and everlasting knowledge."] 'During the period of general annihilation,' says the commentator, the Supreme Being alone existed. Afterwards, during that period, night was produced; in other words, there was universal darkness.' "The universe existed only in darkness, imperceptible, undefinable, undiscoverable by reason, and undiscovered by revelation, as if it were wholly immersed in sleep." (Manu I. 5). Next, when the creation began, the ocean was produced by an unseen power universally diffused: that is, the element of water was first produced, as the means of creation. "He, first, with a thought, created the waters," &c. (Manu I. 8). Then did the Creator, who is Lord of the universe, rise out of the waters. "The Lord of the universe, annihilated by the general destruction, revived with his own creation of the three worlds." Heaven is here explained, the expanse of the sky above the region of the stars. The celestial region is the middle world and heavens above. The author before me has added numerous quotations on the sublimity and efficacy of this text, which Manu compares with the sacrifice of a horse, in respect of its power to obliterate sins.

(10.) The Japa or prayer has been said to be the principal part of Gâyatrî. It is the constant repetition of a word, or a sentence. It might appear to be a useless repetition, but it is not so really. The repetition itself produces a state of consciousness, bordering upon ecstasy, or the Turîya state. The Great Poet Laureate, Tennyson, used to enter into this state by simply repeating his own name (Alfred, Alfred) several times.

In a letter to Mr. B. P. Blood, Tennyson reports of himself as follows:—"I have never had any revelations through anæsthetics, but a kind of waking trance—this for lack of a better word—I have frequently had, quite up from boyhood, when I have been all alone. This has come upon me through repeating my own name to myself silently, till all at once, as it were out of the intensity of the consciousness of individuality, individuality itself seemed to dissolve and fade away into boundless being, and this not a confused state but the clearest, the surest of the surest, utterly beyond words—where death was an almost laughable impossibility—the loss of personality (if so it were) seeming no extinction but the only true life. I am ashamed of my feeble description. Have I not said the state is utterly beyond words?"

Professor Tyndall, in a letter, recalls Tennyson saying of this condition: "By God Almighty! there is no delusion in the matter! It is no nebulous ecstasy, but a state of transcendent wonder, associated with absolute clearness of mind." Memoirs of Alfred Tennyson, ii. 473. (From "The Varieties of Religious Experience" by James, pages 383-384).

This state of consciousness consists "in a feeling of an enlargement of perception," and which is the real meaning of the Saṃskṛit words of the Gâyatrî, "Dhiyaḥ prachodayât," "enlarge our perception." 'Dhiyaḥ is the plural of the word "Dhî" meaning intelligence, intuition, consciousness, prayer. Therefore, by constantly repeating this Gâyatrî, which is a prayer for enlargement of perception or intuition, the man enters into the fourth Koṣa, or sheath, called "Vijñanamaya-koṣa," or the Sheath of Buddhi, or Intuition.

Some misguided people try to stimulate (prachodanaḥ) their mystical faculties (dhiyas). Though it is wrong to use drugs for the "prachodana of dhi" (stimulation of mystical faculties), yet the following quotation from the same author will show that drugs have such an effect:—

The next step into mystical states carries us into a realm that public opinion and ethical philosophy have long since branded as pathological, though private practice and certain lyric strains of poetry seem still to bear witness to its ideality. I refer to the consciousness produced by intoxicants and anaesthetics, especially by alcohol. The sway of alcohol over mankind is unquestionably due to its power to stimulate the mystical faculties of human nature, usually crushed to earth by the cold facts, and dry criticisms of the sober hour. Sobriety diminishes, discriminates, and says no; drunkenness expands, unites, and says yes. It is in fact the great exciter of the *Yes* function in man. It brings its votary from the chill periphery of things to the radiation core. It makes him for the moment one with truth. Not through mere perversity do men run after it. To the poor and the unlettered it stands in the place of symphony concerts and of literature; and it is part of the deeper mystery and tragedy of life that whiffs and gleams of something that we immediately recognize as excellent should be vouchsafed to so many of us only in the fleeting earlier phases of what in its totality is so degrading a poisoning. The drunken consciousness is one bit of the mystic consciousness, and our total opinion of it must find its place in our opinion of that larger whole. (pp. 386-387).

Japa is, therefore, the most important part of Sandhyâ, and we need not further dilate upon it.

The Japa (tenth in order), is preceded by (7) meditation on Gâyatrî, (8) assignment of the various portions of one's body, the various parts of Gâyatrî, and then (9) invokation of Gâyatrî.

(11.) The Japa is followed by bidding farewell to Gâyatrî.

(12) Then follows the parting Arghya to the Sun called the Sûryârghya. This Arghya ceremony is still current in India in showing respect to one's guest by offering him, as soon as he arrives, *pâna* and *utar*, and so also when he departs.

While others offer instead *Hukkâ* or smoke. In ancient India this reception and farewell ceremonies or Arghya Dâna were done in various ways according to the nature of the guest and the god invoked. In the case of the deity invoked the Arghya offering consisted by putting water in a copper vessel called Koṣa, and putting into that water sandal paste scent, flower, uncooked rice, Durvâ grass &c. This water was offered to the Deity invoked with appropriate mantras.

(13.) After offering Arghya, the Deity is further honoured by saluting him with appropriate mantras. In the case of the sun this is done by reciting four mantras of the Ṛigveda III. 59. 6-9.

(14.) Then prayer is offered to the Deity to protect the host, and this is called Âtma-rakṣâ, or prayer for defence of the celebrant, and crushing of one's enemies.

(15.) Then as a preparation to the finishing of Sandhyâ the Devas dwelling in all the quarters,—east, south, west, and north, zenith, and nadir, and in the firmament, as well as the Gâyatrî in Her various forms, are saluted. And lastly, the celebrant is taught to realize his aloofness from all these ceremonies by repeating that all that he has done is really done by his Kamika nature (the desire nature) and by his Mânasika nature, or mental body, called Manyu. This reminds him to remain always aloof from the whole world of ceremonies, and not to attribute them to himself, but to his vehicles, and the gods presiding over those vehicles, *viz.*, to Kâma and Manyu.

(16. & 17.) The whole thing is concluded, then, again offering parting Arghya to Sûrya, and parting Praṇâma to Him.

(18.) The last thing is salutation to the God incarnate as man, to Divine Kriṣṇa, who took human shape to save humanity, at the critical time when the earth was groaning under the ceremonialism of Brâhmaṇas, and the Militarism of the Kṣatriyas. This is done by saluting him at the end of every Sandhyâ by saying:—"Salutation to Brahmaṇya-deva (God of true Brâhmanism, not of rituality, but of spirituality), the God who is born at every age and time, for the welfare of the Brâhmaṇas, for all spiritual men, and for the welfare of cow, the type of earth, *viz.*, when the earth groans under the weight of tyrants, spiritual, or temporal, the Kṛiṣṇa is born to uplift humanity. He is not only born for the sake of earth and Brâhmaṇas, but for the sake of the whole universe. Therefore, in saluting him one says, "Salutation to the God adored by all holy men, to Him who is born for the welfare of earth and the Brâhmaṇas, nay for the welfare of the whole universe, to Kṛiṣṇa, the lord of multitudes of worlds and planets (Govinda)."

That "Go" in this connection means "earth", we know from Nighaṇṭu, the Vaidika Dictionary—"(1) Gao, (2) Gmâ, (3) Jmâ, (4) Ksa, (5) Kama, (6) Ksonih, (7) Kṣitih, (8) Avunih, (9) Urvi, (10) Prithvi, (11) Mahi, (12) Ripah, (13) Aditih, (14) Ila, (15) Niritih, (16) Bhuh, (17) Bhumiḥ, (18) Pusa, (19) Gatuh, (20) Gotra. These 21 are the names of the earth.

Similarly, Brâhmaṇa in this connection does not mean the caste Brâhmaṇa, but a sage, or a saint, as we know from the Brihadâraṇyaka Upaniṣad:—(III. 5. 1):—

"Then Kahola Kausitakeya asked, 'Yâjñavalkya,' he said, 'tell me the Brahman which is invisible, not visible, the Self (Âtman), who is within all.'

Yâjñavalkya replied:—'This, thy Self, who is within all.'

'Which Self, O Yâjñavalkya, is within all?'

6

Yâjñavalkya replied: 'He who overcomes hunger and thirst, sorrow, passion, old age, and death. When Brâhmaṇas know that Self, and have risen above the desire for sons, wealth, and (new) worlds, they wander about as mendicants. For a desire for sons is desire for wealth, a desire for wealth is desire for worlds. Both these are indeed desires. Therefore let a Brâhmaṇa, after he has done with learning wish to stand by real strength; after he has done with that strength and learning, he becomes a Muni (Yogin); and after he has done with what is not the knowledge of a Muni, and with what is the knowledge of a Muni, he is a BRAHMANA. By whatever means he has become a Brâhmaṇa, he is such indeed. Everything else is of evil.' After that Kahola Kausîtakeya held his peace.

That God does incarnate we quote the following from Sir Oliver Lodge. (The words within brackets are ours).

"I believe that the most essential element in Christianity (Hinduism) is its conception of a human God;—of a God, in the first place, not apart from the universe, not outside it and distinct from it, but immanent in it; yet not immanent only, but actually incarnate, incarnate in it and revealed in the Incarnation. The nature of God is displayed in part by everything, to those who have eyes to see, but is displayed most clearly and fully by the highest type of existence, the highest experience to which the process of evolution has so far opened our senses. By what else indeed can it conceivably be rendered manifest? Naturally the conception of Godhead is still only indistinct and partial; but, so far as we are as yet able to grasp it, we must reach it through recognition of the extent and intricacy of the cosmos, and more particularly through the highest type and loftiest spiritual development of man himself.

The perception of a human God, or of a God in the form of humanity, is a perception which welds together Christianity and Pantheism and Paganism and Philosophy. But whatever its unconscious treatment by the sects may have been, this idea the humanity of God or the Divinity of man—I conceive to be the truth which constituted the chief secret and inspiration of Jesus (as well as of Kṛiṣṇa): "I and the Father are one." "My Father worketh hitherto, and I work." "The Son of man," and equally "The son of God." "Before Abraham was I AM." "I am in the Father and the Father in me." And though admittedly "My Father is greater than I," yet "he that hath seen me hath seen the Father," and "he that believeth on me hath everlasting life."

The world has been slow to grasp the meaning of all this. The conception of Godhead formed by some devout philosophers and mystics has quite rightly been so immeasurably vast, though still utterly inadequate and immeasurably beneath reality, that the notion of God revealed in human form-born, suffering, tormented, killed—has been utterly incredible. "A crucified prophet, yes; but a crucified God! I shudder at the blasphemy," yet that apparent blasphemy is the soul of Christianity. It calls upon us to recognize and worship a crucified, as executed, God.

---

## CHAPTER VII.

### THE SANDHYÂ OF THE RIG-VEDINS.

॥ अथ ऋग्वेदीनां सन्ध्याविधिः ॥

*Gâyatrî.*

ओम् । भूर्भुवः स्वः । तत् सवितुर्वरेण्यं भर्गो देवस्य धीमहि धियो यो नः प्रचोदयात् ॥ ओम् ॥

---

*I. Viniyoga.*

ओंकारस्य ब्रह्मा ऋषिर्गायत्री छन्दोऽग्निर्देवता सर्वकर्मारम्भे विनियोगः ।

सप्तव्याहृतीनां विश्वामित्र यमदग्निभरद्वाज गौतम अत्रि वसिष्ठ कश्यपाः ऋषयः
गायत्र्युष्णिगनुष्टुब्बृहती पङ्क्तित्रिष्टुब्जगत्यश्छन्दांसि ।
अग्निवाय्वादित्यबृहस्पतिवरुणेन्द्रविश्वेदेवा देवताः ।
गायत्र्या विश्वामित्रऋषिर्गायत्रीछन्दः सविता देवता ॥
शिरसः प्रजापति ऋषिः यजुश्छन्दो ब्रह्मअग्निवायुसूर्या देवताः प्राणा-
यामे विनियोगः ॥

इति स्मृत्वा तथैव जलगण्डूषं क्रामयित्वा मध्यमानामिकाख्यावामनासापुटं निबन्ध्य दक्षिणनासापुटेन वायुमाकृष्य पुण्डरीकाक्षध्यानमाचरेत ।

## ॥ ततः प्राणायामः ॥

प्रथमं रक्तवर्णं चतुर्मुखं द्विभुजमक्षसूत्रकमण्डलुधरं हंसवाहनस्थं ब्रह्माणं नाभिदेशे ध्यात्वा पूरकोछ्वास-वायुं प्रवेशयन् सप्तव्याहृतिगायत्रीं जपेत् ।

ओं भूः । ओं भुवः । ओं स्वः । ओं महः । ओं जनः । ओं तपः । ओं सत्यम् ।

ओं तत्सवितुर्व्वरेण्यं भर्गोदेवस्य धीमहि ॥ धियो यो नः प्रचोदयात् ॥ ओं आपो-ज्योतीरसोमृतं ब्रह्मभूर्भुवः स्वरोम् ॥

ततो हृदिनीलोत्पलदलप्रभं शङ्खचक्रगदापद्मधरं गरुडारूढं केशवं ध्यायन् ।
वायुं स्तम्भयन् सप्तव्याहृतिगायत्री जपेत् ।
ततो ललाटे श्वेतं द्विभुजं त्रिशूलडमरूकरमर्धचन्द्रविभूषितं वृषभस्थं शम्भुं ध्यायन् श्वासं बहिर्नयन् द्यावापृथिव्योरन्तरसमीक्षमाणः ।
सप्तव्याहृतिगायत्रीं पठन् वायुं रेचयेत् ।
एवं पूरक कुम्भकरे चकमेण प्राणायामं त्रयं कुर्यात् ।
एतेन ब्रह्म विष्णुशिवध्यानपूर्वकपूरककुम्भकरेचकमेण एकप्राणायामः ।

इत्थं त्रयः प्राणायामाः ।

### 1. PRÂṆÂYÂMA.

#### (a) *Pûraka.*

This consists in closing the left nostril with the middle and the ring fingers, and drawing the air through the right nostril, so that it may reach up to the navel, and meditating there on Brahmâ as having red colour, four faces, two hands, holding rosary in one and a Kamandalu in the other, and as seated on a Hamsa or flamingo. While drawing the air in, he should recite the Gâyatrî preceded by seven Vyâhṛitis and succeeded by its Śiras. He should remind himself also, before repeating the mantra, who and what are the Devas, Riṣis, and Chhandas of this mantra.

The full process is this :—

*Viniyoga* :—Of Om, the seer is Brahmâ, the Devatâ is Agni, the metre is Gâyatrî, and it is employed in the beginning of all sacred ceremonies.

Of the seven Vyâhṛitis, the seer is Prajâpati, the Devatâs are Agni, Vâyu, Âditya Bṛihaspati, Varuṇa, Indra, and Viśvedevâs respectively; and their metres are Uṣṇik., Anuṣṭup, Brihatî, Paṅkti, Triṣṭup, and Jagatî ; and it is employed in Upanayana, Prâṇâyâma, and Prâyaschitta.

Of Gâyatrî, the seer is Viśvâmitra, the Devatâ is Savitṛi, the metre is Gâyatrî, and it is employed in Prâṇâyâma and Prâyaschitta.

Of the Śiras, the seer is Prajâpati, the Devatâs are Brahmâ, Agni, Vâyu, Sûrya; the metre is Anuṣṭup, and it is employed in Prâyaśchitta and Prâṇâyâma.

*Prayoga* :—Reciting all these mentally and passing his hand filled with water briskly round, his neck, he should perform the drawing of the breath called Pûraka by closing the left nostril with the ring and the middle fingers, and meditating on Brahmâ in the navel-region, as mentioned above, *viz.*, as having a red colour, four faces, two hands, holding a rosary and a water-pot, and seated on a Haṃsa or flamingo. While thus meditating and drawing in the air, let him recite :—

(*The seven Vyâhṛitis with Om*), Om Bhûḥ, Om Bhuvaḥ, Om Svaḥ, Om Mahaḥ, Om Janaḥ, Om Tapaḥ, Om Satyam.

(*Meaning*) :—God, the Ineffable (Om), is Pure Being, (Bhûḥ), All Knowledge (Bhuvaḥ), Supreme Bliss (Svaḥ), The Almighty (Mahaḥ), The Great Cause (Janaḥ), The Luminous (Tapaḥ), and the True (Satyam).

(*Gâyatrî*). Om Tat Ṣavitur Vareṇyam Bhargo Devasya dhîmahi ; dhiyo yo naḥ prachodayât.

(*Meaning*) :—The Gâyatrî has several meanings, and we give some of them. (1) We meditate on the adorable blissful form of God, the Conscience. May He stimulate all our faculties. (2) I meditate (with my three-fold consciousness) on the adorable divine Fire of the unchangeable Creator : who is called Tat. May Lakṣmî and Nârâyaṇa stimulate my cognitions. (3) I meditate on God (who creates as) Brahmâ, sustains as Viṣṇu, and destroys as Śiva : and who as Turîya is above all these three. May He stimulate my cognitions.

(*Śiras*) :--Om Âpo jyotî raso'mritam Bṛahma, Bhûr Bhuvas, Svar Om.

(*Meaning*) :—The Ineffable God is All-pervading (Âpaḥ), is All-Light, is All-Essence (Rasa), and is Deathless (Amritam), and is Bṛahman (The Full), is Pure Being, Knowledge, and Bliss, Om.

### (*b*) *Kumbhaka.*

After performing Pûraka as mentioned above, while meditating on Keśava in the region of the heart, as having the colour of the petal of a blue lotus, and holding a conch, a discus, a club, and a lotus (in his four hands), and as seated on Garuḍa or Eagle, let him close the right nostril also (with his thumb finger), and while thus restraining the breath, recite the above Gâyatrî with its Vyâhṛitis and Śiras.

### (*c*) *Rechaka.*

Then let him slowly breathe out the air (through his left nostril), reciting the same Gâyatrî with its Vyâhṛitis and Śiras, while meditating all along on Śambhu, in the region of his forehead, as having white colour, two hands, holding a trident and a drum, and as having for his ornament a crescent on his forehead, and seated on a bull.

Thus one full Prâṇâyâma consists of these three processes :—(1) Pûraka, or the filling in of the air, (2) Kumbhaka or the retention of the air, and (3) Rechaka, or expulsion of the breath. In all these processes the above mantra consisting of sixty syllables should be recited. Thus it will take one minute to recite the mantra, or three minutes for the entire process. This constitutes one Prâṇâyâma, in which the three aspects of God, *viz.*, the Creator, (Brahmâ), the Sustainer (Viṣṇu), and the Regenerator (Śiva) are to be meditated upon as existing in one's own body, and presiding over the three functions of the body, *viz.*, of alimentation in the stomach, of the circulation in the heart, and of cognition in the brain, or, in other words, on the vegetative, animal and human functions.

Three such Prâṇâyâmas should be performed in a Sandhyâ.

Thus about ten minutes should be given to Prâṇâyâma.

## II. MORNING ÂCHAMANA.

॥ ततः जलगण्डुषमादाय आचमनं कुर्यात् ॥

ओ३म् सूर्यश्चमेति नारायण ऋषिः सूर्यो देवता गायत्रीछन्दः आचमने विनियोगः ।

ओं सूर्य्यश्च मामन्युश्च मन्युपतयश्च मन्युकृतेभ्यः पापेभ्यो रक्षन्ताम् । यद्रात्र्या पापमकार्षं मनसा वाचा हस्ताभ्यां पद्भ्यामुदरेण शिश्ना रात्रिस्तदवलुम्पतु । यत्किंचिद् दुरितं मयि इदमहमापोऽमृतयोनौ सूर्ये ज्योतिषिपरमात्मनि जुहोमि स्वाहा ॥

(TAITTAREYA ARANYAKA X. 25).

( योऽयम् ) सूर्यः ( अस्ति ) यश्च मन्युः (क्रोधाभिमानी देवः), (ये) च मन्युपतयः (क्रोधस्याभिमानत्वियामका देवाः सन्ति ते सर्वेऽपि ) मन्युकृतेभ्यः ( मदीयकोपनिष्पादितेभ्यः ) पापेभ्यो मा (मां) रक्षन्तां ( पापिनं मां तत्पापविनाशनेन पालयन्तु ) । ( कि चातीतेन ) राज्या ( तस्याम् राज्याम् ) यत्पापमकार्षं ( कृतवानस्मि ) मनसा ( मन आदिभिः शिश्नान्तैरवयवैः ) (तत्सर्वं पापम्) रात्रिरवलुम्पतु ( रात्रिरभिमानी देवो विनाशयतु ) यत्किंच दुरितं मयि ( विद्यते ) इदम् ( पापजातं सर्वं कर्तारं ) अहं माम् ( च लिङ्गशरीररूपम् ) अमृतयोनौ ( मरणरहिते जगत्कारणे ) सूर्ये ज्योतिषि ( स्वयं प्रकाशे वस्तुनि ) जुहोमि ( प्रक्षिपामि, अहमनेन होमेन तत्सर्वं भस्मी करोमीत्यर्थः ) तदर्थमिदमभिमन्त्रितं जलं ) स्वाहा ( मदीयमुखाग्नौ स्वाहुतमस्तु )

अनेन मन्त्रेण ब्राह्मतीर्थेन त्रिराचमेत् ।

Then taking hold of a little water in his hand for Gaṇḍuṣa, let him do the Âchamana with the following mantra :—

*Viniyoga* :—Of the mantra, 'Sûryas' cha mâ &c., the seer is Nârâyaṇa, the Devatâ is Sûrya, the metre is Gâyatri, and it is employed in Âchamana.

*Mantra* :—Sûryaś cha mâ manyuś cha manyu patayaś cha manyu kṛitebhyaḥ Pâpebhyo rakṣantâm yad râtryâ pâpam akârṣam. Manasâvâchâ hastâbhyâm. Padbhyâm udareṇa śiśnâ. Râtris tad avalumpatu. Yat kiñchid duritaṃ mayi. Idam aham âpo' mṛita Yonau. Sûrye jyotiṣi paramâtmani juhomi svâha.

*English meaning* :—सूर्यः = The Sûrya, च = and, मा = me, मन्युः = the Manyu (God of courage, spirit, anger, wrath), च = and, मन्युपतयः = the masters of Manyu, मन्युकृतेभ्यः पापेभ्यः = from the sins caused by wrath, रक्षन्ताम् = may they protect, यत् = what, राज्या = in the night, पापम् अकार्षम् = sin I have committed, मनसा = by mind (sins of thinking evil of another), वाचा = by speech (such as falsehood and harsh words), हस्ताभ्याम् = by hands (in performing homa, &c., with the object of injuring another), पद्भ्याम् = by the feet (the touching of Brâhmaṇas, cows, etc., with the feet), उदरेण = by stomach (in eating forbidden food), शिश्ना = by the organ (in having illicit intercourse), रात्रिः = the God of night, तत् = that, अवलुम्पतु = may destroy, यत् किम् च = and whatever, दुरितम् = sin, मयि = in me, इदम् = all this, अहम् = I, माम् = me, *i.e.*, my astral body, अमृतयोनौ सूर्ये ज्योतिषि = in the immortal cause, the Sûrya, the Luminous, जुहोमि = I offer as oblation, स्वाहा = Svâhâ. That is, may this water sanctified with mantra and poured into my mouth be as if an oblation.

*Translation* :—May Sûrya, and Manyu, and Manyupatis protect me from the sins caused by (my) manyu. Whatever sin I may have committed in the night—whatever by mind, or speech or hands or feet or stomach or organ, may Râtri destroy that. Whatever sin there may be in me, and myself also, all that I offer in the Immortal cause—the Sûrya the self-luminous (to be burnt up). Svâhâ.

May the sun (Sûrya), sacrifice (Manyu), the regent of the firmament, and other deities who preside over sacrifice (Manyupatayas cha), defend me (Rakṣantam) from the sin arising from the imperfect performance of a religious ceremony (Manyukritebhyaḥ pâpebhayaḥ.) Whatever sin I have committed by night, in thought, word or deed, be that cancelled by day. Whatever sin be in me, may that be far removed. I offer this water to the sun, whose light irradiates my heart, who sprung from the immortal essence. Be this oblation efficacious.

Another translation of this mantra is:—May the Supreme Brahman called Sûrya, and may the presiding Dêva of anger and may the Great Souls, who have conquered anger, protect me from the sins committed by my spirit of anger (Manyu). Whatever sin I have committed by night through my mind, speech, or hands or feet, or stomach or the organ, may Day destroy all that sin and its author (my egoism). I throw it (to be consumed) into this Sun, the luminous cause of Immortality, the Supreme Brahman. Svâhâ, let it be efficacious.

*(Prayoga)*— With the above mantra let him sip water thrice through the Brahma Tîrtha.

### III. MÂRJANAM.

॥ ततो मार्जनं कुर्यात् ॥

अर्धर्चया आक्षिपेत् ऊर्ध्वमर्धर्चया क्षिपेदधः ।

ओं आपो हिष्ठेति नवर्चस्य सूक्तस्य सिन्धुद्वीपऋषिरापो देवता गायत्रीछन्दः पञ्चमी वर्धमाना सप्तप्रतिष्ठा अष्टमाद्यनुष्टुपछन्दः आपो मार्जने विनियोगः ।

ओम् । आपोहिष्ठामयोभुवः तान ऊर्जे दधातन । महेरणायचक्षसे ॥ १ ॥

ओम् । यो वः शिवतमोरसः तस्य भाजयतेह नः । उशतीरिव मातरः ॥ २ ॥

ओम् । तस्माअरङ्ग मामवः यस्य क्षयायजिन्वथ । आपो जनयथा च नः ॥ ३ ॥

ओम् । शन्नो देवीरभिष्टये आपो भवन्तु पीतये । शंयोरभिस्रवन्तु नः ॥ ४ ॥

ओम् । ईशानावार्याणां क्षयन्तीश्चर्षणीनाम् । आपो याचामि भेषजम् ॥ ५ ॥

ओम् । अप्सु मे सोमोऽअब्रवीदन्तर्विश्वानि भेषजा । अग्निं च विश्वशम्भुवम् ॥ ६ ॥

ओम् । आपः पृणीत भेषजम् वरूथतन्वे मम । ज्योक् च सूर्यं दृशे ॥ ७ ॥

ओम् । इदमापः प्रवहत यत्किञ्च दुरितं मयि । यद्वाहमभिदुद्रोह यद्वा शेपे उतानृतम् ॥८॥

ओम् । आपोअद्यान्वचारिषं रसेन समगस्महि । पयस्वानग्न आगहि तमासं सृज वर्चसा ॥९॥

ओम् । ससुषीस्तदपसो दिवा नक्तं च ससुषी । वरेण्यक्रतुरहमपो देवी रुपह्वये ॥१०॥

ओं । द्रुपदादिव मुमुचानः स्विन्नःस्नातोमलादिव । पूतंपवित्रेणेवाज्यमापःशुन्धन्तुमैनसः ११

(Yajur Veda. XX. 20)

इत्येतैः कुशै र्मार्जनं कुर्यात् ।

Then let him perform Mârjanam with the following nine mantras. With half of each mantra let him throw the water up, and with the other half let him throw it down.

*Note*:—The mantras are really eleven, but they are treated as nine by considering the mantras 5, 6, and 7 as one composite mantra or a Trich; and so the whole is considered as consisting of nine Riks.

(*Viniyoga*):—Of the Sûkta or hymn consisting of nine Richas beginning with 'Om âpo-hista &c,' the seer is Sindhu-dvîpa, the Devatâ is God the All-pervading, under the name of Apas, and the metre is Gâyatrî, the fifth Ṛik is elongated (consisting of three Riks), while the seventh and eighth Ṛiks are of Anustup-metre and employed in Apo-mârjanam.

(1) O Apas, verily as ye are the giver of mental joy (Mayah), as well as ye give us physical strength by food (Ûrja, so give us the sight of the mighty delight (of emancipation).

(2) Here grant to us a share of bliss (Rasa), that most auspicious bliss (Rasa, of Yours, Like mothers in their longing love.

(3) For you we fain would go to him to whose abode ye send us forth, And, Apas, give us procreant strength.

(4) Ye, Apas, be to us for joy, O Shining One, for our aid and bliss: Let ye stream health and wealth to us.

(5) Ye are lords of food and wealth and giver of abodes to men, O Apas, I pray to ye for balm.

(6) The Beautiful Soma has told me, that all balms are in Apas, stored, As well as Agni who blesseth all.

(7) O Apas, teem with medicine to keep my body safe from harm, So that I long may see the sun.

(8) Ye Apas, wash away this stain and whatsoever taint be here, Each sinful wrong that I have done and every harmless curse of mine.

(9) Ye Apas, I this day have sought, and to your moisture have we come: O Agni, rich in milk, come thou, and with thy splendour cover me.

(10) The constant currents of Apas flow through day and night unceasingly, The shining Apas I beseech, I whose deeds are excellent.

(11) As one unfastened from a stake, or cleansed by bathing after toil, As butter which the sieve hath purged, let Apas clean me from my sin.

*Prayoga*:—With the above mantras let him perform Mârjana by sprinkling water with the Kuśas, by throwing it on his head, (or towards the sky) and on the ground, as directed before.

COMMENTARY ON MÂRJANA MANTRAS.

(Rig Veda, X.9.1., Atharva 1.5.1.)

ओं । आपो हिष्ठा मयोभुवस्तान ऊर्जे दधातन । महे रणाय चक्षसे ॥

आपः । हि । स्थ । मयःऽभुवः । ताः । नः । ऊर्जे । दधातन । महे । रणाय चक्षसे ॥

*Sanskrit Meaning.*

*Sâyana.*—हि (यस्मात् कारणात्) आपः (यायूयम्) मयो भुवः (सुखस्य भावयित्र्यः) स्थ (भवथ) ताः (तादृश्यो यूयं) नः (अस्मान्) ऊर्जे (अन्नाय) दधातन (धत्तः अन्नप्राप्तियोग्यानस्मान् कुरुत

अन्नमस्मभ्यं दत्तेत्यर्थः)। महे (महते) रणाय (रमणीयाय) चक्षसे (दर्शनाय सम्यक् ज्ञानाय च अस्मान् सम्यक् ज्ञानं प्रति योग्यान् कुरुतेत्यर्थः)।

*Word-meaning:* आपः = waters, हि = because, स्था = स्थ = you are, मयोभुवः = sources of happiness, (mayaḥ means pleasantness), ताः = therefore, नः = us (who desire happiness), ऊर्जे = food (*i.e.*, by giving us food) दधातन = support (*i.e.*, nourish us by giving us strengthening food which is pleasant). महे = with the great or the adorable, रणाय = delightful or sounding (sounds which teach the mysteries of the Upaniṣads) चक्षसे = manifesting (by unveiling the desired object which one wanted to see throughout his long life). The word दधातन "support ye" should be supplied to complete the sentence.

*Translation*:—O ye Apas! since you are the sources of pleasure, support us, therefore, by giving us strengthening food, (and nourish us by giving us) great and delightful desired objects (or by teaching us the adorable sounds through which we may find the ineffable bliss of God-vision.)

Since ye are kindly waters, do ye set us unto refreshment (urj), unto sight of great joy.

*Grammatical Notes:* (1) स्थ is 2nd person, plural, present tense of अस् to be, the अ is elided by I. 2. 4. read with VI. 4. 111. The verb retains its accent by VIII. 1. 34; the स् is changed to ष् and thereby थ to ठ, because it is preceded by इ (VIII. 3. 106) the final आ is lengthened by VI. 3. 137.

(2) मयोभुवः pl. of मयोभू is formed by adding क्विप् to the root भू having causative force, and preceded by the upapada मयस्. The व् is not substituted in the plural, *i.e.*, the form is not मयोभ्वः as required by VI. 4. 83, because of the prohibition in VI. 4. 85. The krit formed word भू retains its original accent because of the upapada, see VI. 2. 139.

(3) ऊर्जे is the dative singular of ऊर्ज्. It is derived from ऊर्ज बलप्राणनयोः to be strong, to be alive, by the affix क्विप् (III. 2. 76). The dative has the force of तादर्थ्य "for the purpose of that"; see II. 3. 13 Várt. The accent is on the case affix by VI. 1. 168 as the stem is monosyllabic.

(4) दधातन is the Imperative 2nd person plural of डुधाञ् धारणपोषणयोः "to support, to nourish." The affix त of the Plural is replaced by तनप् by VII. 1. 45. The affix has an indicatory प् and is non-ङित् (I. 2. 4), and therefore the आ of धा is not elided, as otherwise required by VI 4. 112. The whole word is accentless because it is preceded by a noun (VIII. 1. 28.)

(5) महे is dative singular of महत् the final अत् is elided irregularly. Or it is the dative singular of the Noun मह formed from the root मह पूजायाम् to adore, with the affix क्विप्.

(6) रणाय is dative singular of रण. It is formed from the root रम with the affix ल्युट in the sense of भाव or condition. The proper form is रमणाय, but here the final म् of रम् is elided as a Vedic anomaly.*

* The roots रण रव रप शब्दार्थाः mean to 'make sound.' From this root रण the word रण is formed by adding to it the affix अप. (See III. 3. 58.) The affix being पित् is anudâtta, therefore, the root retains its accent in the word रण. The force, of dative in all the above words is that of "for the purpose of."

(7) चक्षसे is dative singular of चक्षस. It is formed from the root चक्ष् with the affix असुन् (Un. IV. 233). The affix is treated as शित्, and being Sârvadhâtuka ख्याञ् is not substituted for चक्ष् to perceive, to tell, otherwise required by II. 4. 54. The word is acutely accented on the first because it is formed by the नित् affix असुन् (VI. I. 197).

Ye waters, truly bring us bliss, so help ye us to strength and power; that we may look on great delight. Or Ye waters are the source of bliss, so help ye us to energy. —Griffith.

MÂRJANA MANTRA II.

(Atharva Veda I. 5. 2. Rig Veda X. 9. 2.)

ओं । वः शिवतमो रसस्तस्य भाजयतेह नः । उशतीरिव मातरः ॥

Pada. यः । वः । शिवऽतमः । रसः । तस्य । भाजयत । इह । नः । उशतीःऽइव मातरः ॥

(हे आपः) वः (युष्माकं स्वभूतः) यो रसः शिवतमः (सुखतमः) इह (अस्मिन् लोके) तस्य (तं रसं) नः (अस्मान्) भाजयत (सेवयत प्रापयतेत्यर्थः) तत्र दृष्टान्तः—उशतीरिव (वत्सल इव पुत्रस्यवृद्धिं कामयमाना) मातरः (स्तन्य रसं यथा भाजयन्ति प्रापयन्ति तद्वत्)

*English meaning* :—यः = That (which is), वः = your, शिवतमः = most auspicious, रसः = essence, तस्य = of that or in that, भाजयत = make us a participator, or nourish ye with that essence, इह = here, in this world, नः = us, उशतीः = well wishing, इव = like, मातरः = mothers.

*Translation* :—O Apas! Nourish us here with that essence of yours which is most auspicious, as the well-wishing mothers (nourish their children with the milk of their breast).

What is your most propitious savor (rasa), of that make us share here, like zealous mothers.

*Grammatical Notes* :—(1) तस्य has the force of dative though the form is genitive, see I. 4. 32 Vâr. 1. Or the genitive has the force of denoting 'a portion'; *i.e.*, "give us a portion of that essence."

(2) भाजयत is imperative, 2nd person, plural of the causative of भज सेवायाम्. The causative णिच is added by III. 1. 26. The force of Imperative is that of entreaty or prayer. The word is thus formed, भज + णिच् + शप् + थ + त = भाजे + अ + त = भाजयत ॥ The शप affix is anudâtta, because it is पित् (III. 1. 4), त is anudâtta by VI. 1. 186; therefore, the word is middle-acute by the चित accent of णिच (VI. 1. 163). It loses this accent also by VIII. 1. 28.

(3) उशतीः is the plural number nominative case of the feminine noun उशती. It is derived from the Adâdi root वश कान्तौ 'to desire or wish.' To the root is added the present participial affix शतृ, which being a Sârvadhâtuka affix and not having an indicatory प् is ङित् (I. 2. 4.) Being ङित it causes the vocalisation of the semi-vowel व into उ by VI. 1. 16. So we have उशत् as pres. part. to which is added ङीप् in the feminine by IV. 1. 6. The participle is acute on उ by the affix accent (III. 1. 2.), but the ई of the feminine becomes acute by V. 1. 273. In the Plural जस is added to उशती and by VI. 1. 106 a single long vowel is substituted for ई × अ. The other form is उशत्यः The word उशतीः is compounded with इव, the case-affix is not elided, and the former word retains its accent, by a Vârtika under II. 2. 18 (see my Ashtâdhyâyi, p. 264.)

**Translation.—Here grant to us a share of dew, that most auspicious dew of yours, like mothers in their longing love.**

**Or**

**Give us a portion of the juice, the most auspicious that ye have. Griffith.**

**MÂRJANA MANTRA. III.**

(Atharva Veda I. 5. 3). (Rig Veda X. 9. 3.)

ओं । तस्मा अरं गमाम वो यस्य क्षयाय जिन्वथ । आपो जनयथा च नः ॥ ३ ॥

तस्मै । अरम् । गमाम । वः । यस्य । क्षयाय । जिन्वथ ॥ आपः । जनयथ । च । नः

(हे) आपो (यूयं) यस्य ( पापस्य ) क्षयाय ( विनाशाय आस्मान् ) जिन्वथ ( प्रीणयथ ) तस्मै ( तादृशाय पापक्षयाय ) अरं ( क्षिप्रं ) वो ( युष्मान् ) गमाम ( गमयाम वयं शिरसि प्रक्षिपामेत्यर्थः ) (यद्वा यस्यान्नस्य ) क्षयाय ( निवासार्थं यूयमोषधीः ) जिन्वथ ( तर्पयथ तस्मै तदन्नमुद्दिश्य वयं अरं अलं पर्याप्तं यथा भवति तथा वो युष्मान् गमाम गच्छाम ) ( किञ्च हे ) आपः नः ( अस्मान् ) जनयथ ( च पुत्रपौत्रादिजनने प्रयोजयतेत्यर्थः ) ।

*English meaning*: तस्मै = for the sake of that (*i.e.*, in order to obtain food for enjoyment as mentioned in the last verse). अरम् = fully, गमाम = let us go, वः = to you, यस्य = of which (food), क्षयाय = for increase, जिन्वथ = you grow (plants, &c.). आपः = O Apas!, जनयथ = give progeny, च = and, नः = to us.

*Another meaning*: हे आपः = O Apas! यस्य = of which, (sins पापस्य), क्षयाय = विनाशाय for destroying, अस्मान् जिनवथ = प्रीणनाय, you are ready, तस्मै = तादृशाय, पापक्षयाय for that destruction of sins, अरं = क्षिप्रं quickly, वः = युष्मान् you, गमाम = गमयाम may carry (*i.e.*, शिरसि प्रक्षिपाम we may pour ye on our heads), हे आपः = O Apas! नः अस्मान् us, जनयथ = पौत्रादिजनने प्रयोजयथ, make us produce progeny.

*Translation*:—O Apas! We fully approach you for the sake of the food, for the increase of which you produce plants; O Apas! reproduce us (in the shape of our sons and grandsons.) O Apas! We quickly pour you (on our heads) for (the destruction) of those (sins) to destroy which you are ready to help us. O Apas! Cause us to produce (sons and grandsons).

We would satisfy you in order to that to the possession of which ye quicken, O waters, and generate us.

*Grammatical Notes :* (1) तस्मा is in the dative case having the force of "for the purpose of that."

(2) अरम् is another form of अलम् the ल is changed to र by a Vârtika under VIII. 2. 18. (see my Ashṭâdhyâyi, page 1551).

(3) गमाम is the Imperative 1st person, plural of गम् 'to go. :' the Imerative has the force of 'entreaty or prayer.' The augment आ is elided by III. 4. 92. The vikaraṇa शप् is elided by II. 4. 37. Or it is the Aorist ( लुङ् ) form of गम् the Aorist having the force of Imperative in the Vedas by III. 4 6. The Aorist is formed by अङ् affix. because the root गम् has an indicatory ऌ in the Dhâtu pâṭha. See III. 1. 55. The augment अट् is not added by VI. 4. 75.

(4) वः is accusative plural of युष्मद्. VIII. I. 21. It is wholly anudâtta by by VIII. 1. 18.

(5) क्षयाय is dative singular of क्षय It is derived from क्षि निवासगत्योः 'to dwell and go,' with the affix अच् III. 3. 56. It would have been finally acute because it is formed with a चित् affix (VI. 1. 163), but it is first acute by VI. 1. 201.

(6) जिन्वथ is 2nd person plural of जिवि प्रीणनार्थः, to satisfy ; as it has an indicatory इ, it takes the न्. The शप् is anudâtta because of प (III. 1. 4) ; the personal ending थ is also anudâtta by VI. 1. 186 ; therefore the accent is on the first syllable, *i.e.*, the root retains its accent as the two affixes शप् and थ added to it are both accentless. The verb does not lose its accent as required by VIII. 1. 28, because it is preceded by यस्य (VIII. 1. 66).

(7) जनयथ is the Causative 2nd per. plural of जन् 'to produce.' This root belongs to Ghatâdi class (Bhuâdi 800, &c.) and is मित् ; and consequently it is not lengthened before the causative णिच्. VI. 4. 92. Of the three affixes added to this root, *viz.*, इ ( णिच् ) अ ( शप् ) and थ the last two are accentless for the reason given above. So the णिच् accent remains. Therefore the accent is on the अ of न ॥ The rule VIII. 2. 28. does not apply because आपः being in the vocative case is considered as non-existent. VIII. 1. 72. The final अ of जनयथ is lengthened by VI. 3. 137.

*Translation* :—For you we fain would go to him to whose abode ye send us forth, and waters, give us procreant strength. Or to you we gladly come for him to whose abode ye send us on.—Griffith.

*Note by Mr. Griffith* :—The purport of this stanza appears to be:—If you direct us and strengthen us for the work, we are ready and willing to visit any worshipper of yours in whose house we may perform sacrifice in your honour. *Give us procreant strength* : ye give us power to generate, that is, to produce or perform the sacrifice which may be regarded as the offspring of the officiating priests. Professor Grassman translates the pâda by :—'Ihr Wasser machet kräftig uns.' Ye waters make us powerful. But t' force of *jan* in *janayatha*, signifying *generation*, procreation, should be preserved. Professor Weber translates the first line differently :—' We bear you thither to the man whose habitation ye befriend.' Sâyaṇa's authority (Commentary on Sâmaveda II. ix. ii. 10. 3) supports this interpretation of *gamâna* as causative-*gama-yâma*; but it is not in accordance with Vedic use. Benfey (Die Hymen des Sâma-Veda) says in note 2, p. 223 :— 'I now take *aram gam* as meaning to go *adorning* to go in order to adorn, to glorify, and accordingly he translates stanza 3 of this Hymn in Sâma-Veda :—We glorify this man of yours, the man whose lordship ye befriend, and, Waters, make us rich in fruit. My version of the stanza is based on Ludwig's translation and Commentary (Der Rigveda, I. p. 189, and IV p. 180).

### MÂRJANA MANTRA IV.

(Rig Veda X. 9. 4. Atharva Veda I. 6. 1).

ओं शन्नो देवीरभिष्टये आपो भवन्तु पीतये । शंयो रभिस्रवन्तु नः ॥

*Pada* :—शम् । नः। देवीः । अभिष्टये। आपः ।भवन्तु। पीतये । शम् । योः । अभि । स्रवन्तु । नः ॥

*Sâyaṇa*.—देवीः (देव्यः द्योतनादिगुणयुक्ताः) आपः नः (अस्माकम् ), अभिष्टये (अभियजनाय or अभितः सर्वतो यागार्थं) शं (सुखं भवन्तु or सुखकारिण्यो भवन्तु ) ; पीतये (पानाय च शं ) भवन्तु ( पीयमानाः आपः स्वादुतमाः सुखाय भवन्तु ); नः (अस्माकं)शं (शमनाय रोगाणाँ), योः ( यावनाय च भयानाम् ), अभिस्रवन्तु (अस्मदाभिमुख्येन गच्छन्तु) or (अस्माकम् उपरि द्रवयर्थे सिंचन्तु ) ॥

*Word-meaning* :—देवीः आप= The Divine or effulgent waters, अभिष्टये = for the sake of sacrifice, शं नः भवन्तु = be propitious to us, पीतये = (so also) for drinking, अभिस्रवन्तु let them be poured over, नः = us, शं = for the sake of destroying (present diseases), योः = and warding (fears of future diseases).

*Translation* :—May the Effulgent Waters be propitious in all our sacrifices, and for our drinking purposes ; may they pour down upon us, removing present diseases and warding off future illnesses.

Or,

Be the divine waters weal for us in order to assistance, to drink; weal (and) health flow they unto us, (Atharva Veda VI. 1).

The Waters be to us for drink, Goddesses, for our aid and bliss; Let them stream health and wealth to us. (Griffith).

Grammatical Notes :—(1) The word Devîḥ is Vedic plural of the singular Devî. The modern plural would be Devyai.

(2) Abhiṣṭaye (dative singular of abhiṣṭi)-abhi-yajanâya. It comes from the √यज् Yaj. The य Ya is changed into इ I by Paṇini VI. 1. 16. read with VI. 1. 15. The ज, Ja, is changed into ष, Ṣa, by Paiṇni VIII. 2. 37.

(3) पीतये, Pitaye, comes from the √पा, Pâ, to drink, and the long आ, Â, is changed into ई, î, by Paṇini VI. 4. 66, and पीतये, Pitaye, पानाय Pânâya. Thus पा + ति (क्तिन्) = पीति the dative singular of which is पीतये Pitaye.

(4) शम् योः Śam yoḥ, शम् Śam means to *heal* the diseases from which one is already suffering, and योः, Yoḥ, means to *remove* the diseases not yet come, but impending. Therefore, शम् योः, Śam yoḥ, means health and prosperity. Śam comes from the √शम्, Śam, to heal, and योः ; Yoḥ, comes from the √यु, Yu, " to join, to separate."

MÂRJANA MANTRA V.

RV. X. 9. 5.

AV. I. 5. 4.

ईशा॑ना॒ वार्या॑णां॒ क्षय॑न्तीश्चर्षणी॒नाम् ।

अ॒पो या॑चामि भेष॒जम् ।

*Padapâṭha*—ईशा॑नाः । वार्या॑णाम् । क्षय॑न्तीः । च॒र्ष॒णी॒नाम् ॥

अ॒पः । या॒चा॒मि॒ भे॒ष॒जम् ॥

*Sâyaṇa*—वार्याणां (वारिप्रभवानां व्रीहियवादीनां यद्वा वरणीयानां धनानां) ईशाना (ईश्वराः) चर्षणी-नाम् (मनुष्याणां) क्षयन्तीः (निवासयित्रीः) अपः (उदकानि) भेषजं (सुखनामैतत् पापापनोदकं सुखं) याचामि (अहं प्रार्थये)।

*Word meaning in English*:—Îśânâḥ, Lords, the Regulators; Vâryâṇâm, of desirable riches. It is said that gold was produced in the waters of the ocean. The story is that Âpas were the wives of Varuṇa, and they meditated on Agni, who appeared before them, and the seed that fell from Agni became gold. It comes from the root "Vṛiñ," "to choose" with the affix "Nyat" by Paṇinî Sûtra III. 1. 24. The Udâtta accent is on the first syllable of Vâryâṇâm. Kṣayantiḥ, abodes, from the root "Kṣi," "to dwell." It is a feminine of the present participle "Kṣayat." The Udâtta accent is on the first syllable by dhâtu-svar. Charṣaṇinâm, of men. The force of genetive is here that of the dative, *viz*., for the sake of men. The accent is on the syllable "Nâm." Apaḥ, the waters. Yâchâmi, I pray to. Bheṣajam, medicine, balm, the remedy to cure diseases etc.

The verb "Yâchâmi" is accentless.

The word "Charṣaṇî" is a Vedic term denoting "man," as we find in the Nirukta III. 7. 1.

*Translation*:—Of the waters, having mastery of desirable things, ruling over human beings (charṣaṇí), I ask a remedy. (Whitney).

I pray the Floods to send us balm, those who bear rule o'er precious things,

And have supreme control of men. (Griffith).

Of the waters, having mastery of desirable things, ruling over human beings (charsani), I ask a remedy.

MÂRJANA MANTRA VI.

RV. X. 9. 6.

AV. I. 6. 2.

अ॒प्सु मे॒ सोमो॑ अब्रवीद॒न्तर्विश्वा॑नि भेष॒जा ।

अ॒ग्निं च॑ वि॒श्वश॑म्भुव॒मा॑पश्च वि॒श्वभे॑षजीः ॥

*Padapâṭha*—अ॒प्ऽसु । मे॒ । सोमः॑ । अ॒ब्र॒वी॒त् । अ॒न्तः । विश्वा॑नि । भे॒ष॒जा ।

अ॒ग्निम् । च॒ । वि॒श्वऽश॑म्भुवम् ॥ आपः॑ । च॒ वि॒श्वऽभे॑षजीः ॥

*Sáyana*—अप्सु ( उदकेषु, जलेषु ); अन्तः ( मध्ये ) विश्वानि (सर्वाणि) × भेषजा =भेषजानि (औषधानि, सर्वरोगनिवर्तकानि औषधानि सन्तीति ); सोमः ( एतन्नामा देवः ) मे ( मह्यम्, मन्त्रदर्शिने ) अब्रवीत् ( उपदिष्टवान् )। ( तथा ) विश्वशंभुवम् ( विश्वस्य जगतः सुखकरम् ) अग्निं ।

*Word meaning* :– Apsu, within the waters. Me, to me, the seer of the hymn. Somaḥ, god Soma. Abravît, has told. Antaḥ, within. Viśvâni, all. Bheṣajâ, remedies. Agniṃ, the god Agni. Cha, and. Viśvaśaṃbhuvaṃ, doing good to all, giving pleasure to the whole world. This word may be taken as a Bahuvrîhi compound also, and then it will be considered as a proper name like Viśvâmitra, Viśvadeva, etc. The accent would then be governed by Paṇinî VI. 2. 106.

*Translation* :– Within the waters, Soma told me, are all remedies, and Agni (fire) wealful for all. (Whitney and Lanman).

Within the Waters—Soma thus hath told me—dwell all balms that heal,

And Agni, he who blesseth all. (Griffith).

*Note by Griffith* :—The meaning is that the poet, under the inspiration produced by draughts of Soma juice, has perceived that water possesses healing virtue, and that the waters of the firmament—that is, clouds—contain purifying and health-giving fire or Agni in the shape of lightning.

### MARJANA MANTRA VII.

AV. I. 6. 3. RV. X. 9. 9 or I. 23. 21.

आपः पृणीत भेषजं वरूथं तन्वे मम ।

ज्योक् च सूर्यं दृशे ॥

*Padapâṭha*—आपः । पृणीत । भेषजम् । वरूथम् । तन्वे । मम ।

ज्योक् । च । सूर्यम् । दृशे ॥

*Sáyaṇa*—( हे ) आपः ( यूयं ) मम तन्वे ( मदीयस्य शरीरस्य )। वरूथं ( वारकं ज्वरादिसर्वरोगनिवर्तनम् ) भेषजम् ( औषधम् ) पृणीत ( पूरयत, यथा मम शरीरं व्याधयो न स्पृशन्ति तथा औषधं प्रयच्छतेत्यर्थः )। ज्योक् ( चिरकालं ) सूर्यं ( सर्वेषां प्राणप्रदत्वेन प्रेरकम् आदित्यं ) दृशे ( द्रष्टुम्, चिरकालं जीवितुम् इत्यर्थः )।

*Word meaning* :—Âpaḥ, waters. Pṛiṇîta, bestow, fill. Bheṣajam, medicine, remedy. Varûthaṃ, destroyer of illness, protection. Tanve, in the body, for my body. Mama, my. Jyok, long, always. Cha, and. Sûryaṃ, the Sun. Dṛiśe, to see.

*Grammatical Notes* :—(1) Pṛiṇîta, comes from the √Pṛi, to nourish, to fill. It is second person, plural, imperative. It belongs to Kriyâdi class, and the â of nâ is changed inte long î by Paṇinî VI. 4. 11 3. The accent is on the last syllable.

(2) Varûthaṃ, comes from the √Vriñ, "to cover." It is formed by Uṇâdi affix 'ûthan.' The accent is on the first syllable, because the affix is nit. Tanve, it has svarita accent, by Paṇinî VIII. 2. 4.

(3) Dṛiśe, is an indeclinable, formed by Paninî III. 4. 11.

*Translation*:—O waters, bestow a remedy, protection (*varûtha*) for my body, and long to see the sun. (Whitney).

### MARJANA MANTRA VIII.

RV. I. 23. 22. or X 9. 8.

इदमापः प्रवहत यत्किंच दुरितं मयि ।
यद्वाहमभिदुद्रोह यद्वा शेप उतानृतम् ॥

*Padapátha*—इदम् । आपः । प्र । वहत । यत् । किम् । च । दुःऽइतम् । मयि ।
यत् । वा । अहम् । अभिऽदुद्रोह । यत् । वा । शेपे । उत । अनृतम् ॥

*Sáyana*—मयि (यजमाने) यत्किं च दुरितं (अज्ञानाद्विरुत्पन्नं), वा (अथवा) अहं (यजमानः) अभिदुद्रोह (सर्वतो बुद्धिपूर्वकं द्रोहं कृतवानस्मि) वा (अथवा) शेपे (साधुजनं शप्तवानस्मि इति यदस्ति) उत (अपि च) अनृतम् (उक्तवान् इति यदस्ति) (तत्) इदम् (सर्वमपराधजातं) (हे) आपः प्रवहत (मत्तोपनीय प्रवाहेणान्यतो नयत) ।

*Word meaning*:—Mayi, in me (the Yajamâna); yat-kim cha, whatever; duritam, bad conduct, sin (committed through ignorance); vâ, or; aham, I, the sacrificer; abhi-dudroha, have committed evil, have hated (fathers etc.), or have worked evil consciously against any body; vâ, or; śepe, I have cursed (good men), or have taken false oath (to get rid of a liability towards my creditor); yat, whatever; uta, also; anṛitam, falsehood; idam, this, the whole mass of my guilt; âpaḥ, O Waters; pravahata, remove away, wash away, carry forth.

*Grammatical Notes*:—(1) Mayi (मयि), has Udâtta accent on the first syllable. It is formed from 'asmad' (अस्मद्) by VIII. 2. 91. and 97 read with VI. 1. 97. and VII. 2. 89. Therefore, the vowel following 'ma' (म), *viz.*, the vowel 'a' (अ) gets Ekadeśa Udâtta accent.

(2) 'Dudroha' (दुद्रोह) is Perfect of "Druh" (द्रुह,) "to hate." The accent is on O (ओ) by VI. 1. 193, because the affix ṇal has an indicatory 'l' (ल).

'Śepe' (शेपे), is perfect of the √Sapa (शप्), "to curse," "to swear." Its accent is on the final by 'Pratyaya svar' (प्रत्ययस्वर).

*Translation*:—Whatever sin is found in me, whatever evil I have wrought,
If I have lied or falsely sworn, Waters, remove it far from me.

**Note**:—The reading of Atharva Veda VII. 89 (94). 3 is somewhat different:—

इदमापः प्र वहतावद्यं च मलं च यत् । यच्चाभिदुद्रोहानृतं यच्च शेपे अभीरुणम् ॥

"O waters, do ye carry forth both this reproach and what is foul (mala), and what untruth I have uttered in hate, and what I have sworn fearlessly (to get rid of the debt of my creditor)."—Whitney.

The word abhîrunam is thus derived by Pt. Ksema-karana-dâsa Trivedi, the learned. Translator of Atharvaveda :—

भी + क्नन् (Un. III. 55). Add augment रुट् + भी + रु + क्नन्. The affix being treated as कित् there is no guna. = भीरुण "fearing." अभीरुणम् "fearless" *i.e.*, sinless.

The meaning then would be "when I have cursed (a sinless and consequently) a fearless person."

See also Vajasaneya Sanhitâ VI 17 and the commentary of Uvata and Mahidhara thereon.

### MARJANA MANTRA IX.

RV. I. 23. 23. or X 9. 9.

आपो॑ अ॒द्यान्व॑चारिषं॒ रसे॑न॒ सम॑गस्महि ।
पय॑स्वानग्न॒ आग॑हि॒ तं मा॒ सं सृ॑ज॒ वर्च॑सा ॥

*Padapátha*—आपः॑ । अ॒द्य । अनु॑ । अ॒चा॒रि॒ष॒म् । रसे॑न । सम् । अ॒ग॒स्म॒हि॒ । पय॑स्वान् । अ॒ग्ने॒ । आ । ग॒हि॒ । तम् । मा॒ । सम् सृ॒ज॒ । वर्च॑सा ॥

*Sáyana*—अद्य अस्मिन् दिने ( अवभृथार्थम् ) आपः अन्वचारिषं ( जलान्यनुप्रविष्टोस्मि प्रविश्य च) रसेन ( जलसारेण ) समगस्महि (संगतास्मः ) ॥ ( हे ) अग्ने पयस्वान् ( जले वर्तमानत्वेन पयोयुक्तस्त्वं ) आगहि ( अस्मिन्कर्मण्यागच्छ ) । तं मां ( तादृशं स्नातं मां) वर्चसा ( तेजसा ) संसृज ( संयोजय )

*Word-meaning in English* :—Adya, अद्य, to-day (for the sake of Avabhritha bath) ; Ápah anva-chárisam, आपः अन्वचारिषं, I have entered the waters (and having entered), rasena, रसेन, through the essence of water ; samagasmahi, समगस्महि, we have come in contact ; Agne, अग्ने O Agni ; payasván, पयस्वान्, O full of milk, or fluid (because Agni dwells in water) ; ágahi, आगहि, come thou (to this sacrifice) ; tam, तं, that me (who was thus bathed) ; varchasá, वर्चसा, with splendour, lustre ; sam-srija संसृज, unite.

*Grammatical Notes* :—'Ápah' आपः, though in the nominative plural, it really has the force of accusative plural here. 'Achárisam,' अचारिषम्, from √Char, 'to go.' It is in aorist, चर + च्लि = चरसिच = च्लि (III. 1. 44) = चर + इट् + सिच्. (VII. 2. 35) = चम् ॥ At this stage, the rule नेटि (VII. 2. 4) would have prevented vriddhi, but for अतोल्रान्तस्य (VII. 2. 2.) and so we have अचारिषम् in the Ist Per. Sing.

अगस्महि is also aorist of गम् "to go" in the Átmanepada by I. 3. 29. गम् + च्लि + गम् + सिच = च्लि. The affix requires to be elided after √Gam by II. 4. 80, but it is not so, as a Chhándas irregularity. The augment इट् (VII. 2. 35) is prevented by VII. 2. 10. The affix सिच is considered as कित by I. 2 13. and the nasal म् is elided by VI. 4. 37. The affix ह of the Imperative in गहि is not elided by VI. 4. 105

because of VI. 4. 22. Thus गम् = अहि = ग + नहि (VI. 4. 37) = गहि or आगोह.

*Translation* :—The Waters I this day have sought, and to their moisture have we come :
O Agni, rich in milk, come thou, and with thy splendour cover me.

A. V. VI. 23. 1.

सुस्रुषीस्तदपसो दिवा नक्तं च सुस्रुषीः ।
वरेण्यक्रतुरहमपो देवीरुप ह्वये ॥

*Padapâṭha.* सस्रुषीः । तत् । अपसः । दिवा । नक्तम् । च । सस्रुषीः । वरेण्यऽक्रतुः । अहम् । अपः । देवीः । उप । ह्वये ॥

*Sáyana.* तत् (प्रसिद्धं सर्वप्राणिजीवनात्मकं रूपं) सस्रुषीः (प्राप्तवतीः), अपसः (अपस्वतीः) (अपसा जगद्रक्षणकर्मणा युक्ताः) दिवा नक्तं च (अहोरात्रोपलक्षितं कृत्स्नं कालम् अविच्छेदेन) सस्रुषीः (सरणशीलाः प्रवहणशीलाः)। (ईदृशीः) देवीरपः वरेण्यक्रतुः (प्रशस्तकर्मा) अहम् उप ह्वये (समीपे आह्वयामि) (यद्वा) उपह्वयः (अनुज्ञा, तां याचामहे)।

तत् tat, 'that' (the well known form which is the life of all living beings); सस्रुषी; sasrusih, 'obtained, flowing, restless'; अपसः apasaḥ, 'containing water, engaged in protecting the world'; दिवा नक्तं च divâ naktam cha, 'day and night'; सस्रुषीः sasrusih, flowing unceasingly in the act of protecting the world'; देवीरपः, devih apah, 'the goddesses waters'; वरेण्यक्रतुः, vareṇeya kratuḥ, 'of excellent activity'; अहम् aham 'I'; उप ह्वये up a hvaye, 'invoke to approach near, or I ask their permission'.

*Grammatical Notes* : अपसः. apasaḥ, is equal to 'apasvatiḥ'. The affix denoting Matup pratyaya is elided.

सस्रुषी : sasruṣiḥ, is derived from the $\sqrt{sri}$, 'to go'. It is formed by the Vedic affix 'kvasu' added with the force of perfect (लिट्, liṭ). The feminine affix ङीप्, ṅip is added by Panini IV. 1. 6. The व va of the affix वस्, vas (a form assumed by क्वसु, kavasu), is changed to उ, u by Pâṇini VI. 4. 131.

सृ + क्वसु (P. III. 2. 107) = सस्र + वस् = सस्र + उस् (P. VI. 4. 131) = सस्रुस्। Add the feminine affix ङीप्, and we get सस्रुषी।

*Translation* :—Here flow the restless ones, the flow unceasing through the day and night.

Most excellently wise I call the Goddess Waters hitherward. (Griffth).

Flowing on, devoted to it; by day and by night flowing on; I, of desirable activity, call upon the heavenly waters. (Whitney).

I invoke (to approach me) the goddesses Âpas, I of the excellent deeds. (I invoke those goddesses) to continually flow day and night, full of water (apasaḥ), and devoted to (sasrusiḥ), or who has attained the position of that (the Life-giver of all creatures). (Sâyana).

8

### IV. AGHAMARṢAṆA.

॥ ततः अघमर्षणम् ॥

ऋतञ्चेत्यघमर्षणऋषिरनुष्टुप्छन्दो भाववृत्तो देवता अश्वमेधावभृथे विनियोगः ।

ओम् । ऋतं च सत्यं चाभीद्धात्तपसोऽध्यजायत । ततो रात्र्यजायत ततः समुद्रो अर्णवः ॥ १ ॥

समुद्रादर्णवादधिसंवत्सरो अजायत । अहोरात्राणि विदधद्विश्वस्य मिषतो वशी ॥ २ ॥

सूर्याचन्द्रमसौ धाता यथापूर्वमकल्पयत् । दिवं च पृथिवीं चान्तरिक्षमथो स्वः ॥ ३ ॥

(Rig. Veda X. 190. 1—3).

इति अनेन जलगण्डूषं भूमौ क्षिपेत् इतिभिः ।

Then let him perform Aghamarṣaṇa.

(*Viniyoga*):—Of the mantras Ṛitam cha satyam cha, the seer is Aghamarṣaṇa, the metre is Anuṣṭup, the Devatâ Bhâvavṛitta (a name of Brahmâ), and they are employed in the final Dikṣa bath (avabhṛitha) at the close of (Aśvamedha sacrifice).

(*Mantra*):—(1) From the highly concentrated meditation came out the Right and the True.

From that the Primal Night arose, from that the Oceanic flood.

(2) From the Ocean flood, thereafter was produced the Year.

The Lord of all living Universe then ordained the Days and Nights.

(3) The Dhâtâ then created the Sun and Moon, as in the past.

He formed the Joyful Heaven and Earth, and the Middle Region too.

(*Prayoga*):—With this he should throw the water held in the palm of his hand on the ground. That is to say,

*Direction*:—Holding some water in the palm of the hand bring it near the nose; repeat once, twice, or thrice, the above mantras; and then throw the water without looking at it on the left, thinking that the person of sin has come out of one's self.

NOTE.

This is done by taking water in the hollow of the palm of the right hand, and thinking of the sin as personified and as coming out of the nostril and entering into this water. The verses Ritam cha satyam cha, &c., should be recited. Drive out the person of sin from the right nostril into this water, and without looking at it throw this water towards one's left on the ground. The Vâjasaneyins read also Drupadadiva. While reciting the Mantras the Prâṇas must be restrained. The sin is personified as having its head consisting of the sin of killing a Brâhmaṇa, the arms consist of the sin of stealing gold, the heart is made up of the sin of drinking wine, the loin is the sin of defiling the bed of one's spiritual preceptor; all the limbs are of sin, the hairs of the body are small sins, the beard and eyes are blood red, and he holds a sword and shield, and of black colour and residing in one's heart.

### V. SÛRYÂRGHA.

॥ ततः सूर्यार्घः ॥

ओम् सन्देहनामानो राक्षसा विनश्यन्तु ।

इत्युक्त्वा सप्रणवव्याहृतिभि र्गायत्र्या जलाञ्जलित्रयं सूर्याय दद्यात् ।

Let him offer Argya to the Sun.

Reciting mentally " Let the Râkṣasâs named Mandehas be destroyed," let him offer three handfuls of water to the sun reciting the Gâyatrî Mantra along with its Praṇava and Vyâhṛitis, *viz.*, reciting the following :—

Om Bhûḥ, Bhuvaḥ, Svaḥ, Tat Savitur Vareṇyam Bhargo Devasya Dhîmahi ; dhiyo yo naḥ prachodayât. Om.

NOTE.

Of course, here also, the recitation of the Gâyatrî should be preceded by the Viniyoga, explaining the Seer and the metre &c., as given in the Prâṇâyâma Section. But here only three Vyâhṛitis are recited, and not all the seven.

The full form is repeated here :—

**(*Viniyoga*):—Of "Om" the seer is Brahmâ, the metre is Gâyatrî, and the Devatâ, is Agni.**

**Of the great Vyâhṛitis Bhuḥ, Bhuvar and Svar, the seer is Prajâpati, the metres are Gâyatrî, Uṣṇik and Anuṣṭup respectively, and the Devatâs are Agni, Vâyu and Âditya, respectively.**

**Of the Gâyatrî the seer is Viśvâmitra, the metre is Gâyatrî, the Devatâ is Savitâ. It is used in offering Arghya to the Sun.**

*Gâyatrî* :—We meditate on the adorable blissful form of God, the Conscience. May He stimulate all our faculties.

*Direction* :—Take a handful (Añjali) of water with darbha, rice, flowers, sanda paste etc., in it, stand facing the sun, recite the Savitṛi preceded by the Vyâhṛitis and the Praṇava, and offer three such handfuls. Then perambulate saying " Asau Âditya Brahma " " That Sun is Brahma" and then sip water.

### VI. SÛRYOPASTHÂNAM.

॥ ततः सूर्योपस्थानम् ॥

चित्रं देवानामिति षड्चस्य सूक्तस्य कुत्सऋषिः सूर्यो देवता त्रिष्टुप छन्दः

सूर्योपस्थाने विनियोगः ।

(Rig. Veda I. 115. 1-6)

ओम् चित्रं देवानामुदगादनीकं चक्षुर्मित्रस्य वरुणस्याऽग्नेः ।

आप्रा द्यावापृथिवी अन्तरिक्ष ꣳ सूर्य आत्मा जगतस्तस्थुषश्च ॥

(AV. X. 121. 2·35).

सूर्यो देवी मुषसं रोचमानां मर्यो न योषामभ्येति पश्चात् ।

यत्रा नरो देवयंतो युगानि वितन्वते प्रति भद्राय भद्रम् ॥ २ ॥

भद्रा अश्वा हरितः सूर्य्यस्य चित्रा एतग्वा अनुमाद्यासः ।
नमस्यंतो दिव आ पृष्ठमस्थुः परि द्यावा पृथिवी यंति सद्यः ॥ ३ ॥
तत्सूर्यस्य देवत्वं तन्महित्वं मध्या कर्तोर्विततं संजभार ।
यदेदयुक्तहरितः सधस्थादाद्रात्री वासस्तनुते सिमस्मै ॥ ४ ॥
तन्मित्र स्य वरुणस्या भिचक्षे सूर्यो रूपं कृणुते द्योरुपस्थे ।
अनन्तमन्यद्रुशदस्य पाजः कृष्णमन्यद्धरितः संभरंति ॥ ५ ॥
अद्या देवा उदिता सूर्यस्य निरंहसः पिपृता निरवद्यात् ।
तन्नो मित्रो वरुणो मामहंतामदितिः सिंधुः पृथिवी उत द्यौः ॥ ६ ॥
एतच्च प्रातः सन्ध्यायां पुटाञ्जलिना कार्यम् ।

Prayer to the Sun.

*Viniyoga* :—Of the six verses beginning with Chitram Devânam &c, the Seer is Kutsa, the Devatâ is Sûrya, the metre is Triṣṭup, and it is employed in praying to the Sun.

*Direction* :—The worship of the Sun is made by standing on one foot, and resting the other against his ankle or heel, looking towards the east, and holding his hands open before him in a hollow form. In this posture he should repeat the following six Riks (115. 1-6) :—

(1) The brilliant presence of the Gods hath risen, the eye of Mitra, Varuṇa and Agni.

The soul of all that moveth not or moveth, the Sun hath filled the air and earth and heaven.

(2) Like as a young man followeth a maiden, so doth the Sun the Dawn, refulgent Goddess :

Where pious men extend their generations, before the Auspicious One for happy fortune.*

(3) Auspicious are the Sun's Bay-coloured Horses, bright, changing hues, meet for our shouts of triumph.

Bearing our prayers, the sky's ridge have they mounted, and in a moment speed round earth and heaven.

(4) This' is the Godhead, this the might of Sûrya : he hath withdrawn what spread o'er work unfinished.

When he hath loosed his Horses from their station, straight over all Night spreadeth out her garment.

(5) In the sky's lap the Sun this form assumeth that Varuna and Mitra may behold it.

* The exact meaning of the second line is somewhat uncertain. As I have rendered it in accordance with Ludwig, it reminds me of Shelley's, 'Man, the imperial shape, then multiplied. His generations under the pavilion of the Suns's throne.' Wilson, following Sâyaṇa, paraphrases, 'At which season pious men perform (the ceremonies established for) ages.'—(Griffith.)

His Bay Steeds well maintain his power eternal, at one time bright and darksome at another.

(6) This day, O Gods, While Sûrya is ascending, deliver us from trouble and dishonour.

This prayer of ours may Varuṇa grant, and Mitra, and Aditi and Sindhu, Earth and Heaven. (Griffith).

### VII. MEDITATING ON GÂYATRÎ.

॥ ततो जलं स्पृष्ट्वा गायत्रीं ध्यायेत् ॥

ओं हंसोपरि पद्मासनस्थां रक्तवर्णां चतुर्मुखीं द्विभुजाम् अक्षसूत्रकमण्डलुकरां रक्ताम्बरधरां ब्रह्मणः सदृशां गायत्रीम् ।

इति ध्यात्वा ( ऋष्यादिन्यासं कुर्यात् ) ।

*Then touching water he should meditate on Gâyatrî.*

In the morning, the Gâyatrî should be meditated upon as a virgin, seated on a flamingo, in the posture of a lotus, red-coloured, having four faces, two hands with a rosary and a water jar in them, wearing a red garment, resembling Brahman.

*After thus meditating he should perform Ṛiṣyâdinyâsa.*

### VIII. ṚIṢYÂDI-NYÂSA.

*or assignment of Ṛiṣis &c.*

गायत्र्या विश्वामित्र ऋषिः सविता देवता गायत्रीछन्दः इयदावृत्तिः गायत्रीजपे विनियोगः।

( १ ) शिरसि विश्वामित्रर्षये नमः । ( २ ) मुखे गायत्रीछन्दसे नमः । ( ३ ) हृदे सवित्रे देवतायै नमः । ( ४ ) ओं भूर्हृदाय नमः । ( ५ ) ओं भुवः शिरसे स्वाहा । ( ६ ) ओं स्वः शिखायै वषट् । ( ७ ) ओं तत्सवितुर्वरेण्यं कवचाय हुं । ( ८ ) भर्गो देवस्य धीमहि नेत्रद्वयाय एवं त्रयाय वौषट् । ( ९ ) धियो यो नः प्रचोदयात् अस्त्राय फट् ॥

(1) Śirasi Viśvâmitrarṣaye namaḥ.
(2) Mukhe Gâyatri-chhandase namaḥ.
(3) Hṛide Savitre Devatâyai namaḥ.
(4) Om Bhûr hṛidayâya namaḥ.
(5) Om Bhuvaḥ Śirase svâha.
(6) Om Svaḥ Śikhâyai vaṣaṭ.
(7) Om tat Savitur vareṇyam kavachâya huṃ.
(8) Bhargo Devasya dhîmahi netra-dvayâya evaṃ trayâya vauṣaṭ.
(9) Dhiyo yo naḥ prachodayât, astrâya phaṭ.

*Direction* :—

1. Salutation to the sage Viśvâmitra on the head.
2. Salutation to the metre Gâyatrî in the mouth.
3. Salutation to the goddess Savitṛi in the heart.

4. Touch the heart with right hand reciting it.
5. Touch the hand do. do.
6. Touch the tuft do. do.
7. Place the left hand on the right shoulder and the right hand on the left shoulder cross-wise.
8. Strike the palm of the left hand with the index and middle fingers of the right hand so as to make a sound.

### IX. ÂVÂHANA.

॥ ततः आवाहनम् ॥

Then invoke Gâyatrî with the following mantras.

ओं आयाहि वरदे देवि जप्ये मे सन्निधौ भव ।

गायन्तं त्रायसे यस्माद् गायत्री त्वं ततः स्मृता ॥

इत्वोचानकरौ प्रातः

इत्यावाह्य सायन्चाधोमुखस्तथा ।

मध्येत्त्वञ्जकराभ्याश्च जपक्रम उदाहृतः ॥

इति आवाह्य यथाशक्ति ( दशधा शतधा सहस्रधा ) गायत्रीं जपेत् ।

Om come boon-giving Goddess and be present at my prayer. Since Thou savest (trâyase) by being sung (gâyantam), therefore thou art called Gâyatrî.

*Direction*:—The method of Japa is (1) to hold the two hands upwards in the morning, (2) to hold them downward in the evening, and (3) to hold them slantingly at noon.

Having thus invoked he should pray to the Gâyatrî ten times, (twenty-eight times), a hundred (and eight) times, or a thousand times.

### X. JAPA.

*Prayer.*

ओं भूर्भुवः स्वः । तत्सवितुर्वरेण्यं भर्गो देवस्य

धीमहि । धियो यो नः प्रचोदयात् ॥ ओम् ॥

*Viniyoga*:—Of the Gâyatrî the Seer is Viśvâmitra, the goddess is Savitâ, the metre is Gâyatrî. It is to be repeated so many times (10, or 28, or 108, or 1000 times), and it is employed in repetition of Gâyatrî.

Om Bhûr Bhuvaḥ svaḥ. Tat Savitur vareṇyam. Bhargo Devasya dhîmahi. Dhiyo yo naḥ prachodayât Om.

*Note.*—This mantra should be repeated ten times, or twenty-eight times, or hundred and eight times. In fact, the more one increases this portion of the Sandhyâ, the better become his spiritual powers, and the Śâstras say that ancient sages by this Japa, or the repetition of a formula over and over again acquired all the power that they had.

### XI. VISARJANAM OR BIDDING FAREWELL TO THE GÂYATRÎ.

॥ जपानन्तरं अनेन मन्त्रेण विसर्जयेत् ॥

ओम् उत्तरे शिखरे जाता भूम्यां पर्वतवासिनी । ब्रह्मणा समनुज्ञाता गच्छ देवि यथेच्छया ॥

After finishing the Japa let him bid farewell to Gâyatrî with the following mantra :

Born on the highest peak, dweller on the mountain in this earth, with the permission of Brahmâ, go O Goddess, wherever Thou likest.

On the highest top of the mountain-summit in earth (*i.e.*, on the Meru mountain), dwells the goddess Gâyatrî. Being pleased with thy worshippers, go back, O Devi, to thy abode as it pleaseth thee. (According to the text in Tait. Ar. X. 36. 1).

### XII. SÛRYÂRGHYA.

*The Offering of Arghya to the Sun.*

॥ ततः सूर्यार्घ्यं दद्यादनेन ॥

हंसः शुचिसदित्यस्य वामदेव्य ऋषिर्जगतीछन्दः सूर्यो देवता राजसूययजमानस्य रथावतरणे सूर्यार्घ्यदाने विनियोगः ।

हंसः शुचिषद्वसुरन्तरिक्षसद्धोता वेदिषदतिथिर्दुरोणसत् ।

नृषद्वरसदृतसद्व्योमसदब्जा गोजा ऋतजा अद्रिजा ऋतं बृहत् ॥

(Rig. IV. 40. 5.)

Then let him offer to the Sûrya with the following mantra :—

*Viniyoga.* Of the mantra "Haṃsa śuchi sat etc.," the seer is Vâmadeva, the metre is Jagatî, the deity invoked is the Sûrya, and it is employed in offering Arghya to the Sûrya, and in alighting from the chariot by the celebrant of the Râja-sûya Yajña.

*Mantra.* The Haṃsa homed in light, the Vasu in mid-air, the priest beside the altar, in the house the guest,
Dweller in noblest place, mid men, in truth, in sky, born of flood, kine, truth, mountain, he is holy Law.

*Note.*—This verse is found in Kaṭhopaniṣat V. 2 Maxmuller translates it thus :—

He (Brahman) is the swan (sun), dwelling in the bright heaven ; he is the Vasu (air), dwelling in the sky ; he is the sacrificer (fire), dwelling on the hearth ; he is the guest (Soma), dwelling in the sacrificial jar ; he dwells in men, in gods (vara), in the sacrifice (Rita), in heaven ; he is born in the water, on earth, in the sacrifice (ṛita), on the mountains ; he is the True and the Great.

According to Madhva this verse means :—

He is Haṃsa (free from all faults and essence of all), residing in the Pure Vâyu, He is Vasu (the best and the blessed) dwelling in the Firmament, He is Hotṛi (the Lord of the senses) dwelling in honoured places, He is Atithi (the rich in food) dwelling in the Soma-jar. He dwells in men, in Devas, in Scriptures, in Space, in the creatures of water and earth. He dwells among the Liberated, and the Mountain-born. He is the Truth (established by the Vedas) and the Great One (full of all qualities).

### XIII. NAMASKÂRA.

इत्यर्घ्यं दत्वा नमस्कुर्यात् ।

After offering Arghya let him salute the Sun with the following four mantras of the Ṛigveda :—

मित्रस्य चर्षणीधृतोऽवो देवस्य सानसि । द्युम्नं चित्रश्रवस्तमम् ॥ ६ ॥

अभि यो महिना दिवं मित्रो बभूव सप्रथाः । अभिश्रवोभिः पृथिवीम् ॥ ७ ॥

मित्राय पञ्चयेमिरे जना अभिष्टिशवसे । स देवान् विश्वान् बिभर्ति ॥ ८ ॥

मित्रो देवेष्वायुषु जनाय वृक्तबर्हिषे । इषइष्टव्रता अकः ॥ ९ ॥ (Ṛig. III. 59. 6-9).

(6) The gainful grace of Mitra, God, supporter of the race of man,
Gives splendour of most glorious fame.

(7) Mitra whose glory spreads afar, he who in might surpasses heaven,
Surpasses earth in his renown.

(8) All the Five Races have repaired to Mitra, ever strong to aid,
For he sustaineth all the Gods.

(9) Mitra to Gods, to living men, to him who strews the holy grass,
Gives food fulfilling sacred Law.

## XIV. ÂTMA-RAKṢÂ.

## ॥ ततः आत्मरक्षा ॥

Then let him perform Âtma-rakṣâ, or the protection of the self :—

काश्यपऋषिस्त्रिष्टुप्छन्दोऽग्निर्देवता आत्मरक्षायां विनियोगः ।

ओं जातवेदसे सुनवाम सोममरातीयतो नि दहाति वेदः ।

स नः पर्षदति दुर्गाणि विश्वा नावेव सिन्धुं दुरितात्यग्निः ॥

(Ṛig. Veda I. 99. 7.)

पिशङ्गभृष्टिमंभृणं पिशाचिमिन्द्र सं मृण । सर्वं रक्षो नि बर्हय ॥

(Ṛig. I. 133. 5.)

एभिः शिरसि रक्षां कृत्वा ।

*Viniyoga.* Of the mantra "Jâtavedasa, &c.," the seer is Káśyapa, the metre is Triṣṭup, the Devatâ is Agni, and it is employed in self-defence.

*Mantra.* We prepare the Soma for the All-knower. May he consume the evil tendencies of our niggardly disposed heart. May he transport us over all difficulties. May the Effulgent convey us as in a boat over the sea, across all Evils.

*Note.*—(1) For Jâtavedasa let us press the Soma : may he consume the wealth of the malignant.

May Agni carry us through all our troubles, through grief as in a boat across the river.

*Mantra.*—O Indra, crush and bray to bits the fearful fiery-weaponed fiend :

Strike every demon to the ground.

*Direction.* With these mantras having prayed for protection for his body and specially for his head, let him salute the quarters as directed in the next paragraph.

### XV. DIK (DEVATÂ) NAMASKÂRA OR SALUTATION TO THE (DEVAS OF) QUARTERS.

॥ ततो दिङ्नमस्कारः ॥

( १ ) ओं प्राच्यां सन्ध्यायै नमः ।

( २ ) ओं दक्षिणस्यां सावित्र्यै नमः ।

( ३ ) ओं प्रतीच्यां गायत्र्यै नमः ।

( ४ ) ओं उदीच्यां सर्वाभ्यो देवताभ्यो नमः ।

( ५ ) ओं कामोकार्षीत् मन्युरकार्षीन्नमो नमः ।

( ६ ) ततः ओं प्राच्यै नमः ।

( ७ ) ओं दक्षिणायै नमः ।

( ८ ) ओं उदीच्यै नमः ।

( ९ ) ओं ऊर्ध्वायै नमः ।

(१०) ओं अधोरायै नमः ।

(११) ओं अन्तरिक्षायै नमः ।

Then let him salute the Quarters.

(1) Om Prâchyâm Sandhyâyai namaḥ.
(2) Om Dakṣiṇasyâm Sâvitryai namaḥ.
(3) Om Pratîchyâm Gâyatryai namaḥ.
(4) Om Udîchyâm sarvâbhyo Devatâbhyo namaḥ.
(5) Om kâmo' kârṣît Manyurakârṣîn namo namaḥ.
(6) Tataḥ Om Prâchyai namaḥ.
(7) Om Dakṣiṇâyai namaḥ.
(8) Om Udîchyai namaḥ.
(9) Om Urddhâyai namaḥ.
(10) Om Adhorâyai namaḥ.
(11) Om Antarikṣâyai namaḥ.

*Meanings.* (1) Salutation to Sandhyâ in the east.
(2) Salutation to Sâvitṛi in the south.
(3) Salutation to Gâyatrî in the west.
(4) Salutation to all gods in the north.
(5) Om Kâma has done it, Manyu has done it, all hail, all hail.

*Note.*—"The mantra, Kamo kârṣit Manyurakârṣit namo namaḥ," is to be found in Âpastamba Sûtras, I. 9. 26, 13 :—"He may either offer oblations to Kâma and Manyu (with the following two mantras), 'Kâma has done it ; Manyu has done it, or he may matter (those mantras)."

The complete mantras will be found in the Taittarîya Âraṇyaka, Ândhra resecension. X. 61., and also in Mahâ Nârâyaṇa Upaniṣad, XVIII. 2 and 3 :—

कर्मोऽकार्षीन्नाहं करोमि कामः करोति कामः कर्त्ता कामः कारयिता ।

एतत्ते काम कामाय स्वाहा ॥ ( २ )

मन्युरकार्षीन्नाहं करोमि मन्युः करोति मन्यु कर्त्ता मन्युः कारयिता ।

एतत्ते मन्यो मन्यवे स्वाहा ॥ ( ३ )

Kâma has done it, I have not done it, Kâma does it, Kâma is the agent, Kâma causes others to do. Svâhâ to Thee, O Kâma (1).

Manyu has done it, I have not done it, Manyu is the agent, Manyu causes others to do. Svâhâ to Thee, O Manyu. (2).

In fact, Kâma represents the emotional and passional nature of man, while the Manyu represents the lower intellectual nature of man, corresponding to Prâṇamaya and Manomayakoṣa of man respectively).

(6) Then salutation to the East.
(7) Om salutation to the South.
(8) Om salutation to the North.
(9) Om salutation to Upwards.
(10) Om salutation to Downwards.
(11) Om salutation to Antarîkṣa.

## XVI. ARGHYA-OFFERING TO THE SUN.

ओं नमो विवस्वते ब्रह्मन् भास्वते विष्णुतेजसे ।

जगत् सवित्रे शुचये सवित्रे कर्मदायिने ॥ १ ॥

ओं एहि सूर्य सहस्रांशो तेजोराशे जगत्पते ।

अनुकम्पय माम् भक्तं गृहाणार्घ्यं दिवाकर ॥ २ ॥

एषोऽर्घः ओं श्रीसूर्याय नमः ।

Then offer Arghya to the Sun with the following mantras :—

Salutation to Vivasvat, O Brahman, salutation to the Luminous One possessing the energy of Viṣṇu. Salutation to The Creator of the world, to the Pure, to the Generator, to the Awarder of the fruit of deeds. (1)

Come O Sûrya, of thousand rays, the Store-house of all energies, the Lord of the world, have mercy on me, Thy devotee; accept this Arghya, O Maker of Day. (2)

This Arghya is to Thee, Om Śri Sûryâya namaḥ.

## XVII. SALUTATION TO SÛRYA.

॥ ततः प्रणमेत् ॥

प्रास्कण्व‍ऋषिर्गायत्री छन्दः सूर्यो देवता सूर्यनमस्कारे विनियोगः ।

ओं जपाकुसुमसङ्काशं काश्यपेयं महाद्युतिम् ।

ध्वान्तारिं सर्वपापघ्नं प्रणतोऽस्मि दिवाकरम् ॥ १ ॥

ओं नमः सवित्रे जगदेकचक्षुषे जगत्प्रसूतिस्थितिनाशहेतवे ।

त्रयीमयाय त्रिगुणात्मधारिणे विरिञ्चिनारायणशङ्करात्मने नमः ॥ २ ॥.

ओं श्रीसूर्याय नमः ।

Then let him offer salutation with the following mantras :—

*Viniyoga.* **The Riṣi is Prâskanna, the metre is Gâyatrî, the Devatâ is Sûrya, and it is employed in salutation to Sûrya.**

Om salutation to the Maker of Day, Whose colour is like that of Javâ flower, Who possesses mighty light, Who is a Child of Kâśyapa and is an Enemy of darkness and the Destroyer of all sins, I reverently bow to that Maker of Day. (1)

Salutation to Sâvitṛi, to the One Eye of the world, to the Cause of the creation, preservation, and destruction of the world, to Him Who consists of trayî Vedas, and Who supports the prakṛiti consisting of three Guṇas, and contains Viriñchi, Nârâyaṇa, and Śaṅkara. (2)

Om salutation to Lord Sûrya.

### XVIII. GENERAL PRAṆÂMA.

॥ सामान्यप्रणामम् ॥

ओं नमो ब्रह्मण्यदेवाय गोब्राह्मणहिताय च ।

जगद्धिताय कृष्णाय गोविन्दाय नमो नमः ॥

॥ इति प्रातःसन्ध्या-विधिः ॥

Om, salutation to Brahmaṇya Deva, to the Well-wisher of the world and the Sages, to the Well-wisher of the universe, to KRISNA, Govinda, hail All, hail.

Here end the Rules of the Morning Sandhyâ.

---

## MID-DAY SANDHYA.

॥ अथ मध्याह्नसन्ध्याविधिः ॥

सर्वं प्रातःसन्ध्यावत् ।

आचमन-सूर्योपस्थान-गायत्र्यावाहनजपसमर्पणादिङ्नमस्कारेष्वेव विशेषः ।

### I. ÂCHAMANA.

॥ अथ आचमनम् ॥

आपः पुनन्त्विति पूतऋषिः पृथ्वी देवता अष्टिछन्दः आचमने विनियोगः ।

ओम् आपः पुनन्त्विति विष्णुऋषिरनुष्टुप्छन्दः आपो देवता आचमने विनियोगः ।

आपः पुनंतु पृथिवीं पृथिवी पूता पूनातु मां । पुनंतु ब्रह्मणस्पतिर्ब्रह्मपूता पूनातु मां ।

यदुच्छिष्टमभोज्यं यद्वा दुश्चरितं मम । सर्वं पुनन्तु मामापोऽसतां च प्रतिग्रहम् ॥ स्वाहा ॥

Tait. A. X. 23. 1.

इत्यनेन त्रिराचम्य पूर्ववन्मार्जनमघमर्षणञ्च कृत्वा, ओं सन्देहनामा राक्षसा क्षिरयन्तु इति विचिन्त्य गायत्र्यै सूर्याय च जलाञ्जलित्रयं दद्यात् ।

## II. SŪRYOPASTHĀNAM.

|| ततः सूर्योपस्थानम् || (Rig. I. 50. 1-13).

उदुत्यमिति त्रयोदशर्चस्य सूक्तस्य प्रस्कण्वऋषिः सूर्यो देवता गायत्री छन्दः सूर्योपस्थाने विनियोगः ।

ओम् उदुत्यं जातवेदसं देवं वहन्ति केतवः । दृशे विश्वाय सूर्यम् ॥ [Av. XIII. 2. 16]

ओं अप त्ये तायवो यथा नक्षत्रा यन्त्यक्तुभिः । सूराय विश्वचक्षसे ॥ २ ॥

ओं अदृश्रमस्य केतवो विरश्मयो जनाँ अनु । भ्राजन्तोऽग्नयो यथा ॥ ३ ॥

ओं तरणिर्विश्वदर्शतो ज्योतिष्कृदसि सूर्य । विश्वमाभासि रोचनम् ॥ ४ ॥

ओं प्रत्यङ्देवानां विशः प्रत्यङ्ङुदेषि मानुषान् । प्रत्यङ्विश्वं स्वर्दृशे ॥ ५ ॥

ओं येनापावक चक्षसा भुरण्यन्तं जनाँ अनु । त्वं वरुण पश्यसि ॥ ६ ॥

ओं वि द्यामेषि रजस्पृथ्वहा मिमानो अक्तुभिः । पश्यन् जन्मानि सूर्य ॥ ७ ॥

ओं सप्त त्वा हरितो रथे वहन्ति देव सूर्य । शोचिष्केशं विचक्षण ॥ ८ ॥

ओं अयुक्त सप्त शुन्ध्युवः सूरो रथस्य नप्त्यः ।
ताभिर्याति स्वयुक्तिभिः ॥ ( ९ )

ओं उद्वयं तमसस्परि ज्योतिः पश्यन्त उत्तरं ।
देवं देवत्रा सूर्यमगन्म ज्योतिरुत्तमम् ॥ ( १० )

ओं उद्यन्नद्य मित्रमह आरोहन्नुत्तरां दिवम् ।
हृद्रोगं मम सूर्य हरिमाणं च नाशय ॥ ( ११ )

ओं शुकेषु मे हरिमाणं रोपणाकासु दध्मसि ।
अथो हारिद्रवेषु मे हरिमाणं निदध्मसि ॥ ( १२ )

ओं उदगादयमादित्यो विश्वेन सहसा सह ।
द्विषन्तं मह्यं रन्धयन्मो अहं द्विषते रधम् ॥ ( १३ )

## III. GĀYATRĪ DHYĀNA.

|| ततो गायत्रीध्यानम् ||.

कृष्णां चतुर्भुजां शङ्खचक्रगदापद्महस्तां गरुडारूढां पीताम्बरधरां विष्णोः सदृशरूपां विष्णुदैवत्यां यजुर्वेदरक्तीं युवतीं रविमण्डलमध्यस्थां सावित्रीं ध्यायेत् ।

## IV. ĀVĀHANA

|| ततः आवाहनम् ||

प्रजापतिऋषिरुपरिष्टाद् गायत्री छन्दः त्रिष्टुमनुष्टुप् छन्दोऽपि मध्याह्ने गायत्र्यावाहने विनियोगः ।

ओं ओजोऽसि सहोऽसि बलमसि भ्राजोऽसि देवानां धामनामासि ।

विश्वमसि विश्वायुः सर्वमसि सर्वायुरभिभूरोम् (Taittiriya-Samhita, II. 4. 3-1 and Mahānārāyaṇa Upanishad XV. 1.)

( गायत्रीं आवाहयामि ) सावित्रीं आवाहयामि ( सरस्वतीं आवाहयामि छन्दऋषीनावाहयामि । श्रियमावाहयामि बलमावाहयामि )

गौरीर्मिमाय सलिलानि तक्षत्येकपदी द्विपदी सा चतुष्पदी ।

अष्टापदी नवपदी बभूवुषी सहस्राक्षरा परमे व्योमन् ॥ (Rig. I. 164-41).

ओं आयाहि वरदे देवित्र्यक्षरे ब्रह्मवादिनी ।

सावित्रीछन्दसां मातरिहागत्य भजस्व माम् ॥

V. GÂYATRÎ JAPA.

## ततो गायत्रीं जप्त्वा ( भूः भुवः इति )

VI. GÂYATRÎ-VISARJANAM.

॥ गायत्री विसर्जनम् ॥

विसर्जयेदनेन मन्त्रेण :—
प्रजापतिर्ऋषिस्त्रिष्टुपछन्दो गायत्री देवता गायत्रीविसर्जने विनियोगः ।

ओं उदीच्यां शिखरे जाते भूम्यां पर्वतवासिनी ।

विष्णुना समनुज्ञाता गच्छ देवि यथेच्छया ॥

महोअर्णः सरस्वती प्रचेतयति केतुना ।

धियो विश्वा विराजति ॥

इति विसर्जयेत् ।

VII. NAMASKÂRA.

## ॥ अथ नमस्कारः ॥

मध्याह्ने आदौ ओं दक्षिणदिशि सन्ध्यायै नमः ।

ओं उदीच्यां गायत्र्यै नमः ।

ओं प्राच्यां सर्वेभ्यो देवेभ्योनमः ।

ओं कामोकार्षीन्मन्यूरकार्षीन्नमोनमः ।

VIII. DINNAMASKÂRA.

॥ ततोदिङ् नमस्कारः ॥

ओं दक्षिणायै नमः ।

ओं प्रतीच्यै नमः ।

ओं उदीच्यै नमः ।

ओं प्राच्यै नमः ।

ओं उर्ध्वायै नमः ।

ओं अधोरायै नमः ।

॥ इति मध्याह्नसन्ध्याविधिः ॥

## MID-DAY SANDHYA.

The mid-day Sandhyâ is like the Morning Sandhyâ, the differences being only in the following five points :—

1. Âchamana.
2. Sûryopasthâna.
3. Gâyâtrî-dhyâna.
4. Gâyatrî-âvâhana.
5. Gâyatrî-visarjana.
6. Salutation to the Quarters.

### I. ÂCHAMANA.

Now as to Âchamana :—

*Viniyoga.* Of the mantra "Âpaḥ punantu etc.," the Ṛiṣi is Pûta, the Devatá is Pṛithivî, the metre is Asṭi (Anuṣṭup), and it is employed in Âchamana.

Om, Âpaḥ punantu prithivîm prithivî pûtâ pûnâtu mâm ; Punantu Brahmaṇaspatir Brahmapûtâ punâtu mâm. Yadu-chchhiṣhṭam abhojyam yad vâ duścharitam mama. Sarvam punantu mâmâpo asatâm cha pratigra ham. Svâhâ.

*Translation* :—Om. Of "Âpo Punantu" the seer is Viṣhṇu, the metre is Anuṣṭup, the god is Apas, and it is used in sipping water.

May the Âpas purify the earth and the earth being purified, purify me. May the waters purify the Brahmanaspati, and the self-purified Brahma (the Vedas) purify me. May the waters purify all sins, such as, eating the remains of another, or improper food, or evil conduct, or accepting gifts from sinners. Svâhâ.

*Note* :—The word "earth" here means the "physical body." The mantra therefore means "May the Waters purify my physical body, which being so purified, in its turn purify "me," namely, my higher bodies" &c.

*Direction* :—Having sipped the water thrice with the above mantra, and having performed Mârjanam and Aghamarṣaṇam as before, and having mentally repeated "Om let the Râkṣasas called Mandehas be destroyed" let him offer

*Jalâñjali*

thrice to the Sun, with the recitation of *Gâyatrî*.

### II. SÛRYOPASTHÂNA.

*Vinioyaga.* Of the hymn consisting of thirteen Riks, the Seer is Praskaṇva, the Devatâ is Sûrya, the metre is Gâyatrî, and it is employed in Sûryopasthâna.

Atharva-Veda XIII 2. 16-24.

(1) This heavenly Jâtavedas the lights (ketu) draw (vah) up, for every one to see the sun.

(2) Away go, like thieves, these asterisms with their rays (aktu), for the all-beholding sun.

(3) The lights (ketu), the rays of him have been seen abroad among the peoples, like shining fires.

(4) Speedy, conspicuous to all, light-making art thou, O sun ; thou shinest unto everything, O bright space (rochana).

(5) In front of the clans of the gods, in front of those of men thou risest; in front of every one, for seeing the sky (svar).

(6) With whom (as) eye thou, O purifying Varuṇa, seest him that busies himself among the people (janân).

(7) Thou goest through the sky, the broad welkin (râjas), fashioning (mâ) the day with (thy) rays, seeing the generations (Janmâni), O sun.

(8) Seven yellow steeds, O heavenly sun, draw in the chariot thee the flame-haired, the out-looking.

(9) The sun hath yoked the seven neat (sundhyu) daughters of the chariot; with them, (who are) self-yoked, he goeth.

(10) Looking upon the loftier light above the darkness we have come

To Surya, God among the Gods, the light that is most excellent.

(11) Rising this day, O rich in friends, ascending to the loftier heaven,

Surya, remove my heart's disease, take from me this my yellow hue.

(12) To parrots and to starlings let us give away my yellowness,

Or this my yellowness let us transfer to Haritâla trees.

(13) With all his conquering vigour this Âditya hath gone up on high.

Giving my foe into mine hand: let me not be my foemân's prey.

### III. GÂYATRÎ DHYÂNA.

Then let him meditate on Gâyatrî as of dark colour, having four hands, holding conch, discus, club, and lotus, and seated on a Garuḍa, and wearing yellow garment, having the same form as Visṇu, and full of Viṣṇu energy and holding Yajurveda, youthful, in the middle of the solar orb, and having the name of Sâvitrî.

### IV. ÂVÂHANA.

Then let him invoke Gâyatrî.

*Viniyoga.* The Riṣi is Prajâpati, the metre is Gâyatrî, and it is employed in invoking Gâyatrî in midday.

*Mantra.*—(1) Thou art energy, Thou art conquering might (patience), Thou art strength, Thou art brilliance, Thou art the abode of Devas (Svarga), Thou art named (such as Indra &c.), Thou art All (inanimate creation), Thou art All Life (animate creation), Thou art All, Thou art All Living Beings, Thou art conquering Might, Om.

(2) I invoke Gâyatrî, I invoke Sâvitrî, I invoke Sarasvatî, I invoke Chhanda-ṛiṣi, I invoke Śrî, I invoke Strength.

(3) Forming the water-floods, the buffalo hath lowed, one-footed, or two-footed or four-footed, she,

Who hath become eight-footed or hath got nine feet, the thousand-syllabled in the sublimest heaven. (Rig. I. 164. 41).

(4) Om come Thou, boon-giving goddess, consisting of three syllables, the Knower of Brahman, Sâvitri, the Mother of metres, coming here help me.

Then having muttered silently (Japa) the Gâyatri, let him bid farewell to Her with the following mantra :—

### V. GÂYATRI-VISARJANAM.

*Viniyoga.* Of the mantra, "Udichyâm etc." the Risi is Prajâpati, the metre is Tristup, the Devatâ is Gâyatri, and it is employed in bidding farewell to the Gâyatri.

*Mantra.*—(1) Om, born on earth on the summit of the northern mountain, O Thou Dweller of mountain, permitted by Viṣṇu, go O goddess, wherever Thou wishest.

(2) Sarasvati, the mighty flood, she with her light illuminates, She brightens every pious thought. (Rig. I. 3. 12).

Thus he should bid farewell to the Gâyatri.

### VII. NAMASKÂRA.

*Then Salutation.*

In the mid-day-at first, (1) Om salutation to Sandhyâ in the south.
(2) Om salutation to Gâyatri in the north.
(3) Om salutation to all gods in the east.
(4) Om Kâma has done, Manyu has done, salutation, salutation.

### VIII. DIK-NAMASKÂRA.

*Salutation to the Quarters.*

(1) Om salutation to the south.
(2) Om salutation to the west.
(3) Om salutation to the north.
(4) Om salutation to the east.
(5) Om salutation to upwards.
(6) Om salutation to downwards.

Here ends the Mid-day Sandhyâ.

---

## EVENING SANDHYA.

## ॥ अथ सायंसन्ध्याविधिः ॥

सर्वं प्रातः सन्ध्यावत् ।

विशेषतस्त्वाचमनसूर्योपस्थानगायत्रीध्यानदिङ्नमस्कारेषु ।

### I. ÂCHAMANA.

॥ आचमनमन्त्रो यथा ॥

ओं अग्निश्चमेति रुद्र ऋषिः प्रकृतिश्छन्दः आपो देवता अपामुपस्पर्शने विनियोगः ।

ओं अग्निश्च मामन्युश्च मन्युपतयश्च मन्युकृतेभ्यः पापेभ्यो रक्षन्तां यदह्ना पापमकार्षं मनसा वाचा हस्ताभ्यां पद्भ्यामुदरेण शिश्ना अहस्तदवलुम्पतु । यत्किंचिद् दुरितं मयि इदमहमापोऽमृतयोनौ सत्ये ज्योतिषि जुहोमि ॥ स्वाहा ॥

इत्यनेन त्रिराचम्य,

II. MÀRJANAM.

पूर्ववन्मार्जनादिकं कृत्वा,

III. SÛRYOPASTHÂNA.

॥ सूर्योपस्थानं कुर्यात् ॥

॥ तद्यथा कृताञ्जलिना सूर्यं पश्येत् ॥

मो षु वरुणेति पञ्चर्चस्य वशिष्ठऋषिर्वरुणो देवता गायत्रीछन्दः सूर्योपस्थाने विनियोगः ।

मो षु वरुण मृन्मयं गृहं राजन्नहं गमम् । मृडा सुक्षत्र मृडय ॥ १ ॥

यदेमि प्रस्फुरन्निव दृतिर्न ध्मातोअद्रिवः । मृडा सुक्षत्र मृडय ॥ २ ॥

क्रत्वः समह दीनता प्रतीपं जगमा शुचे । मृडा सुक्षत्र मृडय ॥ ३ ॥

अपां मध्ये तस्थिवांसं तृष्णाविदज्जरितारम् । मृडा सुक्षत्र मृडय ॥ ४ ॥

यत्किञ्चेदं वरुण दैव्ये जनेऽभिद्रोहं मनुष्या३श्चरामसि ।

अचित्ती यत्तव धर्मा युयोपिम मा नस्तस्मादेनसो देव रीरिषः ॥ ५ ॥

(Rig. VII. 89. 1-5).

IV. GÂYATRÎ DHYÂNA.

॥ ततो गायत्रीध्यानम् ॥

ओं शुक्लां वृषभारूढां द्विभुजां त्रिशूलडमरुकरामर्द्धचन्द्रविभूषितां त्रिनेत्रां रुद्ररुद्रारूपां सामवेदवक्त्रीं रविमण्डलमध्यस्थां ध्यायेत् ।

ओं श्वेतवर्णा समुद्दिष्टा कौशेयवसना तथा । आदित्यमण्डलान्तःस्था ब्रह्मलोकगताथवा ॥

इत्येवं ध्यात्वा,

V. ÂVÂHANA.

॥ आवाहयेत् ॥

ओं आयाहि वरदे देवि त्र्यक्षरे ब्रह्मवादिनि ।

गायत्रीछन्दसां मातर्ब्रह्मयोनि नमोऽस्तु ते ॥

VI. GÂYATRÎ JAPA.

॥ गायत्रीजप ॥

गायत्र्या विश्वामित्रऋषिः सविता देवता गायत्रीछन्द इयदावृत्तिः गायत्रीजपे विनियोगः ।

VII. GÂYATRÎ VISARJANAM.

॥ ततो गायत्रीविसर्जनम् ॥

ओं उत्तमे शिखरे जाता भूम्यां पर्वतमूर्धनि । ब्राह्मणेभ्योऽभ्यनुज्ञाता गच्छ देवि यथासुखम् ॥

### VIII. DIK-NAMASKÂRA.

॥ ततो दिङ्नमस्कारः ॥

ओं प्रतीच्यां सन्ध्यायै नमः ।

ओं उदीच्यां सावित्र्यै नमः ।

ओं प्राच्यां गायत्र्यै नमः ।

ओं दक्षिणस्यां सर्वाभ्यो देवताभ्यो नमः

ओं कामोकार्षीन्मन्यूरकार्षीन्नमोनमः ।

ओं प्रतीच्यै नमः ।

ओं उदीच्यै नमः ।

ओं प्राच्यै नमः ।

ओं दक्षिणायै नमः ।

ओं ऊर्ध्वायै नमः ।

ओं अधरायै नमः ।

ओं अन्तरिक्षायै नमः ।

॥ इति ऋग्वेदीनां सन्ध्याविधिः समाप्ता ॥

॥ ओं तत्सत् ॥

### EVENING SANDHYÂ.

Now the rules about the Evening Sandhyâ.

Everything is like the Morning Sandhyâ. The difference consists in (1) Âchamana, (2) Sûryopasthâna, (3) Gâyatri-dhyâna, [(4) Âvâhana, (5) Visarjana ], and (6) Dik-namaskâra.

### I. ÂCHAMANA.

The Âchamana mantra is as follows :—

*Viniyoga.* Of the Mantra, "Agniś cha mâ etc.," the Riṣi is Nârâyaṇa, the metre is Gâyatrî of the natural form (perhaps prose), the Devatâ is Agni, and it is employed in Âchamana.

*Meaning.*—May Agni, and Manyu, and the Lords of Manyu protect me from the sins committed by my Manyu. Whatever sin I may have committed by day through my mind, speech, or hands, or feet, or stomach, or the organ [of generation], may the Night destroy all that sin whatsoever, which may be in me, its author. I throw it into the Truth, the Light, The Supreme Self, the Womb of Immortality, as an oblation. Let it be efficacious, Svâhâ.

Having thus performed Âchamana rites, and having performed Mârjana rites as mentioned above, let him perform Sûryopasthâna, with the mantras given below.

### II. SÛRYOPASTHÂNA.

The Sûryopasthâna should be done thus:—Having put his hand in the form of Añjali let him look at the Sun and recite :—

*Viniyoga.* Of the five mantras "Mo ṣu Varuṇa," the seer is Vasiṣṭha, the Devatâ is Varuṇa, the metre is Gâyatrî, and they are employed in Sûryopasthâna.

*Meaning.* (1) Let me not yet, King Varuṇa, enter into the house of clay :

Have mercy, spare me, Mighty Lord.

(2) When, Thunderer ! I move along tremulous like a wind-blown skin,

Have mercy, spare me, Mighty Lord.

(3) O Bright and Powerful God, through want of strength I erred and went astray :

Have mercy, spare me, Mighty Lord.

(4) Thirst found thy worshipper though he stood in the midst of water-floods :

Have mercy, spare me, Mighty Lord.

(5) O Varuṇa, whatever the offence may be which we as men commit against the heavenly host,

When through our want of thought we violate thy laws, punish us not, O God, for that iniquity.

### III. GÂYATRÎ DHYÂNA.

Then let him meditate on Gâyatrî thus :—

She is dressed in white, seated on a bull, has two hands, holding a trident and a drum (Ḍamaru) respectively, is adorned with a crescent, has three eyes, and a form resembling Rudra, and recite Sâma-Veda, and is in the middle solar orb, I meditate on Her thus.

Om ! She who has white colour and wears silken dress, and is in the middle solar orb, and resides in the Brahma-loka. (This is an alternative dhyâna).

Having thus meditated on Gâyatrî, let him invoke Her by saying :—

### IV. ÂVÂHANA.

*Meaning.*—Om ! Come Thou, O Boon-giving Goddess, consisting of three syllables, and Revealer of Brahman, Gâyatrî, the mother of all metres, salutation to Thee, O Source of Brahman (Vedas).

After this recite Gâyatrî as before, ten, twenty-eight, hundred and eight times etc.

### V. VISARJANA.

Then bid farewell to Gâyatrî by saying :—

Born on the summit of the mountain in the north, as well as in the middle of the earth, and permitted by Brahmâ, Thou Who hadst come to help Thy devotees, now being permitted go O Lady, wherever Thou desirest to go.

*Note.*—According to the Dipikâ of Nârâyaṇa on Mahânârâyaṇa Upaniṣad, Ch XV, verse 5, where this mantra occurs with some variation, the Sandhyâ mountain is explained to be a hill, west of Gayâ.

VI. THEN LET HIM SALUTE THE QUARTERS.

(1) Oṃ Pratîchyâṃ Sandhyâyai namaḥ.
(2) Oṃ Udîchyâṃ Sâvitryai namaḥ.
(3) Oṃ Prâchyâṃ Gâyatryai namaḥ.
(4) Oṃ Dakṣiṇasyâṃ sarvâbhyo Devatâbhyo namaḥ.
(5) Oṃ Kâmo' kârṣin manyûra kârṣin namo namaḥ.
(6) Om Pratîchyai namaḥ.
(7) Oṃ Udîchyai namaḥ.
(8) Oṃ Prâchyai namaḥ.
(9) Oṃ Dakṣînâyai namaḥ.
(10) Oṃ Ûrddhâyai namaḥ.
(11) Oṃ Adharâyai namaḥ.
(12) Oṃ Antarîkṣâyai namaḥ.

*Meaning.* (1) Salutation to Sandhyâ in the west.
(2) Salutation to Sâvitrî in the north.
(3) Salutation to Gâyatrî in the east.
(4) Salutation to all gods in the south.
(5) Kâma has done, Manyu has done, salutation, salutation.
(6) Salutation to the west.
(7) Salutation to the north.
(8) Salutation to the east.
(9) Salutation to the south.
(10) Salutation to upwards.
(11) Salutation to downwards.
(12) Salutation to Antarîkṣa.

Here ends the Evening Sandhyâ.

Here end the Sandhyâ Rituals of the Rigvedins.

*Note.*—This Rigvedi Sandhyâ is taken from a manuscript in the possession of Babu Gopal Chandra Lahiri, and it is written in neat Bengali characters, and the colophon says "written by Śrî Mahesh Chandra Śarmâ in the Śâka era 1813, and in the San 1298, on the 9th of Aṣâdha." The manuscript consists of 21 folios of eight-half inches by three-half inches, each page containing five lines. Besides the Sandhyâ which ends at folio 16, the rest contains the ritual of Brahma-Yajña, Gâyatri-Stava, Gâyatrî-Kavacha.

Pandit Mahesh Chandra Śarmâ was the father-in-law of Babu Gopal Chandra Lahiri, and he died in Benares in the year 1908 A.D.

## CHAPTER VIII.

### THE SÂMA-VEDI SANDHYA.

After tarpana, the morning Sandhyâ should be performed. The Vedic Sandhyâ consists of the following parts according to the Sâma-Vedins:—

I. Ordinary âchamana or the sipping of water.

II. Mârjana or the sprinkling of water with a Kuśâ blade, accompanied by the recitation of certain mantras.

III. Prâṇâyâma or the regulation of breath. It consists of:—

(a) Pûraka or the drawing in of breath by reciting the Gâyatrî.

(b) Kumbhaka or the retention of breath for the period till the Gâyatrî is recited.

(c) Rechaka or the expelling of breath with the same recitation.

IV. Âchamana with appropriate mantras, according as the Sandhyâ is of morning, of midday or of evening.

V. Punar-mârjana or the second sprinkling of water.

VI. Agha-marṣana or the expulsion of sin from the body, by mentally burning up the Person of Sin.

VII. Sûryopasthâna or the hymn addressed to the Sun.

VIII. Gâyatrî-japa or the silent recitation of Gâyatrî. This is the principal portion of Sandhyâ. In cases of emergency, other portions might be omitted, but *never* this. It consists of—

1. Invocation of Gâyatrî,
2. Riṣi Nâysa
3. Ṣaḍaṅga Nâysa or assignment of the various parts of the body to different deities.
4. Dhyâna or meditation, *i.e.*, the mental image making of the goddess Gâyatrî. It is three-fold according to the time of the day.

   Morning = Brahmâṇi.
   Mid-day = Vaiṣṇavi.
   Evening = Rudrâṇi.

5. Japa or the silent recitation 10 times or 108 times of Gâyatrî.
6. Farewell to the Gâyatrî and Prayer.

IX. Âtmarakṣâ or the prayer for protection of self.

X. Rudra-upasthâna or hymn to Rudra.

#### I.—ORDINARY ÂCHAMANA.

Perform the Âchamana as already described before by reciting:—

ओं तद्विष्णोः परमं पदं सदा पश्यन्ति सूरयः ।

दिवीव चक्षुराततम् ॥

Om tad viṣṇoḥ paramam padam sadâ paśyanti Sûrayaḥ.
Divîva chakṣur âtatam. Rigveda I. 22. 20.

That supreme state of Visṇu, the Suris always see. In the Heaven, as wanders the eye.

[*N.B.*—The proper time for morning Sandhyâ is before the sun-rise. But if the time be past, then the Gâyatri should be repeated *ten* times after Âchamana, as a reminder to be more punctual in future.]

[*N.B.*—The full process of Âchamana is given before at pages 13 and the following.]

### II.—MÂRJANA.

Then let him perform the mârjana by reciting the following mantras, and pour the water in the koşâ (copper vessel) with the kuśi (small copper spoon,. :—

ओं शं न आपो धन्वन्याः शमु नः सन्त्वनूप्याः ।

शं नः समुद्रिया आपः शमु नः सन्तु कूप्याः ॥

Om ! śaṃ na âpo dhanvanyâḥ śamu naḥ santv anûpyâḥ.

Śan naḥ samudriyâ âpaḥ śamu naḥ santu kûpyâh. (Atharva Veda I, I. 6. 4.)

Om ! auspicious be to us the waters of the desert places ; auspicious be the waters of well-watered land ; auspicious be to us the waters of the sea ; auspicious be to us the waters of the well.

Then with this mantra throw the water on the body.

ओं द्रुपदा दिवमुमुचानः स्विन्नः स्नातो मलादिव ।

पूतं पवित्रेणेवाज्यमापः शुन्धन्तु मैनसः ॥

(Yajur Veda XX. 20.)

Om, Drupadâdiva mumuchânaḥ svinnâḥ snâto malâdiva ;
Pûtam pavitreṇev âjyam âpaḥ śundhantu mainasaḥ.

Om even as the perspiring gets relief from the shade of the tree, as bathing removes the impurities of the body, as the ghee becomes purified by its purifying agents, so let the waters purify me from all sins.

ओम् । आपोहिष्ठामयोभुवः तान ऊर्जे दधातन ।

महे रणाय चक्षसे ॥

ओं यो वः शिवतमो रसः तस्य भाजयतेह नः ।

उशतीरिव मातरः ॥

ओं तस्मा अरङ्ग मामवः यस्य क्षयाय जिन्वथ ।

आपो जनयथा च नः ॥

(Rig. X. 9. 1. to 3, Atharva. I. 5. 1.)

Om ; Âpo hiṣṭhâ mayobhuvaḥ, tâna ûrje dadhâtana, mahe raṇâya chakṣase.

Om ; Yo vaḥ śivatamo rasaḥ, tasya bhâjayate ha naḥ ; uśatîr iva mâtaraḥ.

Om ; Tasmâ araṅgamâma vaḥ yasya kṣayâya jinvatha ; Âpo janayathâ cha naḥ.

O ye Apas (All-pervading Divine Currents) since you are the sources of pleasure, help us therefore by giving us energy, so that we may feel the Mighty Sound.

That essence of yours which is most auspicious, of that a share give us here. As loving mothers (suck the babe).
O Waters! we approach thee all for our sins to be destroyed, Give us strength to cope with sin.

ओम् ऋतं च सत्यंचाभीद्धात्तपसोऽध्यजायत ।
ततो रात्र्यजायत ततः समुद्रोऽर्णवः ॥ १ ॥
समुद्रादर्णवादधि संवत्सरो ऽजायत ।
अहोरात्राणि विदधद्विश्वस्य मिषतोवशी ॥ २ ॥
सूर्याचन्द्रमसौ धाता यथापूर्वमकल्पयत् ।
दिवं च पृथिवीं चान्तरिक्षमथो स्वः ॥ ३ ॥

Rig. X. 190. 1.

Om ṛitam cha satyam châbhîdhât tapaso' dhyajâyata;
Tato râtry ajâyata tataḥ samudro arṇavaḥ.
Samudrâd arṇavâd adhi samvatsaro' jâyata;
Ahorâtrâṇi vidadhat viśvasyâ miṣato vaśi;
Sûryâchandramasau dhâtâ yathâ pûrvam akalpayat;
Divam cha prithivîm chântarikṣam atho svaḥ.

From the highly concentrated meditation came out the Right and the True.
From that the Primal Night arose, from that the Oceanic flood.
From the Ocean flood, there after was produced the Year.
The Lord of all living Universe then ordained the Days and Nights.
The Dhâtâ then created the Sun and Moon, as in the past.
He formed the Joyful Heaven and Earth, and the Middle Region too.

[*N.B.*—The Sâma-vedis recite ten times Gâyatrî at this stage, if the proper Sandhyâ time be past.]

Then let him recite the following in the *morning* Sandhyâ only:—

ओं नत्वा तु पुण्डरीकाक्षं उपात्ताघःप्रशान्तये ।
ब्रह्मवर्च्चसकामार्थं प्रातः सन्ध्यामुपास्महे ॥

Om! Natvâ tu Puṇdarikâkṣam upâttâghaḥ praśântaye.
Brahma-varchasa Kâmârtham prâtaḥ sandhyâmupâsmahe.

Om! Having bowed to the Lotus-eyed and to remove the sins performed, and to obtain the strength of spirit, the morning prayer, we commence.

### III.—PRÂṆÂYÂMA.

Then let him perform Prâṇâyâma, reciting:—
(Then with this Mantra sprinkle water on the pot.)

ओंकारस्य ब्रह्मा ऋषिर्गायत्री छन्दोऽग्निर्देवता
(शुक्लो वर्णः) सर्वकर्म्मारम्भे विनियोगः ॥

Oṃkârasya Brahmâ risi Gâyatrî chhando' gnir Devatâ, (śuklo varnaḥ) sarva karmârambhe viniyogaḥ.

Of Om, the seer is Brahmâ, the metre is Gâyatrî, the Devatâ is Agni, the color is white, and it is employed in reciting all sacred formulas.

ओं सप्तव्याहृतीनां प्रजापतिर् ऋषिर्गायत्र्युष्णिगनुष्टुब्बृहतीपङ्क्तित्रिष्टुब्जगत्य-
श्छन्दांस्यग्निवायुसूर्यवरुणबृहस्पतीन्द्रविश्वेदेवा देवताः प्राणायामे विनियोगः ।

Om; Sapta vyâhṛitînâm Prajâpatir Riṣir Gâyatry Uṣnig, Anuṣṭub, Brihatî, Pankti Triṣṭub, Jagatyas Chhandâmsy, Agni, Vâyu, Sûrya, Varuṇa, Brihaspatîndra Viśvedevâ devatâḥ Prâṇâyâme viniyogaḥ.

Of the seven Vyâhritis, the Riṣi is Prajâpati, the metres are Gâyatrî, Uṣnik, Anuṣṭup, Brihati Pankti, Triṣṭup, and Jagati; the Devatas are Agni, Vâyu, Sûrya, Varuṇa, Brihaspati, Indra, and Viśvedeva, they are employed in Prâṇâyâma.

ओं गायत्र्या विश्वामित्रऋषिर्गायत्री छन्दः सविता देवता प्राणायामे विनियोगः ॥

Om! Gâyatryâ Viśvâmitrar Ṛiṣir Gâyatrî Chhandaḥ Savitâ Devatâ Prâṇâyâme viniyogaḥ.

Om! of Gâyatri the seer is Viśvâmitra, the metre is Gâyatri, the Devatâ is Savitâ and it is employed in Prâṇâyâma.

ओं शिरसः प्रजापतिऋषिर्गायत्री छन्दो ब्रह्मवाय्वग्नि-सूर्याश्चतस्रो देवताः प्राणायामे विनियोगः ॥

Om! Śirasaḥ Prajâpatir Ṛiṣir, Gâyatrî chhando Brahma Vâyu agni Sûrya Devatâḥ, Prâṇâyâme viniyogaḥ.

Om! of the Śirasa, the seer is Prajâpati, the metre is Gâyatrî, the Devatas are Brahmâ, Vâyu, Agni, and Sûrya, and it is employed in Prâṇâyâma.

Having recited the above four preliminary mantras, and having sprinkled water about the head, let him meditate on Brahmâ in the navel, while inspiring breath through the left nostril, the right nostril being closed with the right thumb. While drawing in the breath let him recite :—

ओं भूः । ओं भुवः । ओं स्वः । ओं महः । ओं जनः । ओं तपः । ओं सत्यम् ॥ तत्सवितुर्वरेण्यं भर्गो देवस्य धीमहि । धियो यो नः प्रचोदयात् ॥ ओं आपो ज्योतीरसोऽमृतं ब्रह्मभूर्भुवस्स्वरोम् ॥

*Note*:—The sacred syllable ओं Om consists of three letters अ उ and म् expressive of three aspects of God, (Creator, Preserver and Regenerator), the three states of consciousness, *i.e.*, waking, dreaming and deep sleep, &c. See Mândukya Upaniṣad. The seven syllables, Bhuh, &c., denote the seven planes, Physical, Astral, Mental, Buddhik, Nirvânik, Mahâ Nirvânik and Paramahânirvânik. In exoteric religion (1) Bhuḥ extends upto Meru; (2) Bhuvah, the land of enjoyment after death, from Meru upto Dhruva; (3) Svaḥ, the land of the virtuous after death, from Dhruva upto Svarga loka of five kinds; (4) Mahaḥ, the middle plane and the largest of all planes; (5) Janaḥ, the land of archetypal *births*, for the first *birth* of every type takes place on this plane after the end of a Paralaya and at the beginning of a new Kalpa, the starting plane of Creation; (6) Tapaḥ, the land of the Siddhas where, they live undisturbed by Pralaya, the land of Sanaka, &c.; (7) Satyam the plane of Brahmâ, free from all changes. The jñânîs live here. On reaching this plane there is no longer any compulsory re-incarnation.

These seven syllables are the names of God also, as explained by Sri Sankarâcharya, see commentary.

The Gâyatri has already been explained. See pages 29 and the following.

ओं रक्तवर्णं चतुर्मुखं, द्विभुजं, अक्षसूत्रकमण्डलुकरं, हंसासनसमारूढं ब्रह्माणं ध्यायेत् ॥

Om Bhuḥ, Om Bhuvaḥ, Om Svaḥ, Om Mahaḥ, Om Janaḥ, Om Tapaḥ, Om Satyam.

Om Tat Savitur Vareṇyam Bhargo Devasya dhîmahi ; dhiyo yo naḥ prachodayât.

Om Âpo jyotî raso ' mritam Brahma Bhur Bhuvas Svar Om.

Om, Raktavarṇam chatur mukham dvi-bhujam, akṣa sûtra kamaṇḍalu karam, Haṃsâsana samârûḍham Brahmâṇam dhyâyet.

Let him meditate on Brahmâ, as seated on Haṃsa, having two hands, holding a rosary and water-pot and of red color.

Then let him close the left nostril also, with his ring and little fingers, and keep the breath in, performing kumbhaka while reciting the *same* mantras and meditating on Keśava in the heart :—

ओं भूः ओं भुवः ओं स्वः ओं महः ओं जनः ओं तपः ओं सत्यम् । ओं तत्सवितुर्व्वरेण्यं भर्गो देवस्य धीमहि ॥ धियो यो नः प्रचोदयात् ॥ ओं आपोज्योतीरसोमृतं ब्रह्म भूर्भुवः स्वरोम् ॥

ओं नीलोत्पलदलप्रभं, चतुर्भुजं, शंखचक्रगदापद्महस्तं, गरुडासनसमारूढं, केशवं ध्यायेत्

Om, Nilot-paladala-prabham, chatur-bhujam śaṅkhachakra-gadâ-padma-hastam, Garuḍâsana-samârûḍham Keśavam dhyâyet.

Let him meditate on Keśava as seated on Garuda, having four hands holding a conch, a discus, a club and a lotus in each hand, and of lotus-blue colour.

Then he should expel the air slowly through the right nostril, by removing the thumb, keeping the left closed, and meditating on Śiva in the forehead, reciting the same mantras :—

ओं भूः । ओं भुवः । ओं स्वः । ओं महः । ओं जनः । ओं तपः । ओं सत्यम् ओं तत्सवितुर्व्वरेण्यं भर्गो देवस्य धीमहि ॥ धियो यो नः प्रचोदयात् ॥ ओम् आपो ज्योतीरसोमृतं ब्रह्मभूर्भुवः स्वरोम् ॥

ओं श्वेतवर्णं, द्विभुजं, त्रिशूलडमरुकरमर्द्धचन्द्रविभूषितं, त्रिनेत्रं, वृषभस्थं शम्भुं ध्यायेत् ॥

Om, Śvetavarṇam, dvi-bhujam triśûla-ḍamaru karam ardhachandra vibhûṣitam trinetram vṛiṣabhastham Sambhum dhyâyet.

Let him meditate on Śambhu seated on Vṛiṣabha, having three eyes and two hands, holding a Trident and a drum, and having the crescent on his forehead and of white color.

### IV.—ÂCHAMANA.

Then let him perform (the morning) Âchamana reciting the following :—

ओं सूर्य्यश्चमेति ब्रह्मा ऋषिः प्रकृतिश्छन्दः आपो देवता आचमने विनियोगः ॥

ओं सूर्य्यश्च मामन्युश्च अन्युपतयश्च मन्युकृतेभ्यः । पापेभ्यो रक्षन्तां । यद्रात्र्या

पापमकार्ष । मनसा वाचा हस्ताभ्यां । पद्भ्यामुदरेण शिश्ना । अहस्तदवलुम्पतु । यत्किंच दुरितं मयि । इदमहमाममृतयोनौ । सूर्ये ज्योतिषि परमात्मनि जुहोमि स्वाहा ॥

इति प्रातराचामेत् ॥ T. A. X. 25·1.

Om, Sûryaśchameti, Brahmâ ṛisiḥ, prakritiś chhandaḥ, Âpo devatâ, âchamane viniyogaḥ.

Om, Sûryaś cha mâ manyuś cha manyu patayaś cha manyukritebhyaḥ pâpebhyo rakṣantâm. Yad râtryâ pâpam akârṣam, manasâ vâchâ hastâbhyâm, padbhyâm udareṇa śiśnâ ahas tad avalumpatu.

Yat kiñcha duritam mayi idam ahammâmamrita yonau Sûrye jyotishi paramâtmani juhomi svâhâ.

May Sûrya and Manyu and Manyupatis protect me from the sins caused by my Manyu. Whatever sins I may have committed in the night—whether by mind, or speech or hands or feet or stomach or organ—may Râtri destroy that, whatever sin there may be in me, all that I offer in the Immortal cause, the Sûrya, the Self-luminous (to be burnt up). Svâhâ.

The mid-day âchamana mantra is :—

ओं आपः पुनंत्विति विष्णुर्ऋषिरनुष्टुपछंदः आपो देवता आचमने विनियोगः ॥ आपः पुनंतु पृथिवीं पृथिवी पूता पुनातु मां ॥ पुनंतु ब्रह्मणस्पतिर्ब्रह्म पूता पुनातु मां ॥ यदुच्छिष्टमभोज्यं यद्वा दुश्चरितं मम । सर्वं पुनन्तु मामापोऽसतां च प्रतिग्रहम् ॥ स्वाहा ॥

Tait, A. X. 23·1.

Om Âpaḥ punantviti viṣṇur ṛiṣir anuṣṭup chhandaḥ Âpo devatâ âchamane viniyogaḥ. Om, Âpaḥ punantu prithivîm prithivî pûtâ punâtu mâm ; Punantu Brahmaṇaspatir Brahma pûtâ punâtu mâm. Yad uchchhiṣṭam abhojyam yad vâ duścharitam mama. Sarvam punantu mâmâpo asatâm cha pratigraham. Svâhâ.

May the Âpas purify the earth and the earth being purified, purify me. May the waters purify the Brahmaṇaspati, and the self-purified Brahma (the Vedas) purify me. May the waters purify all sins, such as, eating the leavings of another, or improper food, or evil conduct or accepting gifts from sinners. Swâhâ.

The evening Âchamana mantra' is the same as that of the morning, with a slight difference, as shown below :—

ओं अग्निश्चमेति रुद्र ऋषिः प्रकृतिश्छन्द आपो देवता आचमने विनियोगः ॥ ओं अग्निश्च मा मन्युश्च मन्युपतयश्च मन्युकृतेभ्यः पापेभ्यो रक्षन्तां यदह्ना पापमकार्षं मनसा वाचा हस्ताभ्यां पद्भ्यामुदरेण शिश्ना रात्रिस्तदवलुम्पतु यत्किंच दुरितं मयि इदमहं माममृतयोनौ सत्ये ज्योतिषि परमात्मनि जुहोमि, स्वाहा ॥

T. A. X. 24·1.

NOTE—In Northern India, there is a slight difference of reading in these Mantras. While according to the Sâmaveda school of Bengal, Âpa is the Devata of all the three Mantras, here Sûrya, Âpa and Agni are the respective Devatas of the Morning, Mid-day and Evening.

The other difference is that in the morning Mantra रात्रि is read instead of अहस् and in the evening Mantra अहस् is read instead of रात्रि

### V.—PUNAR MÂRJANA.

Then let him perform Punarmârjana by sprinkling water seven times on the head, by reciting each time one of the lines given below: by reciting the eighth line he should sprinkle water on the earth, with the ninth line he should again sprinkle on the head with three kuśa grass. The mantras are as follows :—

ओं आपो हिष्ठेत्यादित्र्यृगत्रयस्य सिन्धुद्वीप ऋषिर्गायत्री छन्दः आपो देवता मार्जने विनियोगः ॥

(1) ओम् । आपो हिष्ठामयो भुवः (2) ओं तान ऊर्जे दधातन (3) ओं महेरणाय चक्षसे ॥ (4) ओं यो वः शिवतमो रसः (5) ओं तस्य भाजयतेह नः (6) ओम् उशतीरिव मातरः (7) ओं तस्मा अरङ्गमामवः (8) ओं यस्य क्षयाय जिन्वथ (9) ओम् आपो जनयथा च नः ॥

*N.B.*--For translation and Explanation See p 78.

### VI.—AGHAMARSAṆA.

Let him next perform Aghamarṣaṇa reciting the following, while holding a little water in the palm of the right hand near the nose :—

ओं ऋतञ्च सत्यञ्च इति मन्त्रस्याघमर्षण ऋषिरनुष्टुप्छन्दो भाववृत्तं दैवतमश्वमेधावभृथे विनियोगः ॥

Om Ṛitam cha satyam cha iti mantrasyâ-ghamarṣaṇa Ṛiṣir anuṣṭup Chhando Bhâva vṛittam daivatam, aśvamedhâ vabhṛithe viniyogaḥ.

ओम् ऋतं च सत्यं चाभीद्धात्तपसोऽध्यजायत ।
ततो रात्र्यजायत ततः समुद्रो अर्णवः ॥ १ ॥
समुद्रादर्णवादधिसंवत्सरो अजायत ।
अहोरात्राणि विदधद्विश्वस्य मिषतो वशी ॥ २ ॥
सूर्याचन्द्रमसौ धाता यथापूर्वमकल्पयत् ।
दिवं च पृथिवीं चान्तरिक्षमथो स्वः ॥ ३ ॥

Of the Mantras Ritam cha satyam cha, the Seer is Aghamarṣaṇa, the metre is Anuṣṭup, the Devatâ is Bhâva vṛitta (or Bhâva-bhṛitta, a name of Brahmâ), and they are employed in the final Dikṣâ bath (avabhṛitha at the close of Aśvamedha sacrifice).

Having recited this, and drawing in the air through the left nostril, and throwing it out through the right nostril, with the black sin personified, let him throw the water on the left palm, imagining it to be a rock. This should be done thrice. Then reciting Gâyatri, three offerings of water should be made to the Sun in the morning and evening, but *one* only at mid-day, and then he should perform Sûryopasthâna.

### VII.—SURYOPASTHÂNAM.

After aghamarṣaṇa let him perform oblation offering to the Sun reciting the following :—

ओं उदुत्यमित्यस्य प्रस्कण्व ऋषिर्गायत्रीछन्दः सूर्यो देवता सूर्योपस्थाने विनियोगः ॥

Om, Udutyam ity asya Praskaṇva Ṛiṣir Gâyatrî chhandaḥ Sûryo Devatâ Suryopasthâne viniyogah.

**Om, of the mantra Udutyam, &c., the seer is Praskaṇva, the metre is Gâyatri, the Devatâ is the Sun, and it is employed in Suryopasthâna.**

**ओम् उदुत्यं जातवेदसं देवं वहन्ति केतवः ।**

**दृशे विश्वाय सूर्य्यम् ।**

(Rig. Veda I. 50. 1.)

Om, Udutyam Jâtavedasam Devam vahanti ketavaḥ; Driśe Viśvâya Sûryam.

**His heralds bear Him up aloft, the God who knoweth all that lives; Surya that all may look on Him.**

**उत्**, Ut = up, qualifying vahanti; **उ**, U = mere expletive; **त्यम्**, tyam = Him; **जातवेदसं**, Jâta-Vedasam = Knower of all living things; **देवं** devam = god; **वहन्ति**, vahanti = bear; **केतवः**, Ketavaḥ = heralds, rays of the sun; **दृशे**, driśe = that (he may) be seen; **विश्वाय**, viśvâya = for all; **सूर्यम्**, Sûryam = Sûrya.

**N. B.—The above mantras should be recited by holding the sacred thread round the two thumbs and raising the hands with the thread stretched towards the sun.**

**ओं चित्रमित्यस्य कौत्स ऋषिस्त्रिष्टुप्छन्दः सूर्यो देवता सूर्योपस्थाने विनियोगः ॥**

Om chitram ity asya Kautsa Riṣis Triṣṭup Chhandaḥ, Suryo Devatâ Sûryopasthâne viniyogaḥ.

**Om! Of the mantra Chitram, &c., the seer is Kautsa, the metre is Triṣṭup, the Devatâ is Sûrya; and it is employed in Sûryopasthâna.**

**ओं चित्रं देवानामुदगादनीकं चक्षुर्मित्रस्य वरुणस्याऽग्नेः ।**

**आप्रा द्यावापृथिवीअन्तरिक्ष ꣳ सूर्य्य आत्मा जगतस्तस्थुषश्च ।**

(Ṛig. Veda I. 115. 1)

Om! Chitram Devânâm udagâd anîkam; Chakṣur Mitrasya, Varuṇasyâgneḥ; Âprâ Dyâvâ Prithivî antarikṣam; Sûrya âtmâ jagatas tasthuṣas cha.

**The brilliant Presence of the gods hath risen, the eye of Mitra, Varuṇa and Agni.**

**The soul of all that moveth not or moveth, the sun hath filled the air, earth and heaven (Griffith).**

Then he should offer an *añjali* of water to each of the following Devas with these mantras:—

**ओं ब्रह्मणे नमः ॥ ओं ब्राह्मणेभ्यो नमः ॥ ओं आचार्येभ्यो नमः ॥ ओं ऋषिभ्यो नमः ॥ ओं देवेभ्यो नमः ॥ ओं मृत्यवे नमः ॥ ओं वायवे नमः ॥ ओं विष्णवे नमः ॥ ओं वैश्रवणाय नमः ॥ ओं उपजाय नमः ॥**

(1) Om Brahmaṇe Namaḥ, (2) Om Brâhmaṇebhyo Namaḥ, (3) Om Âchâryebhyo Namaḥ, (4) Om Ṛiṣibhyo Namaḥ, (5) Om Devebhyo Namaḥ, (6) Om Mṛityave Namaḥ, (7) Om Vâyave Namaḥ, (8) Om Viṣṇave Namaḥ, (9) Om Vaiśravaṇâya Namaḥ, (10) Om Upajâya Namaḥ.

At this point the person should perform Tarpana (as already taught before); provided that his father be not alive.

### VIII.—GÂYATRI JAPA

Then he should perform the Japa or silent repetition of Gâyatri mantra 108 times, &c. There are some preliminaries to Japa as shown below :—

1. Invocation of Gâyatri.
2. Riṣi Nyâsa.
3. The nyâsa of six organs or assignment of the various parts of the body to different deities.
4. Dhyâna.
5. Japa.
6. Salutation and Farewell.

#### 1. INVOCATION.

With joined palms recite—

आयाहीत्यस्य विश्वामित्र ऋषिर्गायत्रीच्छन्दः सविता देवता जपोपनयने विनियोगः।

Âyâhîtyasya viśvâmitra ṛiṣir gâyatri chchhandaḥ savitâ devatâ japopanayane viniyogaḥ.

Of the Mantra Âyahi, &c., the seer is Viśvâmitra, the metre is Gâyatri, the Devatâ is Savitâ and it is employed in japa and upanayana.

ओं आयाहि वरदे देवि त्र्यक्षरे ब्रह्मवादिनि।

गायत्रि छन्दसां मातर्ब्रह्मयोने नमोऽस्तु ते ॥

Om Âyâhi varade devi tryakṣare brahmavâdini,
Gâyatri chhandasâm mâtar brahma yone namo stute.

Om O Goddess, come Thou showering boons. Oh Thou of three syllables (or consisting of three imperishable essences). Oh Thou knower or revealer of Brahm, Oh Gâyatri, mother of Chhandas, Oh Thou source of the Vedas, salutation be to Thee. *

#### 2. RISI NYÂSA.

Then let him perform Ṛiṣi Nyâsa or the assignment of the head, mouth and heart to Viśvâmitra, Gâyatri and Sâvitri by reciting the following mantras, touching those places with the fingers of the right hand :—

शिरसि विश्वामित्रऋषये नमः Śirasi Viśvâmitra riṣaye namaḥ ; मुखे गायत्रीच्छन्दसे नमः, Mukhe Gâyatri-chchhandase namaḥ ; हृदि सवित्रे देवतायै नमः। Hridi Savitre devatâyai namah.

#### 3. SADÂNGA NYÂSA.

Then let him perform Ṣaḍanga Nyâsa by reciting the following mantras :—

| | |
|---|---|
| ओं हृदयाय नमः। | Om, hridayáya namaḥ. |
| ओं भूःशिरसे स्वाहा | Om, bhûḥ śirase swáhá. |

---

* NOTE.—The reading in Taitt. Aranyaka X. 26·1 is as follows :—

आयातु वरदा देवी अक्षरं ब्रह्म संमितम्।

गायत्री छन्दसां माता इदं ब्रह्मजुषस्व मे ॥

"May the Divine Gâyatri, showering boons, come to instruct us about the Imperishable well-established Brahman; may Gâyatri the mother of all harmony teach us this Brahman."

ओं भुवः शिखायै वषट् Om, bhuvah śikháyái vaṣaṭ.
ओं स्वः कवचाय हुं । Om, swaḥ kavacháya hum.

ओं भूर्भुवः स्वः नेत्रत्रयाय वौषट् ।

Om, bhur bhuvaḥ svaḥ netra-trayâya vouṣaṭ.

ओं भूर्भुवः स्वः करतलपृष्ठाभ्यां अस्त्राय फट् ।

Om, bhur bhuvaḥ svaḥ karatala priṣṭhâbhyâm astrâya phaṭ.

Then having performed aṅga-nyâsa, he should clap three times and perform Dig-bandhana, or the closing up of all quarters against the entrance of bad influences. This process must be learnt from the teacher, for it differs in different schools. Then holding a flower in the palm of the left hand and covering it up with the right hand in the form of pûrṇa mudrâ he should perform meditation.

### 4. DHYÂNA.

Then he should perform dhyâna of Gâyatrî, *i.e.*, he should try to make the mental image of the Goddess in the heart. It will differ according to the time of the day when the Sandhyâ is performed. In the morning, she is Brahmâṇî, in the mid-day, she is Vaiṣṇavî, and in the evening, she is Rudrâṇî. The following are the Dhyâna mantras describing the Gâyatrî in her three stages called Gâyatrî, Sâvitrî and Saraswatî.

In the morning, he should recite the following Dhyâna mantra :—

ओं प्रातर्गायत्री रविमण्डलमध्यस्था, रक्तवर्णा, द्विभुजा, अक्षसूत्रकमण्डलुधरा हंसासनमारूढा, ब्रह्माणी, ब्रह्मदैवत्या, कुमारी ऋग्वेदोदाहृता ध्येया ।

Om, prâtar Gâyatrî ravimaṇḍala madhyasthâ, raktavarṇâ, dvibhujâ, akṣa sûtra kamaṇḍalu dharâ haṃsâsanam âruḍhâ, Brahmâṇî, brahma daivatyâ, kumârî Ṛig vedodâhritâ dhyeyâ.

In the morning the Gâyatrî should be meditated upon as a virgin of the nature of Ṛigveda and Brahma-natured, seated on a swan, holding in her two hands a rosary and a water jar, the color being rosy red.

In the mid-day he should recite the following mantra, which should bring up the proper picture of the Gâyatrî.

ओं मध्याह्ने सावित्री रविमण्डलमध्यस्था, कृष्णवर्णा, चतुर्भुजा, त्रिनेत्रा, शङ्खचक्रगदापद्महस्ता, युवती, गरुडारूढा, वैष्णवी, विष्णुदैवत्या, यजुर्वेदोदाहृता ध्येया ।

Om madhyâhne Sâvitrî ravimaṇḍala madhyasthâ, kṛiṣṇavarṇâ, chaturbhujâ, trinetrâ, śaṅkha chakra gadâ padmahastâ, yuvatî garuḍâ rûḍhâ, Vaiṣṇavî, viṣṇudaivatyâ Yajur vedodâhṛitâ dhyeyâ.

At mid-day Sâvitrî should be meditated upon in the form of the essence of Yajurveda, dark-colored, having four arms, three eyes, holding conch-shell, discus, club and lotus, a young woman, seated on Garuḍa, and of Vaiṣṇavî form.

In the evening, he should recite the following dhyâna mantra :—

ओं सायाह्ने सरस्वती रविमण्डलमध्यस्था, शुक्लवर्णा । द्विभुजा, त्रिशूलडमरुकरा वृषभासनमारूढा, वृद्धा, रुद्राणी, रुद्रदैवत्या सामवेदोदाहृता ध्येया ।

Om sâyâhne Saraswatî ravi maṇḍala madhyasthâ, śuklavarṇâ, dvibhujâ, triśûla ḍamaru karâ vriṣavâsanaṃ ârûḍhâ, vṛiddhâ, Rudrâṇi, rudra daivatyâ Sâmavedodâhṛitâ dhyeyâ.

In the evening Sarasvatî should be meditated upon in the form of the Essence of the Sâma veda, white-colored, having two arms, holding the Trident and the Drum, seated on the bullock, old and as Rudrâṇî.

## 5. *Japa.*

Having thus formed the appropriate image of Gâyatrî, he should recite (japa) the Gâyatrî mantra ten times at least, and if possible one hundred and eight times. The following is the Gâyatrî as used in Japa :—

ओं भूर्भुवः स्वः तत्सवितुर्वरेण्यं भर्गो देवस्य धीमहि ।

धियो यो नः प्रचोदयात् ॥ ओं ॥

The counting is performed on the phalanges of the fingers of the right hand, by placing the thumb on each of them in succession. It commences with the second phalanx of the ring finger of the right hand and is continued thus :—(1) the middle phalanx of the ring finger; (2) the first phalanx of the same; (3) the first phalanx of the little finger; (4 and 5) the middle and last phalanges; (6) the last phalanx of the ring finger; (7) the phalanx of the middle finger; (8) the last phalanx of the index finger; (9 and 10) the middle and first phalanges of the index finger.

This completes the counting of ten times. Then, if necessary, the same process of counting is performed again to complete the second ten and so on. While the tens are counted on the corresponding phalanges of the left hand.

## 6. *Farewell.*

Then farewell should be bidden by reciting the following Mantra :—

ओं महेशवदनोत्पन्ना विष्णोर्हृदयसम्भवा ।

ब्रह्मणा समनुज्ञाता गच्छ देवि यथेच्छया ॥

Om Maheśa vadanotpannâ Viṣṇor hṛidaya sambhavâ.
Brahmaṇâ samanujñâtâ gachchha Devi yathechhayâ.

Oh goddess (Gâyatri) thou comest out of the mouth of Mahesa and dwellest in the heart of Viṣṇu, being ordered thereto by Brahmâ. Now, depart, wherever it pleases Thee.

Then he should pour a little water on the copper vessel in front of him, reciting the following :—

अनेन जपेन भगवन्तावादित्यशुक्रौ प्रीयेताम् ।

ओं आदित्यशुक्राभ्यां नमः ॥

Anena japena bhagavantâvâditya śukrau priyetâm.
Om, Âditya śukrâbhyâṃ namaḥ.

May this Japa of mine please the Lords Âditya and Sukra.
Om, Salutation be to Âditya and Sukra.

### IX.—ÂTMA-RAKṢÂ.

Then let him recite the following, the sacred thread should be circled round the thumb which should touch the right ear :—

जातवेदस इत्यस्य काश्यप ऋषिस्त्रिष्टुप्
छन्दोऽग्निर्देवता आत्मरक्षायां जपे विनियोगः ।

Jâtavedasa ity asya Kâśyapa Ṛiṣistriṣṭup Chhando' gnir Devatâ, Âtma-rakṣâyâm jape viniyogaḥ.

Of the mantra "Jâtavedasa, etc.," the seer is Kâśyapa, the metre is Triṣṭup, the Devatâ is Agni, and it is employed in Âtma-rakṣâ.

ओं जातवेदसे सुनवाम सोममरातीयतो नि दहाति वेदः ।
स नः पर्षदति दुर्गाणि विश्वा नावेव सिन्धुं दुरितात्यग्निः ॥

(Ṛig Veda I. 99. 7.)

Oṃ ! jâtavedase sunavâma somaṃ arâtîyato nidahâti vedaḥ.
Sa naḥ Parṣad ati durgâṇi viśvâ nâveva sindhuṃ duritâty Agniḥ.

We prepare the Soma for the All-knower. May he consume the evil tendencies of our niggardly disposed heart. May he transport us over all difficulties. May the Effulgent convey us as in a boat over the sea, across all Evils.

### X.—RUDRÂ UPASTHÂNÂ.

Then let him with folded hands bow to Rudra reciting :—

ऋतमित्यस्य कालाग्निरुद्र ऋषिरनुष्टुप् छन्दो रुद्रो देवता रुद्रोपस्थाने विनियोगः ।

Ṛitam ity asya Kâlâgni Rudra Ṛiṣir Anuṣṭup Chhando, Rudro Devatâ Rudropasthâne viniyogaḥ.

Of the Mantra Ritam, &c., the seer is Kâlâgni Rudra, the metre is Anuṣṭup, and it is employed in Rudropasthâna.

ओं ऋतं सत्यं परं ब्रह्म पुरुषं कृष्णपिङ्गलम् ।
ऊर्ध्वरेतं विरूपाक्षं विश्वरूपाय वै नमः ॥

Oṃ, ṛitaṃ satyaṃ paraṃ Brahma puruṣaṃ Kriṣṇa piṅgalaṃ.

Ûrddha retaṃ virûpâkṣaṃ viśvarûpâya vai namaḥ. Tait. Ar. X. 12.1.

Om, Salutation be to that All-pervading, All-eyed, whose Energy flows upwards, who is Eternal, True Righteousness, the Supreme Brahma, the Violet-colored Puruṣa.

Then let him offer a handful of water to each of the following and reciting :—

| | |
|---|---|
| ओं ब्रह्मणे नमः | Oṃ Brahmaṇe namaḥ. |
| ओं अद्भ्यो नमः | Oṃ Adbhyo namaḥ |
| ओं वरुणाय नमः | Oṃ Varuṇâya namaḥ. |
| ओं शिवाय नमः | Oṃ Śivâya namaḥ. |
| ओं ऋषिभ्यो नमः | Oṃ Ṛiṣibhyo namaḥ. |
| ओं देवेभ्यो नमः | Oṃ Devebhyo namaḥ. |
| ओं वायवे नमः | Oṃ Vâyave namaḥ. |
| ओं विष्णवे नमः | Oṃ Viṣṇave namaḥ. |

| | |
|---|---|
| ओं प्रजापतये नमः | Om Prajâpataye namaḥ. |
| ओं रुद्राय नमः | Om Rudrâya namaḥ. |
| ओं सर्वेभ्यो नमः | Om Sarvebhyo namaḥ. |
| ओं देवेभ्यो नमः | Om Devebhyo namaḥ. |

Then let him offer arghya to Sûrya, reciting :—

ओं नमोविवस्वते ब्रह्मन् भास्वते विष्णुतेजसे। जगत्सवित्रे शुचये सवित्रे कर्मदायिने ॥ इदमर्घ्यम् ओं श्रीसूर्याय नमः ॥

Om, Namo vivasvate Brahman bhâsvate Viṣṇu tejase, Jagat savitre śuchaye Savitre karma dâyine. Idam arghyam Om Śri Sûryâya namaḥ.

Om, Salutation be to Vivasvat, Brahman, to the effulgent Viṣṇu energy, to the World Creator, the pure, the creator, the Karma fruit awarder. This offering is to Om Śri Sûrya, namaḥ.

Then let him bow down to Sûrya, reciting :—

ओं जपाकुसुमसङ्काशं काश्यपेयं महाद्युतिम्।
ध्वान्तारिं सर्वपापघ्नं प्रणतोस्मि दिवाकरम् ॥

Om, Javâ-kusuma saṃkâśam kâśyapeyam mahâdyutim.
Dhvântârim sarva pâpaghnam praṇato'smi Divâkaram.

*Translation* :—Om ! I bow to the Maker of the Day, the Destroyer of all sins, the Enemy of Darkness, the Great Light, the Kâśyapeya, whose colour is like that of Javâ-flower.

BRAHMA-YAJNA.

Then he should recite the first mantra of each one of the four Vedas. This is called Brahma-Yajña.

Ṛig. Veda I. 1. 1.

मधुच्छन्द ऋषिर्गायत्री छन्दः, अग्निर्देवता ब्रह्मयज्ञजपे विनियोगः ॥

ओं अग्निमीळे पुरोहितं यज्ञस्य देवमृत्विजम्। होतारं रत्नधातमम् ॥

*Pada* : अग्निम्। ईळे। पुरः-हितम्। यज्ञस्य। देवम्। ऋत्विजम् ॥ होतारम्। रत्नधातमम् ॥

*Transliteration* :—Agnim île purohitam, yajñasya devam ṛitvijam ; Hotâram ratna dhâtamam.

*Word-meaning* :—अग्निम् = Agni, God, ईळे = I implore, पुरोहितं = the Provident, or chief Priest, यज्ञस्य = of the sacrifice, देवं = the divine, ऋत्विजं = the Ṛitvij priest or minister, होतारं = the Hotri priest, रत्नधातमम् = the best reservoir of wealth.

*Translation* :—I adore Agni, the Provident, the divine Time-Priest of sacrifice, the Invoker, the best giver of what is good.

*Note* :— Purohita = the Provident, Ritvij = the priest who performs at the great seasons (ṛitu) of the year, Hotṛi = the priest who invokes and pours out the libations, the Invoker.

Yajur Veda I. 1. 1.

याज्ञवल्क्य ऋषिस्त्रिष्टुप् छन्दो वायुर्देवता ब्रह्मयज्ञ जपे विनियोगः ॥

ओं इषे त्वोर्जेत्वा। वायवः स्थ। देवो वः सविता प्रार्पयतु श्रेष्ठतमाय कर्मणे ॥

*Pada* :—इषे । त्वा । ऊर्जे । त्वा । वायवः । स्थ । देवः । वः । सविता । प्र । अर्पयतु । श्रेष्ठतमाय । कर्मणे ॥

*Transliteration* :—Oṃ, 1. Iṣe tvo'rje tvâ, 2. Vâyavaḥ stha, 3. Devo vaḥ Savitâ prârpayatu śreṣṭhatamâya Karmaṇe.

*Word-meaning* :—इषे = for food, त्वा = thee, ऊर्जे = for strength, त्वा thee, ( हे शाखे इषर्थं त्वां छिनद्मि । ऊर्गर्थं त्वां छिनद्मि ) O branch! I cut thee, in order to get food. I cut thee, for the sake of strength. The Adhvaryu priest utters these, while cutting the sacrificial twig on Amâvasya day. The verb छिनद्मि 'I cut' has been supplied to complete the sentence. When applied to God, the verb 'I pray' should be supplied. "I pray Thee for food, I pray Thee for strength).

वायवः = Winds ( गन्तारः ) or the goers, the moving (calves), स्थ = be ye, हे वत्साः मातृसकाशाद् गन्तारो भवत "O ye calves, go to your mothers." This is addressed to the calves. स्थ is the Imperative plural of the verb अस् "to be."

देवः God, refulgent, वः = you, सविता = the Creator, प्रार्पयतु May establish, श्रेष्ठतमाय कर्मणे = for the highest work (or Sacrifice), ["यज्ञो हि श्रेष्ठतमं कर्म" = for the Sacrifice is the highest work].

*Translation* :—(I pray) to Thee for food, (I pray) to Thee for strength. Be (swift as) winds. May the Divine Creator fit you for the highest work.

or

(I cut) thee (O twig) for the sake of food, (I cut) thee, for the sake of strength. (Ye calves) be (swift as) winds (to approach your dams).

(Ye Cows) may the Divine Sâvitri establish you for the highest work.

Sâma Veda I. 1.

गौतम ऋषिरनुष्टुप् छन्दः सूर्यो देवता ब्रह्मयज्ञजपे विनियोगः ॥

ओम् अग्न आयाहि वीतये गृणानो हव्यदातये । निहोता सत्सि बर्हिषि ॥

*Pada* :—अग्न । आ । याहि । वीतये । गृणानः । हव्यदातये । नि । होता । सत्सि । बर्हिषि ॥

*Transliteration* :—Oṃ, Agna âyâhi vitaye griṇâno havya-dâtaye, Nihotâ satsi barhiṣi.

*Word-meaning* :—अग्ने = O Agni, आयाहि = Come, वीतये ( हविषां भक्षणार्थं or तर्पणार्थं ) = in order to eat the (oblations), or to satisfy (the sacrificers); हव्यदातये (हव्यानि हवींषि देवेभ्यो दातुम् ) = and to give (or carry) the offerings (to the Devas), गृणानः ( स्तूयमानः ) = praised (thou who art being praised), बर्हिषि (आस्तीर्णे दर्भे ) = on the (spread out) Kuśa grass, होता (being a) Hotṛi priest, निषत्सि ( निषीद, उपविश ) = sit down.

*Translation* :—O Agni! Come to eat (the oblations) and give the offerings (to Devas). (Thou art) being praised; (like a) Hotṛi (priest) sit (Thou) down on (this seat of) kuśa grass.—(Ṛig Veda VI, 16, 10).

Atharva Veda I. 1.

पिप्पलाद ऋषिरुष्णिक् छन्दो वरुणो देवता ब्रह्मयज्ञजपे विनियोगः ॥

शन्नो देवीरभिष्टये आपो भवन्तु पीतये । शंयोरभिस्रवन्तु नः ॥

*Transliteration*:—Śanno devi rabhiṣtaye âpo bhavantu pîtaye. Śaṃyo rabhisravantu naḥ.

*Pada* :—शम् । नः । देवीः । अभिष्टये । आपः । भवन्तु । पीतये । शम् योः । अभि । स्रवन्तु । नः ॥

*Sanskrit-meaning*:—देवीः ( देव्यः द्योतनादिगुणयुक्ताः ) आपः नः ( अस्माकम् ) अभीष्टये ( अभियजनाय or अभितः सर्वतो यागार्थं ) शं ( सुखं भवन्तु or सुखकारिण्यो भवन्तु ) पीतये ( पानाय च शं ) भवन्तु ( पीयमानाः आपः स्वादुतमाः सुखाय भवन्तु ) नः ( अस्माकं ) शं ( शमनाय रोगाणां ) योः ( यावनाय च भयानाम् ), अभिस्रवन्तु ( अस्मदाभिमुख्येन गच्छन्तु ) or ( अस्माकम् उपरि शुद्ध्यर्थं सिंचन्तु ) ॥

*English meaning* :—देवीः आपः = The Divine or effulgent waters, अभिष्टये = =for the sake of sacrifice, शं नः भवन्तु = be propitious to us, पीतये = (so also) for drinking, अभिस्रवन्तु = let them be poured over, नः = us, शं = for the sake of destroying (present diseases), योः = and warding (fears of future diseases).

*Translation* :—May the Effulgent Waters be propitious in all our sacrifices, and for our drinking purposes ; may they pour down upon us, removing present diseases and warding off future illnesses.

*Griffith* :—The Waters be to us for drink, Goddesses, for our aid and bliss ; Let them stream health and wealth to us.

Here ends the Sandhyâ of the Sâma Vedins.

---

## CHAPTER IX.

### THE YAJUR VEDI SANDHYÂ.

ACCORDING TO MÂDHYANDINÂS.

We give below the Sandhyâ as it is current in these United Provinces, from the excellent edition of Pt. Devidatta Jyotirvid and published by Pt. Ram Narain Varmana of Allahabad.

The Sandhyâ has twenty-eight parts.

Separate enumeration of 28 parts.

#### I.—VISṆU-SMARAṆAM.

or

*Meditation on Viṣṇu.*

MANTRA.

ओं अपवित्रः पवित्रो वा सर्वावस्थां गतोऽपि वा ।

यः स्मरेत् पुण्डरीकाक्षं स बाह्याभ्यन्तरः शुचिः ॥

*Transliteration* :—Oṃ Apavitraḥ pavitro vâ, sarvâvasthâṃ gato pi vâ;

Yaḥ smaret Puṇḍarîkâkṣaṃ, sa bâhyâbhyantaraṃ śuchiḥ.

*Word-meaning* :—1. Apavitraḥ=not pure, impure. 2. Pavitraḥ= pure. 3. Vâ=or. 4. Sarvâvasthâṃ=(in) all conditions. 5. Gataḥ= gone, existing. 6. Api=even. 7. Vâ=or. 8. Yaḥ=who. 9. Smaret=may remember. 10. Puṇḍarîkâkṣaṃ=the lotus-eyed. 11. Sa= he. 12. Bâhyâbhyantaram=outside and inside. 13. śuchiḥ=cleansed, sanctified.

*Translation* :—Whether pure or impure, in whatever condition one may be, he who meditates on the Lotus-eyed, becomes cleansed within and without.

*Directions* :—Reciting this mantra and thinking on Viṣṇu, let him hold a little water in the palm of the right hand, and sprinkle that water all around himself.

### II.—ÂCHAMANAM.

or *sipping of water.*

1. ओं ऋग्वेदाय स्वाहा ॥ Oṃ Ṛig-vedâya swâhâ.
2. ओं यजुर्वेदाय स्वाहा । Oṃ Yajur-vedâya swâhâ.
3. ओं सामवेदाय स्वाहा । Oṃ Sâma-vedâya swâhâ.
4. ओं अथर्ववेदाय नमः । Oṃ Atharva-vedâya namaḥ.

*Directions* :—Let him sip water three times reciting the first three mantras: reciting the fourth mantra let him throw the water on the ground and wash his hands.

*Note* :—The word swâhâ means "prosperity to all"—"(su) good wishes, (âhâ) to all"=" god-speed."

### III.—ŚIKHÂ BANDHANAM.

or *tying the tuft.*

ओं ब्रह्मवाक्यसहस्रेण शिववाक्यशतेन च ।

विष्णोर्नामसहस्रेण शिखाग्रन्थिं करोम्यहम् ॥

*Transliteration* :—Oṃ Brahma vâkya sahasreṇa, Śiva vâkya śatena cha.

Viṣṇor nâma sahasreṇa, Śikhâ granthiṃ karomyahaṃ.

*Translation* :—With the thousand names of Brahmâ and hundred names of Śiva, with the thousand names of Viṣṇu, I tie the tuft.

ओं भूर्भुवः स्वः । तत्सवितुर्वरेण्यं भर्गो देवस्य धीमहि । धियो यो नः प्रचोदयात् । ओ३म् ॥

This is the Gâyatrî. (See pages 29 and the following).

*Directions* :—Reciting the above two mantras let him tie the tuft by 2½ turns and putting a knot. If the tuft be already tied, he should merely touch it reciting these mantras.

### IV.—KHA-SPARŚA.

or *touching the various centres of the body.*

ओं वाक् Om Vâk (speech) (touch the lips with middle and ring finger of the right hand).

ओं मनः Om Manaḥ (mind) (touch similarly the lower lip).

ओं प्राणः Om Prâṇaḥ (breath) (touch the nostrils).

ओं चक्षुः चक्षुः Om Chakṣuḥ chakṣuḥ (eyes) (touch two eyes).

ओं श्रोत्रम् श्रोत्रम् Om Śrotram śrotram (ears) (touch both ears).

ओं नाभिः Om Nâbhiḥ (navel) (touch the navel).

ओं हृदयम् Om Hṛidayam (heart) (touch the heart).

ओं कंठः Om Kaṇṭhaḥ (throat) (touch the throat).

ओं ललाटम् Om Lalâṭam (forehead) (touch the forehead).

ओं शिरः Om Śiraḥ (head) (touch the head).

ओं शिखा Om Śikhâ (tuft) (touch the tuft).

ओं बाहू Om Bâhû (hands).

ओं यशोबलमस्तु Om Yaśo balam astu. "Let there be fame and strength." With this make namaskâra.

*Directions* :—Uttering the above mantras touch the various organs indicated. Reciting Om Bâhû put the right hand on the left shoulder, and the left hand on the right shoulder. With the last mantra clasp the hands and bow down. In touching, where there are two organs, such as eyes, ears, &c., always touch the right first. The object of such touching is to invoke the blessing of God on the senses, the prayer being "let the organs be strong, and work for the good of all so that they bring fame. Let them never do anything of which one may be ashamed."

### V. PÂVANAM

or *purification.*

ओं ओं पुनातु Om Om punâtu (may Om purify) (with this sprinkle water on the head).

ओं भूः पुनातु Om Bhûḥ punâtu (with this sprinkle water on feet).

ओं भुवः पुनातु Om Bhuvaḥ punâtu (with this sprinkle on heart).

ओं स्वः पुनातु Om Svaḥ punâtu (with this sprinkle water on heart).

ओं महः पुनातु Om Mahaḥ punâtu (with this sprinkle water on throat).

ओं जनः पुनातु Om Janaḥ punâtu (with this sprinkle water on eyes).

ओं तपः पुनातु Om Tapaḥ punâtu (with this sprinkle water on forehead).

ओं सत्यं पुनातु Om Satyam punâtu (again on the head).

ओं तत्सवितुर्वरेण्यं भर्गो देवस्य धीमहि ।

धियो यो नः प्रचोदयात् ।

ओं सर्वं पुनातु Om Sarvam punâtu (sprinkle water all round).

*Directions*:—Taking water in the palm of the left hand, let him sprinkle water on himself with the ring finger of the right hand as directed above. If one be standing in a current water, then he need not take water in the palm of his hand. If he can get kuśa grass he should use it, instead of finger, to sprinkle water.

### VI. ÂSANOPAVEŚANAM

or *taking the seat.*

पृथ्विव्यवेति मेरुपृष्ठ ऋषिः सुतलं छन्दः कूर्मो देवता आसनोपवेशने विनियोगः ।

ओं पृथ्वि त्वया धृता लोका देवि त्वं विष्णुना धृता ।

त्वं च धारय मां देवि पवित्रं कुरु चासनम् ॥

*Transliteration*:—Prithvi tvayâ dhṛitâ lokâ, devi tvam Viṣṇunâ dhṛitâ.

Tvam cha dhâraya mâm Devi, pavitram kuru châsanam.

*Word-meaning*:—Prithvi=O Earth. Tvayâ=by Thee. Dhṛitâḥ= are upheld. Lokâḥ=The creatures. Devi=O Shining One. Tvam= Thou. Viṣṇunâ=by Viṣṇu. Dhṛitaḥ=art upheld. Tvam=Thou. Cha= and. Dhâraya=uphold. Mâm=me. Devi=O Shining One. Pavitram=sacred. Kuru=make. Cha=and. Âsanam=the seat.

**Translation**:—O Earth, all creatures are upheld by Thee; O Devi, thou art supported by Viṣṇu; support me thou, O Shining One, and sanctify my seat.

*Directions*:—Reciting this mantra, let him touch the ground with the little finger of the right hand.

### VII. SANDHYÂ SANKALPA

or *Resolve to perform Sandhyâ.*

ओं अद्योपात्त सकल दुरितक्षयाय श्रीपरमेश्वरप्रीत्यर्थं (प्रातः मध्याह्न सायं) सन्ध्योपासनमहं करिष्ये।

*Transliteration*:—Om ! adyopâtta-sakala-duritakṣayâya, Śrî Parameśvara prîty-artham (Prâtaḥ, Madhyâhna or Sâyam) Sandhy opâsanam aham kariṣye.

*Word-meaning*:—adya=to-day ; upâtta=performed ; sakala=all ; durita=sin ; kṣayâya=for destroying ; Śrî Parameśvara prîtyartham= and for the sake of pleasing the supreme God ; Sandhyopâsanam kariṣye=I shall perform the (morning, mid-day or evening) ; Sandhyâ= meditation.

*Directions*:—Taking water in the palm of the right hand and reciting this mantra, let him throw the water on the ground.

*Note* :—The efficacy of every religious act depends upon Sankalpa—the strong determination, the mental effort. If the mind is not put in the act, but it is done mechanically, no fruit is produced. Hence the necessity of Sankalpa in the beginning of every act.

### VIII. KARA-NYÂSA.

or *the hand nyâsa.*

अस्या अग्निमुख्याः गायत्र्याः परंब्रह्म ऋषिऋंग्यजुःसामाथर्वछन्दः सविता देवता परंब्रह्म-भानुर्न्यासे विनियोगः ॥

1. ओं भूः अङ्गुष्ठाभ्यां नमः Oṃ Bhûḥ angusṭhâbhyâṃ namaḥ.
   Oṃ Bhúḥ—salutation to the thumbs.

2. ओं भुवः तर्जनीभ्यां नमः Oṃ Bhuuvaḥ tarjanîbhyâṃ namaḥ, Index finger).

3. ओं स्वः मध्यमाभ्यां नमः Oṃ Svaḥ madhyamâbhyâṃ namaḥ (middle finger).

4. ओं तत् सवितुर्वरेण्यं अनामिकाभ्यां नमः Oṃ Tat savitur vrreṇyaṃ anâmikâbhyâṃ namaḥ. (Ring finger).

5. ओं भर्गोदेवस्य धीमहि कनिष्ठिकाभ्यां नमः Oṃ Bhargo devasya dhîmahi kaniṣthikâbhyâṃ namaḥ. (Little finger).

6. ओं धियो यो नः प्रचोदयात् करतलकरपृष्ठाभ्यां नमः Oṃ dhiyo yo naḥ prachodayât, karatala karapriṣṭhâbhyâṃ namaḥ. (Palm and back of hand).

*Directions* :—

1. Reciting this touch the two thumbs with the index fingers.
2. Reciting this touch the index fingers with the thumbs.
3. Reciting this touch the middle fingers with the thumbs.
4. Reciting this touch the ring fingers with the thumbs.
5. Reciting this touch the little fingers with the thumbs.
6. Reciting this turn the right hand round the left.

*Note* :—The word nyâsa means the assignment of the various members of the body to various portions of a mantra, or to various deities. The salutation is offered to 1. Thumbs, 2. Index fingers, 3. Middle fingers, 4. Ring fingers, 5. Little fingers, 6. The palm and the back of the hand. The mantras assigned are the portions of the Gâyatrî.

### IX. AṄGA-NYÂSA

or *assignment of bodily members.*

1. ओं भूः हृदयाय नमः Oṃ Bhûḥ Hridayâya namaḥ.

2. ओं भुवः शिरसे स्वाहा Oṃ Bhûvaḥ Śirase Swâhâ.

3. ओं स्वः शिखायै वषट् Oṃ Svaḥ Śikhâyai vaṣaṭ.

4. ओं तत् सवितुर्वरेण्यं कवचाय हुम् Oṃ Tat Savitur Vareṇyaṃ Kavachâya Huṃ.

5. ओं भर्गो देवस्य धीमहि नेत्रत्रयाय वौषट् Oṃ Bhargo Devasya dhîmahi netratrayâya vauṣaṭ.

6. ओं धियो यो नः प्रचोदयात् अस्त्राय फट् Oṃ Dhiyo yo naḥ prachodayât, astrâya phaṭ.

*Directions* :—

1. Touch the ***heart*** with right hand reciting it.
2. Touch the hand do. do.
3. Touch the tuft do. do.
4. Place the left hand on the right shoulder and the right hand on the left shoulder cross-wise.
5. Touch the right eye with the index finger, and the left eye with the middle finger, of the right hand.
6. Strike the palm of the left hand with the index and middle fingers of the right hand so as to make a slight sound.

*Note* :—

1. Namaḥ means salutation. from √nam to 'bow.'
2. Svâhâ "welcome," from su 'good,' √hve 'to call" or from √svad 'to taste.
3. Vaṣaṭ "offering to Devas," from √vah to carry.
4. Huṃ from √hu 'to give' or 'to eat,' syllable of interrogation, doubt, assent, anger, fer, censure.
5. Vauṣaṭ from √vah 'to carry,' the same as Vaṣaṭ.
6. Phaṭ from √sphut "to break," in destructive acts, such as removing serial obstacles, aghamarṣana etc.

## X.

### SANDHYÂ DHYÂNAM ÂVÂHANAM CHA.

प्रातः सन्ध्यायाम्

In the morning Sandhyâ.

ओम् गायत्रीं त्र्यक्षरां बालां साक्षसूत्रकमण्डलुम् ।
रक्तवस्त्रां चतुर्वक्त्रां हंसवाहनसंस्थिताम् ॥ १ ॥
ऋग्वेदकृतोत्सङ्गां रक्तमाल्यानुलेपनाम् ।
ब्रह्माणीं ब्रह्मदैवत्यां ब्रह्मलोकनिवासिनीम् ॥२॥
आवाहयाम्यहं देवीमायान्तीं सूर्यमण्डलात् ॥ ३ ॥
आगच्छ वरदे देवि त्र्यक्षरे ब्रह्मवादिनि ।
गायत्रि छन्दसां मातर्ब्रह्मयोने नमोस्तुते ॥४॥

*Transliteration.*

Oṃ ! 1. Gâyatrîm tryakṣarâṃ bâlâṃ Sâkṣa-sûttra-Kamaṇḍaluṃ ;
Raktavastrâṃ chatur vaktrâṃ Hamsa-vâhana-samsthitâṃ.

2. Ṛig-veda-kṛitotsaṅgâṃ Rakta-mâlyânulepanâṃ ;
Brahmâṇîṃ brahma-daivatyâṃ Brahma-lokanivâsinîṃ.

3. Âvâhayâmy ahaṃ Devîṃ Âyântîṃ sûrya-maṇḍalât.

4. Âgachchha varade Devi try-akṣare brahma-vâdinî,
Gâyatri chandasâṃ mâtar Brahma-yone namo'stu te.

*Word-meaning* :—I. 1. Gâyatrîṃ = Gâyatri, accusative case governed by "I invoke" of the third verse; 2. Tryakṣaraṃ=three syllabled. *i.e.*, a, u and m. 3. Bâlâṃ=virgin; 4. Sa-akṣa-sûtra-Kamaṇḍaluṃ= with rosary and water-pot; 5. Rakta-vastrâṃ=red-dressed; 6. Chatur-vaktrâṃ=four-faced; 7. Haṃsa-vâhana-saṃsthitâṃ=Swan-vehicle-seated, *i.e.*, sitting on a swan.

II. 1. Ṛigvedakritotsaṅgâṃ=Ṛigveda-held-on lap, *i.e.*, holding the Ṛigveda on her lap; 2. Rakta-mâlyâ-nulepanâṃ=(wearing) red garland and (red) sandal paste; 3. Brahmâṇîṃ=Brahmâṇi; 4. Brahma daivatyâṃ=(consecrated to) Brahmâ as its Deity; 5. Brahmaloka-nivâsinim=residing in Brahmâ world;

III. 1. Avâhayâmi=invoke; 2. aham=I; 3. Devîṃ=The goddess; 4. âyântîṃ=descending from; 5. Sûrya maṇḍalât=the solar orb.

IV. 1. Âgachchha=come; 2. varade=O boon-conferring; 3. Devi= goddess; 4. Tryakṣare=O three=syllabled; 5. Brahmavâdini= Instructor of Brahma-knowledge; 6. Gâyatri=O Gâyatri; 7. Chhandasâṃ Mâtar=mother of sacred hymns; 8. Brahma-yone=O source of Vedas; 9. Namaḥ=salutation; 10. Astu=be; 11. te=to Thee.

*Translation*:—I invoke the goddess Gâyatrî to come down from the solar orb. She consists of three syllables (or three indestructible principles), is a Virgin, has a rosary and a Kamaṇḍalu in her two hands, she is dressed in red, has four faces, and is seated on a swan. She has the Ṛigveda on her lap; and wears red garland of red flowers, and is anointed with red sandal wood paste. She is the energy of Brahmâ, and is sacred to Brahmâ as her Deity, and dwells on the plane of Brahmâ.

Come, O Boon-giving Goddess, O three syllabled teacher of Brahma-wisdom. Salutation be to Thee, O Gâyatri, the mother of hymns and the womb of Vedas.

*Directions*:—Reciting the above Mantras, with clasped palms, let him invoke the Goddess. He should form a mental picture of the Goddess as described above, all red dress, flowers, sandal paste, &c. It represents the first life-wave or Brahmâ energy.

The invocation and Dhyâna Mantras for midday are as follows:—

ओं सावित्रीं युवतीं शुक्लां शुक्लवस्त्रां त्रिलोचनाम् ।
त्रिशूलिनीं वृषारूढां श्वेतमाल्यानुलेपनाम् ॥ १॥
यजुर्वेदकृतोत्सङ्गां जटामुकुटमण्डिताम् ।
रुद्राणीं रुद्रदैवत्यां रुद्रलोकनिवासिनीम् ॥२॥
आवाहयाम्यहं देवीमायान्तीं सूर्यमण्डलात् ॥३॥
आगच्छ वरदे देवि त्र्यक्षरे रुद्रवादिनि ।
सावित्रिच्छन्दसां मातर् रुद्रयोने नमोऽस्तु ते ॥४॥

*Transliteration*:—

1. Oṃ Sâvitrîṃ yuvatîṃ śuklâm śuklavastrâṃ trilochanâṃ,
Triśûlinîṃ vriṣârûḍhâṃ śveta mâlyânulepanâṃ,
2. Yajur-veda-kṛitotsaṅgâm jaṭâ mukuṭa maṇḍitâṃ.
Rudrâṇîṃ rudra daivatyâṃ rudra-loka nivâsinîṃ.
3. Âvâhayâmy ahaṃ Devîṃ âyântîṃ sûrya maṇḍalât.
4. Âgachchha varade Devi try-akṣare rudra-vâdini,
Gâyatri chhandasâṃ mâtar rudra-yone namo' stu te.

*Translation* :—I invoke the goddess Sâvitrî to come down from the solar orb. She is a youthful maiden, white in color, dressed in white, having three eyes; carrying a trident, seated on a bull, and wearing a garland of white flowers, and having white sandal wood paste. On her lap is Yajur Veda, and her crown is of matted hair. She is the energy of Rudra, sacred to Rudra, dweller of the Rudra plane.

Come, O boon-giving Goddess of three syllables, teacher of the Science of Rudra, O Sâvitri, the mother of hymns, O womb of Rudra, salutation be to Thee.

The invocation and Dhyâna mantras for the evening are :—

ओं वृद्धां सरस्वतीं कृष्णां पीतवस्त्रां चतुर्भुजाम् ।
शङ्खचक्रगदाशार्ङ्ग-हस्तां गरुडवाहिनीम् ॥१॥
सामवेदकृतोत्सङ्गां वनमालाविभूषिताम् ।
वैष्णवीं विष्णुदैवत्यां विष्णुलोकनिवासिनीम् ॥२॥
आवाहयाम्यहं देवीमायान्तीं सूर्यमण्डलात् ॥३॥
आगच्छ वरदे देवि त्र्यक्षरे विष्णुवादिनि ।
सरस्वतिच्छन्दसां मातर् विष्णुयोने नमोस्तुते ॥४॥

*Transliteration* :—

1. Vṛiddhâṃ Sarasvatîṃ kṛiṣṇâṃ pîtavastrâṃ chaturbhujâṃ,
   Śankha-chakra-gadâ-śarṅga hastâṃ garuḍa-vâhinîṃ,
2. Sâma-veda-kṛitotsaṅgâm Vanamâlâ vibûṣitâṃ,
   Vaiṣṇavîṃ viṣṇu daivatyâṃ viṣṇuloka nivâsinîṃ.
3. Âvâhayâmy-ahaṃ Devîm Âyântîm sûrya manḍalât.
4. Âgachchha varade Devi try-akṣare viṣṇuvâdini,
   Sarasvatichchhandasâm mâtar viṣṇu yone namo stu' te.

*Translation* :—I invoke the goddess Sarasvatî to descend from the solar sphere. She is old, dressed in yellow, having four hands, holding a conch, a discus, a club and a bow in each hand, and seated on Garuḍa. The Sâma Veda is on her lap, and a garland of wild flowers adorns her. She is the energy of Viṣṇu, sacred to Viṣṇu, dweller of the plane of Viṣṇu. Come, O boon-conferring Goddess of three syllables, the teacher of Viṣṇu-lore, O Sarasawati! mother of hymns! O womb of Viṣṇu! salutation to Thee.

### XI. PRÂṆÂYÂMA.

or *Regulation of Breathing*.

Then let him perform Prâṇâyâma, reciting :—

*N.B.*—See pp. 43-44, for fuller description.

ओंकारस्य ब्रह्मा ऋषिर्गायत्री छन्दोऽग्निर्देवता ।

सप्त व्याहृतीनां विश्वामित्रजमदग्निभरद्वाजगौतमात्रिवसिष्ठकश्यपा ऋषयः गायत्र्युष्णिगनुष्टुब्‌-
हती पङ्क्तित्रिष्टुब्जगत्यश्छन्दांसि । अग्निवाय्वादित्यबृहस्पतिवरुणेन्द्रविश्वेदेवा देवताः ।

गायत्र्या विश्वामित्रऋषिर्गायत्रीछन्दः सविता देवता ॥

शिरसः प्रजापतिऋषिः यजुश्छन्दो ब्रह्माग्निवायुसूर्या देवताः प्राणायामे विनियोगः ॥

*Transliteration* :—Omkârasya ṛiśi Gâyatrî chhando' gnir Devatâ.

Sapta vyahṛitînam Viśvâmitra, Yamadagni, Bharadvâja, Gautama, Atri, Vasiṣṭha, Kâśyapâḥ Ṛiṣayaḥ. Gâyatry Uṣṇig Anuṣṭub, Bṛihatî

Paṅkti. Tristub Jagatyas Chhandâṃsi, Agni, Vâyu, Âditya, Bṛihaspati Varuṇa, Indra, Viśvedeva devatâḥ.

Gâyatrya Viśvâmitra Riṣir Gâyatrî chhandaḥ Savitâ Devatâ.

Śirasaḥ Prajâpatir Riṣir yajus chhando Brahm Agni Vâyu Sûryâ Devatâḥ Prânâyâme viniyogaḥ.

*Translation*:—Of Om the seer is Brahmâ, the metre is Gâyatrî, the Devatâ is Agni.

Of the seven Vyâhṛitis, the Riṣis are Viśvâmitra, Jamadagni, Bharadvâja, Gautama, Atri, Vasiṣṭa, and Kâśyapa, the metres are Gâyatrî, Uṣṇik, Anuṣṭup, Bṛihati, Paṅkti, Triṣṭup, and Jagati; the Devatâs are Agni, Vâyu, Sûrya, Indra, Varuṇa, Bṛihaspati, and Viśvedevâ.

Om! of Gâyatrî the seer is Viśvâmitra, the metre is Gâyatrî, the Devatâ is Sâvitrî.

Om! of the Śirasa, the seer is Prajâpati, the metre is Gâyatrî, the Devatâs are Brahmâ, Agni, Vâyu and Sûrya and it is employed in Prâṇâyâma.

Then let him inhale, retain and expel air each time reciting the following:—

ओं भूः ॥ ओं भुवः ॥ ओं स्वः ॥ ओं महः ॥ ओं जनः ॥ ओं तपः ॥ ओं सत्यं ॥

ओं तत्सवितुर्वरेण्यं भर्गोदेवस्य धीमहि । धियो यो नः प्रचोदयात् ॥ ओं आपो ज्योतीरसो-मृतं ब्रह्म भूर्भुवस्स्वरोम् ॥

*Transliteration*:—Om Bhûḥ, Om Bhuvaḥ, Om Svah, Om Mahaḥ, Om Janaḥ, Om Tapaḥ, Om Satyam.

Om Tat Savitur Vareṇyam Bhargo Devasya dhîmahi; dhiyo yo naḥ prachodayât.

Om Âpo jyotî raso' mṛitam Brahma Bhûr Bhuvas Svar Om.

XII.—*Âchamana.*

Then let him perform (the morning) Âchamana reciting the following:—

ओं सूर्य्यश्चमेति ब्रह्मा ऋषिः प्रकृतिश्छन्दः आपो देवता अपामुपस्पर्शने विनियोगः ॥

ओं सूर्यश्च मामन्युश्च मन्युपतयश्च मन्युकृतेभ्यः पापेभ्यो रक्षन्ताम् । यद्रात्र्या पापमकार्षं मनसा वाचा हस्ताभ्यां पद्भ्यामुदरेण शिश्ना रात्रिस्तदवलुम्पतु । यत्किंचिद् दुरितं मयि इदमहमापोमृतयोनौ सूर्य्ये ज्योतिषि जुहोमि स्वाहा ॥ इति प्रातराचमेत् ॥

*Transliteration*:—Om, Sûryaś-chameti Brahmâ ṛiṣiḥ prakṛitiś-chhandâḥ âpo devatâ apâm upasparśane viniyogaḥ.

Om, Sûryaś cha mâ manyuś cha manyu patayaś cha manyu-kṛitebhyaḥ pâpebhyo rakṣantâm. Yad râtryâ pâpam akârṣam manasâ vâchâ hastâbhyâm padbhyâm udareṇa śiśnâ râtris tad avalumpatu.

Yat kiñchid duritam mayi idam ahamâpo mṛita yonau Sûrye Jyotiṣi juhomi svâhâ.

*Translation*:—Om! Of "Sûryaś chame" the seer is Brahmâ, the metre is Prakṛiti, the god is Apas, and it is used in sipping water.

May Sûrya and Manyu and Manyu-patis protect me from the sins caused by my Manyu. Whatever sins I may have committed in the night, whether by mind, or speech or hands or feet or stomach or organ, may Râtri destroy that; whatever sin there may be in me, all that I offer to the Immortal cause, the Sûrya, the Self-luminous (to be burnt up). Svâhâ.

The mid-day âchamana mantra is :—

ओं आपः पुनन्त्विति विष्णुऋषिरनुष्टुप्छन्दः आपो देवता आपामुपस्पर्शने विनियोगः ॥

ओं आपः पुनन्तु पृथिवीं पृथ्वी पूता पुनातु माम् । पुनन्तु ब्रह्मणस्पतिर्ब्रह्मपूता पुनातु माम् ॥ यदुच्छिष्टमभोज्यं यद्वा दुश्चरितं मम । सर्वं पुनंतु मामापोऽसतां च प्रतिग्रहम् ॥ स्वाहा ॥

*Transliteration* :—Om Âpaḥ punantviti viṣṇur ṛiṣir anuṣṭup chhandaḥ apodevatâ apâm upasparśane viniyogaḥ.

Om, Âpaḥ punantu prithivîm prithvî pûtâ punâtu mâm ; Punantu Brahmaṇaspatir Brahmapûtâ punâtu mâm. Yad-uchchhiṣṭam abhojyam yad vâ duśchâritam mama. Sarvam punantu mâmâpo asatâm cha pratigraham. Svâhâ.

*Translation* :—Om. Of "Âpaḥ Punantu" the seer is Viṣṇu, the metre is Anuṣṭup, the god is Apas, and it is used in sipping water.

May the Âpas purify the earth and the earth being purified, purify me. May the waters purify the Brahmaṇaspati, and the self-purified Brahma (the Vedas) purify me. May the waters purify all sins, such as, eating the remains of another, or improper food, or evil conduct, or accepting gifts from sinners. Svâhâ.

*The evening Âchamana mantra is the same as that of the morning, with a slight difference, as shown below* :—

ओं अग्निश्चमेति रुद्रऋषिः प्रकृतिश्छन्दः आपो देवता आपामुपस्पर्शने विनियोगः ॥

ओं अग्निश्चमामन्युश्च मन्युपतयश्च मन्युकृतेभ्यः पापेभ्यो रक्षन्तां यद्ह्ना पापमकार्षं मनसा वाचा हस्ताभ्यां पद्भ्यामुदरेण शिश्ना अहस्तदवलुम्पतु । यत्किंचित् दुरितं मयि इदमहमापोऽमृतयोनौ सत्ये ज्योतिषि जुहोमि ॥ स्वाहा ॥

For word-meaning, translation, &c., see p. 45.

## XIII. MÂRJANAM.

### or *sprinkling of water.*

Then let him perform mârjana reciting

"आपोहिष्ठा" इत्यादि त्र्यृचस्य सिन्धुद्वीप ऋषि गायत्रीछन्दः आपो देवता मार्जने विनियोगः ।

*Transliteration* :—"Âpo hiṣṭhâ" ityâdi tryṛichasya Sindhudvîpa Riṣir Gâyatrî chhandaḥ Âpo devatâ, mârjane viniyogaḥ.

*Translation* :—Of the three verses—"Âpo hiṣṭhâ, &c., the seer is Sindhudvîpa, the metre is Gâyatrî, the devatâ is waters and it is used in mârjana.

Then recite and sprinkle water as directed at page 46.

( 1 ) ओं आपोहिष्ठामयो भुवः ( 2 ) ओं तान ऊर्जे दधातन ( 3 ) ओं महेरणाय चक्षसे ( 4 ) ओं योवः शिवतमो रसः ( 5 ) ओं तस्य भाजयतेह नः ( 6 ) ओं उशतीरिव मातरः ( 7 ) ओं तस्मा अरंगमामवः ( 8 ) ओं यस्य क्षयाय जिन्वथ ( 9 ) ओं आपो जनयथा च नः ॥

## XIV. AVABHRITHAH.

"द्रुपदादिव" इति कोकिलो राजपुत्र ऋषिरनुष्टुप्छन्दः आपोदेवताः, सौत्रामन्यवभृथे विनियोगः ॥

***Transliteration*** **:—"Drupadâdiva" iti kokilo râjaputra Riṣir. anuṣṭup chhandaḥ âpo devatâ, sautrâ-manyavabhṛithe viniyogaḥ.**

***Translation*** **:—Of the verse "Drupadâdiva" the seer is Prince Kokila, the metre is Anuṣṭup, and it is used in Sautrâmaṇi, and Avabhṛitha.**

Then with this mantra throw the water on the body.

(AV. 6. 115. 3. VS. 20. 20.)

ओं द्रुपदादिव मुमुचानः स्विन्नः स्नातो मलादिव ।
पूतं पवित्रेणेवाज्यमापः शुन्धन्तु मैनसः ॥

Pada:—द्रुपदात्, इव, मुमुचानः, स्विन्नः, स्नातः, मलात् इव । पूतं, पवित्रेण, इव, आज्यम्, आपः, शुन्धन्तु, मा, एनसः ॥

*Transliteration* :—Om, Drupadâdiva mumuchânaḥ svinnaḥ snâto malâdiva ; pûtam pavitreṇev âjyam âpaḥ śundhantu mainasaḥ.

(Yajur Veda, XX. 20.)

*According to Uvaṭa.*

*Sanskrit Meaning* :—

( द्रुममयः पदः ) द्रुपदः ( पादुका बध्यन्ते ) मुमुचानः ( यथा द्रुमसत्पादात् मुच्यमानः पुरुषः तज्जैर्दोषैरपी असंबध्यमानः पृथग्भवेद् ) । ( यथा च ) स्विन्नः ( प्रस्विन्नः पुरुषः ) स्नातः ( मलात्पृथग्भवेत्, प्रस्विन्नस्य हि कृत्स्नो मल उपैति ) । ( यथा च ) पूतं पवित्रेण ( कम्बलमयेन ) आज्यं ( घृतं पृथग्भवेत् कीटिकातः ), ( एवम् ) आपः शुन्धन्तु ( पृथक्कुर्वन्तु ) मामेनसः ( पापात्सकाशात् ) ।

*According to Mahidhara.*

स्विन्नः = स्वेदयुक्तः । पूतः = गलितमाज्यं घृतं कीटेभ्यः पृथग्भवति ।

*Word-meaning* :—(1) Drupadât = from a tree, a post, Drupada means "tree." Or drupada may mean "a wooden sandal for the feet," *i.e.*, dru = tree or wood ; pada = foot, a covering for the feet made of wood, sandals. (2) Iva = like unto. (3) Mumuchânaḥ = freed. He who has thrown off or put off the shoes and has thus become free from the impurities that have stuck to the shoes. (4) Svinnaḥ = Sweating or perspiring. (5) Snâtaḥ = bathed. (6) Malât = from impurity. (7) Iva = like. As a perspiring or fatigued person becomes free from impurities by bathing. (8) Pûtam = strained. (9) Pavitreṇa = through a blanket or a strainer. (10) Iva = like. (11) Âjya = sacrificial butter. As ghee when heated and melted is purified of all its impurities, like insects, &c., by being strained through a woollen cloth. (12) Âpaḥ = Waters, All-pervading. (13) Śûndhantu = may purify. (14) Mâ = me. (15) Enasaḥ = from sin.

***Translation*** **:—Being freed as if from a post, as one that has sweated from filth on bathing, like sacrificial butter purified by a purifier,——— let the All-pervading cleanse me of sin.**

Or,—Om, even as the perspiring gets relief from the shade of the tree, as bathing removes the impurities of the body, as the ghee becomes purified by its purifying agent,—so let the Waters purify me from all sins.

## XV. AGHAMARSANA.

ओं ऋतञ्च सत्यञ्च इति मन्त्रस्याघमर्षण ऋषिरनुष्टुप्छन्दो भाववृत्तं दैवतमश्वमेधावभृथे विनियोगः ॥

*Transliteration* :—Om Ritam cha satyam cha iti mantrasyâghamarṣaṇa Riṣir anuṣṭup chhando Bhâvavṛittam daivatam, aśvamedhâ vabhṛithe viniyogaḥ.

*Translation* :—Of the Mantras Ritam cha satyam cha, the Seer is Aghamarṣaṇa, the metre is Anuṣṭup, the Devatâ Vṛitta (or Bhâvavṛitta, a name of Brahmâ), and they are employed in the final Dikṣâ bath (avabhṛitha) at the close of (Aśvamedha sacrifice).

ओं ऋतं च सत्यं चाभीद्धात्तपसोध्यजायत ।

ततो रात्र्यजायत ततः समुद्रो अर्णवः ॥

समुद्रादर्णवादधिसंवत्सरो अजायत ।

अहोरात्राणिविदधद्विश्वस्य मिषतो वशी ॥

सूर्याचन्द्रमसौ धाता यथापूर्वमकल्पयत् ।

दिवं च पृथिवीं चान्तरिक्षमथो स्वः ॥

*Translation* :—The Right and True was born from kindled heat, then the night was born and the surging sea. From the surging sea the annual son was born, he who orders day and night, the lord of all that sees. The Creator made sun and moon in turn, the sky and the air, and then the Heaven.

*Direction* :—Holding some water in the palm of the hand bring it near the nose; repeat once twice or thrice the above mantras; and then throw the water without looking at it on the left, thinking that the person of sin has come out of one's self. Sometimes these three mantras are read at the time of bathing in a river. It is mentally repeated while diving down with head under water, having closed the orifices with fingers.

## XVI.

### *Upasparśaḥ.*

(अन्तश्चरसीति तिरश्चीन ऋषिः, अनुष्टुप छन्दः, आपो देवता, अपामुपस्पर्शने विनियोगः ॥)

*Transliteration* :—"Antaś charasi" iti Tiraśchina Riṣiḥ anuṣṭup chhandaḥ Apo Devatâ, apâmupasparśane viniyogaḥ.

*Translation* :—Of the hymn "Antaś charasi, &c.," the seer is Tiraśchina, the metre is Anuṣṭup, the Devatâ is Apas, and it is used in touching the waters.

ओं अन्तश्चरसि भूतेषु गुहायां विश्वतो मुखः ।

त्वं यज्ञस्त्वं वषट्कार आपोज्योती रसोऽमृतम् ॥

*Transliteration* :—

Om! Antaś charasi bhûteṣu Guhâyâm viśvato mukhaḥ;

Tvam Yajñas Tvam Vaṣaṭkâra Âpo Jyotî Raso mṛitam.

*Word-meaning* :—Antar=Inside, within; charasi=thou movest; bhuteṣu=in the beings; guhâyâm=in the cavity; viśvataḥ=on all sides,

Mukhaḥ = face ; Tvam = Thou ; Yajña = Sacrifice ; Tvam = Thou ; Vaṣaṭ-kâra = the syllable Vaṣaṭ ; Apaḥ = all = pervading ; Jyotiḥ = Light; Rasaḥ = Essence, Amṛitam = the Immortality.

*Translation* :—O All pervading! Thou movest within the cavity (or heart) of (all) living beings. Thy face is on all sides. Thou the Sacrifice, Thou the sacrificial formula, Thou the Light, the rasaḥ, the immortal nectar.

*Direction* :—Perform the second âchamana with this mantra.

## XVII.

### Suryârghya Dânam

or

### *Offering of Arghya to the Sun.*

This is done by reciting the Gâyatrî.

ओंकारस्य ब्रह्मा ऋषिर्गायत्रा छन्दोऽग्निर्देवता । महाव्याहृतीनां प्रजापतिरृषि-र्गायत्र्युष्णिगनुष्टुभश्छन्दांसि । अग्निवाय्वादित्या देवताः । गायत्र्या विश्वामित्र ऋषिर्गायत्री छन्दः सविता देवता सूर्यार्घ्यदाने विनियोगः ॥

*Transliteration* :—Oṅkârasya Brahmâ Ṛiṣir Gâyatrî chhando' gnir Devatâ, Mahâvyâhṛitînâm Prajâpatir Ṛiṣir, Gâyatry-Uṣṇig-Anuṣṭubhas chhandâṃsi Agni-Vâyu-Âdityâ devatâḥ. Gâyatryâ Viśvâmitra Ṛiṣir Gâyatrî chhandaḥ, Savitâ devatâ ; Sûryârghya dâne viniyogaḥ

*Translation* :—Of "Aum" the seer is Brahmâ, the metre is Gâyatrî, and the Devatâ is Agni.

Of the Great Vyâhṛitis Bhuḥ, Bhuvar and Svar the seer is Prajâpati, tne metres are Gâyatrî, Uṣṇik Anuṣṭup respectively, and the Devatâs are Agni, Vâyu and Âditya, respectively.

Of the Gâyatrî the seer is Viśvâmitra, the metre is Gâyatrî, the Devatâ is Savitâ. It is used in offering Arghya to the Sun.

ओं भूर्भुवः स्वः । तत् सवितुर्वरेण्यं भर्गो देवस्य धीमहि । धियो यो नः प्रचो-दयात् ॥ ओं ॥

*Directions* :—Putting some flowers in water offer it to the Sun thrice in the morning and evening; and once at mid-day Sandhyâ ; just after Aghamarṣaṇa. Three handfuls of water are offered to the Sun, standing with face towards it while the Gâyatri is recited by the offerer.

## XVIII.—SÛRYOPASTHÂNAM.

or

### *praise of the Sun.*

उद्वयमिति प्रस्कण्व ऋषिरनुष्टुप् छन्दः सूर्यो देवता सूर्योपस्थाने विनियोगः ॥

*Transliteration* :—Udvayamiti Praskaṇva Ṛiṣir, Anuṣṭup chhandaḥ, Sûryo Devatâ, Sûryopasthâne viniyogaḥ.

*Meaning* :—Of "Udvayam," &c., the seer is Praskaṇva, the metre is Anuṣṭup, the Devatâ is the Sun and it is employed in Sûryopasthâna.

ओं उद्वयं तमसस्परि स्वः पश्यन्त उत्तरम् ।
देवं देवत्रा सूर्यमगन्म ज्योतिरुत्तमम् ॥

*Transliteration* :—

Aum ! Udvayam tamasas pari Svaḥ paśyanta uttaram ;

Devam Devatrâ Sûryam, Aganma jyotir uttamam.

*Word-meaning* :—Ut=out or away ; vayam=we ; tamasas=from darkness ; pari=around ; svaḥ=heaven ; paśyantaḥ=seeing ; uttaram=the superior.

Devam=the shining ; devatrâ=in the heaven-world ; Sûryam=the Sun ; aganma=we have gone ; jyotir=light ; uttamam=best.

**Translation** :—**We have gone, out of the encircling darkness, and have seen the high heaven, and the Divine Sun full of great light in the sky.**

ओं उदुत्यमिति मन्त्रस्य प्रस्कण्व ऋषिर्गायत्री छन्दः सूर्योदेवता सूर्योपस्थाने विनियोगः ॥

*Transliteration* :—Om, Udutyamityasya Praskaṇva Ṛiṣir Gâyatrî chhandaḥ Sûryo Devatâ Sûryopasthâne viniyogaḥ.

**Translation**:—**Of the mantra Om, Udutyam, &c., the seer is Parskaṇva, the metre is Gâyatrî, the Devatâ is the Sun, and it is employed in Sûryopasthâna.**

ओम् उदुत्यं जातवेदसं देवं वहन्ति केतवः । दृशे विश्वाय सूर्यम् ।

*Transliteration* :—

Om, Udutyam Jâtavedasam Devam vahanti ketavaḥ ;
Driśe Viśvâya Sûryam.

*Word-meaning* :—Ut=up, qualifying vahanti ; U=mere expletive, tyam=Him ; Jâta-vedasam=Knower of all things ; devam=god ; vahanti =bear ; Ketavaḥ=heralds, rays of the sun ; driśe=that (he may) be seen ; viśvâya=for all ; Sûryam=Sûrya.

**Translation** :—**His heralds bear Him up aloft, the God who knoweth all that lives ; Sûrya that all may look on Him.—(*Griffith.*)**

ओं चित्रमित्यस्य कौत्सऋषिस्त्रिष्टुप्छन्दः सूर्यो देवता सूर्योपस्थाने विनियोगः ॥

*Transliteration* :—Om chitram ityasya Kautsa Ṛiṣis Triṣṭup Chhandaḥ, Sûryo Devatâ, Sûryopasthâne viniyogaḥ.

**Meaning** :—**Of the mantra Om ! Chitram, &c., the seer is Kautsa, the metre is Triṣṭup, the Devatâ is Sûrya ; and it is employed in Sûryopasthâna.**

ओं चित्रं देवानामुदगादनीकं चक्षुर्मित्रस्य वरुणस्याग्नेः ॥ आप्राद्यावा पृथिवी अन्तरिक्षꣳ सूर्य आत्मा जगतस्तस्थुषश्च स्वाहा ।

(Rig. I. 115. 1.)

*Transliteration* :—

Om ! Chitram Devânâm udagâd anikam ; Chakṣur Mitrasya, Varuṇasyâgneḥ ;

Âprâ Dyâvâ Pṛithivî antarikṣam ; Sûrya âtmâ jagatastasthuṣaś cha.

**Translation** :—**The brilliant Presence of the gods hath risen, the eye of Mitra, Varuṇa and Agni.**

The soul of all that moveth not or moveth, the sun hath filled the air, earth and heaven (Griffith.).

तच्चक्षुरिति दध्यङ्ङाथर्वण ऋषिरक्षरातीत पुर उष्णिक् छन्दः सूर्यो देवता सूर्योपस्थाने विनियोगः ॥

*Transliteration* :—Tach chakṣur iti dadhyañ Âtharvaṇa Ṛiṣir akṣarâtîta pura uṣṇik chhandaḥ, Sûryo devatâ, Sûryopasthâne viniyogaḥ.

*Meaning* :—Of the verses "Tach chakṣur," the seer is Dadhyañ Atharvaṇa, the metre is irregular Uṣṇik, the Devatâ is the Sun, and it is employed in Sûryopasthâna.

ओं तच्चक्षुर्देवहितं पुरस्ताच्छुक्रमुच्चरत् । पश्येम शरदः शतं; जीवेम शरदः शतम् । शृणुयाम शरदः शतं; प्रब्रवाम शरदः शतम् । अदीनाः स्याम शरदः शतम्, भूयश्च शरदः शतात् ॥

*Transliteration* :—Aum ! Tach chakṣur devahitam purastâch chhukram uchcharat.

Paśyema śaradaḥ śatam, Jîvema śaradaḥ śatam, śṛiṇuyâma śaradaḥ śatam, Prabravâma śaradaḥ śatam, Adînâḥ syâma śaradaḥ śatam, bhûyaś cha śaradaḥ śatât.

*Word-meaning* :—Tach = that ; chakṣur = eye ; devahitam = beloved of the Devas ; purastât = in the East ; śukram = brilliant, pure ; uchcharat = arises, lit. ; moves up.

Paśyema = may we see ; Śaradaḥ = autumns ; Śatam = hundreds ; Jîvema = may we live ; śaradaḥ śatam = hundred autumns ; śṛiṇuyâma = may we hear ; śaradah śatam = hundred autumns ; prabravâma = may we speak ; śaradaḥ śatam = hundred autumns ; Adînâḥ syâma = may we not be humiliated ; śaradaḥ śatam = hundred autumns ; Bhûyas = more than ; cha = and ; śaradaḥ śatât = hundred autumns.

*Translation* :—That Eye (of the universe), the beloved of the Gods, the Brilliant (Sun) arises in the East.

May we see for a hundred autumns, live for a hundred autumns, hear for a hundred autumns, speak for a hundred autumns, be rich for a hundred autumns—yea, more than hundred autumns.

*Direction* :—Raising his hands up, let him recite the above four Mantras in praise of the Sun. These should be recited standing on tiptoes, the heels not to touch the ground. Or he may stand on one leg, and reciting these verses, revolve round himself looking at the Sun so far as possible ; and then bowing to the Sun, should sit down, facing east or north.

The verses in praise of the Sun are many in the Vedas. He may recite them as well ; if he likes.

The hands should be in Swastika posture at morning Sandhyâ, straight up at mid-day Sandhyâ, and open palms at evening Sandhyâ, when performing the Upasthâna.

### XIX.—GÂYATRYÂVÂHANAM.

or *the Invocation of the Gâyatrî.*

1. *The Vaidic Invocation.*

तेजोसीति देवा ऋषयः शुक्रं दैवतं गायत्री छन्दः गायत्र्यावाहने विनियोगः ।

*Transliteration* :—"Tejosi" iti Devâ Riṣayaḥ, Śukram Daivatam, Gâyatrî chhandaḥ, Gâyatry âvâhane viniyogaḥ.

**Meaning** :—Of the hymn "Tejosi, &c.," the seers are the Devas, the Devatâ is Śukra, the metre is Gâyatrî, and it is employed in invoking the Gâyatrî.

ओं तेजोसि शुक्रमस्यमृतमसि। धाम नामासि प्रियं देवानामनाधृष्टं देव यज्ञनमसि ॥

(Yaj. Veda I, 31.)

*Transliteration* :—Om! Tejosi Śukram asi amṛitam asi, Dhâma nâma asi, priyam devânâm, anâdhṛiṣṭam devayajñanam asi.

*Word-meaning* : —Tejas = light; asi = thou art; Śukram = brilliant; asi = thou art; dhâma = "above" (or seat of mental concentration); nâma = name or honor; asi = thou art; priyam = beloved; devânâm = of the Devas; anâdhṛiṣṭam = excellent; devayajñanam = the sacrifice or worship of the Devas; asi = thou art.

**Translation** :—Om! Thou art Light, Thou art brilliant, Thou art Immortal, Thou art the honored abode, Beloved of the Devas, Thou art the excellent sacrifice of the Devas.

*II. The non-Vaidic Invocation.*

ओं आगच्छ वरदे देवि जपे मे सन्निधौ भव । गायन्तं त्रायसे यस्माद् गायत्री त्वं ततः स्मृता ॥

*Transliteration* :—

Om! Âgachchha varade Devi jape me sannidhau bhava;

Gâyantam trâyase yasmâd Gâyatrî tvam tataḥ smṛitâ.

**Translation** :—Om! O thou boon-conferring goddess, come, be present at my japa. Since thou savest him who sings (gâyantam, thy praise) therefore art thou called Gâyatrî.

*Directions* :—With joined palms recite the above mantras and invoke the Devatâ, by will-power.

### XX.—GÂYATRY UPASTHÂNAM.

गायत्र्यसीति विमलः ऋषिः पंक्ति छन्दः, परमात्मा देवता गायत्र्युपस्थाने विनियोगः ॥

*Transliteration* :—Gâyatryasîti Vimalaḥ Riṣiḥ, Paṅkti chhandaḥ, Paramâtmâ Devatâ, Gâyatry upasthâne viniyogaḥ.

**Meaning** :—Of the verse "Gâyatryasi," the seer is Vimala, the metre is Paṅkti. the Devatâ is the Supreme self, and it is employed in the praise of Gâyatrî.

ओं गायत्र्यस्येकपदी द्विपदी त्रिपदी चतुष्पद्यपदसि नहि पद्यसे नमस्ते तुर्याय दर्शताय पदाय परो रजसेऽसावदो मा प्रापत् ।

(Bṛihad. Up. V. 14. 7.)

*Transliteration* :—Om ! Gâyatryasyeka-padî dvipadî tri-padî chatuṣ-pady apadasi, nahi pady ase namas te turîyâya darśatâya padâya paro rajase, sâvado mâ prâpat.

*Word-meaning* :—Gâyatri = O Gâyatri ; asi = thou art ; eka-padî = one-footed (in the form of Triloki) ; dvi-padî = two-footed (the Trayî-vidyâ from thy second foot) ; tripadi = three-footed (all Prana &c., are thy third foot) ; Chatuṣ-padi = four footed (as the Puruṣa) ; apad = without foot ; asi = thou art ; na = not ; hi = because ; padyase = art reached or known. Namaḥ = salutation ; te = to thee or thy ; turîyâya = fourth ; darśatâya = beautiful ; padâya = foot ; paraḥ rajase = above the Rajas or Dust ; asau = that ; adaḥ = this ; mâ = not ; prâpat = may obtain.

*Translation* :—O Gâyatri ! Thou art of one foot, of two feet, of three feet, and of four feet – thou art without foot, because thou art not obtained. Salutation to thy beautiful fourth foot which is above the Triloki (Rajas). This cannot obtain that.

### XXI.—GÂYATRÎ DHYÂNAM.

or *meditation on Gâyatrî.*

ओं श्वेतवर्णा समुद्दिष्टा कौशेयावसना तथा। श्वेतैर्विलेपनैः पुष्पैरलंकारैश्च भूषिता ॥
आदित्यमण्डलस्था च ब्रह्मलोकगता तथा। अक्षसूत्रधरा देवी पद्मासनगता शुभा ॥

*Transliteration* :—

Om ! Sveta-varṇa sam-ud-diṣṭâ Kauśeyâ-vasanâ tathâ ;
Śvetair vilepanaiḥ puṣpair Alaṅkârais cha bhûṣitâ ;
Âditya-maṇḍalasthâ cha Brahma-loka-gatâ tathâ ;
Akṣa-sûtra-dharâ Devî Padmâsana-gatâ śubhâ.

*Word-meaning* :—Śveta varṇa = white-colored ; samuddiṣṭâ = is described ; Kauśeya-vasanâ = silken-dressed ; tathâ = also ; Śvetaiḥ = with white ; vilepanaiḥ = sandal-paste ; puṣpaiḥ = (with) flowers ; alaṅkâraiḥ = ornaments ; cha = and ; bhûṣitâ = adorned.

Âditya-maṇḍala-sthâ = dwelling in Solar orb ; Brahmaloka-gatâ = and in Brahma-world residing ; Akṣa-sûtra-dharâ = holding the rosary ; Devî = the shining one ; padmâsanagatâ = seated on a lotus-seat ; śubhâ = auspicious.

*Translation* :—Om ! White-colored they say is Gâyatrî in silken-shining garment dressed.
White sandal-paste perfumes her skin with flowers white and jewels decked.
In Solar orb her home you find in Brahma-world also she dwells.
With rosary in hand is she on Lotus flower auspicious one.

### XXII.—GÂYATRÎ JAPAḤ.

or *mental recitation of Gâyatrî.*

ओंकारस्य ब्रह्मा ऋषिर्गायत्री छन्दोऽग्निर्देवता ।

*Transliteration* :—Oṅkârasya Brahmâ Ṛiṣir, Gâyatrî chhando' gnir devatâ.

*Translation* :—Of the syllable Om, the seer is Brahmâ, the metre is Gâyatri, and the Devâta is Agni.

महाव्याहृतीनां प्रजापतिरृषिर्गायत्र्युष्णिगनुष्टुभश्छन्दांसि अग्निवाय्वादित्या देवताः।

*Transliteration* :—Mahâ-vyâhṛitinâm Prajâpatir Riṣir, Gayatry-uṣṇig-anuṣṭubhaś chhandâṁsi Agni-vâyu-âdityâ devatâḥ.

*Translation* :—Of the Great-vyahṛitis, the seer is Prajâpati, the metres are Gâyatrî, Uṣṇik and Anuṣṭup respectively, and their respective Devatâs are Agni, Vâyu and Âditya.

गायत्र्या विश्वामित्र ऋषिर्गायत्री छन्दः सविता देवता ।

*Transliteration* :—Gâyatryâ Viśvâmitra Riṣir Gâyatri chhandaḥ, Savitâ Devatâ.

*Translation* :—Of Gâyatri the seer is Viśvâmitra, the metre is Gâyatrî, and the Devâta is Savitâ.

सवितुः प्रीतये (दश, अष्टाविंशति, अष्टोत्तरशतसहस्रसंख्यया जपे विनियोगः ।

*Transliteration* :—Savituḥ prîtaye (daśa aṣṭâviṁśati, aṣṭottara śata, sahasra, &c.) saṁkhyayâ jape viniyogaḥ.

*Translation* :—In order to please Savitâ, the Mantra is used for Japa 10 or 28 or 108 or 1000 times, &c.

(NOTE :—Here insert the proper numeral 10, &c., showing how many times one intends to recite it.)

ओँ भूर्भुवः स्वः । ओं तत्सवितुर्वरेण्यं भर्गो देवस्य धीमहि । धियो यो नः प्रचोदयात् ॥ ओं ॥

*Transliteration* :—Om Bhûr, Bhûvaḥ, Svaḥ. Om Tat savitur vareṇyam bhargo devasya dhîmahi. Dhiyo yo naḥ prachodayât. Om.

*Direction* :—Facing the Sun, in the morning, let him mentally repeat the Gâyatrî with the Praṇava and the three Vyâhṛitis, as shown in the above mantra, 108 times, 28 times or 10 times. The repetition should not be mechanical, but with meditation over the sense of the words. In the evening, he should sit facing the Vâyu-corner, just as the Sun is setting and go on repeating till the stars arise. On Holidays (days on which the reading of Vedas is suspended) 28 repetitions in the morning and 10 in the evening are enough. The rosary may be of Rudrâkṣa, Indrákṣa, crystal or Vidruma or on fingers. The rosary should contain 108 beads or half of it, *i.e.*, 54, or its half, *i.e.*, 27 beads. The Japa should be with concentrated mind. One should not talk nor shake the body or head or neck, or open his mouth at the time of Japa. The place should be pure and solitary.

At the time of Japa, one foot should not be pressed by the other foot. Meditation should not be performed with head covered by any cloth. In the morning, the hand should be near the naval, at midday near the heart, and in the evening near the face. The Japa should never be performed in water. The rosary in the right hand should be covered up with cloth

The number should *always* be counted. The Japa without keeping any count leads to a state of mental vacuity and passivity which is extremely undesirable. Countless-Japa is therefore called Asuric Japa.

As a general rule, the counting is done on the phalanges, as mentioned at page 87.

The âsana (seat) may be of a piece of silk spread on the ground, or a blanket, or a skin of antelope, or linen, or wood, or leaves, &c. No one else should use it. The bed, âsana, dress, and drinking vessel should never be used by another—they are pure so long as they are used by one's own self.

The posture to be adopted at the time of Japa is that which is most convenient.

The Praṇava must be recited both at the beginning and at the end, as shown above, that is to say, begin with Praṇava, then say Bhûḥ, Bhuvaḥ, Svaḥ. Then again recite the Praṇava and repeat the Gâyatri and finish with the Praṇava.

The repetition 1000 times is the best, 100 times is middling and ten times the lowest, at morning. In the evening 30 or 10 times. The students and house-holders should recite 108 times: the ascetics 2000 times.

The Gayatri-Japa is one of the Great Yajñas.

## XXIII. Japa-nivedana

### or *Ending the Japa.*

अनेन (दश, अष्टाविंशति ) संख्यया जपेन भगवान्(ब्रह्म रुद्र विष्णु ) स्वरूपी सविता प्रीयतां नमः ।।

*Transliteration*:—Anena saṁkhyayâ Japena Bhagavân svarûpî Savitâ prîyatâm Namaḥ.

By this (10, 28 or 108, &c., in number) Japa, may the Lord Savitâ, having the form of (Brahmâ in the morning, Rudra at midday, and Visṇu in the evening) be pleased. Salutation.

*Directions*:—Taking some water in the right palm, and reciting the above mantra, put that water into the right hand of the Deity, thinking Him sitting in the front. The words Brahmâ, &c., should be supplied in the mantra, according to the time of the day. Such as, in the morning Japa of 108 times the words should be "Anena anena aṣṭottara śatâ saṅkhyayâ Japena, Bhagavân Brahma-svarûpî Savitâ prîyatâm, Namaḥ."

## XXIV. Surya Pranâma.

### or *Bow to the Sun.*

एकचक्रइत्यस्य नारायण ऋषिः, उष्णिक् छन्दः, सूर्यो देवता, सूर्यनमस्कारे विनियोगः ॥

*Transliteration*:—Eka chakra ity asya Nârâyaṇa Riṣiḥ usṇik chhandaḥ, Sûryo Devatâ, Sûrya namaskâre viniyogaḥ.

*Translation*:—Of the mantra "Eka chakra", the seer is Nârâyaṇa, the metre is Uṣṇik, the Devatâ is the Surya, and it is used in making bow to the Sun.

ओं एकचक्रो रथो यस्य दिव्यकनकभूषितः ।
समे भवतु सुप्रीतः, पद्महस्तो दिवाकरः ॥

*Transliteration* :—

Om! Eka chakro ratho yasya divya kanaka-bhûṣitaḥ;
Sa me bhavatu supritaḥ Padma hasta Divâkaraḥ.

*Word-meaning* :—Yasya = whose, rathaḥ = chariot, ekachakro = one wheeled, divya = shining, kanaka = gold, bhuṣitaḥ = adorned. Sa = He, me = to me, bhavâtu = let be, supritaḥ = well-pleased, padmahastaḥ = lotus handed, Divâkaraḥ = the Maker of Day.

*Translation* :—May that Maker of Day, Sun, the lotus-handed, be well-pleased with me—He whose chariot has one wheel and is refulgent with burnished gold.

*Directions* :—Bow with clasped hands to the Sun reciting this.

XXV. GÂYATRI-VISARJANA

or *Farewell to Gâyatri.*

उत्तम इति प्रजापतिर्ऋषिरनुष्टुप् छन्दो गायत्री देवता गायत्रीविसर्जने विनियोगः ॥

*Transliteration* :—Uttama iti Prajâpatir Riṣir, anuṣṭup chhando, Gâyrtrî Devatâ, Gâyatrî visarjane viniyogaḥ.

*Translation* :—Of the mantra "Uttama, &c.," the seer is Prajâpati, the metre is anuṣṭup, the Devatâ is Gâyatri, and it is employed in bidding farewell to Gâyatri.

ओं उत्तमे शिखरे देवि भूम्यां पर्वतमूर्धनि ।
ब्राह्मणेभ्योऽभ्यनुज्ञाता गच्छ देवि यथासुखम् ॥

*Transliteration* :—

Om! Uttame śikhare Devi Bhûmyâm parvata mûrdhani;
Brâhmaṇebhyo' bhyanujñâtâ Gachchha Devi yathâ sukham.

*Word-meaning* :—Uttame = on the highest, sikhare = top or summit, Devi = Goddess, Bhumyam, = on Earth, parvata-mûrdhani = on the summit of the mountain, Brâhmaṇebhyaḥ = by the worshippers, abhyanujñâtâ = being satisfied, gachchha = go, Devi = O Goddess, yathâ sukham = as it pleaseth Thee.

*Translation* :—On the highest top of the mountain-summit in earth (*i.e.*, on the Meru mountain), dwells the Goddess Gâyatri. Being pleased with Thy worshippers, go back, O Devi, to Thy abode as it pleaseth Thee.

*N.B.*—The word Brâhmaṇebhyaḥ has been translated as "worshippers." The most ancient meaning of this word is "the praise-singer," hence "the adorer, the worshipper."

XXVI. DEVATÂ VISARJANAM PRÂRTHANÂ CHA.

or *Farewell to the Devatâ and Prayer*

देवागातुविदिति मनसस्पतिर्ऋषिर्विराट् छन्दः वातो देवता पूर्वार्धेन देवताविसर्जने उत्तरार्धेन चंद्रप्रार्थने विनियोगः ॥

*Transliteration*:—Devâ gâtu iti Manasaspatir Riṣir, virâṭ chhandaḥ, Vâto Devatâ, pûrvardhena Devatâ visarjane, uttarârdhena Chandra prârthane viniyogaḥ.

**Translation**:—Of the mant . "Devi gâtu, &c.," the seer is Manasaspati, the metre is Virât, the Devatâ is Wind, the first hemistich is used in bidding farewell to Devatâ, the second half is used in prayer to the Moon.

ओं देवा गातु विदोगातुं वित्वा गातुमित ।
मनसस्पत इमं देव यज्ञं स्वाहा वातेधा ॥

(Yajur Veda, VIII. 21)

*Transliteration*:—

Om! Devâ gâtu-vido gâtum vitvâ gâtum ita,
Manasas-pata imam Deva yajñam svâhâ vâtedhâ.

*Word-meaning*:—Devâḥ=O Devas, Gâtu-vidaḥ=O knowers of Gâtu (=yajña, sacrifice, or song or hymn), knowers of Path (ga=to go), gâtum =sacrifice, vittvâ=having known, gâtum=to the sacrifice, ita=come or gâtum=Path, ita=go.

Manasaspate—O Lord of Manas, imam=this (sacrifice), Deva=O Deva, yajña=Sacrifice, svâhâ=offered (to thee), vâte=in the air, dhâ= place thou.

**Translation**:—Ye Devas, who know the Path! having known our Path, go ye on (your) Path.

O Lord of Manas! O Deva! May this sacrifice be welcome to thee. Fix it in the air.

*Directions*:—Take some water in the palm of the hand, and finish the Japa by reciting the above mantra.

XXVII.—DEVA-BRÂHMANA NAMASKÂRAH.

or *Salutations to Devas and Brâhmanas.*

ओं तत् सत् Om Tat Sat,
ओं सन्ध्यायै नमः Om Sandhyâyai Namaḥ.
ओं गायत्र्यै नमः Om Gâyatryai Namaḥ.
ओं सावित्र्यै नमः Om Sâvitryai Namaḥ.
ओं सरस्वत्यै नमः Om Sarasvatyai Namaḥ.
ओं सर्वाभ्यो देवताभ्यो नमः Om Sarvâbhyo Devatâbhyo Namaḥ.

ओं आसत्यलोकात् पातालाद् आलोकालोकपर्वतात् ।
ये सन्ति ब्राह्मणा देवास्तेभ्यो नित्यं नमोनमः ॥

*Transliteration*:—

Om Âsatya-lokât pâtâlâd Âlokâloka parvatât,
Ye santi Brâhmaṇâ devâs Tebhyo nityam Namo Namaḥ.

**Translation**:—From Pâtala up to Satya-loka, yea up to mountain Lokâloka whatever Brahmaṇas or Devâs live, to them I always salutations give.

*Directions* :—Reciting let him bow down. He *may* recite the following also at the end and then finish the Sandhyâ with âchamana again :—

( १ ) ब्रह्मार्पणम् ।

ओं कायेन वाचा मनसेन्द्रियैर्वा बुद्ध्यात्मना वानुसृतिः स्वभावात् ।
करोमि यद्यत्सकलं परस्मै नारायणायेति समर्पयामि ॥

( २ ) यज्ञात्मने नमस्कारः ।

चतुर्भिश्च चतुर्भिश्च द्वाभ्यां पञ्चभिरेव च ।
हूयते च पुनर्द्वाभ्यां तस्मै यज्ञात्मने नमः ॥

( ३ ) विष्णुस्मरणम् ।

प्रमादात्कुर्वतां कर्म प्रच्यवेताध्वरेषु यत् ।
स्मरणादेव तद्विष्णोः सम्पूर्णं स्यादिति स्मृतिः ॥
यस्य स्मृत्या च नामोक्त्या तपोयज्ञक्रियादिषु ।
न्यूनं सम्पूर्णतां याति सद्यो वन्दे तमच्युतम् ॥

( ४ ) अच्युत नमस्कारः

ओं अच्युताय नमः । ओं अच्युताय नमः । ओं अच्युताय नमः ।

( ५ ) अन्ते पुनराचमनम् ।

ओं ऋग्वेदाय स्वाहा । ओं सामवेदाय स्वाहा ।
ओं यजुर्वेदाय स्वाहा । ओं अथर्ववेदाय नमः ॥
ओं तत्सत् परं ब्रह्मार्पणमस्तु ओं ॥

### XXVIII. PARISISTAM OR END.

(1) *Brahmârpanam*
or
Offering to Brahmâ.

Om! Whatever I do with body, speech, mind, or senses or with reason and soul or whatever is automatically done by my nature—all that I offer to the Supreme Nârâyaṇa.

(2) *Salutation to Yajña-Puruṣa.*

I bow to that self of sacrifice who is adored in sacrifices by the utterance of the seventeen syllables, namely, the four syllables âśrâvaya ( आश्रावय ), the four syllables astu śrauṣaṭ ( अस्तु श्रौषट् ), the two syllables yaja ( यज ), the five syllables ye yajâmahe ( ये यजामहे ) and the two syllables vaṣaṭ ( वषट् )

(3) *Viṣṇu Smaranam.*

" Whatever defects occur in any ceremony through oversight or carelessness, they all become rectified by remembering Viṣṇu "—so declare the Scriptures.

I praise that Eternal Lord by remembering whom and uttering whose name all deficiencies are supplied in every sacrifice and ceremony.

(4) *Salutation to the Eternal.*

Om Achyutâya Namaḥ. Om Achyutâya Namaḥ. Om Achyutâya Namaḥ.

(5) *Âchamana.*

Om Rig Vedâya svâhâ, Om Yajur Vedâya svâhâ, Om Sâma Vedâya svâhâ, Om Atharva Vedâya namaḥ.

Om Tat Sat, Para-Brahmârpaṇam astu.

---

## CHAPTER X.

## THE TÂNTRIKÎ SANDHYÂ.

The Sandhyâs given before are Vaidikî. Though in the ancient times, according to some authorities, all mankind were entitled to Vaidikî Sandhyâ, yet in modern days lower castes are debarred from it. The reason of it is clear. The Vaidik language is difficult; even the best of the Pandits cannot understand it without the help of commentaries; so the masses would not have benefited by it. Therefore, for them Tântrikî Sandhyâ was promulgated by the Riṣis. Brahmins even perform it, in addition to their Vaidikî Sandhyâ. The forms are different, according to the different Iṣṭa Devatâ. The general outline is given below.

### I.—ÂCHAMANA.

ओं आत्मतत्त्वाय स्वाहा Om Âtma-tattvâya Svâhâ.

ओं विद्यातत्त्वाय स्वाहा Om Vidyâ-tattvâya Svâhâ.

ओं शिवतत्त्वाय स्वाहा Om Śiva-tattâya Svâhâ.

*Note*:—The Soul, the Nature and the God are the Three Eternal entities in a manifested universe. The Souls, or Jivâtmas are innumerable—from the highest Devas to the lowest minerals, all Jîvas belong to the category of Âtmâ. Man is such an Âtmâ. This is the consciousness side of the universe. On the form or matter side, we have Prakṛiti or Mahâmâyâ—the object of knowledge, the Vidyâ. All the Vidyâ or Science depends upon the knowledge of Nature, the Mula Prakṛiti. As the *Knower* is Âtmâ, so the *Known* is Vidyâ or Prakṛiti or Achit Tattvâ. The third is God, or Śiva-tattva controlling both, establishing relations between them. For fuller details, see my tract on "The Three Truths of Theosophy."

*Direction*:—Sip water thrice, reciting the above three mantras, and touch the various orifices as taught in the chapter on bathing--pp. 16-18.

### II. MÂRJANA.

This has two parts. First sanctifying the water and then sprinkling that water over the head.

*Sanctification mantra.*

ओं गङ्गे च यमुने चैव गोदावरि सरस्वति ।

नर्म्मदे सिन्धु कावेरि जलेऽस्मिन् सन्निधिं कुरु ॥

Om. Gaṅge! cha Yamune! chaiva, Godâvari! Sarasvati! Narmade! Sindhu! Kâveri! Jale' smin sannidhim kuru.

*Note* :—These are the five well-known rivers of India. They are invoked to approach the water. In fact these *five* streams are the *five* currents that are constantly pouring down from the Sun. Not only heat, light and electricity come from the Sun, but life-forces also come from Him. They are called "rivers" in mystic literature. These currents are conscious *living* streams; and do come when properly invoked.

*Direction* :—Reciting this mantra, make the sign of the Cow (Dhenumudrâ) over the water. Then with the thumb, middle and ring-finger joined together, sprinkle the water three times on the ground, and seven times on the head, reciting the following :—

*Note* :—The blank represents the Seed Mantra (Bija). It is different for different deities. Learn it from your Guru.

THE ÂCHAMANA AND MARJANA PURIFY THE DENSE BODY.

### III. PRÂṆYÂMA.

Then perform regulation of breath, as taught before reciting the Seed Mantra. The proportion of 1, 4, 2 should be kept. That is, if the breath is drawn in by reciting the Seed Mantra four times, it should be retained for the period taken up in reciting it 16 times, and then slowly exhaled reciting it eight times.

THE PRANAYAMA PURIFIES THE PRANA AND ETHERIC BODY.

### IV. ṢAḌAṄGA-NYÂSA.

The same as in the Vaidikî Sandhyâ, the difference consists in reciting the Seed Mantra, instead of the Vyâhṛitis. Thus :—

ओं (Seed Mantra) हृदयाय नमः
ओं Do. शिरसे स्वाहा
ओं Do. शिखायै वषट्
ओं Do. कवचाय हुम्
ओं Do. नेत्रत्रयाय वौषट्
ओं Do. करतलपृष्ठाभ्यां अस्त्राय फट्

*Note* :—The six organs here referred to are the six most vital and important parts in the human body. This process is one of self-magnetisation of these, by means of the divine force hidden in the Seed Mantra through the meditation of the sound of the last syllables.

The object of Nyâsa is to *put in, to store up* energy. While reciting the above mantras and touching the various parts, such as the heart, the fore-head, the top, the shoulders, the eyes and the palms, strongly *think* that energy is being poured in them. Thought creates energy.

### V. PUṆAR-MÂRJANA.

Take some water in the palm of the left hand, and cover it up with the right hand. Then sanctify the water by reciting twice the following five syllables :—

हं Haṃ
यं Yaṃ
वं Vaṃ
लं Laṃ
रं Raṃ

The water being thus sanctified, sprinkle over the head *seven* times with Seed Mantra as directed before (*i.e.*, with the thumb, middle and the ring-finger of the right hand joined together).

*Note*:—The above five syllables are the symbols of the *five* elements, and the five *senses*. As the senses are in the Manomaya sheath or the Astral body, the object of this mârjana or baptism is to purify the astral body. While sanctifying the water, *imagine* the five energies entering it. While sprinkling it, *imagine* all your astral and lower mental impurities (such as anger, lust, hatred, &c.) washed away. These five mystic syllables should be meditated upon to unfold their inner secret.

*Direction*:—Some portion of the water should be left in the palm, for the next process.

### VI. AGHAMARṢAṆA.

With the remaining water that was left in the palm of the left hand, perform the Aghamarṣaṇa. Pour this water on the palm of the right hand, and go through the same process as taught in the Vaidikî Sandhyâ. Go back in thought, to the time when there was no manifestation and no sin, and the universe first came out from the Thought of the Supreme. Having then *smelt* the water, or rather breathing over it, *imagine* that the Person of Sin has come out of you and is sunk in the water. Throw the water with force on the ground, reciting

फट् Phaṭ.

*Note*:—This process purifies the Higher Mental body, the Causal-body of Theosophy. "It is expiatory of all sins to which the Ego, not the Personality, is attached."

By these six preparatory holy communions—the Dense, the Etheric, the Mental and the Causal bodies are purified, and you are now fit to stand in the presence of Higher Intelligences and God and invoke them.

### VII. SECOND OR VAIDIKA ÂCHAMANA.

Wash your hands and again perform âchamana with the Vaidika mantra as taught on page 13.

Om Tad Viṣṇoḥ paramam padam sadâ paśyanti Sûrayaḥ Divîva chakṣur âtatam.

### VIII Recite the following Gâyatrî.

*Note*:—The student must learn the Gâyatrî from his Guru, also consult various forms given at the end of the chapter.

Pour water thrice into a copper vessel reciting the above Gâyatri each time, in honour of the THREE. (Brahmâ, Viṣṇu and Śiva.)

### IX.—TARPANA (*abridged*).

Then perform Tarpaṇa of the other Intelligences by offering water thrice to each, reciting:—

ओं देवांस्तर्पयामि Om Devâṃs tarpayâmi.

ओं ऋषींस्तर्पयामि Om Riṣîṃs tarpayâmi.

ओं पितॄंस्तर्पयामि Om Pitṛîṃs tarpayâmi.

ओं मनुष्यांस्तर्पयामि Om Manuṣyâṃs tarpayâmi.

ओं गुरूंस्तर्पयामि Om Gurûṃs tarpayâmi.

ओं परमगुरूंस्तर्पयामि Om Parama Gurûṃs tarpayâmi.

ओं परापरगुरूं स्तर्पयामि Om Parâpara Gurûṃs tarpayâmi.

ओं परमेष्ठि गुरूं स्तर्पयामि Om Parameṣṭhi Gurûṃs tarpayâmi.

ओं (Mûla Mantra) *so and so* देवतां तर्पयामि,

X.—SÛRYA-ARGHYA.

Then offer water to the Sun, the manifested God of our system, by reciting :—

ओं ह्रीं हं स मार्तण्डभैरवाय प्रकाशशक्तिसहिताय इदमर्घ्यं श्री सूर्याय नमः ।

Om Hrîm Ham Sa Mârtaṇḍa-bhairavâya prakâśaśakti-sahitâya, idam arghyam Śrî Sûryâya *Namaḥ*.

or

घृणि सूर्य आदित्य इदमर्घ्यं श्रीसूर्याय नमः ।

Ghriṇi Sûrya Âditya idam arghyam Śrî Sûryâya Namaḥ.

XI.—DEVATÂ-ARGHYA.

Then recite the Gâyatrî of your Devatâ and offer arghya to Him.

or

Recite the following mantra and offer arghya.

सूर्यमण्डलमध्यस्थायै———देवतायै नमः ॥

Sûrya maṇḍala madhyasthâyai———Devatâyai Namaḥ.

XII.—DHYÂNA OF GÂYATRÎ.

Then perform meditation of Gâyatrî. Form a mental image of Her, as taught before.

*Morning-Mantra.*

उद्यदादित्यसङ्काशां पुस्तकाक्षकरां स्मरेत् ।

कृष्णाजिनधरां ब्राह्मीं ध्यायेत् तारकितेऽम्बरे ॥

Udyad Âditya saṅkâśâm pustakâ-kṣa-karâm smaret.

Krisṇâjina-dharâm Brâhmîm dhyâyet târakite'mbare.

Refulgent red as the rising Sun, The Book and Rosary in hand, The Brâhmic force in deer-hide clad, Such form think ye, while stars still shine.

*Mid-day-Mantra.*

श्यामवर्णां चतुर्बाहुं शङ्खचक्रलसत्कराम् ।

गदापद्मकरां देवीं सूर्यासनकृताश्रयाम् ॥

Śyâma-varṇâm chatur bâhum, Śaṅkha-chakra-lasat-karâm.

Gadâ-padma-karâm Devîm Sûryâsana kritâśrayâm.

Azure-coloured and four-armed, Conch and discus in each hand
Club and Lotus holding Goddess Seated in the Solar orb.

*Evening-Mantra.*

शुक्लां शुक्लाम्बरधरां वृषासनकृताश्रयाम् ।

त्रिनेत्रां वरदां पाशं शूलञ्च नृकरोटिकाम् ॥

Śuklâm Śuklâmbaradharâṃ vṛiṣâsana-kritâśrayâm,

Tri-netrâm varadâm pâśaṃ śûlañ cha nṛikaroṭikâm.

White-hued, in snow-white garment clad, Seated on the Bull of Might

Three-eyed, with boon and bond in hand, With lance and drum reative armed.

*Note*:—The word Gâyatrî means "that which *chanted saves*." It is therefore the Eternal *Sound*, the word that was in the beginning, the Saviour. This sound pervades the whole universe, yea, it, creates, maintains and destroys it. Those three aspects of the Logos—the Gâyatrî, the Song-Saviour, are symbolised above. This is the highest meditation, *hearing* of this Cosmic chant—the Śruti—is the highest revelation. While meditating on the Gâyatrî let us aspire towards this goal.

XIII.—JÁPA.

Then recite the Gâyatrî ten times.

XIV.—PRAYER.

ओं गुह्यातिगुह्यगोप्त्री त्वं गृहाणास्मत्कृतं जपम् ।

सिद्धिर्भवतु मे देवि त्वत्प्रसादात् महेश्वरि ॥

Then pray:

Om, Guhyâti guhya goptrî tvam grihâṇ âsmat kṛitaṃ japam,
Siddhir bhavatu me Devi Tvat prasâdât maheśvari.

*Translation*:—Hidden most hidden Saviour Thou Accept this prayer of mine
Perfection be to me, O Light! Through grace of Thee, Great God.

In the case of a Deity symbolised as Male, read "Goptâ," "Deva" and "Maheśvara" respectively.

Here ends the Gâyatrî Sandhyâ proper. Next comes the worship of the Iṣṭa-devatâ, as part of the Sandhyâ.

XV.—GURU-PRAṆÂMA.

Then sprinkle your head with water once uttering

Raṃ.

Then salute on the *left* side, bringing each time the joined palms to the corners of the *left* eye reciting.

ओं गुरुभ्यो नमः Om Gurubhyo namaḥ.

ओं परमगुरुभ्यो नमः Om Paramagurubhyo namaḥ.

ओं परापरगुरुभ्यो नमः Om Parâpara Gurubhyo namaḥ.

ओं परमेष्ठि गुरुभ्यो नमः Om Parameṣṭhi Gurubhyo namaḥ.

Then salute on the *right* side.

ओं गणेशाय नमः Om Gaṇeśâya namaḥ.

Then salute in *front* the Iṣṭa-devatâ.

ओं __________ देवाय नमः __________ devâya namah.

### XVI.—SECOND PRÂṆÂYÂMA.

Then perform prâṇâyâma as taught before.

### XVII.

Then again perform Nyâsa as before.

### XVIII.—IṢṬA-DEVATÂ DHYÂNA.

Then meditate on the Iṣṭa-devatâ, slowly forming the mental picture as complete as you can.

### XIX.—JAPA.

Then recite the *Seed* Mantra 108 times.

### XX.—PRAYER.

Offer water, reciting the prayer Guhyâti guhya, &c., (p. 117.)

### XXI.—FINAL PRÂṆÂYÂMA.

Then perform prâṇâyâma for the last time.

### XXII.—SALUTATION.

Then bow down to the Iṣṭa-devatâ, reciting the appropriate Praṇâma mantras.

### XXIII.—GURU PRAṆÂMA.

Then salute the Gurudeva reciting the mantras given at page 18.

*Notes on the Tântrikî Sandhyâ.*

Some of the Seed Mantras (Bîja Mantras) and the corresponding Gâyatris of the various deities are given below. They are taken from the Tantra Sâra of Kṛṣṇânanda Bhattacharya.

(1) *Viṣṇu Gayatri.*

त्रैलोक्यमोहनाय विद्महे कामदेवाय धीमहि; तन्नो विष्णुः प्रचोदयात् ।

Om Trailokya Mohanâya vidmahe, Kâmadevâya dhîmahi, Tan no Viṣṇuḥ prachodayât.

*Mantra* :—ओं नमो नारायणाय Om namo Nârâyaṇâya.

नारायणाय विद्महे वासुदेवाय धीमहि तन्नो विष्णुः प्रचोदयात् ।

(2) Om Nârâyaṇâya vidmahe, Vâsudevâya dhîmahi, Tan no Viṣṇuḥ prachodayât.

(3) *Râma Gâyatri.*

दाशरथाय विद्महे सीतावल्लभाय धीमहि तन्नो रामः प्रचोदयात् ।

Om Dâśarathâya vidmahe, Sitâvallabhâya dhîmahi, Tan no Râmaḥ prachodayât.

*Mantra* :—रॉं रामाय नमः Râṃ Râmâya namaḥ.

(4) *Śiva Gâyatri.*

तत्पुरुषाय विद्महे महादेवाय धीमहि तन्नो रुद्रः प्रचोदयात् ।

Tat Puruṣâya vidmahe, Mahâdevâya dhîmahi, Tan no Rudraḥ prachodayât.

*Mantra*—हौं Hauṃ. Another mantra is :—ह्रीं ओं नमः शिवाय Hrim Om namaḥ Śivâya Hrim

GAṆEŚA GÂYATRÎ.

तत्पुरुषाय विद्महे वक्रतुण्डाय धीमहि तन्नो दन्ती प्रचोदयात् ।

Tat Puruṣâya vidmahe. Vakratuṇḍâya dhîmahi, Tan no Dantî prachodayât.

*Mantra* :—ओं श्रीं ह्रीं क्लीं ग्लौं गंगणपतये वर वरद सर्वजनं मे वशमानय स्वाहा ।

DAKṢIṆA MÛRTI GÂYATRÎ.

दक्षिणामूर्त्तये विद्महे ध्यानस्थाय धीमहि तन्नो धीशः प्रचोदयात्

Dakṣiṇâmûrtaye vidmahe, Dhyânasthâya dhîmahi, Tan no' dhîśaḥ prachodayât.

SÛRYA GÂYATRÎ.

आदित्याय विद्महे मार्तण्डाय धीमहि तन्नः सूर्यः प्रचोदयात्

Âdityâya vidmahe, mârtaṇḍâya dhîmahi, Tan naḥ sûryaḥ prachodayât.

*Mantra* :—ओं घृणि सूर्य आदित्यः Om Ghṛini Sûrya âdityaḥ.

DURGÂ GÂYATRÎ.

महादेव्यै विद्महे, दुर्गायै धीमहि, तन्नो देवी प्रचोदयात् ।

Mahâdevyai vidmahe, Durgâyai dhîmahi, Tan no Deî prachodayât.

*Mantra* दूं dûm.

---

## CHAPTER XI.

### UNIVERSAL SANDHYÂ.

This Sandhya is meant for all, Hindus and non-Hindus, Brahmins and non-Brahmins, men and women, in fact all mankind, irrespective of colour, caste, creed, race, sex, or nationality. It is generally said that the Hindu religion does not admit proselytes, a Hindu is born, not made. This is true for general forms of Hinduism, but there is one aspect of it which enjoins on its followers, to preach their teachings to all; and to induce all mainkind to accept that saving faith. That form of Hinduism is called Kula-dharma or the religion of universal love, or humanity. It considers humanity to be a family, in which there are elders, youths, infants, etc., having different rights and privilages; different duties and obligations, but all bound by one tie of love, there being no competition between each other, but emulation to serve one another. This Family Religion or Kula-Dharma has been proclaimed as the best suited for this age. We, therefore, give this Sandhyâ as taught in the handbook of Kula-Dharma (Mahânirvâna Tantra).

*The Mantra.*

The Sacred Mantra in this Sandhyâ is :—ओं सच् - चिदेकं ब्रह्म

Om sach-chid-ekam Brahma.

*Translation.* Om, the God is Good, Wise and One.

*Note.*—This Mantra should be repeated 108 times or as many times as one likes.

*Explanation.*

ओम् Om, It consists of three letters, A. U. M. The letter A means the Preserver of the World. The letter U means "the destroyer or regenerator of the World." The letter M,Means "the creator of the World." Thus the whole syllable Aum, means "the Creator, the Preserver, the Destroyer of the world."

सत् Sat, Ever-existent, The Good. चित् Chit, Intelligence, Wise. एकम् Ekam, One, the Peerless, the Unique, ब्रह्म Brahma, The Supreme, the Great, the Full; God.

The whole Mantra thus means " Brahma is One, all intelligence and all-existence.

The above mantra contains five words, every one of which is full of deep and various meanings and may be differently explained.

Thus the word Om or Aum has been explained as the secret name of God, in His aspects of creation, preservation, and destruction of the world ; as possessing the true powers or Saktis called the Ichchhâ-Sakti or will power, Kriyâ-śakti or Creative-power and Jñâna-śakti or the wisdom-power. सत् Sat, is the same word as the Latin word 'est' and means existent, being, good etc. चित् Chit, is the same word as Chaitanya, and means consciousnes,

Intelligence, wisdom, Knowledge. एकम् Ekam, means One, Chief, Supreme. ब्रह्म Brahma, literally comes from a root meaning great, Big, Full.

The mantra therefore means :—

The Preserver, Destroyer and Creator (of the World) is God the Good, the Wise, and the One.

## NYÂSA.

or

### *The Consecration of the Body.*

Before entering into the worship of God, the whole body with its various organs, must be dedicated to God, Who should be considered as dwelling in every part of it. As a temple is consecrated before it becomes a sacred place of worship, so before God is invoked, this body, (the true temple of God) should be dedicated to him. This dedication or assignment of the body is called Nyâsa.

#### I. RISI NYÂSA.

**अस्य परमब्रह्म मन्त्रस्य सदाशिव ऋषिरनुष्टुप् छन्द :**

**सर्वान्तर्यामि-निर्गुण-परमब्रह्म देवता धर्मार्थ-काम-मोक्ष-चतुर्वर्ग-फलाप्तये विनियोग : ॥**

Of this mantra of the Supreme God, the Ṛiṣi or seer is Sadâ-śiva, the metre is anuṣṭup, the Supreme, God Who is attributeless and the Inner-ruler of all is the deity, and it is employed for the acquisition of four-fold fruits—Religion, Wealth, Pleasure and Salvation.

Then dedicate the head, mouth and heart with the following three mantras :—

**शिरसि सदाशिवाय ऋषये नम : ।**

1. Śirasi Sadâ-śivâya ṛiṣaye namaḥ. Salutation to the Ṛiṣi sadâśiva, in the head.

**मुखे अनुष्टुप् छन्दसे नमः ॥**

2. Mukhe anuṣṭup chhandase namaḥ. Salutation to the metre Anuṣṭup in the mouth.

**हृदि सर्वान्तर्यामि-निर्गुण- परम-ब्रह्मणे देवतायै नम : ॥**

3. Hṛidi sarva-antaryâmi-nirguṇa-parama-Brahmaṇe devatâyai namaḥ. Salutation to the deity, the Supreme God, Who is without

(material) attributes, and is the Inner-ruler of all, salutation to Him, in the heart.

### II. KARA-NYÂSA

The five fingers of the body are to be next purifed by the following Mantras :—

Om angusthâbhyâm namaḥ. Om salutation to the two thumb fingers.

Sat tarjanibhyâm svâhâ. Sat, Svâhâ to the two index fingers. Chin madhyamâbhyâm vaṣaṭ. Chit is welcome to the middle fingers. Ekam anâmikabhyâm hum, One is welcome to the two ring fingers. Brahma kaniṣṭhâbhyâm vauṣaṭ. Brahma is welcome to the two little fingers.

Om sach-chid-ekam brahma karatala priṣṭhâbhyâm phaṭ. May the supreme Brahma who is one the all intelligence and all existence whose name is Om, protect by two hands the palms and the backs.

*Note.*—This is the method of kara-nyasa or invoking God to sanctify the fingers and the hands.

### III.—AṄGA-NYÂSA.

*Mantra.*

Then recite the following six mantras to consecrate the six limbs of the body *viz* : the Heart, the Head, the Crown of the head, the Shoulders, the Eyes, and the Palm of the hand.

1. ओं हृदयाय नमः ॥

Om Hṛidayâya namaḥ. Salutation to Om, to the *heart.*

2. सत् शिरसे स्वाहा ॥

Sach-chhirase Svâhâ. Svâhâ to the Good, to the *head.*

3. चित्शिखायै वषट् ॥

Chich-chhikhâyai vaṣaṭ. Vaṣaṭ to the Wise to the *crown* of the head.

4. एकम् कवचाय हुं ॥

Ekam kavachâya huṃ. Huṃ to the One to the *shoulders.*

5. ब्रह्म नेत्रत्रयाय वौषट् ॥

Brahma netra-trayâya vauṣaṭ. Vauṣaṭ to God to the three eyes.

6. 'ओं सत्चित् एकम् ब्रह्म करतलपृष्ठाभ्यां फट् ॥

Om sach-chid-ekam Brahma karatala-priṣṭhâbhyâm phaṭ. Phaṭ to the palms and back of the two hands, to Om the God the Good, the Wise and the One.

### IV.—PRÂṆÂYÂMA OR BREATH-REGULATION.

(*a*) *Pûraka or inspiration.*

Then perform the regulation of breath, while drawing it in through the right nostril, the left nostril being closed with the ring and middle fingers. This is called Pûraka. While drawing in the breath let him recite ;—eight times either the full mantra or merely Om thus :—

Om Sach-Chid-Ekam Brahma, or Om. (*Eight* times).

(*b*) *Kumbhaka or retention.*

Then close the right nostril with the thumb finger and retain the breath, by thus closing both the nostrils. Repeat the same mantra thirty two times. This is called Kumbhaka or retention of breath. The mantra is the same :—

Om Sach-Chid-Ekam Brahma or Om. (*Thirty-two* times.)

(*c*) *Rechaka or expiration.*

Then expire the air slowly through the same right nostril, by which it was filled, reciting the same mantra *sixteen* times, *viz.*:—

Om Sach-Chid-Ekam Brahma, or Om. (*Sixteen* times).

*Note.*—This triple process constitutes *one* prâṇâyâma. It is different from the previous processes described in Vedic Sandhyâ, in as much as the *left* nostril is to be closed and the air *is drawn* through the *right* nostril and expired also through the *same* nostril, in the *first* process.

*Note.*—The Prâṇâyâma is to be repeated *thrice.* But in the second Prâṇâyâma, the *right* nostril is to be closed with the thumb finger, and the air drawn through the *left* nostril, and after Kumbhaka, expelled through the same *left* nostril.

The third Prâṇâyâma is like the first.

In every Sandhyâ at least *three* prâṇâyâmas should be performed.

### V.—DHYÂNA.

Then perform dhyâna with the following mantra :—

हृदयकमलमध्ये निर्विशेषं निरीहम् ।

हरिहरविधिवेद्यं योगिभिर्ध्यानगम्यम् ।

जननमरणभीतिभ्रंशि सच्चित्स्वरूपम् ।

सकलभुवनबीजं ब्रह्मचैतन्यमीडे ॥

Hṛidaya-Kamala-madhye nirviśeṣam nirîham,

Hari-Hara-Vidhi-vedyam yogibhir dhyâna-gamyam.

Janana-maraṇa-bhiti-bhraṁśi sach-chit-svarûpam,

Sakala-bhuvana-bîjam Brahma chaitanyam iḍe.

*Word-meaning* :—

Hṛidaya, Heart. Kamala, Lotus. Madhye, In the middle. Nirviseṣam, Free from all specific differences. Nirîham, Without any desire. (Because he is the Lord over all). Hari-Hara-Vidhi-vedyam, Known by Hari (Viṣṇu), Hara (Śiva) and Vidhi (Brahmâ). Yogibhir, By the seers, contemplative sages. Dhyâna-gamyam, Obtained through mystic meditation called dhyâna. Janana, Birth. Maraṇa, Death. Bhîti, Fear. Bhraṁśi, Destroyer. Sach-chit-savarûpam, Whose essential form is Existence and Knowledge. Sakala-bhuvana-bîjam, The seed or cause of the entire Universe or cosmos. Brahma, God. Chaitanyam, All-consciousness. Iḍe, I meditate, I gloryfy.

*Translation* :—I meditate on God, the All-knowing, within the lotus of my heart. He is free from all limiting attributes and desires, and is the object of knowledge to the highest intelligences like Brahmâ, Viṣṇu and Maheśa, Who is known by mystic meditation by the contemplative sages, Who destroys the fear of birth and death, Whose essential nature is pure existence and knowledge, and Who is the cause of the entire universe.

*Directions* :—

The God must be meditated in the heart, as possesing the above attributes. He has no form but for conveniance of fixing the mind He may be considered as a steady flame of life burning in the heart.

### VI.—PÛJA.

Having thus meditated on God, offer him pûjâ with scents, flowers, incense, light and food. Of course these things are all to be offered metaphorically. The five primordial elements or states in which matter exists are the five offerings to God *viz* :—the solid or physical, the liquid or astral, the gaseous or mental, the luminous or Heavenly and the etheric or Atmic conditions of matter. Recite the following mantras in making these mental offerings :—

1. Lam prithvy-âtmakam gandham samarpayâmi namaḥ.

Lam I offer scent in the shape of solid matter or earth-tattva Hail.

2. Ham âkâśatamakam puṣpam samarpayâmi namaḥ.

Ham I offer flower in the shape of etheric matter or âkâśa tatva.

3. Yam vâyu-âtmakam dhupam samarpayâmi namaḥ. Yam I offer incense in the shape of gaseous matter, Hail !

4. Ram teja-âtmakam dîpam samarpayâmi namaḥ. Ram I offer light in the shape of luminous matter, Hail.

5. Vam amṛitâtmakam naivedyam samarpayâmi namaḥ. Vam I offer food in the shape of nectar, Hail.

After having made these five offerings with the five fingers in the manner kara-nyâsa *viz* :—With the two ring fingers, the two thumbs, the index fingers, the two middle fingers and the two ring fingers respectively, let him join both hands in the form of Añjali offering with the following mantras.

6. Aim sarvâ-tmakam tâmbulam samarpayâmi namaḥ. Aim I offer betel in the shape of the whole world, Hail.

After performing this mental offering let him consecrate the food &c., with the mantra given in the next page.

### VII. JAPA.

Having finished the mental pûjâ, let him recite the mantra, Om Sach-Chid Ekam Brahma, mentaly hundred and eight times, and then finish the japa by saying :—

Om Brahmarpaṇam astu. Let the fruit of all this go to God.

### VIII. EXTERNAL PÛJÂ.

After finishing Japa prayer let perform external pûjâ with external objects such as scents, flowers, clothes, ornaments, food, drink &c. The great consecration mantra should be recited to sanctyfy all these objects and to convert them into sacraments.

Brahmarpaṇam Brahma-havir brahm-âgnau Brahmaṇa hutam,
Brahmaiva tena gantavyam Brahma karma-samâdhina,

*Translation.*—God is the sacrificial vessel, God is the sacrificial offering, God is the sacrificial fire, in which the offering is poured, and by God is the offering made. Verily to God does he go by performing this act of conscentrating on God.

*Direction.*—Having thus consecrated these objects let him close his eyes and meditate on Brahman and recite the sacred mantra, Om, Sach-Chid Ekam Brahma, hundred and eight times or as many times as he likes, and then finish the Japa by saying Om Brahmarpaṇam astu, as before.

Then he should open his eyes and recite the Mûla mantra, Om Sach-Chid Ekam Brahma. Om God is the One the All knowing and the True being. Then he should offer the fruit of this Japa or Prayer by saying "O Lord I do not want any merit for this Prayer but let the result of it I offer to God."

Then let him recite the following hymn in praise of God.

### IX. BRAHMA STOTRA.

ओं नमस्ते सते सर्वलोकाश्रयाय ।
नमस्ते चिते विश्वरूपात्मकाय ।
नमोऽद्वैततत्त्वाय मुक्तिप्रदाय
नमो ब्रह्मणे व्यापिने निर्गुणाय ॥

Om namaste state sarva-lok-âśrayaya,
Namaste Chite Viśva-rûp-âtmakaya,
Namo-dvaita-tattvâya mukti-pradyya,
Namo Brahmaṇe vyâpine nir-guṇâya.

*Translation.*—Om Salutation to Thee the All-being, the refuge of all worlds.

Salutation to thee O All-Intelligence who art the soul of all forms of consciousness.

Salutation to Thee O One without a second, O Giver salvation.

Salutation to Thee O God All pervading and without attributes.

त्वमेकं शरण्यं त्वमेकं वरेण्यम्
त्वमेकं जगत्कारणं विश्वरूपम् ।
त्वमेकं जगत्कर्तृपातृप्रहर्तृ
त्वमेकं परं निश्चलं निर्विकल्पम् ॥

2. Tvam Ekam Śaraṇyam Tvam Ekam Vareṇyam,
Tvam Ekam Jagat-Kâraṇam Viśva Rûpam,
Tvam Ekam Jagat-Kartṛi-Pâtṛi-Prahartṛi,
Tvam Ekam Param Niśchalam Nirvikalpam.

*Translation.*—Thou art the Sole Refuge, Thou art the sole adorable.

Thou art the One cause of the Universe under all forms.

Thou art alone the Creator, the Preserver and Destroyer of the world.

Thou alone art the Highest Immutable and the ineffable.

भयानां भयं भीषणं भीषणानाम्
गतिः प्राणिनां पावनं पावनानाम् ।
महोच्चैः पदानां नियन्तृत्वमेकम्
परेषां परं रक्षकं रक्षकाणाम् ॥

3. Bhayânâm bhyam bhîṣaṇam bhîṣaṇânâm ;
Gatiḥ prâṇinâm pâvanam pâvanânâm ;
Mahochchaiḥ padânâm niyantṛi tvam ekam ;
Pareṣâm param rakṣakam rakṣakânam.
*Translation.*—Dread of the dreadful, Terror of the terrible.
Refuge of all beings, Purificator of all purificators.
Thou alone rulest the high-placed ones,
Supreme over the Supreme Protector of the Protectors.

परेश प्रभो सर्वरूपाप्रकाशिन्
अनिर्देश्य सर्वेन्द्रियागम्य सत्य ।
अचिन्त्याक्षर व्यापकाव्यक्ततत्त्व
जगद्भासकाधीश पायादपायात् ॥

4. Pareśa prabho sarva-rup-aprakaśin ;
Anirdśya sarvendriy-agamya satya ;
Achintyakṣara vyâpakâvyaktatattva ;
Jagad-bhâṣakadhîśa ; pâyâd apât.

*Translation.*

O supreme Lord in whom all things are, yet Unmanisfest in all,
Imperceptible by the senses, yet the very truth.
Incomprehensible, Imperishable, All-pervading hidden Essence.
Lord and Light of the Universe ! save us from harm.

तदेकं स्मरामस्तदेकं जपामः
तदेकं जगत्साक्षिरूपं नमामः ।
सदेकं निधानं निरालम्बमीशम्
भवाम्भोऽधिपोतं शरण्यं व्रजामः ॥

5. Tad ekam smarâmas tad ekam japâmḥ;
Tad ekam Jagat-sâkṣi-rûpam namâmaḥ;
Sad ekam Nidhânam nirâlambamîśam;
Bhâvambhodhi-potam Śaraṇyam vrajâmaḥ.

*Translation.*

On that One alone we meditate, that One alone we in mind worship,
To that one alone the witness of the Universe we bow.
Refuge we seek with the One who is our sole Eternal Support,
The self-existent Lord, the Vessel of safety in the ocean of being.

### X.—BRAHMA KAVACHA.

After reciting the Prayer or Stotra let him recite the following verses to protect his body, and praying to God for health. These verses are called the amulet or Kavacha. Some write these verses and wear it as an amulet or Kavacha:—

Paramâtma śiraḥ pâtu, hridayam parameśvaraḥ,
Kaṇṭhkan pâtu jagat-pâta vadanam sarva drig bibhûḥ,
Karau me pâtu viśvâtmâ padau rakṣatu chin-mayaḥ,
Sarvâṅgam sarvadâ pâtu parama Brahma Sanâtanam.

*Translation*:—

May the Supreme Soul protect the head,
May the Supreme Lord protect the heart,
May the Protector of the World protect the throat,
May the All-pervading, All-seeing Lord protect the face.
May the soul of the Universe protect my hands,
May He Who is Intelligence itself protect the feet,
May the Eternal and Supreme Brahman protect the feet,
May the Eternal and Supreme Brahman Protect my body in all its parts always.

*Note*:—The Riṣi of this world-beneficent amulet is Śada-śiva; the verse is anuṣṭup, its presiding Devatâ is the Supreme Brahman and object of its use is the attainment of Dharma, Artha, Kâma, and Mokṣa. He who recites this protective Mantra after offering it to its Riṣi attains knowledge of Brahman, and is one immediately with the Brahman. If written on birchbark and encased in a golden ball, it be worn round the neck or on the right arm, its wearer attains all kinds of powers.

### XI.—PRAṆÂMA.

Then let him salute the supreme Brahman with the following prayer:—

Om Namaste Paramam-Brahma namaste paramâtmane,

Nirguṇaya namas tubhyam sad-rûpâya namo-namaḥ.

*Translation.*

I bow to the Supreme Brahman.

I bow to the Supreme Soul.

I bow to Him Who is above all qualities.

I bow to the Ever-existent again and again.

### XII.—THE DISTRIBUTION OF THE HOLY FOOD.

After purification by the Brahma-mantra, whatever food or drink is offered to the Supreme Lord becomes itself purifying. The touch of inferior castes may pollute the water Gangâ and the Śâligram, but nothing which has been consecrated to the Brahman can be so polluted. If dedicated to Brahman with this Mantra, the worshipper with his people may eat of any thing whether cooked or uncooked. In the partaking of this food no rule as to caste or time need be observed. No one should hesitate to take the leavings from the plate of another, whether such another be pure or impure.

Whenever and whatsoever the place may be howsoever it may have been attained, eat without scruple or inquiry the food dedicated to the Brahman. Such food, O Devi! even the Devas do not easily get, and it purifies mouth of a dog. As to that which the partaking of such food affects in men, what O Adored of the Devas! shall we say of? It is deemed excellent even by the Devas. Without a doubt the partaking of this holy food be it but once only frees the greatest of sinners and all sinners of their sins. The mortal who eats of it acquires such merit as can only otherwise be earned by bathing and alms at thirty-five millions of holy place.

### XIII.—GÂYATRÎ.

After the distribution of Prasâda (holy food) let him perform the Sandhyâ strictly so called, by the recitation of the following Gâyatrî 108 times:—

*Gâyatrî.*—"Parmeśvarâya vidmahe Paratattvâya dhîmahi, Tanno Brahma prachodayat."

*Translation.*—"May we know the Supreme Lord; let us contemplate the Supreme Essence, and may that Brahman direct us."

### XIV.—PRAṆÂMA.

Then let him make obeisance to the Supreme with the Mantra previously given *viz*:—

Om Namaste Pramam-Brahma Namaste paramâtmane,

Nirguṇâya namas tubhyam sad-rûpâya namo namaḥ.

*Translation.*—I bow to the Supreme Brahman, I bow to the Supreme Soul, I bow to Him Who is above all qualities, I bow to the ever-existent again and again.

*Note.*—Thus ends the Universal Sandhyâ, which differs from the ordinary Sandhya in as much as it combines the elements of Pûjâ also. It may properly be called Pûjâ plus Sandhyâ. The ceremonial purity required in ordinary Sandhyâ is not a *sine qua non* in this mode of worship and meditation. To get perfection in the japa of Brahma Mantra (Om Sach-Chid Ekam Brahma) it should be recited thirty two thousand times accompanied by fire oblations three thousand two hundred times and offering of water to the Devata three hundred and twenty times and for mental purification before worship and sacred bath thirty two times. In other words thirty two with its multiple of ten should be employed for this puras-charaṇa.

---

## CHAPTER XII.

## PÛJÂ OR WORSHIP.

After Brahma-yajña or the study of the sacred scriptures, the pious Hindu performs the worship of his tutelary deity. Though one may belong to any one of the various sects into which the Hindu religious community is divided, yet, so great is the tolerance of the people, both learned and illiterate that every one worships the Pañcha Devatâs (the five deities). The Iṣṭa Devatâ is the principal deity in one's Pûjâ, but the worship is not considered complete, till the honor is paid to the others.

The five deities are the Âditya (the Solar Logos), Gaṇeśa (the Lord of Hosts), the Devî (the Word), Rudra (Śiva), and Nârâyaṇa (the Saviour of souls).

After finishing the worship of the Pañcha Devatâs, he should worship the family deity (Kula-Devatâ) who is generally the Iṣṭa Devatâ.

As a sample, we give below the method of Viṣṇu Pûjâ.

### THE PÛJÂ OF VIṢṆU.

Being seated on a pure âsana, perform the âchamana (see pp. 13—14), and perform snâna of the Śâligrâma with the following mantras :—

ओं सहस्रशीर्षा पुरुषः सहस्राक्षः सहस्रपात् ।

स भूमिं विश्वतो वृत्वाऽत्यतिष्ठद् दशाङ्गुलम् ॥ १ ॥

(Rig. Veda. X. 90. 1.)

Pada Pâṭha :—सहस्रऽशीर्षा। पुरुषः । सहस्रऽअक्षः। सहस्रऽपात् । सः। भूमिम् । विश्वतः । वृत्वा । अति । अतिष्ठत् । दशऽअङ्गुलम् ।

Om ! Sahasra śîrṣâ puruṣaḥ Sahasrâkṣaḥ sahasrapât, sa bhûmim viśvato vritvâ tyatiṣṭhad daśâṅgulam,

*Word meaning* :—सहस्रशीर्षा=Thousand-headed, पुरुषः=Puruṣa, the spirit, सहस्राक्षः=Thousand-eyed, सहस्रपात्=Thousand-footed, सः = He, भूमिं =earth, विश्वतः =on every side, वृत्वा=pervading अत्यतिष्ठत्=stands over, दशाङ्गुलम्=ten fingers.

1. A thousand heads hath the Puruṣa, a tnousand eyes, a thousand feet.

Though He pervades the universe on all sides, yet He occupies a space ten fingers wide (the heart). Or on every side pervading the universe, He extends beyond the space ten fingers wide.

पुरुष एवेदं सर्वं यद् भूतं यच्च भाव्यम् ।

उतामृतत्वस्येशानो यदन्नेनातिरोहति ॥ २ ॥

Pada Pâṭha :—पुरुषः । एव । इदम् । सर्वम् । यत् । भूतम् । यत् । । च भाव्यम् ।
उत । अमृतऽत्वस्य । ईशानः । यत् । अन्नेन । अतिरोहति ।

Puruṣaevedam sarvam yadbhûtam yachcha bhâvyam

Utâmṛitatvasyeśâno yadannenâtirohati.

*Word meaning* :—पुरुषः =Puruṣa, एव=even, इदं=this (world), सर्वम्=all, यत्=that, भूतं past (world), यत् that, च and, भाव्यम्=is to be, future (world), उत =so, अमृतत्वस्य=of Immortality, यत्=which, अन्नेन=by food अतिरोहति=waxes.

2. This Puruṣa is all that yet hath been and all that is to be.

Though Lord of immortality yet through Matter He evolves (that the Jîvas may get their Karmaphala, the fruition of action).

एतावानस्य महिमातो ज्यायांश्च पूरुषः ।

पादोऽस्य विश्वा भूतानि त्रिपादस्यामृतं दिवि ॥ ३ ॥

Pada Pâṭha :—एतावान् । अस्य । महिमा । अतः । ज्यायान् । च । पूरुषः ।
पादः । अस्य । विश्वा । भूतानि । त्रिऽपात् । अस्य । अमृतम् । दिवि ।

Etâwânasya mahimâ'to jyâyâṃścha Pûruṣaḥ.

Pâdo'sya viśvâbhûtâni tripâdasyâ mṛitaṃ divi.

*Word meanning* :—एतावान्=So much, अस्य=His, महिमा=greatness, अतः=from this, ज्यायान्=greater, च=and, पूरुषः=Pûruṣa, पादः=a foot, quarter, अस्य=his, विश्वाभूतानि=all creatures, त्रिपात्=three-fourths, अस्य=his, अमृतम्=eternal life, दिवि=in heaven.

3. All this proclaims His greatness, but greater than this is the Puruṣa.

All creatures are one-fourth of him, three-fourths eternal life in heaven.

त्रिपादूर्ध्व उदैत्पुरुषः पादोऽस्येहाभवत्पुनः ।

ततो विष्वङ् व्यक्रामत्साशनानशने अभि ॥ ४ ॥

Pada Pâṭha :—त्रिपात् । ऊर्ध्वः । उत् । ऐत् । पुरुषः । पादः । अस्य । इह । अभवत् । पुनरिति । ततः । विष्वङ् । वि । अक्रामत् । साशनानशने । इति । अभि ।

Tripâdûrdhva udait Puruṣaḥ Pâdo'sye hâbhavat punaḥ.
Tato viṣvaṅ vyakrâmat sâśanâ naśane abhi.

*Word meanning* :—त्रिपात्=Threefourths, ऊर्ध्वः=up, high, उदैत्=went up, पादः=a quarter, अस्य=his, इह—in this, अभवत्=was, पुनर्=again, ततः=thence, विष्वङ्=all, वि, अक्रामत्=strode out, साशनानशने,=what eats not and what eats.

4. With three fourths the Puruṣa went up ; one-fourth of him again was here.

Thence he strode out to every side over what eats not and what eats.

तस्माद्विराडजायत विराजो अधि पूरुषः ।

सजातो अत्यरिच्यत पश्चाद्भूमिमथो पुरः ॥ ५ ॥

Pada Pâṭha :—तस्मात् । विऽराट् । अजायत । विऽराजः । अधि । पूरुषः । सः । जातः । अति । अत्यरिच्यत । पश्चात् । भूमिम् । अथ । पुरः ।

Tasmâd virâṭajâyata virâjo adhipûruṣaḥ ; sajâto atya richyata paśchâd bhûmim atho puraḥ.

*Word meanning* :—तस्मात्=from him, विराट=Virâja, अजायत=was born, विराजः=from Virâja, अधि=great, पूरुषः=Pûruṣa, सः=he, जातः=was born, अत्यरिच्यत=spread, पश्चात्=behind or westward, भूमिम्=over the earth, अथ=so, पुरः=before.

5. From him Virâja was born ; again a Person from Virâj was born. As soon as he was born he spread, eastward and westward o'er the earth.

यत्पुरुषेण हविषा देवा यज्ञमतन्वत ।

वसन्तोऽस्यासीदाज्यं ग्रीष्म इध्मः शरद्धविः ॥ ६ ॥

Pada Pâṭha :—यत् । पुरुषेण । हविषा । देवाः । यज्ञम् । अतन्वत । वसन्तः । अस्य । आसीत् । आज्यम् । ग्रीष्मः । इध्मः । शरत् । हविः ।

Yat puruṣeṇa haviṣâ devâ yajñam atanvata
Vasanto asyâśîd âjyam grîṣma idhmaḥ śarad haviḥ.

*Word meaning* :—यत्=when, पुरुषेण=by or with Pûruṣa, हविषा=as offering, देवाः=Gods, यज्ञम्=the sacrifice, अतन्वत=prepared, वसन्तः=spring, अस्य=its, आसीत्=was, आज्यम्=oil, ग्रीष्मः=summer, इध्मः=wood, शरत्=autumn, हविः=holy gift.

6. When Gods prepared the sacrifice with Puruṣa as their offering, Its oil was spring, the holy gift was autumn, summer was the wood.

तं यज्ञं बर्हिषि प्रौक्षन्पुरुषं जातमग्रतः ।

तेन देवा अयजन्त साध्या ऋषयश्च ये ॥ ७ ॥

Pada Pâṭha :—तम् । यज्ञम् । बर्हिषि । प्र । औक्षन् । पुरुषम् । जातम् । अग्रतः । तेन । देवाः । अयजन्त । साध्याः । ऋषयः । च । ये ।

Tam yajñam barhiṣi praukṣan puruṣam jâtam agratah
Tena devâ ayajanta sâdhyâ ṛiṣayaś cha ye.

*Word meaning* :—तम् = that, यज्ञम् = sacrifice, बर्हिषि = (lit.) on the *kuśa* grass or in the mental sacrifice, प्रौक्षन् = sprinkled, balmed, जातम् = born, अग्रतः = in early time, तेन = with him, देवाः = the gods, अयजन्त = performed, साध्याः = sâddhyas, ऋषयः = Riṣis च = and, ये who.

7. They balmed as victim on the grass Puruṣa born in the earliest time.

With him the deities and all Sâdhyas and Riṣis sacrificed.

तस्माद् यज्ञात् सर्वहुतः संभृतं पृषदाज्यम् ।
पशून् तांश्चक्रे वायव्यान् आरण्यान् ग्राम्याश्च ये ॥ ८ ॥

Pada Pâṭha :—तस्मात् । यज्ञात् । सर्वऽहुतः सम् ऽभृतम् । पृषत् आज्यम् । पशून् । तान् । चक्रे । वायव्यान् । आरण्यान् । ग्राम्याः । च । ये ।.

Tasmâd yajñât sarva hutaḥ sambhṛitam pṛiṣadâjyam,
Paśûn tâmś chakre vâyavyân âraṇyân grâmyâś cha ye.

*Word meaning* :—तस्मात् = from that, यज्ञात् = sacrifice, सर्वऽहुतः = fully offered, संभृतं = performed, पृषत् आज्यम् = curd and Ghee, पशून् = animals, तान् = them, वायव्यान् = creatures of the air, आरण्यान् = animals of the forest, ग्राम्याः = animals of the village, च = and ये = who.

8. From that great general sacrifice the dripping fat was gathered up.

He formed the creatures of the air, and animals both wild and tame.

तस्माद् यज्ञात् सर्वहुत ऋचः सामानि जज्ञिरे ।
छन्दांसि जज्ञिरे तस्माद् यजुस्तस्मादजायत ॥ ९ ॥

Pada Pâṭha :—तस्मात् । यज्ञात् । सर्वऽहुतः । ऋचः । सामानि । जज्ञिरे । छन्दांसि । जज्ञिरे । तस्मात् । यजुः । तस्मात् । अजायत ।

Tasmâd yajñât sarva huta Richaḥ Sâmâni jajñire,
Chhandâmsi jajñire tasmâd yajus tasmâd ajâyata.

*Word meaning* :—तस्मात् = from that, यज्ञात् = sacrifice, सर्वहुतः = fully offered, ऋचः = Richas, सामानि = Sâmas, जज्ञिरे = were born, छन्दांसि = Vedas or spells and charms or गायत्री, तस्मात् = from that, यजुः = Yajur veda, तस्मात् = from that, अजायत = was born.

9. From that great general sacrifice Richas ahd Sâma hymns were born :

Therefrom were spells and charms produced ; the Yajus had its birth from it.

तस्माद् अश्वा अजायन्त ये के चोभयादतः ।

गावो ह जज्ञिरे तस्मात् तस्माज् जाता अजावयः ॥ १० ॥

pada Pâṭha :—तस्मात् । अश्वाः । अजायन्त । ये । के । च । उभयादतः गावः।

ह । जज्ञिरे । तस्मात् । तस्मात् जाताः । अजावयः ।

Tasmâd aśvâ ajâyanta, ye ke cha ubbhayâdataḥ.

Gâvo ha jajñire tasmât, tasmât jâtâḥ ajâvayaḥ.

*Word meaning* :—तस्मात् = from that, अश्वाः = horses, अजायन्त = were born, ये = who, के च = so ever, (besides horses) उभयादतः = cattle with two rows of teeth, ह = also, गावः = cows, जज्ञिरे = were generated, तस्मात् = from that, जाताः = were born, अजावयः = goats.

10. From it were horses born, from it all cattle with two rows of teeth :
From it were generated kine, from it the goat and sheep were born.

यत् पुरुषं व्यदधुः कतिधा व्यकल्पयन् ।

मुखं किम् अस्य कौ बाहू का ऊरू पादा उच्येते ॥ ११ ॥

Pada Pâtha :—यत् । पुरुषम् । वि । अदधुः। कतिधा । वि । अकल्पयन् । मुखम् । किम् । अस्य । कौ । बाहू इति । किम् । ऊरू इति । पादौ । उच्येते । इति ।

Yat Puruṣam yadadhuḥ katidhâ vyakalpayan.

Mukham kim asya kau bâhû kâ ûrû pâdâ uchyete.

*Word meaning* :—यत् = when that, पुरुषम् = Puruṣa, व्यदधुः = created by thought power, कतिधा = in how many ways, व्यकल्पयन् created in diverse ways, मुखम् = mouth, किम् = what, अस्य, = his, कौ, = what, बाहू = two arms किम् = what, ऊरू = two thighs, पादौ = two feet, उच्येते = were called.

11. When they divided Puruṣa how many portions did they make ? What do they call his mouth, his arms ? What do they call his thighs and feet ?

ब्राह्मणोऽस्य मुखम् आसीद् बाहू राजन्यः कृतः ।

ऊरू तदस्य यद् वैश्यः पद्भ्यां शूद्रो अजायत ॥ १२ ॥

Pada Pâtha :—ब्राह्मणः । अस्य । मुखम् । आसीत् । बाहू इति । राजन्यः । कृतः । ऊरू इति । तत् । अस्य । यत् । वैश्यः । पद्ऽभ्याम् । शूद्रः । अजायत ।

Brâhmano'sya mukham âsid. bâhû Râjanyaḥ kṛitaḥ.

Urû tad asya yad Vaiśyaḥ, padbhyâm Śûdro ajâyata.

*Word meaning* :—ब्राह्मणः—Brâhmaṇa, अस्य, = his, मुखं = mouth, आसीत् = was, बाहू (two) hands, राजन्यः = the Kṣatriyas, कृतः = made, ऊरू = (two) thighs, तत् = that, अस्य = his, यत् वैश्यः = Vaiśya, पद्भ्याम् = from two legs, शूद्रः = Śûdra, अजायत = was born.

12. The Brâhman was his mouth, of both his arms was the Râjanya made.

His thighs became the Vaiśya, from his feet the Śûdra was produced.

चन्द्रमा मनसो जातश्चक्षोः सूर्यो अजायत ।

मुखाद् इन्द्रश्चाग्निश्च प्राणाद् वायुरजायत ॥ १३ ॥

Pada Pâṭha :—चन्द्रमाः । मनसः । जातः । चक्षोः । सूर्यः । अजायत । मुखात् । इन्द्रः । च । अग्निः । च । प्राणात् । वायुः अजायत ।

Chandramâ manaso jâtaś chakṣoḥ Sûryo ajâyata,

Mukhâd Indraś châgnis cha, Prâṇâd Vâyur ajâyata.

*Word meaning* :—चन्द्रमाः = the moon, मनसः = from mind, जातः = was born, चक्षोः = from eye, सूर्यो = the sun, अजायत = was born, मुखात् = from mouth, इन्द्रः = Indra, च = and, अग्निः = the fire, प्राणात् = from breath, वायुः = the air, अजायत = was born.

13. The Moon was gendered from his mind, from his eye the sun had birth;

Indra and Agni from his mouth were born and Vâyu from his breath.

नाभ्या आसीदन्तरिक्षं शीर्ष्णो द्यौः समवर्तत ।

पद्भ्यां भूमिं दिशः श्रोत्रात् तथा लोकां अकल्पयन् ॥ १४ ॥

Pada Pâṭha :—नाभ्या । आसीत् । अन्तरिक्षम् । शीर्ष्णः । द्यौः । सम् । अवर्तत । पद्भ्याम् । भूमिः दिशः । श्रोत्रात् । तथा । लोकान् । अकल्पयन् ।

Nâbhyâ âsîd antariksam śirṣṇo Dyauḥ samavartata,

Padbhyâm Bhûmir, diśaḥ śrotrât, tathâlokân akalpayan.

*Word meaning* :—नाभ्या = from navel, आसीत् = was, अन्तरिक्षम् = mid air, शीर्ष्णः = from head, द्यौः – sky, समवर्तत = was fashioned, पद्भ्याम् = from two feet, भूमिः = earth, दिशः = regions, श्रोत्रात् = from ear, तथा = thus, लोकान् = the worlds, अकल्पयन् = formed.

14. Forth from his navel came mid-air; the sky was fashioned from his head;

Earth from his feet and from his ear the regions. Thus they formed the worlds.

सप्तास्यासन् परिधयस्त्रिःसप्त समिधः कृताः ।

देवा यद् यज्ञं तन्वाना अबध्नन् पुरुषं पशुम् ॥ १५ ॥

Pada Pâṭha :—सप्त । अस्य । आसन् । परिऽधयः । त्रिः । सप्त । सम्ऽइधः । कृताः । देवाः । यत् । यज्ञम् । तन्वानाः । अबध्नन् । पुरुषम् । पशुम् ।

Saptâsyâsan paridhayas triḥ sapta samidhaḥ kṛitâḥ,

Devâ yad yajñam tanvânâ abadhnan puruṣam paśum.

*Word meaning* :—सप्त = seven, अस्य = his, आसन् = were, परिधयः = fencing sticks, त्रिः सप्त = thrice seven, समिधः = layers of fuel, कृताः = were prepared, देवाः = gods, यत् = when, यज्ञम् = sacrifice, तन्वानाः = offering, अबध्नन् = bound, पुरुषम् = Purûṣa, पशुम् = victim, as sacrificial animal.

15. Seven fencing sticks had He, thrice seven layers of fuel were prepared ;

When the Gods offering sacrifice, bound, as their victim, Puruṣa.

यज्ञेन यज्ञमयजन्त देवास्तानि धर्माणि प्रथमान्यासन् ।

तेह नाकं महिमानः सचन्त यत्र पूर्वे साध्याः सन्ति देवाः ॥ १६ ॥

Pada Pàṭha :—यज्ञेन । यज्ञम् । अयजन्त । देवाः । तानि । धर्माणि । प्रथमानि । आसन् । ते । ह । नाकम् । महिमानः । सचन्त । यत्र । पूर्वे । साध्याः । सन्ति । देवाः ।

Yajñena Yajñam ayajanta devâs, tâni dharmâṇi prathamâny âsan.

Te ha nâkam mahimânaḥ sachanta, yatra pûrve sâdhyâḥ santi devâḥ.

*Word meaning* :—यज्ञेन, with the Puruṣa as the sacrificial victim, यज्ञम् = sacrifice, अयजन्त = performed, देवाः = gods, तानि = these, धर्माणि = ordinances, प्रथमानि = first, आसन् = were, ते = They, the gods, ह = verily, नाकम् = heaven, महिमानः = greatnes, height, सचन्त = attained, यत्र = where, पूर्वे = in anterior kalpas, साध्याः = became perfected, देवाः = The gods.

16. Gods sacrificing, sacrificed the victim. These were the earliest holy ordinances.

The mighty ones attained the height of heaven, there where the Sâdhyas, Gods of old, are dwelling.

*Tulasi offering.*

Then take up a Túlasi leaf with the thumb and the forefinger, immerse it in white sandal paste, and offer it to Nârâyaṇa placing it on Śaligrâma, reciting the following mantra.

इदं स चन्दनं तुलसीपत्रं ओं नमस्ते बहुरूपाय विष्णवे परमात्मने स्वाहा ।

Idam sa chandanam tulasîpatram Om namaste bahurâpâya Viṣṇave Parmâtmane Svâhâ.

This Tulsi leaf with sandal paste, (I offer) Om, salutation to Thee, multiform ! Viṣṇu ! Highest Self ! Svâhâ.

SURYÂRGHYA.

Then give arghya offering to the sun with the mantra.

ओं नमो विवस्वते ब्रह्मन् भास्वते विष्णुतेजसे ।

जगत् सवित्रे शुचये सवित्रे कर्मदायिने ।

इदं अर्घ्यम् ओं श्रीसूर्याय नमः ।

The arghya offering consists of water with durvâ grass, unhusked rice, sandal paste and flowers. That is take the copper kosâ (vessel), fill it with water, and throw a few blades of durvâ grass, a few grains of unhusked rice, a little of sandal paste and red flowers in it and then offer the arghaya to the sun with the above mantra.

SVASTI VACHANA.

Then let him recite Peace Mantras.

[Of these seven mantras, six are taken from the Rig Veda, and one from the Yajur Veda.]

स्वस्ति न इन्द्रो वृद्धश्रवाः स्वस्ति नः पूषा विश्ववेदाः ।

स्वस्ति नस्तार्क्ष्यो अरिष्टनेमिः स्वस्ति नो बृहस्पतिर्दधातु ॥

(Rig. Veda I. 89. 6.)

Svasti na Indro Vriddhas'ravâ Svasti naḥ Pûṣâ Viśvavedâḥ,

Svasti nas Târkṣyo Arishṭanemih, Svasti no Brihaspatir dadhâtu.

*Word meaning* :—स्वस्ति = Svasti, prosperity; immortality; indestructibility; welfare. नः = Naḥ, us. इन्द्रः = Indraḥ, Inera or the Powerful, a name of Viṣṇu. वृद्धश्रवाः = Vriddhaśravâḥ, illustrious; far-praised (śrava); whose praises are sung far and wide, of ancient fame; praised of yore. स्वस्ति = Svasti, prosperity. नः = Naḥ, us. पूषा = Pûṣâ, Pûṣân, the nourisher, a name of Viṣṇu. विश्ववेदाः = Viśvavedâḥ, the Knower of all or the possessor of all wealth (Vedâṇsi, Dhanâni.) स्वस्ति = Svasti, welfare. नः = Naḥ, us. तार्क्ष्यः = Târkṣyah, the son of Trikṣa or motion, *i.e.*, Garuḍa, a name of Viṣṇu. अरिष्टनेमिः = Ariṣta-nemi, uninjured chariot felly. (Nemi) the rim of whose chariot wheel is perfect and imperishable, whose weapons (nemi) are not injured (ariṣṭa) by any opponent; safety-wheeled. स्वस्ति नः = Svasti naḥ, preperity to us. बृहस्पतिः = Brihaspatih, the Lord of Mighty ones, a name of Viṣṇu. दधातु = Dadhâtu, may vouchsafe.

May Viṣṇu the powerful, the Ancient of days, vouchsafe unto us prosperity, may Viṣṇu the nourisher, the knower of all hearts, give us what is well for us, may Viṣṇu the Lord of swift motion, the felly of whose wheel never wears out, be propitious to us, may Viṣṇu the protector of the great ones, protect us too.

गणानां त्वा गणपति ꣳ हवामहे प्रियाणां त्वा प्रियपति ꣳ हवामहे निधीनां त्वा

निधिपति ꣳ हवामहे वसो मम । ओं स्वस्ति ओं स्वस्ति ओं स्वस्ति ।

Yajur Veda XXIII. 19.

Gaṇânâṁ tvâ Gaṇapatiṁ havâmahe Priyâṇâṁ tvâ priyapatiṁ havâmahe.

Nidhinâm tvâ nidhipatiṁ havâmahe, Vaso! mama. Om Svasti, Om Svasti. Om, Svasti.

*Word meaning*:—गणानां = of forces, त्वा = Thee. गणपतिं = Lord of the troops, हवामहे = we invoke, प्रियाणां = of all the beloved things, त्वा = Thee. प्रियपतिं = Lord of the loved one, हवामहे = we invoke, निधीनां = of treasures, त्वा = Thee, निधिपतिं = Lord of Treasures, हवामहे = we invoke. वसो = Oh wealth, मम = my, ओं स्वस्ति = Om peace.

Thee we invoke, Troop-lord of troops.

Thee we invoke, the loved ones' Lord.

Thee, Lord of treasures, we invoke, my Precious Wealth! Om Peace! Om Peace! Om Peace!

स्वस्ति नो मिमीतामश्विना भगः स्वस्ति देव्यदितिरनर्वणः ।

स्वस्ति पूषा असुरो दधातु नः स्वस्ति द्यावापृथिवी सुचेतुना ॥ ११ ॥

Rig. Veda V. 51, verses 11 to 15.

Svasti no mimitâm Aśvinâ Bhagaḥ Svasti Devî Aditir anarvaṇaḥ,

Svasti Pûṣâ asuro dadhâtu naḥ. Svasti Dyâvâ-Pṛithivî suchetunâ.

*Word meaning*:—स्वस्ति = prosperity, imperishable good, नः = to us. मिमीताम् = may do, अश्विना = the two Asvins, भगः Bhagaḥ, स्वस्ति = prosperity, देवी = Goddess, अदितिः = Aditi, अनर्वणः = Irresistible, स्वस्ति = Svasti, पूषा = the Nourisher, असुरः = giver of life, दधातु = may give, नः = to us, स्वस्ति = Svasti, द्यावापृथिवी = the Heaven and Earth, सुचेतुना = with good intelligence.

May Bhaga and the Aśvinas grant us health and wealth and Goddess Aditi and He whom none resist, the Life-giving Pûṣan grant us all prosperity, and Heaven and Earth most wise vouchsafe us happiness.

स्वस्तये वायुमुपब्रवामहै सोमं स्वस्ति भुवनस्य यस्पतिः ।

बृहस्पतिं सर्वगणं स्वस्तये स्वस्तय आदित्यासो भवन्तु नः ॥ १२ ॥

Svastaye Vâyum upa bravâmahai Somam svasti bhuvanasya yas patiḥ;

Bṛihaspatim sarva gaṇam svastaye, Svastaya âdityâso bhavantu naḥ.

*Word meaning*:—स्वस्तये = for the sake of prosperity, वायुम् = Vâyu, उपब्रवामहै = we praise, solicit, सोमं = Soma, स्वस्ति = prosperity, भुवनस्य = of the world, यः = who, पतिः = the protector, the preserver, the Lord, बृहस्पतिं = Brihaspati or protector of mantras ( बृहत् ) सर्वगणं = with all hosts of Devas, स्वस्तये = for the sake of prosperity, स्वस्तये = for the sake of prosperity; आदित्यासः = the sons of Aditi, *viz.*, all the Devas or the twelve Adityas called Aruṇa, &c., भवन्तु = may be, नः = to us.

Let us solicit Vâyu for prosperity, and Soma who is Lord of all the world for weal; for weal Brihaspati with all his company. May the Âdityâs bring us health and happiness.

विश्वे देवानो अद्या स्वस्तये वैश्वानरो वसुरग्निः स्वस्तये ।

देवाः अवन्त्वृभवः स्वस्तये स्वस्तिनो रुद्रः पात्वंहसः ॥ १३ ॥

Viśve devâno adyâ svastaye Vaiśvânaro vasur Agniḥ svastaye.

Devâḥ avantu Ribhavaḥ svastaye Svasti no Rudraḥ pâtu aṁhasaḥ.

*Word meaning* :—विश्वे = All, देवाः = devas, the shining ones, नः = to us, अद्या = to-day, स्वस्तये = for the sake of prosperity, वैश्वानरः = the leader (nara) of all ( विश्व ), God of all men, वसुः = the receptacle of all, the Home of all, the Benificent, अग्निः = Agni, स्वस्तये = for the sake of prosperity, देवाः = the divine ones, अवन्तु = may protect, ऋभवः = the Ribhavas, स्वस्तये = for our good, स्वस्ति = prosperity, नः = to us, रुद्रः = Rudra or destroyer of sorrow, पातु = may protect, अंहसः = from sins.

May all the Gods, may Agni the beneficent, God of all men, this day be with us for weal; help us the Ribhus, the Divine ones, for our good May Rudra bless and keep us from calamity.

स्वस्ति मित्रावरुणा स्वस्ति पथ्ये रेवति ।

स्वस्ति न इन्द्रश्चाग्निश्च स्वस्ति नो अदिते कृधि ॥ १४ ॥

Svasti mitrâ Varuṇâ svasti pathye revati.

Svasti na Indraśchâgniścha Svasti no adite kṛidhi.

*Word meaning* :—स्वस्ति = Svasti, मित्रा वरुणा = O Mitra and Varuṇa, Lords of day and night, स्वस्ति = Svasti, पथ्ये = O Pathyâ, the goddess of the path of heaven, रेवति = possessing wealth, स्वस्तिनः good to us, इन्द्रः = Indra, च = and, अग्निः = Agni, च = and, स्वस्तिनः = prosperity to us, अदिते = O Aditi, कृधि = do.

Prosper us Mitra, Varuṇa, O wealthy Pathyâ prosper us.

Indra and Agni prosper us; prosper us thou, O Aditi.

स्वस्ति पन्थामनु चरेम सूर्याचन्द्रमसाविव ।

पुनर्ददताघ्नता जानता संगमेमहि ॥ १५ ॥

Svasti panthâm anucharema Sûryâ chandramasâviva.

Punar dadatâ ghnatâ jânatâ saṅgame mahi.

*Word meaning* :—स्वस्ति = Svasti, पन्थानम् = path, अनुचरेम = may we pursue, सूर्याचन्द्रमसौ-इव = like the sun and moon, as they move unobstructed and unsupported in their heavenly path, so may we pursue our path unobstructed by any one, पुनः = again, ददता = the giver, the benefactor, अघ्नता = the non-killer, who does not slay us, जानता = who knows us and therefore does not suspect us, who does not forget us, संगमेमहि = may we meet (again with our friend).

Like sun and moon may we pursue in full prosperity our path, and meet with one who gives again, who knows us well and slays us not.

Then, (if he is a Trivedi), he should recite also :

सूर्यः सोमो यमः कालः संध्ये भूतान्यहः चपा ।

पवनो दिक्पतिर्भूमिराकाशं खचरामराः ।

ब्राह्मं शासनमास्थाय कल्पध्वं इह सन्निधिम् ॥

Om ! Sûryaḥ Somo Yamaḥ Kâlaḥ Sandhye Bhûtâny Ahaḥ Kṣapâ. Pavano Dikpatir Bhûmir Âkâśam khacharâ marâḥ. Brâhmam śâsanam âsthâya kalpadhvam iha sannidhim.

Om ! May the Sun, the Moon, the Lord of death, the Time, the two Twilights, the Day, the Night.

The Wind, the Lord of quarters, the Earth, the Âkâśa and the Immortals that move in the depths of space, may they all approach here, fulfilling the ordinances of the Supreme Brahman.

This is an invocation to that hierarchy of divinities of time, space and worlds, which is the active agent in carrying out the divine will in creation, the so-called laws of nature.

Then taking a flower each time and immersing it in sandal paste let him offer it to every one of the following deities.

एते गन्धपुष्पे ओं विघ्ननाशाय नमः ।

Ete gandha-puṣa Om Vighna-nâśâya namaḥ !

These flower and scent, Om ! to the destroyer of all obstacles ! Hail (offer to Ganeṣa).

एते गन्धपुष्पे ओं आदित्यादिनवग्रहेभ्यो नमः ।

Ete gandha-puṣpe Om Âdityâdi Navagrahebhyo namaḥ.

These flower and scent, Om ! to the nine planets, Âditya and the rest ! Hail !

एते गन्धपुष्पे ओं नमो नारायणाय नमः !

Ete gandha-puṣpe Om ! namo Nârâyaṇâya namaḥ.

These flower and scent, Om ! Hail to Nârâyaṇa Hail.

Having thus worshipped in brief, let him bow down reciting the following Mantra :—

ओं त्रैलोक्यपूजित श्रीमन् सदा विजयवर्धन ।

शान्तिं कुरु गदापाणे नारायण नमोस्तु ते ॥

Om ! Trailokya-pûjita ! Śrîman ! sadâ vijaya vardhana !

Śântim kuru Gadâpâṇe ! Nârâyaṇa ! Namo'stu Te !

Om ! Adored of the three-worlds ! Lord of Śri ! Always victory increasing ! O wielder of the club ! grant peace. O Nârâyaṇa ! All hail to Thee !

Having thus finished the brief pûjâ, he should proceed to consecrate the water.

*The general consecration of water*

or

SÂMANYA ARGHYA.

The method of general consecration of water is applicable to every pûjâ; while there are special methods of the same, when particular deities are worshipped. The method briefly consists in sanctifying first the ground, by invoking the lords of the earth; then placing the Arghya, copper vessel on it, and filling it in slowly with water, reciting certain mantras, and then throwing into it flowers, scent, unhusked rice, Durvâ grass, &c., and lastly, making certain mystical signs and uttering of a Mantra.

First draw a triangle on the ground towards the left hand; the size of the triangle to depend on the size of the copper arghya vessel to be placed on it. Then consecrate this spot with the following mantras:—

ओं आधारशक्त्यै नमः Om Âdhâra śaktyai namaḥ, Om! Hail to the force that sustains the whole cosmos.

ओं कूर्माय नमः Om Kûrmâya namaḥ, Om! Hail to the force that keeps the worlds in their orbit.

ओं अनन्ताय नमः Om Anantâya namaḥ, Om! Hail to the endless force!

ओं पृथिव्यै नमः Om Pṛithivyai namaḥ, Om! Hail to the terrestrial force!

While reciting the above, place with each recitation, flower and unhusked rice on the triangle. Then place on the ground so sanctified, the arghya vessel (the copper Kośâ and Kuśi) uttering फट् Phaṭ. Then fill the arghya vessel with water, uttering नमः namaḥ. Then put in this water, some durvâ grass, unhusked rice, flowers and sandal paste. Then hold the palms of the hand over the water, with fingers bent in the sign called aṅkuśa mûdra and recite.

ओं गङ्गे च यमुने चैव गोदावरि सरस्वति।
नर्म्मदे सिन्धु कावेरि जलेऽस्मिन् सन्निधिं कुरु॥

Om! Gaṅge! cha Yamune! chaiva, Godâvari! Sarasvati!
Narmade! Sindhu! Kâveri! Jale' smin san-niddhiṃ kuru.

Om! O Gaṅgâ! O Yamunâ! O Godâvari! O Sarasvati! O Narmadâ! O Sindhu! O Kâveri! approach and enter this water.

Then show the "Dhenu-mudrâ*" on the water, uttering vaṁ, recite Praṇava (Om) ten times; and sprinkle the head, as well as the pûjâ ingredients with such water.

ÂSANA ŚUDDHI.

or *The purification of the Seat.*

The next thing to do is the sanctifying of the seat, on which the

* अन्योन्याभिमुखा श्लिष्टा कनिष्ठानामिका पुनः।
तथैव तर्ज्जनीमध्या धेनुमुद्रा प्रकीर्त्तिता॥

worshipper sits. It is similar to what has already been described before, in the chapter VI on the Sandhyâ, (pages. 32 and the following.)

Draw a triangle under the âsana, and place on it a flower immersed in sandal paste with the mantra :—

एते गन्धपुष्पे आधारशक्तिकमलासनाय नमः ।

Ete gandha puṣpe Âdhâraśakti kamalâsanâya namaḥ.

These scent and flower to the Lotus Seat, the sustaining Force all Hail!

Then recite—

ओं आसनमन्त्रस्य मेरुपृष्ठ ऋषिः सुतलं छन्दः कूर्मो देवता आसनपरिग्रहे विनियोगः ।

Om! âsanamantrasya Merupṛiṣṭha Ṛiṣiḥ, Sutalaṁ chhandaḥ, Kûrmo Devatâ, âsana parigrahe viniyogaḥ.

Om! of the Âsana mantra, the seer is Meru Pṛiṣṭha; the metre is Sutalam; the Devatâ is Kûrma; and its application is in taking the seat.

ओं पृथ्वि त्वया धृता लोका देवि त्वं विष्णुना धृता । त्वं च धारय मां देवि पवित्रं कुरु चासनम् ॥

*Transliteration* :—Oṁ Pṛithvi tvayâ dhṛitâ lokâ, devi tvam Viṣṇunâ dhṛitâ, tvaṁ cha dhâraya mâm devi, pavitram kuru châsanam.

*Translation* :—O Earth, all creatures are upheld by thee : O Devi, thou art supported by Viṣṇu ; support me thou O Goddess, and sanctify my seat.

Then let him salute on the left side the Gurus, on the right Gaṇeśa, on the Nadir Ananta ; on the zenith Brahman and in the middle (in front) Nârâyaṇa reciting,

ओं ( वामे ) गुरुभ्यो नमः Om (vâme) Gurubhyo namaḥ.

Om salutation to all gurus, (on the left.)

ओं ( दक्षिणे ) गणेशाय नमः Om (Dakṣiṇe) Gaṇeśâya namaḥ.

Om salutation to Gaṇeśa, (on the right.)

ओं ऊर्द्ध्वे ब्रह्मणे नमः Om (Ûrddhve) Brahmaṇe namaḥ.

Om salutation to Brahman, on the zenith.

ओं मध्ये नारायणाय नमः Om (Madhye) Nârâyaṇâya namaḥ.

In the middle, Om salutation to Nârâyaṇa.

Reciting these touch the respective sides.

PUṢPA ŚUDDHIḤ.

or *The purification of flower.*

Touching the flowers, recite the following :—

ओं पुष्पे पुष्पे महापुष्पे सुपुष्पे पुष्पसम्भवे ।

पुष्पचयावकीर्णे च हुं फट् स्वाहा ॥

Om! Puṣpe puṣpe mahâ puṣpe, Supuṣpe Puṣpa sambhave.
Puṣpa chayâva kîrṇe cha. Huṁ Phaṭ Svâhâ.

Then taking one flower squeeze it with both hands, uttering :—ऐं रं अस्त्राय फट् aim ram astrâya Phat.

Then throw the flower to the left side and sprinkle the remaining flowers with a litte water.

### Driving away of the Evil Elementals

### or *Bhûta apasarpaṇam.*

Then drive away all evil elementals, by reciting the following:—

ओं अपसर्पन्तु ते भूता ये भूता भुवि संस्थिताः ।

ये भूता विघ्नकर्तारस्, ते नश्यन्तु ममाज्ञया ॥

Om ! Apasarpantu te bhutâ, Ye bhutâ bhuvi samsthitâḥ ;
Ye bhutâ vighna kartâras Te naśyantu mamâjñayâ.

Let all those Elementals go away, the Elementals, that on earth do dwell; and the Elementals that obstacles raise, may they be destroyed by my command.

Reciting the above, scatter some unhusked rice, on all sides.

### Closing of ten quarters from further attack

### or *Dasa-dik-Bandhanam.*

Then strike the earth with the left foot three times, and uttering Phaṭ, clap thrice raising the hands above the head; and by making "sounds with the fingers" (turi) close all the ten directions to the attack of the insidious.

### Purification of the Bodily Elements

### or *Bhûta Śuddhiḥ.*

Then purify the various subtle bodies by reciting the following four mantras :—

ओं भूतश्रृङ्गाटाच्छिरः सुषुम्ना पथेन जीवशिवं परमशिवपदे योजयामि स्वाहा ।

Om Bhûta-śriṅgâṭâch chhiraḥ Suṣumnâ pathena jîva-śivam Parama-śiva-pade yojayâmi Svâhâ !

Om ! Raising the Jîva-monad from the Mulâdhâra (lit. Elemental-Mountain), slowly through the Suṣumnâ channel of the spinal cord, I unite it with the Supreme Monad in the head. Svâhâ.

ओं यं लिङ्गशरीरं शोषय शोषय स्वाहा ।

Om ! Yam Liṅga Śarîram Śoṣaya śoṣaya svâhâ.

Om Yam ! dry up, dry up (the impurities of the) Liṅga Body (subtle body), svâhâ.

ओं रँ सङ्कोचशरीरं दह दह स्वाहा ।

Om ! Ram ! Saṅkochaśarîra mdaha daha svâhâ !

Om ! Ram ! Burn up, burn up, the body of selfishness, svâhâ !

ओं परमशिव सुषुम्नापथेन मूलश्रृङ्गाटम् उल्लस उल्लस ज्वल ज्वल प्रज्वल प्रज्वल सोऽहं हंसः स्वाहा ।

Om Parama Śiva suṣumnâ pathena mûla-śriṅgâṭaṁ ullasa ullasa, jvala jvala, prajvala prajvala, So' ham, haṁsah, svâhâ.

Om! Supreme Śiva! blow upon, blow upon, inflame, inflame, illumine, illumine (the spiritual spark immersed in the) mountain of matter, So'ham (I am He); Hamsaḥ (the eternal swan): Svâhâ.

The above is a short method of performing the purification of the various elements of one's body. The fuller method is this. Imagine the Jiva to be in the heart as a flame of light. Take it down to the Kula Kuṇḍalini in the mulâdhâra or sacral plexus, and then uttering so'haṁ, raise it up through the spinal cord (suṣumnâ) to the top and join it with the supreme Śiva there. In doing so, of course, one has to pass successively through the various chakras that lie between the mulâdhâra and the thousand petalled Lotus or Brain; namely, 1. Mûlâdhâra, 2. Svadhisthâna, 3. Manipuraka, 4. Anâhata, 5. Viśuddha and sixthly Ajña chakras. Having effected the unity of the Trinity, imagine that all the 24 tattvas have come to latency there. Then perform prâṇâyâma.

### PRÂṆÂYÂMA

*or Regulation of Breath.*

Then perform Prâṇâyama as already taught before. (See p. 33.) Form the mental picture of the deity to be worshipped.

---

### *Ganeśa-Pujâ.*

The various steps in every pûjâ are (1) Nyâsas, (2) Dhyâna, (3) Offering of upachâras, (4) Japa, (5) Prayer and (6) Praṇâma. First perform the two Nyâsas, that of the fingers and that of the limbs, as taught in before by uttering :—

### 1. *Kara-nyâsa.*

1. ओं गां अंगुष्ठाभ्यां नमः Om Gâṁ anguṣṭhâbhyâm namaḥ.

Om Gâṁ—salutation to the thumbs.

2. ओं गीं तर्जनीभ्यां स्वाहा Om Gîṁ tarjanîbhyâm svâhâ. (Index finger).

3. ओं गूं मध्यमाभ्यां वषट् Om Gûṁ madhayamâbhyâm vaṣaṭ (middle finger).

4. ओं गैं अनामिकाभ्यां हुं Om Gaiṁ anâmikâbhyâm huṁ. (Ring-finger),

5. ओं गौं कनिष्ठिकाभ्यां वौषट् Om Gauṁ kaniṣṭhikâbhyâm vauṣaṭ. (Little-finger).

6. ओं गः करतलकरपृष्ठाभ्यां अस्त्राय फट् Om Gaḥ karatala karapṛiṣṭhâbhyâm astrâya Phaṭ. (Palm and back of hand).

### (2) ANGA-NYÂSA

*or assignment of bodily members.*

1. गां हृदयाय नमः Gaṁ Hridayâya namaḥ.
2. गीं शिरसे स्वाहा Gîṁ Śirase swâhâ.
3. गूं शिखायै वषट् Gûṁ Śikhâyai vaṣaṭ.

4. गैं कवचाय हुम् Gaiṁ Kavachâya Huṁ.

5. गौं नेत्रत्रयाय वौषट् Gauṁ netratrayâya vauṣaṭ.

6. गः अस्त्राय फट् Gaḥ astráya phaṭ.

It will help the student to remember, if he knows that the first letter of the mantra, in the two nyâsas, is taken from the name of the deity : and then add to it the long vowels and the anusvâra (nasal), thus in the case of Gaṇeśa, the letter ग is taken, in the case of Śiva, the letter श and so on.

(3) DHYÂNA

or *Mental Picture making.*

Then form a mental picture of Gaṇeśa while reciting the following mantra, which gives the description of the form of the deva.

ओं खर्व्वं स्थूलतनुं गजेन्द्रवदनं लम्बोदरं सुन्दरं,

प्रस्यन्दन्मदगन्धलुब्धमधुपव्यालोलगण्डस्थलम् ।

दन्ताघातविदारितारिरुधिरैः सिन्दूरशोभाकरं,

वन्दे शैलसुतासुतं गणपतिं सिद्धिप्रदं कर्मसु ॥

Om! kharvam sthûlatanum gajendra vadanam lambodaram sundaram,

Prasyandan-mada-gandha-lubhdha-madhupa-vyâlola-gaṇḍasthalam.

Dantâghâta vidâritâri-rudhiraiḥ sindûra śobhâkaram,

Vande śaila-sutâ-sutam Gaṇapatim siddhi pradam karmasu.

*Word meaning* :—खर्व्वं—short statured, स्थूलतनुं—stout bodied, गजेन्द्रवदनं—elephant faced, लम्बोदरं—of protuberant body or belly, सुन्दरं—beautiful, प्रस्यन्दम्—flowing out, मद—Ichor, गन्ध—fragrance, sweet smell, लुब्ध—entrapped, enamoured, captivated, मधुप—bees, व्यालोल—shaking about, moving about, गण्डस्थलम्—staying in the cheeks, whose cheeks are surrounded by swarms of bees attracted by the sweet scented exudation from his temples, दन्ताघात—blow of the tusks, विदारित-अरि—pierced his enemies, रुधिरैः—by Blood, सिन्दूर—vermilion, शोभाकरं—beautified, वन्दे—I bow, शैल-सुता-सुतं—the son of the daughter of Himâlaya; Parvati's son, गणपतिं—The Lord of Hosts, सिद्धिप्रदं—The giver of success, कर्मसु—In undertakings.

**Translation**—I salute Ganesa, the son of Pârvati, the giver of success in all undertakings, who is of short stature, stout body, elephantface, protuberant belly, and is beautiful; whose cheeks are surrounded by swarms of bees attracted by the sweet-scented exudation from his temples; the blood of his enemies pierced by his tusks adds the magnificent vermillion color to his forehead.

(4) *Upachâra-Offering.*

Having thus pictured the Deity in his heart, offer to this luminious image mental *Pujâ* (worship). Then taking a flower in the hand, project this mental figure on the flower and place it on a flat copper plate used for worship. This flower now forms the external representatiou of Gaṇeśa and external pûjâ is offered to it. Thus :—

एतत् पाद्यं ओं गणेशाय नमः Etat pâdyaṁ oṁ Gaṇeśâya namaḥ. This pâdya (water for washing the feet) I offer to Gaṇeśa. Salutation (Put a little water on the Symbolic flower).

इदमर्घ्यं ओं गणेशाय नमः Idam arghyaṁ oṁ Gaṇeśâya namaḥ.

This arghya to Gaṇeśa. Salutation.

इदं आचमनीयं ओं गणेशाय नमः Idam âchamanîyam &c. This âchamanîya (water) to Gaṇeśa. Salutation.

एष गन्धः, &c., eṣa gendhaḥ, &c. This scent, &c.

एतत् पुष्पं, &c. etat puṣpaṁ, &c. This flower, &c.

एष धूपः, &c., eṣa dhûpaḥ, &c. This dhupa, &c.

एष दीपः, &c., eṣa dîpaḥ, &c. This lamp, &c.

एतन्नैवेद्यं, &c., etan naivedyam, &c. This food, &c.

इदं पानार्थं जलं, &c., Idam pânârthaṁ jalaṁ, &c. This drinking water, &c.,

इदं पुनराचमनीयं &c., Idaṁ punar âchamanîyam, &c. This water for rinsing the mouth again, &c.

एतत् ताम्बूलं, &c. Etat tâmbûlaṁ, &c. This betel leaf, &c.

(The word *etcetra* above means Om Gaṇeśâya namaḥ which is to be added to the end of the above sentences.)

This is the tenfold *upachâra* or offerings ; of course, flowers and water should always be offered. Other offerings like dhûpa, light, &c., are generally repl: ced by water.

### (5) *Japa.*

Having thus performed the pûja, one should repeat the mantra of Gaṇeśa, one hundred and eight times. The mantra is ओं गणेशाय नमः Om Gaṇeśâya namaḥ. Another mantra of Ganeśa is :—ओं श्रीं ह्रीं क्लीं ग्लौं गं गणपतये वर वरद सर्वजनम् मे वशमानय ठः ठः । Oṁ Śrîṁ Hrîṁ, klîṁ, Glauṁ Gaṁ Gaṇapataye vara varada sarva janam me vaśamânaya ṭhaḥ ṭhaḥ.

### (6) *Prayer.*

Then offer the following prayer :—

ओं देवेन्द्र मौलि मन्दार मकरन्द कणारुणाः ।
विघ्नं हरन्तु हेरम्ब चरणाम्बुज रेणवः ॥

Oṃ devendra mauli mandâra makaranda kaṇâruṇâḥ
Vighnam harantu Heramba charaṇâmbuja reṇavaḥ.

*Translation.*—May the dust of the Lotus feet of Ganeśa destroy all obstacles—that luminous dust which is mixed with the pollen of the Heavenly flower fallen from the crown of the Lord of the Devas [Indra] when he bowed to him.

(7) *Bow or Pranâma.*

Then finish the pûjâ with the following pranâma :—

ओं एकदन्तं महाकायं लम्बोदरं गजाननम् ।

विघ्ननाशकरं देवं हेरम्बं प्रणमाम्यहम् ॥

Om ekadantam mahâkâyam lambodaram gajânanam ;
Vighna nâśakaram devam Herambam pranamâmyaham.

*Translation.* I bow to Heramba the Deity who is destroyer of all obstacles, elephant faced, one tusked, big bodied, and protuberant bellied.

*Sûrya Pûjâ.*

Perform then the pûjâ of the Sun in a manner similar to that of Ganeśa, *i. e.*, perform—

(1) Karanyâsa, (2) aṅganyâsa, (3) dhyâna, (4) Offering of the ten upacharas, padya, arghya, &c. (5) Japa of the mantra of the deity, (6) Prârthana or prayer, and (7) pranâma or Salutation.

The dhyâna of Sûrya is performed by the following which describes the mental picture to be formed.

ओं रक्ताम्बुजासनमशेषगुणैकसिन्धुं,

भानुं समस्तजगतामधिपं भजामि ।

पद्मद्वयाभयवरं दधतं कराब्जै-

र्माणिक्यमौलिमरुणाङ्गरुचिं त्रिनेत्रम् ॥

Om raktâmbujâsanamaśeṣa gunaika sindhum,
Bhânuṁ samasta jagatâmadhipam bhajâmi ;
Padma dvayâbhaya varam dadhatam karâbjair,
Mânikya mauli marunaṅga ruchim trinettram.

*Word meaning* :—रक्त-अम्बुज = Red-lotus, आसनम् = seat, रक्ताम्बुजासनम् = who is seated on a red lotus, अशेष = Infinite, गुण = auspicious qualities, एक = only, सिन्धु = ocean, अशेषगुणैकसिन्धुं = who is the ocean of infinite good qualities, भानुं = the sun, समस्तजगतां = of all worlds, अधिपं = Lord, भजामि = I worship, पद्मद्वय = two lotuses, अभयवरं = the boon and protection (lit. fearlessness), दधतं = holding, कराब्जैः = By lotus-like hands, माणिक्य = Jewels, मौलिं = crown, अरुणाङ्गरुचिं = whose rays are pleasant, त्रिनेत्रम् = who has three eyes.

*Translation* :—I worship the Sun, the presiding lord of all worlds, who is seated on a red lotus and is the ocean of infinite auspicious qualities. Whose four hands hold two lotuses, one in each hand ; and the other two are raised in the form of giving boon and protection to his worshippers ; whose crown is bedecked with jewels, whose rays are pleasant and who has three eyes.

Note.—Offer red sandal and bilva leaf to the Sun.

The mantra of Sûrya is ओं सूर्याय नमः Om Sûryâya namaḥ

The nyâsas of Sûrya may be done by affixing merely ओं also, exactly as in pp. 142 and 143. Another mantra of Sûrya is ओं घृणिः सूर्य आदित्यः (T. A. xxxvii. 1. 1). Om ghriniḥ sûrya âdityaḥ.

*Word meaning* :—घृणिः = refulgent, सूर्यः = The Creator, आदित्यः = the Lord of Infinity.

*Translation* :—The Lord of Infinity is the refulgent Creator.

*Devî Pûjâ.*

In a similar way he should worship Durgâ.

The mantra is ओं ह्रीं दुं दुर्गायै नमः Om Hrim Dum Durgâyai namaḥ. The Nyâsas are performed by the mantras ह्रां ओं ह्रीं दुन्दुर्गायै अंगुष्ठाभ्यां नमः &c.

The syllable is ह hra ; which is successively changed to ह्रां ह्रीं ह्रूं ह्रैं ह्रौं and ह्रः before the various fingers and limbs.

The Dhyâna mantra is—

सिंहस्था शशिशेखरा मरकतप्रख्यैश्चतुर्भिर्भुजैः
शङ्खञ्चक्रधनुःशरांश्च दधती नेत्रैस्त्रिभिः शोभिता ।
आमुक्ताङ्गदहारकङ्कणरणत्काञ्चीक्वणन् नूपुरा
दुर्गा दुर्गतिहारिणी भवतु नो रत्नोल्लसत् कुण्डला ॥

Simhasthâ śâśiśekharâ marakata prakhyaiś chaturbhir bhujaiḥ,
Śankhañ chakra dhanuḥ śarâñścha dadhatî netrais tribhiḥ śobhitâ ;
Âmuktâṅgada hâra kaṅkaṇa raṇat kâñchi kvanan nûpurâ,
Durgâ durgati hâriṇi bhavatu no ratnollasat kuṇḍalâ.

*Translation.*—May the goddess Durgâ, whose earrings sparkle with gems, who is seated on a lion, and is crowned with the moon, whose four arms resembling emerald, hold in them the conch shell, discus, bow and arrow, and who has three eyes, whose necklace and bracelet emit sweet sound along with the girdle zone, and whose anklets are adorned with small tinkling bells, be the remover of miseries.

Or, one may repeat the following :—

सिंहस्कन्धसमारूढान्नानालङ्कारभूषिताम् ।
चतुर्भुजाम्महादेवीन्नागयज्ञोपवीतिनीम् ॥ १ ॥
रक्तवस्त्रपरीधानाम्बालार्कसदृशीतनुम् ।
नारदाद्यैर्मुनिगणैः सेविताम्भवगेहिनीम् ॥ २ ॥
त्रिवलीवलयोपेतनाभिनालसुवेशिनीम् ।
रत्नद्वीपे महाद्वीपे सिंहासनसमन्विते ॥
प्रफुल्लकमलारूढान्ध्यायेत्ताम्भवगेहिनीम् ॥ ३ ॥

---

*Śiva Pûjâ.*

Then he should offer pûjâ to Śiva similarly. The mantra is ओं नमः शिवाय नमः । Om namaḥ Śivâya namaḥ.

The Dhyâna mantra is :—

ओं ध्यायेत् नित्यं महेशं रजतगिरिनिभं चारुचन्द्रावतंसम् ।
रत्नाकल्पोज्ज्वलाङ्गं परशुमृगवराभीतिहस्तं प्रसन्नम् ॥

पद्मासीनं समन्तात् स्तुतममरगणैर्व्याघ्रकृत्तिं वसानम् ।
विश्वाद्यं विश्वबीजं निखिलभयहरं पंचवक्त्रं त्रिनेत्रम् ॥

Om! Dhayâyet nityam Mahesam rajata-giri nibham chârucbandrâ vatamsam. Ratnâ kalpojjvalângam parasu mrigavarâ bhiti hastam prasannam. Padmâsînam samantât stutam amaraganair vyâghra-krittim vasânam. Visvâdyam visva bîjam nikhila-bhaya-haram pañcha vaktram tri netram.

*Word meaning* :—ध्यायेत् = Let him meditate, नित्यं = always, महेशं = the Great Lord, रजत = silver, गिरि = mountain, निभं = brilliaut, Refulgent as a silver hill. चारु = beautiful, चन्द्र = moon. अवतंसं = ornament or crest-jewel, adorned with, decked with the beautiful moon as crest-jewel, रत्न jewel, आकल्प = like, उज्ज्वलाङ्गं = whose body is shining, परशु = axe, मृग = antelope, वर = boon, अभीति = protection, हस्तं = hand, whose hands shower boon and protection, प्रसन्नम् = happy, पद्मासीनं = seated in lotus posture, समन्तात् = on all sides, स्तुतम् = being praised, अमरगणैः = by hosts of gods, व्याघ्रकृत्तिं = skin of the tiger, वसानम् = dress, विश्वाद्यं = who is the beginning of the world, विश्वबीजं = who is the seed of the world, निखिलभयहरं = who is the destroyer of all fears, पञ्चवक्त्रं = who has five faces, त्रिनेत्रम् = who has three eyes.

**Translation.**—Let him always meditate on the mighty Lord whose body is as white as a silver mountain, whose head jewel is a beautiful crescent, whose limbs are refulgent as if adorned with gems, and who holds in his two hands an axe, and an antelope, and whose other two hands shower boon and protection [on his votaries.] Who is seated in the Lotus posture and who is on all sides surrounded by a host of immortals, who chant his praises, and whose dress is the skin of a tiger, who is the beginning of the Universe and its seed, who is destroyer of manifold fears, who is five faced and has three eyes.

———

*Brief Pûjâ.*

Then he should offer the brief pûjâ to all devas by the following :—

ओं एते गन्धपुष्पे ओं शिवादिपंचदेवताभ्यो नमः ।

Om Ete gandha puṣpe Om! Śivâdi Pañcha devatâbhyo namaḥ.

**These scent and flower Om! to Śiva and the rest—the Five Devatâs all Hail.**

एते गन्धपुष्पे ओं आदित्यादिनवग्रहेभ्यो नमः ।

Ete gandha puṣpe Om! Âdityâdi nava grahebhyo namaḥ.

**These scent and flower Om! to the Sun and the rest—the Nine Planets—namaḥ.**

एते गन्धपुष्पे ओं इंद्रादि दशदिक्पालेभ्यो नमः ।

Ete gandha puṣpe Om! Indrâdi daśa ḍikpâlebhyo namaḥ.

**These scent and flower Om! to Indra and the rest—the ten Wardens of the Quarters Namaḥ.**

एते गन्धपुष्पे ओं सर्वेभ्यो देवेभ्यो नमः ।

Ete gandha puṣpe Om sarvebhyo devebhyo namaḥ.

**These scent and flower Om to all Devis, namaḥ.**

एते गन्धपुष्पे ओं सर्वाभ्यो देवीभ्यो नमः ।

Ete gandha puṣpe Om ! Sarvâbhyo Devîbhyo namaḥ.

**The scent and flower Om ! to all Devîs, namaḥ.**

एते गन्धपुष्पे श्रों गुरवे नमः ।

Ete gandha puṣpe Om Gurave namaḥ.

**These scent and flower Om to Guru Hail.**

Offer a flower immersed in sandal paste each time, while reciting the above.

---

*Nârâyaṇa Pujâ.*

After all these preliminary pujâs now enter into the essential pujâ, that of Viṣṇu called Nârâyaṇa. Like all the previous pujâs, it also consists of (1) Karanyâsa (2) aṅga nyâsa (3) Dhyâna, (4) Viśeṣa Arghya, (5) Offerings of the ten Upachâras (6) Japa (7) Prayer (8) Praṇama. The special point is the second sanctifying of water called viśeṣa arghya.

*Kara Nyâsa.*

नां अङ्गुष्ठाभ्यां नमः Nâṁ aṅguṣṭhâbhyâm namaḥ.

नीं तर्जनीभ्यां स्वाहा Nîṁ tarjanîbhyâm svâhâ &c., &c., (with नूं, नैं; नौं नः )

*Aṅga Nyâsa.*

नां हृदयाय नमः náṁ hridayâya namaḥ.

नीं शिरसे स्वाहा niṁ śirase svâhâ &c., &c.,

*Guru Praṇâma.*

*On the left.*

श्रों गुरुभ्यो नमः Om Gurubhyo namaḥ.

श्रों परमगुरुभ्यो नमः Om Parama Gurubhyo namaḥ.

श्रों परापरगुरुभ्यो नमः Om Parâpara Gurubhyo namaḥ.

श्रों परमेष्ठिगुरुभ्यो नमः Om Parameṣṭhi Gurubhyo namaḥ.

Then salute on the *right* side.

श्रों गणेशाय नमः Om Gaṇeśâya namaḥ.

Then salute in *front* the Iṣṭa-devatâ.

श्रों नारायणाय नमः Om *Nârâyaṇâya* namaḥ.

*Dhyâna.*

Then form the mental picture of Nârâyaṇa, as described in the following mantra, with a flower in hand, with Kûrma Mudrâ.

श्रों धेयः सदा सवितृमण्डलमध्यवर्त्ती ।

नारायणः सरसिजासनसन्निविष्टः ॥

केयूरवान् कनककुण्डलवान् किरीटी ।

हारी हिरण्मयवपुर्धृतः शङ्खचक्रः ॥

Om ! Dheyaḥ sadâ savitṛi maṇḍala madhya vartî
Nârâyaṇaḥ sarasijâsana san niviṣṭhaḥ.
Keyûravân kanaka kuṇḍalavân kirîṭî.
Hâri hiraṇmaya vapur dhṛitaḥ śankha chakraḥ.

*Word meaning* :—ध्येयः=should be meditated upon, सदा=always, सवितृ=the sun, मण्डल=the orb, मध्य=middle, वर्ती=dwelling, savitṛi maṇdala madhya vartin means He who dwells in the midst of the solar orb, नारायणः=the saviour (ayana) or goal of men (nara) or the spirit moving (ayana) over the waters (nârâ), सरसिज=lotus, (lit.) born-in-the-tank, आसन=seat. lotus-seated, sitting in the lotus posture, सन्-निविष्टः=seated firmly, केयूर-वान्=having the armlet, कनक=gold, कुण्डलवान्=having the ear-ring, किरीटी=having the diadem-crown, हारी=the Saviour, हिरण्मय-वपुः=golden body, धृतः=holding, शङ्ख=conch, चक्रः=discus.

*Translation* :—Nârâyana should always be meditated upon as in the midst of the Solar orb, seated on a lotus, decked with armlet, golden ear rings and diadem crown. The Saviour, Golden bodied, holding conch and discus.

After such meditation, put the flower which was kept in the hand with Kûrma Mudrâ on one's own head, identifying himself with the deity.

Then offer mental upachâras.

Then consecrate the Special Arghya.

*Special Arghya.*

The method of establishing Viśeṣa Arghya is as follows :—On one's left make a triangle, circumscribe round it a circle, around the circle make a square. On this place a brass tripod : and on it a hollow conch shell. The water is to be placed in this *shell.* Before placing the tripod, sanctify the square by offering scent and uuhusked rice, repeating : ओं आधारशक्त्यै नमः ओं अनन्ताय नमः ओं कूर्माय नमः Om âdhâraśaktyai namaḥ. Om Anantâya namaḥ. Om Kûrmâya namaḥ. Then place the tripod on the sanctified ground. Then wash the conch with uttering नमः namaḥ ; and place it on the tripod.

Then fill three-fourths of the shell with water, and sanctify the ground, the tripod and the conch shell by the following three mantras respectively :—

ओं वह्निमण्डलाय दशकलात्मने नमः । इति त्रिपादिकायाम् ।

Om ! vahnimaṇḍalâya daśakalâtmane namaḥ.

Om ! to that who has ten kalâs to the orb of Fire, Hail.

ओम् अर्कमण्डलाय द्वादशकलात्मने नमः । इति शङ्खे ।

Âm Arka maṇḍalâya dvâdaśa kalâtmane namaḥ.

Âm ! To the sphere of the Sun consisting of 12 kalâs, Hail.

ऊम् सोममण्डलाय षोडशकलात्मने नमः । इति जले ।

Ûm Soma maṇḍalâya ṣodaṣa kalâtmane namaḥ.

Ûm ! to the Lunar Orb, consisting of 16 kalâs. Hail

Then put some durvâ grass, unhusked rice, scent, flowers, &c., in the water of the conch, and showing dhenu mudrâ, repeat ओं Om eight times; and invoke the streams by "Gange cha Yamune, &c." (page 139, and sprinkle a little of this water on one's own head and on the Pûjâ ingredients. This is the special Arhgya water.

*Second Dhyâna.*

Then again meditate on Nârâyaṇa. And offer a flower to the Sâlagrâma after mental projection of the picture of Nârâyaṇa on such flower. This flower is now the symbol to whom offerings are made.

*Upachâra offerings.*

Then offer the ten upachâras as before.

*Japa.*

Then after having again performed Kara and Aṅga Nyâsas; perform the silent repetition of the Mantra at least 108 times. The mantra is ओं नमो नारायणाय Om namo Nârâyaṇâya.

After finishing the Japa, recite :—

ओं गुह्यातिगुह्यगोप्ता त्वं गृहाणास्मत्कृतं जपम् ।

सिद्धिर्भवतु मे देव त्वत्प्रसादात् महेश्वर ॥

Om, Guhyâti guhya goptâ tvam grihâṇ âsmat kṛitaṃ japam,
Siddhir bhavatu me Deva tvat prasâdât Mahesvara.

*Translation* :—Om, Thou, the Protector of the secret of Great secrets, accept the Japa performed by us. O Deva, O Mahesvara, by Thy grace, may success be mine.

*Prayer.*

Then offer the following prayer :—

ओं मन्त्रहीनं क्रियाहीनं भक्तिहीनं जनार्दन ।

यत् पूजितं मया देव परिपूर्णं तदस्तु मे ।

Om, Mantra hînam kriyâhînam bhaktihînam Janârdana
Yat pûjitam mayâdeva paripûrṇam tadastu me.

*Translation* :—Whatever shortcomings there may be in this pûjâ, whether defects of mantras or defects of rituals, or defects in devotion, may all that become remedied, O Sifter of men!

*Praṇâma.*

Then finish the Pûjâ with the following salutation mantras :—

ओं नमो ब्रह्मण्य देवाय गोब्राह्मणहिताय च ।

जगद्धिताय कृष्णाय गोविन्दाय नमो नमः ॥

Om! Namo Brahmaṇya devâya go Brâhmaṇa hitâya cha,
Jagad Dhitâya Kṛishṇâya govindâya namo namaḥ.

*Translation* :—Om! Salutation to the Brahmanya-Deva, to the well-wisher of the worlds (Go) and Sages (Brâhmaṇa), to the well-wisher of the whole Universe, to Kṛishṇa, to Govinda, all Hail, all Hail.

ओं कायेन वाचा मनसेन्द्रियैर्वा
बुद्ध्यात्मना वानुसृतः स्वभावात् ।
करोमि यद्यत्सकलं परस्मै
नारायणायेति समर्पयामि ॥

Om Kâyena vâchâ manasendriyair vâ
Buddhy âtmanâ vâ nusritaḥ svabhâvât.
Karomi yad yat sakalam parasmai.
Nârâyaṇayeti samarpayâmi.

Om! Whatever I do with body, speech, mind or senses, or with Buddhi or Âtman, or whatever is automatically done by nature—all that I offer to the Supreme Nârâyaṇa.

प्रमादात्कुर्वतां कर्म प्रच्यवेताध्वरेषु यत् ।
स्मरणादेव तद्विष्णोः सम्पूर्णं स्यादितिस्मृतिः ॥
यस्य स्मृत्या च नामोक्त्या तपोयज्ञक्रियादिषु ।
न्यूनं सम्पूर्णतां याति सद्यो वन्दे तमच्युतम् ॥

Pramâdât kurvatâm karma prachyavetâdhvareṣu yat
Smaraṇâdeva tad Viṣṇoḥ sampûrṇam syâditi smrith.
Yasya smrityâ cha nâmoktyâ tapo yajña kriyâdiṣu
Nyûnam sampûrṇatâm yâti sadyo vande tam achyutam.

"Whatever defects occur in any ceremony through oversight or carelessness, they all become rectified by rembering Viṣṇu"—so declare the Scriptures.

"I praise that Eternal Lord, by remembering whom and uttering whose name, all deficiencies are supplied in every sacrifice and ceremony."

---

## CHAPTER XIII.

### THE SIVA PÛJÂ.

Sitting on a pure seat, first perform the âchamana (p. 13 and 44). Then offer arghyam to the Solar Logos with the mantra ओं नमो विवस्वते ब्रह्मन् भास्वते विष्णुतेजसे, जगत्सवित्रे शुचये सवित्रे कर्मदायिने । इदमर्घ्यं ओं नमो भगवते श्री सूर्याय नमः

*Common Arghya.*

Then sanctify water as taught before. (Make the clay Lingam if so inclined) see note at the end of the chapter.

*Kara nyâsas.*

ओं अंगुष्ठाभ्यां नमः &c. Or with शां, शीं &c. Or with the letters of ओं नमः शिवाय as, ओं हृदयाय नमः, नं शिरसे स्वाहाः, मं शिखायै वषट्, शिं कवचाय हुम् ; वां नेत्रत्रयाय वौषट्, यः करतलपृष्ठाभ्यां फट् ।

### *Guru Pankti salutation.*

Then salute all Gurus as taught before.
Left. ओं गुरुभ्यो नमः । ओं परमगुरुभ्यो नमः । Right. ओं परापरगुरुभ्यो नमः Front ओं गणेशाय नमः । ओं नमः शिवाय नमः ।

### *Dhyâna.*

Then meditate on Śiva and form as clear a mental image as possible. The dhyána mantra has been taught before.

ओं ध्यायेन्नित्यं महेशं रजतगिरिनिभं चारुचन्द्रावतंसम्

### *Mental Pûjâ.*

Then offer mental pûjâ to the Deity.

### *Specific or Viśeṣa Arghya.*

Then establish the specific arghya in a conch shell, as taught before.
**Note:—Perform invocation if clay lingam is worshipped, see note.**

### *Pûjâ.*

Then offer the Ten Upachâras, –

( १ ) एतत् पाद्यं ओं नमः शिवाय नमः ।

( २ ) इदमर्घ्यम् ओं नमः शिवाय नमः ।

( ३ ) इदमाचमनीयम् ओं नमः शिवाय नमः ।

( ४ ) इदं स्नानीयम् ओं नमः शिवाय नमः ।

( ५ ) इदम् पुनराचमनीयम् ओं नमः शिवाय नमः ।

( ६ ) एषः गन्धः ओं नमः शिवाय नमः ।

( ७ ) एतत् पुष्पम् ओं नमः शिवाय नमः ।

( ८ ) एतद् बिल्वपत्रम् ओं नमः शिवाय नमः ।

( ९ ) एषः धूपः ओं नमः शिवाय नमः ।

(१०) एषः दीपः ओं नमः शिवाय नमः ।

(११) एतन्नैवेद्यम् ओं नमः शिवाय नमः ।

(१२) इदम् पुनराचमनीयम् ओं नमः शिवाय नमः ।

(१३) एतत् ताम्बूलं ओं नमः शिवाय नमः ।

### *The Pûjâ of the Eight Forms of Śiva.*

Then give offerings of scent and flower to the eight forms of Śiva presiding over the eight quarters.

East पूर्वस्यां, एते गन्धपुष्पे ओं शर्वाय क्षितिमूर्तये नमः । Śarva—Earth.

N.-E ईशाने, ओं भवाय जलमूर्तये नमः । Bhava—Water.

North उत्तरस्याम्, ओं रुद्राय अग्निमूर्तये नमः । Rudra – Fire.

N.-W. वायुकोणे, ओं उग्राय वायुमूर्त्तये नमः Ugra—Air.

West पश्चिमस्यां, ओं भीमाय आकाशमूर्त्तये नमः। Bhima—Âkâśa.

S.-W. नैऋते, ओं पशुपतये यजमानमूर्त्तये नमः। Paśupati—Yajamâna.

South दक्षिणस्यां, ओं ईशानाय सूर्यमूर्त्तये नमः। Îśâna—Sun.

S.-E. अग्निकोणे, ओं महादेवाय सोममूर्त्तये नमः। Mahâdeva—Moon.

Middle मध्ये, ओं नन्दिने नमः, ओं भृंगिणे नमः, ओं क्षेत्रपालाय नमः, ओं वामदेवाय नमः।

*Japa.*

Then perform japa of the mantra ओं नमः शिवाय नमः।

*Samarpana.*

Then finish the japa by the following Mantra:

गुह्यातिगुह्यगोप्ता त्वं, गृहाणास्मत्कृतं जपम्।
सिद्धिर्भवतु मे देव त्वत्प्रसादात् महेश्वर॥

*Praṇâma.*

Then offer salutation reciting:

नमस्तुभ्यं विरूपाक्ष नमस्ते दिव्यचक्षुसे।
नमः पिनाकहस्ताय वज्रहस्ताय वै नमः॥

Namas tubhyam Virûpâkṣa Namaste divya chakṣuse,
Namaḥ pinâka hastâya Vajra hastâya vai namaḥ.

All hail to Thee O Oblique Eyed; Hail O Divine Eyed one to Thee! Salutation to Thee that bearest the Trident! Verily all hail who holds the thunderbolt.

नमस्ते शूलहस्ताय दण्डपाशासिपाणये।
नमस्त्रैलोक्यनाथाय भूतानां पतये नमः॥

Namaste śûla hastâya Daṇḍa pâṣâsipâṇaye,
Namas Tailokya nâthâya Bhutânâm pataye namaḥ.

All Hail to Thee who holds the Lance, The sceptre, noose and sword in hands All hail to the Lord of the three worlds Salutation to the Lord of all Beings.

ओं नमः शिवाय शान्ताय कारणत्रयहेतवे।
निवेदयामि चात्मानं त्वं गतिः परमेश्वर!॥

Om Namaḥ Śivâya śântâya kâraṇatraya hetave,
Nivedayâmi châtmânam Tvam gatiḥ parameśvara,

Om! Om Salutation to Śiva the Peaceful, The Caus of the Three Causes. I offer myself to Thee, O Lord Thou art my goal and end, O God.

*Finishing the Pûjâ.*

Then after making the sound of बं बं बं, finish the pûjâ by asking forgiveness of sins and faults.

आवाहनं न जानामि नैव जानामि पूजनम् ।
विसर्जनं न जानामि क्षमस्व परमेश्वर ! ॥

"I do not know how to invoke, nor how to worship, nor how to bid Thee farewell, pardon my delinquencies, O Lord!"

*Note.*

If Pûjâ is to be offered to an extemporised clay image of Śiva (the Liṅgam); then the following procedure should be observed:—

After making the sâmânya arghya; take a small lump of pure clay with the mantra ओं हराय नमः Om Harâya namaḥ. Make a Liṅgam of it and wash it with the mantra ओं महेश्वराय नमः Om maheśvarâya namaḥ, and place it facing north on an entire untorn bilva leaf. Then bathe it with water uttering: इदम् स्नानीयं ओं पशुपतये नमः idam snâniyam Om Paśupataye namaḥ. Then perform the vitalisation of the image by saying ओं शूलपाणे इह सुप्रतिष्ठितो भव Om Śûlapâne iha supratiṣṭhito bhava.

Then perform the Nyâśa, &c., as told above. After establishing the specific arghya, address the following invocation:—

ओं पिनाकधृक् इहागच्छ आगच्छ Om Pinâkadhrik ihâgachchha âgachchha O holder of Pinâka, come hither, come.

इह तिष्ठ तिष्ठ iha tiṣṭha, tiṣṭha, stay here stay.

अत्र अधिष्ठानं कुरु atra adhiṣṭhânam kuru, preside here.

मम पूजां गृहाण mama pûjâm grihâṇa, accept my pujâ.

Then offer pâdya, &c., first having recited with folded hands:

स्थां स्थीं स्थिरोभव यावत् पूजां करोम्यहम् ।

Sthâm Sthim, Stay here so long as I offer Thee pûjâ.

---

## CHAPTER XIV.

### MID-DAY DUTIES.

From noon till 1-30 P. M. is the proper time to perform the Mid-day duties. They consist of (1) Deva-Yajña or the offering to fire, called also Homa, or Viśva offering, (2) Bhûta-Yajña or Bali karma, (3) Manuṣya Yajña or feeding of the guest, (4) Pitri-Yajña or the daily Śrâddha, (5) Go-grâsa-dâna or giving mouthful of cooked food to the cow, and (6) Bhojanam, or taking one's own food. The fifth mahâ yajña, namely, the Brahma-jajña is generally performed before the noon: or even after, and therefore is not mentioned here along with the other four mentioned above.

It is not possible to give full details of these ceremonies here, all that we can do is to give a brief account of them.

## THE SANCTIFICATION OF FIRE.

(1) Erection of Fire-altar and consecration ceremony :—The practitioner whether a student or a householder should set apart a particular place in which perpetual fire should be kept burning. The fire-pit (or kuṇḍ) or the fire altar (or sthaṇḍila) should be prepared according to the rules laid down in the particular śâkhâ to which one belongs. Any good priest would be able to make this for him. For the ordinary homa of the householder, if the digging of the pit be not convenient, a fire altar may be erected on a piece of ground 18 inches square and a little raised from the general level. Fire should be brought from the house of a Brâhmaṇa, and placed on this altar. The consecration of fire is one which should generally be performed by a priest. If no priest be available one may do it himself in the abridged form here given. Place the fire on the altar and look at it and sanctify it with the mûla mantra uttering the word *vauṣat* : then utter the mantra हुं फट् क्रव्यादिभ्यो नमः huṃ phat kravyâdebhyo namaḥ. Then recite the following mantras :—

ओं वह्नेर्योगपीठाय नमः Om Vahner yoga-piṭhâya namaḥ.

ओं वामायै नमः Om Vâmâyai namaḥ.

ओं ज्येष्ठायै नमः Om Jyeṣṭhâyai namaḥ.

ओं रौद्रै नमः Om Raudryai namaḥ.

ओं अम्बिकायै नमः Om Ambikâyai namaḥ.

With the last four mantras, the four sides of the altar should be sanctified. Then having meditated on the fire, recite the following mantras :—

ह्रीं वह्निमूर्त्तये नमः Hrîṁ vahni-mûrttaye namaḥ ; and salute the fire by bowing down.

वं वह्निचैतन्याय नमः Vaṃ-vahni-chaitanyâya namaḥ.

With this mantra he should endow the fire with consciousness.

Then he should lighten the fire by the following mantra :—

ओं चित् पिङ्गल हन हन दह दह पच पच सर्वं ज्ञापय ज्ञापय स्वाहा

Om ! chit piṅgala hana, daha daha, pacha pacha, sarvam jñâpaya svâhâ.

Then let him stand saluting the fire reciting the following mantra :—

अग्निं प्रज्वलितं वन्दे जातवेदं हुताशनम् ।
सुवर्णवर्णममलं समिद्धं विश्वतो मुखम् ॥

Agniṁ prajvalitaṁ vande jâta-vedaṁ hutâśanaṁ.
Suvarṇa-varṇaṁ amalaṁ samiddhaṁ viśvatomukhaṁ.

"I bow to the adorable Agni who knows all, who is of golden color, pure and facing all quarters."

Then he should name the fire with the following :—

अग्ने त्वं अमुक देवता नामासि

Agne tvam (amuka) devatâ nâmasi. (The particular name to be given to the fire must be learned from one's family priest).

(2) *Homa.*

Then meditate upon the three nâḍis—iḍâ, piṅgalâ and suṣumnâ, as situated on the right, left and the middle of one's body and commence Homa or pouring in of offerings into the fire. The Fire-Devatâ should be pictured as a being of great refulgence: and those upachâras which are offered in pûjâ to the Iṣṭa devatâ are now to be offered in the fire, thinking that one's Iṣṭa is present there in fire to receive the offerings. Then reciting the following mantra, invoke the fire :—

ओं वैश्वानर जातवेद इहावह लोहिताक्ष सर्वकर्माणि साधय स्वाहा

Om Vaiśvânara Jâtaveda ihâvaha Lohitâkṣa sarva karmâṇi sâdhaya svâhâ.

O Lord of all men! Omniscient! Come here, Thou with red eyes! and accomplish all my work.

Then offer arghya, &c., upachâras to the fire, as offered in the pûjâ.

After the pûjâ of fire recite :—

ओं अग्नेर्हिरण्यादिसप्तजिह्वाभ्यो नमः ।

Om! Agner Hiraṇyâdi sapta jihvâbhyo namaḥ. (Om salutations to the seven tongues of Agni, called golden, &c.).

ओं सहस्रार्चिषे हृदयाय नमः ।

Om! sahasrârchiṣe hridayâ namaḥ. (Om! adoration to the thousand rayed One: adoration to the heart, namaḥ).

With the same mantra make offerings to the other five members as in *sandhyâ, viz.*, to śirasa, śikhâ, Kavacha, netratraya, and kara-tala-karapriṣtha. (see page 61). Or merely say :—Om! sahasrârchiṣe Haridayâya namaḥ, ityadi Agni Ṣadaṅgebhyo namaḥ.

ओं अग्नये जातवेदसे इत्याद्यष्टमूर्त्तिभ्यो नमः ।

Om! Agnaye Jâtavedase ityâdy aṣṭamûrtibhyo namaḥ.

ओं ब्राह्म्याद्यष्टशक्तिभ्यो नमः Om! Brâhmy âdy aṣta śaktibhyo namaḥ.

ओं पद्मादि अष्टनिधिभ्यो नमः Om! Padmâdi aṣṭa Nidhibhyo namaḥ.

ओं इन्द्रादिलोकपालेभ्यो नमः Om! Indrâdi Loka-pâlebhyo namaḥ.

ओं वज्रादि अस्त्रेभ्यो नमः Om! Vajrâdi astrebhyo namaḥ.

Then recite the following mantra, offering with the wooden spoon ghee to the fire, thinking that the fire has three eyes and the three offerings are made in those eyes respectively :—

ओं अग्नये स्वाहा Om! Agnayo svâhâ, and pour the offering into the right eye of the fire.

ओं सोमाय स्वाहा Om! Somâya svâhâ, and pour the offering into the left eye of Agni.

Then reciting the following mantra pour the offering into the third eye of the fire :—

ओं अग्नीषोमाभ्यां स्वाहा Om ! Agni-ṣom-âbhyâm svâhâ.

Then pour offering into the mouth of Agni with the following mantra :—

ओं अग्नये स्विष्टकृते स्वाहा-। Om ! Agnaye sviṣtakrite svâhâ.

Then pour offering three times into the fire reciting :—

ओं भूः स्वाहा Om ! Bhûḥ svâhâ.

ओं भुवः स्वाहा Om ! Bhuvaḥ svâhâ.

ओं स्वः स्वाहा Om ! svar svâhâ.

Then reciting Om ! Vaiṣvânara Jâtaveda, &c. pour three offerings into the fire.

*A brief method of Homa.*

All this is preliminary and may be dispensed with.

The essential portion is to lighten the fire and strongly thinking that it is the symbol of the adorable Iṣṭadevatâ, offer 25 times ghee and other preparations into the fire, reciting once the mûla mantra. Or if one is not initiated, he should recite the Gayatri 25 times. Or he may offer it only 11 times, identifying one's self with one's Iṣṭa-devatâ as present in the fire. Or he may recite any Vedic or other hymn that he may remember, such as the "Agnimîde" mantra of the Sandhya or any other mantra and pour offerings with the word "svâhâ."

THE FIVE MAHA-YAJNAS.

*1. Deva Yajna.*

(A portion of Viśva-deva offering.)

This is an offering to all the devas in the aggregate. This may be briefly done by reciting the following mantra :—

ओं विश्वदेवाय नमः Om ! Viśvadevâya namaḥ.

According to Manu, Viśva deva offerings are made with the cooked food to the following :—(1) Agni, (2) Soma, (3) Agni-Soma, (4) Viśve devas, (5) Dhanvantari, (6) Kuhu, (7) Anumati, (8) Prajâpati, (9) Dyâvâ-Prithivi and (10) Agni-Sviṣṭakrit. The mantras can be easily formed. Put these words in the dative case, and add "svâhâ" in the end. Thus ओं अग्नये स्वाहा Om ! Agnaye svâhâ, &c. The offerings are made in the domestic fire.

"A Brahman shall offer according to the rule of his Grihya-Sutra, a portion of the cooked food destined for the Viśva deva in the sacred domestic fire to the following deities :—

"First to Agni, and next to Soma, then to both these gods conjointly, further to all-the-gods (Viśve Devâh) and then to Dhanvantari.

"Further to Kuhu (the goddess of the moon day), to Anumati (the goddess of the full moon day), the Prajâpati (the lord of creatures ; to heaven and earth conjointly, and finally to Agni-Sviṣṭarkrit (the fire that performs the sacrifice well.)"

(Manu III. 84 to 94.)

The object of the Vaiśvadeva Homa is not so much the sanctification of the food, as the attainment of the proper condition of sanctity by the sacrificer to fit him to eat that food.

According to Âśvaláyana Grinya Sûtra the following mantras are used in the Vaiśvadeva Yajña when it is done in full.

ओं सोमाय वनस्पतये स्वाहा - Om ! Somâya Vanaspataye svâhâ. (Adoration to Soma, the lord of the Forests.)

ओं अग्नीषोमाभ्यां स्वाहा Om ! Agnî-somâbhyâm svâhâ.

ओं इन्द्राग्निभ्यां स्वाहा Om ! Indrâgnibhyâm svâhâ.

ओं द्यावापृथिवीभ्यां स्वाहा Om ! Dyâvâ-Prithivibhyâm svâhâ.

ओं धन्वन्तरये स्वाहा Om ! Dhanvantaraye svâhâ.

ओं इन्द्राय स्वाहा Om ! Indrâya svâhâ.

ओं विश्वेभ्यो देवेभ्यः स्वाहा Om ! Viśvebhyo Devebhyo svâhâ.

ओं ब्रह्मणे स्वाहा Om ! Brahmaṇe svâhâ.

ओं अग्नये स्वाहा Om ! Âgnaye svâhâ.

ओं सोमाय स्वाहा Om ! Somâya svâhâ.

2. *Bhûta Yajña.*

(The second portion of Vaiśvadeva offering).

The Bali mantras given in the Âśvalâyana Grihya Sûtra are as follows, and the offerings may be made with water only, when food is not given to each.)

ओं ओषधिवनस्पतिभ्यः स्वाहा Om ! Oṣadhivanaspatibhyaḥ svâhâ. (Salutations to herbs and trees.)

ओं गृहाय स्वाहा Om ! Grihâya svâhâ, (to house).

ओं गृहदेवताभ्यः स्वाहा Om ! Griha-devatâbhyaḥ svâhâ. (to the tutelary deity of the house).

ओं वास्तुदेवताभ्यः स्वाहा Om ! Vâstu-devatâbhyaḥ svâhâ, (to the tutelary deity of the house).

Then offer Bali to the four quarters saying :—

ओं इन्द्राय स्वाहा ! Om ! Indrâya svâhâ.
ओं इन्द्रपुरुषेभ्यः स्वाहा Om ! Indra-Puruṣebhyaḥ svâhâ.—East

ओं यमाय स्वाहा Om ! Yamâya svâhâ.
ओं यमपुरुषेभ्यः स्वाहा Om ! Yama-puruṣebhyaḥ svâhâ.—South.

ओं वरुणाय स्वाहा Om ! Varuṇâyasvâhâ.
ओं वरुणपुरुषेभ्यः स्वाहा Om ! Varuṇa-Puruṣebhyaḥ svâhâ.—West.

ओं सोमाय स्वाहा Om ! Somâya svâhâ.
ओं सोमपुरुषेभ्यः स्वाहा Om ! Soma-Puruṣebhyaḥ svâhâ.—North.

In the middle offer one Bali to Brahman, and one to Viśvedevas and one to all creatures, saying :—

ओं ब्रह्मणेभ्यः स्वाहा Om ! Brahmaṇebhyaḥ svâhâ.

ओं विश्वेभ्यो देवेभ्यः स्वाहा Om ! Viśvebhyo devebhyaḥ svâhâ.

ओं सर्वेभ्यो भूतेभ्यो दिवाचारिभ्यः स्वाहा Om ! Sarvebhyo bhûtebhyo divâchâribhyaḥ svâhâ. (To goblins roaming about by day).

(In the night Bali, substitute ओं सर्वेभ्यो भूतेभ्यो नक्तंचारिभ्यः स्वाहा ' to goblins roaming about by night, (naktachâribhyaḥ).

ओं रक्षेभ्यः स्वाहा Om ! Rakṣebbyaḥ svâhâ.

This Bali properly, however, consists in offering food to lower creatures as well as to superhuman beings. Take a portion of the food prepared for one's own eating and give it to some animal, such as dogs, cats, &c., reciting.

देवा मनुष्याः पशवो वयांसि सिद्धाः सयक्षोरगदैत्यसङ्घाः ।
प्रेताः पिशाचास्तरवः समस्ता ये चान्नमिच्छन्ति मया प्रदत्तम् १ ॥
पिपीलिकाकीटपतङ्गकाद्या बुभुक्षिताः कर्मनिबद्धबद्धाः ।
प्रयान्तु ते तृप्तिं इदम् मयान्नं तेभ्यो विसृष्टं मुदिता भवन्तु २ ॥
येषां न माता न पिता न बन्धुर्नैवान्नसिद्धिर्न तथान्नमस्ति ।
तत्तृप्तयेऽन्नं भुवि दत्तमेतत् प्रयान्तु तृप्तिं मुदिता भवन्तु ॥ ३ ॥
ये चान्ये पतिताः केचित् अपात्राः पापयोनयः ।

Devâ manuṣyâḥ paśavo vayâmsi Siddhâḥ Sayakṣoraga daitya sanghaḥ ;
Pretâḥ Piśâchâs taravaḥ samastâ Ye chânnam ichchhanti mayâ pradattam.
Pipilikâ kiṭa patangakâdyâ Bubhuksitâḥ karmanibaddha baddhâḥ,
Prayântu te tṛiptim idam mayânnam Tebhyo visṛiṣṭam muditâ bhavantu.
Yeṣâm na mâtâ na pitâ na bandhur Naivânnasiddhir na tathânnam asti ;
Tat triptaye' nnam bhuvi dattametat Prayântu tṛiptim muditâ bhavantu.

Ye chânye patitâḥ kechid Apâtrâḥ pâpayonayaḥ.

Those who are in need of food given by me, I offer this to them be they devas or men, beasts or birds, siddhas, yakṣas, dragons, or the host of demons, ghosts, spooks, or immovable trees ;

The insects, ants, moths, or other small creatures, whoever they be, who bound by kârmic chains are suffering hunger and thirst, may they get all joy and satisfaction by this food scattered by me for them.

Those who have no father, no mother, nor friends, those who have no kitchen to cook their food or food to cook therein, for their satisfaction and joy, I throw this food on earth. May they feel satisfied and happy.

*Give food to all fallen beings and others who have taken birth in sinful races. Manu thus describes it (Manu III, 81-92).*

" After having thus duly offered the sacrificial food, let him throw Bali offerings in all directions of the compass, proceeding (from the east) to the south, to Indra, Yama, Varuṇa and Soma, as well as to the servants (of those deities).

Saying " adoration to the Maruts," he shall scatter (some food) near the door, and (some) in water, saying " adoration to the water " ; he shall throw some on the pestle and the mortar, speaking thus, " adoration to the trees."

" Near the head (of the bed) he shall make an offering to Śri (fortune), and near the foot (of his bed) to Bhadrakâlî ; in the centre of the house let him place a bali for Brahman and for Vâstoṣpati (the Lord of the dwelling) conjointly.

"Let him throw up into the air a bali for all the gods, and (in the day time) one for the goblins that walk at night.

"In the upper story let him offer a bali to Sarvâtmabhûti; but let him throw what remains (from these offerings) in a southerly direction for the manes.

"Let him gently place on the ground (some food) for dogs, outcastes, Chandâlas (Svapâk), those afflicted with diseases that are punishments of former sins, crows and insects."

### (3) *Pitṛi Yajña.*

(Also included in Vaiśvadeva).

Then wearing the sacred thread on the right shoulder (prâchîṇâvîtî, see tarpaṇa, pages 21 and the following) he should offer food to the manes; using the word "svadhâ" at the end. This constitutes the Pitṛi-Yajña. Instead of naming all the ancestors, one may shortly say :—

ओं स्वधा पितृभ्यः Om! Svadhâ Pitṛibhyaḥ.

This daily śrâddha may be performed with food or with water or also with milk, roots or fruits. (Manu III, 82). Very little or no preparation is necessary for this purpose. The ordinary food cooked for one's own purpose, should be offered in small balls to one's father, grandfather great grandfather and maternal grandfather and great-grandfather and great-great grandfather.

### (4) *The Brahma Yajña.*

It consists of the study of the Vedas. It may be done either before or after the above two Yajñas. The brief method of doing it has been taught before.

For fuller details consult Manu, Chapter III.

### 5. *Manuṣya Yajña.*

This consists in feeding a stranger. It should be performed after the Pitṛi Yajña

The feeding of the guest is also one of the five great Yajñas which a Hindu is daily enjoined to perform. Says Manu, (III, 94) "having performed this bali offering, he shall first feed his guest and according to the rule, give alms to an ascetic and to a student."

The best way in modern times of performing this portion of the Pañcha Yajña is to daily feed some sick or helpless man in the hospital, and a student reading in any school or college, who stands in need of such help. Feeding professional beggars is not discharging this duty. Hospitality is a well-known quality of Asiatic races, but of late it has been abused by some people. The best substitute, therefore, is what we have suggested above. If, however, a *stranger* asks your hospitality, do not refuse it, give him food without questioning.

Thus have been described the Pañcha Mahâ Yajñas, or the five great sacrifices. The offering in fire is (1) Deva Yajña, the throwing of Bali is (2) Bhûta Yajña; the offering to the Pitṛis is (3) Pitṛi Yajña, the study of the Vedas is (4) Brahma Yajña and lastly, the feeding of the stranger, *i.e.*, (5) Manuṣya Yajña. Of these five Yajñas or the great sacrifices, the four (1, 2, 3, and 5) appertain to food and are collectively called

"Pâka-Yajñas." They are generally performed at the time of meals. The fifth or Brahma-Yajña or the study of the sacred literature, is necessarily performed separately.

Yâjñyavalka lays down the following rules for the house-holder. It is an abridged form of Daily Practice.

"Let the house-holder daily perform the *Śmârta* ceremonies on the marriage-fire, or the fire taken at the time of taking the heritage; and the *Srauta* ceremonial on the *Vaitânika* (or the three sacred fires).

After finishing the care and attention with respect to the body, a twice-born, making the purificatory rites, should first clean his teeth, and then say the morning-prayer.

Having offered sacrifices to the fires, let him, with collected thoughts, repeat prayers sacred to the sun; let him study the meaning of the *Vedas* and of the various *śastras*.

Let him approach the ruler in order that what he has not may be obtained, and what he has may be preserved; (afterwards) bathing, let him offer libation of water to the gods, the *manes* and worship the gods.

Let him (then) repeat the *Vedas*, the *Atharvan*, the *Purâṇas* together with the *Itihâsas* (epics), according to ability, in order that the rite of uttering prayers may be completed, and let him likewise meditate on the science of self-knowledge.

The great sacrifices to the *Bhûtas*, the manes, the gods, the *Brahma* and men, are—(1) the *Bali-karma* (making of the *Bali* sacrifice), (2) the *svadhâ* offering, (3) the offering of food to fire, (4) the repeating the Vedas, and (5) the honouring of guests.

Let him offer the sacrifice to the Bhûtas from the remains of food after sacrifice has been offered to gods; let him then place on the ground food for dogs, *chaṇḍâlas* and crows.

Food (is) to be daily given to the *manes*, and men, and water also, daily; the *Vedas* to be (likewise) daily repeated; food is not to be cooked simply for oneself.

Children, the married girls, the old, the pregnant, the distressed, the unmarried girls, the guests and the servants, are to be fed and the man and his wife are to eat of the remaining food.

Let the twice-born diner take food covered and sweet, by means of the *Aposana* in the beginning as well as in the end.

Gift is to be made to men of the four classes (coming) as guests according to ability; giving precedence (according to the order of the classes); even in the evening a guest is not to be turned away, and hospitality is to be shown (if there be no food to give,) at least with kind) words, (and giving) room, grass and water.

To the *Sannyâsin* and to the *Brahmachârin*, alms are to be given with kind treatment; also friends, relatives and brethren who come at (dinner) time, should be fed.

Let him give a big ox or a big goat to a Brâhmaṇa knowing the Vedas, and (let him give him) also good reception, delicious food, sweet speech, and precedence in sitting.

Let him once a year worship (with a *Madhuparka*), the *snâtaka*, the *âcharya*, the ruler, the friend, the son-in-law, and again the *ritvij* (the officiating priest should be worshipped) at each sacrifice (with a *Madhuparka*).

He who is a traveller is to be understood to be an *Atithi* (guest); the *Śrotriya* and one versed in one of the Vedas (who come as guests) are to be honoured by the house-holder who wishes (to attain) the world of Brahma.

Without unexceptionable invitation, let there be not (a desire to) taste another's food; let him avoid (abuse) of speech, hands, feet, &c., and too much food-taking.

The satisfied Śrotriya guest is to be escorted to the boundary; the rest of the day, let him remain (or spend) with superior men, the friends, and brethren.

### (6). *Go-Grâsadâna.*

The cow is such a useful animal, that every pious Hindu thinks it his duty to feed it with one mouthful of cooked food daily, before taking his own food. He should feed the cow with the following mantra :—

सौरभेयाः सर्वहिताः पवित्राः पुण्यराशयः ।

प्रतिगृह्णन्तु मे ग्रासं गावस्त्रैलोक्यमातरः ॥

Saurabheyâḥ sarvahitâḥ pavitrâḥ punyarâśayaḥ.

Pratigrihṇantu me grâsam, gâvas trailokyamâtaraḥ.

The cows who are of universal utility, pure and holy, may they accept this food, they who are mother of the three worlds.

The cows are typical here of the intelligence that particularly presides over our earth and of the globes connected with it.

(7). *Eating.*

A man should eat such food as is suitable according to his country, age and health. Says the Śruti, "Ahâraśuddhau sattva śuddhih :—" On the purity of food depends the purity of mind." (Chhândogya Upaniṣad VII. 25. 2). No hard and fast rules can be laid down as to what a man should eat and what he should not. In a hot country like India, vegetarianism is necessary. Fruits and farinaceous articles should be the staple diet. Meat should be avoided, as far as possible. Even among non-meat substances, the following directions of Manu should be remembered.

As says Manu (Chapter V, verses 5 to 27) :—

Garlick, leeks and onions, mushrooms and (all plants), springing from impure (substances), are unfit to be eaten by twice-born men.*

One should carefully avoid red exudations from trees and (juices), flowing from incisions, the Selu (fruit), and the thickened milk of a cow (which she gives after calving).

Rice boiled with sesamum, wheat mixed with butter, milk and sugar, milk-rice and flour-cakes which are not prepared for a sacrifice, meat which has not been sprinkled with water while sacred texts were recited, food offered to the gods and sacrificial viands.

The milk of a cow (or other female animal) within ten days after her calving, that of camels, of one-hoofed animals, of sheep, of a cow in heat, or of one that has no calf with her.

(The milk) of all wild animals excepting buffalo-cows, that of women and all (substances turned) sour must be avoided.

Among (things turned) sour, sour milk and all (food) prepared of it may be eaten, likewise what is extracted from pure flower, roots and fruit.

India however is not inhabited by spiritual souls alone. There are born here, as in every other country, souls in various stages of evolution ; and they perhaps require a meat and a fish diet.

The Kṣattriyas were always allowed to hunt and take meat diet. But even in taking meat and fish the śâstric injunctions should be observed. No butcher's meat should be taken. The animal must be duly sacrificed and the flesh sanctified by appropriate mantras. The Brahmachâris (*i. e.*, the school and college students) should under no circumstances take meat, for in that âśrama meat is strictly prohibited. When they enter the household life they may do so, if allowed by their caste rules. As regards students, Manu lays down the following rules:—

Let him abstain from honey, meat, perfumes, garlands, substances (used for flavouring (food), women, all substances turned acid, and from doing injury to living creatures." (Manu III, 177).

* Dr. Alexander Haig, in his wellknown work on "Uric acid in Disease" advises not to take these articles because these contain Uric Acid.

As regards meat and fish also restrictions are imposed, as will appear from the following extract from Manu :—

Let him avoid all sorts of carnivorous birds and those living in villages. and-one-hoofed animals which are not specially permitted (to be eaten), and the Tittibha (parra-jacana).

The sparrow, the plava, the Hamsa, the Brâhmaṇi duck, the village-cock, the strasa crane, the Rajjudala, the woodpecker, the parrot, and the starling.

Those which feed striking with their beaks, web-footed birds, the Koyaṣṭi, those which scratch with their toes, those which dive and live on fish, meat from a slaughter house and dried meat.

The Baka and the Balaka crane, the raven, the khangaritaka, animal that eat fish, village-pigs, and all kinds of fishes.

He who eats the flesh of any (animal) is called the eater of the flesh of that (particular creature), he who eats fish is an eater of every (kind of) flesh ; let him therefore avoid fish.

(But the fish called) pathina and (that called) Rohita may be eaten, if used for offerings to the gods or to the manes ; (one may eat) likewise Ragivas, simhatuṇḍas, and Sasalaks on all (occasions).

Let him not eat solitary or unknown beasts and birds, though they may fall under (the categories of) eatable (creatures), nor any five-toed animals.

The porcupine, hedgehog, the iguana, the rhinoceros, the tortoise, and the hare they declare to be eatable : likewise those (domestic animals) that have teeth in one jaw only, excepting camels.

Beasts and birds recommended (for consumption) may be slain by Brâhmaṇas for sacrifice and in order to feed those whom they are bound to maintain; for Agastya did this of old.

For in ancient (times) the sacrificial cakes were (made of the flesh) of eatable beasts and birds at the sacrifices offered by Brâhmaṇas and Kṣatriyas.

One may eat meat when it has been sprinkled with water, while Mantras were recited, when Brâhmaṇas desire (one's doing it), when one is engaged in the performance of a rite) according to the law, and when one's life is in danger.

### *The method of Eating food.*

The method of eating food is as follows :—Taking his seat on the floor, he should sit facing east or west, and making a square on the ground (chouka or chatuṣkona) place the dish of food in this square. Before taking his seat, he should wash his hands, feet and mouth. As a rule he should begin with liquid food first, then solid and end with liquid. The food of course has already been sanctified by the previous ceremonies of homa, Vaiśvadeva and Bali. Yet when food is placed before him, he should offer thanks to the Almighty and sprinkle a little water on it, reciting the Gâyatri (Om Bhur Bhuvaḥ Svaḥ Tat savitur, &c.). As fas as possible, two solid meals should not be taken in a day. In addition to the Gâyatri, he should recite also the following mantra during the day meal :—

ओं सत्यं त्वर्तेन परिषिञ्चामि । Om Satyam tvartena pariṣiñchâmi. Om Truth! I sprinkle thee with Right. In the night time he should recite :—

ओं ऋतं त्वा सत्येन परिषिञ्चामि । Om ṛitam tvâ satyena parisiñchâmi. Om Right! I sprinkle thee with Truth. Then he should put a little food on the ground, on his right, with salutations to the ruling powers, reciting the following mantra :—

ओं भूपतये नमः । Om Bhûpataye namaḥ, (salutation to the King.)

ओं भुवनपतयेनमः Om bhuvanapataye namaḥ, (salutations to the Lord of the earth, *i.e.*, the planetary Logos).

ओं भूतानां पतये नमः । Om Bhûtânâm pataye namaḥ, (salutations to the Lord of all beings, *i. e.*, the Supreme God).

Then wash the hand and sip a little water reciting the following mantra :—

ओं अमृतोपस्तरणमसि स्वाहा । (T. A. X 32. I) Om amṛitopastaraṇamasi svâhâ. (This is called gaṇḍuṣa mantra).

*Word meaning* :—O water, thou, असि=art, अमृत= Immotral, indestructible ; thou art, उपस्तरणम्=the bed sheet of the Prâna-Devatâ.

*Translation* :—O water ! Thou art the Industructible covering of Prâna.

Then he should perform the inner yâga or offering to the fire within, by reciting the following five mantras and putting a little food into his mouth each time and eating it. He should think strongly that these five life-currents go to regulate the functions of his body.

ओं प्राणाय स्वाहा । Om práṇâya svâhâ.

ओं अपानाय स्वाहा । Om apânâya svâhâ.

ओं समानाय स्वाहा । Om samânâya svâhâ.

ओं उदानाय स्वाहा । Om udânâya svâhâ.

ओं व्यानाय स्वाहा । Om vyânâya svâhâ.

He may add here a sixth offering to his Iṣṭa devatâ or Kula devatâ if he likes. After finishing this internal homa, he should eat the food in silence, and when he feels satisfied, he should finish it with sipping a little water (gaṇḍuṣa) with the following mantra :—

ओं अमृतापिधानमसि स्वाहा Om amṛitapidhânamasi svâhâ. (T. A. X. 86 1)

*Word meaning* :—O water, thou, असि= art, अमृत= Immortal, Indestructible, अपिधानम्=covering.

*Translation* :—O water, Thou art the Imperishable covering.

The theory of gaṇḍuṣa is that the food is to be covered up between these two sheets of water. Upastaraṇam means a bed or anything spread out as covering, it means also the lower bed sheet. The word apidhânam means the under covering. The food is imagined to rest in the stomach between these two coverings of nectar or amṛitam. Then he should rinse his mouth thoroughly, wash his hands and feet again.

*Verses in praise of food.*

There is a very good custom, amongst the religious communities in India, that when they sit down to take their meals, they sing in a chorus, praises of the food placed before them, blessing the giver of the food and the king and his officials.

The verses differ with each community and some time with the idiosyncracy of the individual eater. It is a good custom and keeps alive in us a feeling of thankfulness to the great Lord who gives us food and loyalty to the sovereign under whose rule we live. Even in the best families, it is not always possible to prevent accidents, such as over-cooking or under-cooking or omitting to add some ingredients, &c. This praising the food before eating, puts one in proper humour not to quarrel with his food.

अन्नाद्वै प्रजाः प्रजायन्ते ॥ याः काश्च पृथिवीꣳश्रिताः ॥ अथो अन्नेनैव जीवन्ति ॥ अथैनदपि यन्त्यन्ततः ॥ अन्नꣳहि भूतानां ज्येष्ठम् ॥ तस्मात्सर्वौषधमुच्यते ॥ सर्वं वै तेऽन्न-माप्नुवन्ति ॥ येऽन्नं ब्रह्मोपासते ॥ अन्नाद्भूतानि जायन्ते ॥ जातान्यन्नेन वर्धन्ते ॥ अद्यतेऽत्ति च भूतानि तस्मादन्नं तदुच्यत इति ॥

अन्नं न निन्द्यात् ॥ तद्व्रतम् ॥ प्राणो वा अन्नम् ॥ शरीरमन्नादम् ॥ प्राणे शरीरं प्रतिष्ठितम् ॥ शरीरे प्राणः प्रतिष्ठितः ॥ तदेतदन्नमन्ने प्रतिष्ठितम् ॥ स य एतदन्नमन्ने प्रति-ष्ठितम् वेद प्रतितिष्ठति ॥ अन्नवानन्नादो भवति ॥ महान् भवति प्रजया पशुभिर्ब्रह्मवर्चसेन ॥ महान् कीर्त्या ॥

न कंचन वसतौ प्रत्याचक्षीत ॥ तद्व्रतम् ॥तस्माद्यया कया च विधया बह्वन्नं प्राप्नुयात् ॥ अराध्यस्मा अन्नमित्याचक्षते ॥ एतद्वै मुखतोऽन्नꣳराद्धम् ॥ मुखतोऽस्मा अन्नꣳराध्यते ॥ एतद्वै मध्यतोऽन्नꣳ राद्धम् ॥ मध्यतोऽस्मा अन्नꣳ राध्यते ॥ एतद्वा अन्ततोऽन्नꣳ राद्धम् ॥ अन्ततो-ऽस्मा अन्नꣳ राध्यते ॥

"From food are produced all creatures which dwell on earth. Then they live by food and in the end they return to food. For food is the oldest of all beings and therefore it is called the panacea (sarvauṣadha, i. e., consisting of all herbs or quieting the heat of the body of all beings)".

"They who worship food as Brahman, obtain all food. For food is the oldest of all beings, and therefore it is called panacea. From food all creaturse are produced; by food when born they grow. Because it is fed on, or because it feeds on beings, therefore it is called food (anna)." (Tai. Up. II. 2, 1 and 2).

Let him never abuse food that is the rule.

Breath is food, the body eats the food. The body rests on breath, breath rests on the body. This is food resting on food. He who now knows this food resting on food, rests exalted, becomes rich in food and able to eat food (healthy), becomes great by offspring, cattle and the splendour of his knowledge (of Brahman) great by fame." (Tai. Up., III. 7, 1).

"Let him never turn away (a stranger) that is the rule. Therefore a man should by all means acquire much food for good people say (to the stranger): there is food ready for him. If he gives food amply, food is given to him amply. If he gives food fairly, food is given to him fairly. If he gives food meanly, food is given to him meanly." (Tai. Up., III. 10, 1).

### *A warning.*

The cook or the person who serves the food should never touch it with his hand, but give it with spoons or other vessels, specially with regards to (*a*) salt (*b*) Curries, ghee, oils, drinkables, &c. In short, liquid and semi-liquid articles of food should never be touched by the hands of the persons distributing them. The place where, and the vessels in which, one eats should be both cleansed at once, and not kept over for the next day, for a man is not really purified so long as those are not cleansed.

# APPENDIX.

## SOME OF THE VEDIK MANTRAS EXPLAINED.

### Âchamana Mantra.

*Page 77.*

ओं तद्विष्णोः परमं पदं सदा पश्यन्ति सूरयः । दिवीव चक्षुराततम् ॥

Rig Veda 1.21.20.

Pada : तत्, विष्णोः, परमम्, पदम्, सदा, पश्यन्ति, सूरयः ॥ दिवि, इव, चक्षुः, आऽततम् ॥

*Word-meaning* :—तत् = That, विष्णोः = of Viṣṇu, परम् = highest, पदं = step (heaven), सदा = always, पश्यन्ति = see, सूरयः = the wise ones, दिवि = in the sky, इव = as if, चक्षुः = eye, आतत = spread.

The highest abode of Viṣṇu, the Devas always see, like a broad eye fixed in heaven.
The highest step or the supreme abode of Viṣṇu is seen by the wise men with unobstructed gaze : as the eye fixed in heaven sees every thing without let or hindrance, so the wise see the highest step of Viṣṇu.

*Grammatical notes* :—सदा = is formed by the affix दा added to सर्व, whereby the र्व is elided (see Panini V. 3, 15 and 6). It is acutely accented on the first syllable anomalously. दिवि is locative singular of dyu ; the accent is on the case-affix by VI. 1.171 the इ of the case-affix is elided before the इ of इव, but the first word still retains its original accent, चक्षुः is acutely accented on the first syllable by Phit. II. 3. (आतत) is the past-participle of तन् तनोति (to stretch) the augment इट् is not added because of the prohibition of VII. 2. 15, the न् is elided by VI. 4. 37, the accent is on the gati आ by VI. 2. 49.

### Mârjana Mantra.

*Page 78.*

शं न आपो धन्वन्या३ः, शमु सन्त्वनूप्याः । शं नः खनित्रिमा आपः शमु या कुम्भ आभृताः शिवा नः सन्तु वार्षिकीः ॥

(Atharva Veda I. 1. 4.)

Pada : शम् । नः । आपः । धन्वन्याः । शम् । ऊँ इति । सन्तु । अनूप्याः । शम् । नः । खनित्रिमाः । आपः । शम् । ऊँ इति । याः । कुम्भे । आभृताः । शिवाः । नः । सन्तु । वार्षिकीः ॥

*Word-meaning* :—शम् = Propitious, नः = to us, आपः = waters, धन्वन्याः (of) the desert places ; the word dhanvan = marubhúmi, the water existing there is called dhanvanya, शम् = propitious, उ and, सन्तु, may be, अनूप्याः अनुगता आपो यस्मिन् देशे स अनूपो देशः = the water of the country which is full of water, शं = propitious, नः = to us, खनित्रिमा (of) wells, literally that which has been dug out. शम् उ = and propitious, याः = those (waters), कुम्भे = by pots, आभृताः = are brought, शिवाः = propitious, नः = to us, सन्तु = may be, वार्षिकीः = of the rains.

*Translation* :—Propitious be to us the waters of desert places, and propitious may be those of humid lands. Propitious be to us the waters of the wells, propitious be those brought in pots, and may the rain waters do good to us.

*Grammatical notes* :—(1.) धन्वन्याः plural of धन्वन्य from the root धवि to go, with the affix कनिन् (Unâdi I. 156), as धन्व + अन् = धन्वन् ॥ The न् is inserted because of the indicatory इ (VII. 1. 58.). To this is added the affix यत् (IV. 4. 110), in the sense of staying there. Rule VI, 4. 144, required the elision of the final अन् of धन्वन् before the affix यत् but is prohibited by VI. 4. 168. (2) अनूप्याः plural of अनूप्य similarly formed from the word अ by the affix यत् (VI. 4. 110). The word अनूप is formed by adding अनु to the word अप् as अनु + अप. Now the अ is changed to ऊ by VI. 3. 98, = अनु + ऊप = अनूप the samâsanta अ is added by V. 4. 74, and we have अनूपः (3) खनित्रिमा from the root खनु अवदारणे to dig. To this is added anomalously the affix क्त्री, (III. 3. 88) and then the augment इट् (VII. 2. 35), and then the affix मप् (IV. 4. 20) and we get खनित्रिमा (4) आभृताः from the root हृञ् हरणे to carry away. The ह is changed to भ by a Vârtika under VIII. 2. 35. See my Aṣṭâdhyâyi, page 1560. The gati आ retains its accent by VI. 2. 49. (5) वार्षिकी. The affix ठञ् is added to the word वर्षा by IV. 3. 19, and then the feminine ङीप् by IV. 1. 15. It is acutely accented on the first syllable by VI. 1. 197. (6) सन्तु is the Imperative plural of the root अस 'to be.' The अ is elided by VI. 4. 111.

**The waters bless us, all that rise in desert lands or marshy pools! Bless us waters brought in jars, bless us the waters of the rains.**

**AGHAMARSANA MANTRAS.**

**Page 79.**

**MANTRA I.**

ओम् ऋतं च॑ स॒त्यं चा॒भी᳚द्धा॒त्तप॒सोऽध्य॑जायत ।

तत॒ो रात्र्य॑जायत॒ तत॑ः समु॒द्रो अ॑र्ण॒वः ॥

R. V., X. 190. 1.

*Sâyana:* ऋतम् (इति सत्यनाम ऋतं मानसं यथार्थसंकल्पनं) सत्यं (वाचिकं यथार्थं भाषणं) चकाराभ्याम् ( अन्यदपि शास्त्रीयं धर्मजातं समुच्चीयते ) । ( तत्सर्वम् ) अभीद्धात् ( अभितसात् अद्भुता पुरातनत्वयं कृतात्) तपसोधि (अधि उपर्यर्थे उपरि) अजायत ( अदपद्यत ) । ततः (तस्मादेव ईश्वरात्) रात्री ( उपलक्षणमेतत् अह्नोपि अहश्च रात्रिश्च ) अजायत ॥ ततः (तस्मादेव ईश्वरात्) अर्णवः ( अर्णोभिरुदकेन युक्तः ) समुद्रश्चाजायत ( समुद्रशब्दोन्तरिक्षो दध्यो साधारण इति ) ।

*Word-meaning* :—ऋतं = True thoughts, च = and, सत्यं = True speech, च = and (referring to other sacred virtues), अभीद्धात् = from the highly concentrated or gloriously luminous, तपसः = reflection (meditation as to the mode of creating the cosmos), अध्यजायत = were produced or came up, ततः = from that, रात्री = the night (and day), अजायत = was produced, ततः = from that, अर्णवः = watery, समुद्र := ocean.

*Translation:*—From the highly concentrated (of the Supreme) came out right thinking and true speaking. From Him was born the Night, from Him the watery ocean.

*Note* :—The translation is according to Sâyana's gloss. But it is now admitted by almost all Sanskrit scholars that Rita means "the Law" the force that governs the universe; and Satya means "True," that which constitutes the Be-ness of a thing: *i.e.*, Essence, *i. e.*, Spirit and Matter.

Mr. Griffith translates it as follows :—From fervour kindled to its height eternal Law and Truth were born.: Thence both the Day and Night and thence the billowy flood of sea arose.

*Grammatical Notes* :—अभीद्धात् is ablative singular of अभीद्ध which is the past participle of the root इन्ध् "to burn" preceded by the preposition अभि । The augment इट् is not added by Pâṇini VII. 2 14. The Gati अभि retains its accent on the final by P. VI. 2. 49. The long ई is ekâdeśa for the इ of अभि and the इ of इद्ध, and this long ई becomes svarita by P.VIII. 2. 6. It is in the Ablative case by P. I. 4. 30. (2) रात्री is feminine in ङीप् of रात्रि See P. IV. 1. 31. (3) अर्णव is formed by adding व to अर्णस् and eliding the स before this व. The affix has the force of Matup.

*Note.*—Another explanation of these Aghamarṣana mantras is given in Taittarîya Âraṇyaka Prapâṭhaka X, Anuvâk 1, Section 13. The word-meaning according to commentary given there is somewhat different from what Sâyaṇa gives in the Rig Veda. There he says :—These mantras are for Aghamarṣaṇa and should be recited restraining the breath, while immersed in water (at the time of bathing).

*Word-meaning* :—अभिद्ध *Abhiddha.* It is a compound of "abhi" and "iddha," meaning "luminous on all sides, therefore the ever-effulgent Supreme Self." From this "abhiddha," or the ever-effulgent Supreme Self अजायत was produced the Ritam, or the Real, consisting of the five elements, earth etc., and the Satyam, or The True, consisting of the fourteen worlds. The force of the two "chas" is to indicate that other living creatures were also produced besides the five primordial elements, and the fourteen Lokas.

How were these produced? The answer is Tapasaḥ adhi, *viz.*, after meditation. The Lord meditated "I shall create the world in such and such a manner."

Tataḥ, after this. After creating the five elements and the fourteen worlds. रात्रिरजायत Râtrira jâyata, the night was produced. This is an illustration only and improves the creation of day also.

Tataḥ, then. After the creation of day and night, Samudraḥ, the seven-fold ocean was produced; so also Arṇava, अर्णव, or the waters existing in places other than the ocean, such as in wells, tanks, etc.

*Translation* :—After meditation the ever-effulgent produced the real and the true, then he produced the day and night, and the waters of the (celestial) ocean and of land.

*Note* :—Samudra means the "heavenly ocean"—the waters above the firmament. Arṇava means the waters on the land, *i.e.*, seas &c. Compare Genesis I. 6 and 7.

"And God said, Let there be a firmament in the midst of the waters, and let it divide the waters from the waters.

"And God made the firmament, and divided the waters which were under the firmament from the waters which were above the firmament: and it was so."

MANTRA II.

समुद्रादर्णवादधि संवत्सरो अजायत ।
अहोरात्राणि विदधद्विश्वस्य मिषतो वशी ॥

R. V., X. 190. 2.

*Sâyana:* अर्णवात् समुद्रात् ( सृष्टात् ) अधि ( ऊर्ध्वं ) संवत्सरः ( संवत्सरोपलक्षितः सर्वः कालः ) अजायत । (स ईश्वरः) अहोरात्राणि (एतदुपलक्षितानि सर्वाणि भूतजातानि) विदधत् ( कुर्वन्,-सृजन् ) मिषतो ( निमिषादियुक्तस्य ) विश्वस्य ( सर्वस्य प्राणिजातस्य ) वशी ( स्वामी भूत्वा वर्तते )

*Word-meaning* :—अर्णवात् समुद्रात् = From the watery ocean, अधि = afterwards, संवत्सरः = year (all seasons), अजायत = was produced, अहोरात्राणि =

Days and nights, विदधत् = He re-ordained, मिषतःविश्वस्य = of the whole universe of moments, वशी = the Lord.

Or, समुद्रादर्णवादधि, after the production of (celestial) ocean and other waters, संवत्सरो अजायत, the year (consisting of eleven, twelve, or thirteen months) was produced. अहोरात्राणि विदधत्, ordaining days and nights (including hours and minutes, etc). वशी, the independent creator, the Lord over all. विश्वस्य, of the world.

मिषतो, of the beings that wink, *viz.*, of the living beings who move. It is illustrated and includes the beings that do not move, *viz.*, the plants.

The sense is that the Year means "kâla, or the time." When this Time was produced by the Lord, it brings under its control the whole universe consisting of mobile and immobile creation—those that wink and those that do not wink.

*Grammatical Notes* :—दधत् is acutely accented on the first syllable, by VI. 1. 189; being compounded with वि it still retains its accent, by VI 2. 139.

*Translation* :—After the watery ocean year was produced. The Lord of all living universe then ordained nights and days.

Or,

From that same billowy flood of sea, the year was afterwards produced, Ordainer of the Days and Nights, lord over all who close the eyes.

Or,

After producing the (celestial) ocean and the waters of the land (the Ever-Effulgent) produced the Year (the Time), Who is the Ordainer of days and nights, and is Lord over all that wink (or do not wink).

MANTRA III.

सूर्याचन्द्रमसौ धाता यथापूर्वमकल्पयत् ।
दिवं च पृथिवीं चान्तरिक्षमथो स्वः ॥

R. V. X., 190. 3.

*Sâyana*: सूर्याचन्द्रमसौ (कालस्य ध्वजभूतौ) दिवं च पृथिवीं चान्तरिक्षं (इत्थं त्रिभुवनं) स्वः (स्वः शब्दः सुखवाची दिवो विशेषणं सुखरूपां दिवं) (तदेतत्सर्वं) धाता (विधाता) यथापूर्वम् (पूर्वस्मिन् काले) अकल्पयत् (सृष्टवान् तथैवागामिन्यपि कल्पे कल्पयिष्यतीत्यर्थः) ।

*Word-meaning* :—धाता = The Creator, यथा पूर्वम् अकल्पयत् = as He created in the Past, (so He creates in the present cycle also), सूर्याचन्द्रमसौ = the Sun and the Moon, दिवं स्वः = the happy Heaven, पृथिवीं = the Earth, च = and, अन्तरिक्षम् = the intermediate region, अथ = as well.

*Another word-meaning* :—It has been said above that the Supreme Self created the cosmic egg which contains all other creatures. Then arises the question "In what manner did He create these"? This verse answers that question.

धाता the Supreme Lord. सूर्याचन्द्रमसौ the Sun and the Moon, the two holy luminaries. पृथिवीम् अन्तरिक्षम् दिवम् सुवर्, Prithivim, Antarikṣam, Divam, Suvar, the Earth, the Middle Region, and the delightful Heaven, as well as all the objects of enjoyment (Suvar), that exist in these three regions.

अथो, atho, is an indeclinable word meaning अधः adhaḥ, below. It is a word ending in ओ, 'O.' Namely the worlds below these three, that is, the seven lower Lokas. यथापूर्वम्, yathâ pûrvam, as before, that is, as in former Kalpas or creations. अकल्पयत्, akalpayat, had created. As He created in the former Kalpas, so He created in this Kalpa also.

The two चs indicate that all other objects not included above should also be understood.

*Translation*:—As the Creator created in the past the Sun and the Moon, the joyful Heaven, the earth and the middle region (Kâma-loka), (so He creates them in the present cycle also).

Or,

Dhâtar, the great Creator, then formed in due order the Sun and the Moon. He formed in order the heaven and earth, the regions of the air and light.

Or,

The Supreme Lord created as before (He had created in the former Kalpas) the Sun and the Moon, the Earth, the Middle Region, and the Heaven, with all the objects of enjoyment therein, as well as the regions below them.

## COMMENTARY ON SÛRYOPASTHÂNA MANTRA.

### RIG-VEDA, MANDALA I. SUKTA 115.

Page 59.

### MANTRA 1.

चित्रं देवानामुदगादनीकं चक्षुर्मित्रस्य वरुणस्याग्नेः ।

आप्रा द्यावापृथिवी अन्तरिक्षं सूर्य आत्मा जगतस्तस्थुषश्च ॥

*Padapâtha*: चित्रम् । देवानाम् । उत । अगात् । अनीकम् । चक्षुः । मित्रस्य । वरुणस्य । अग्नेः । आ । आप्रा । द्यावापृथिवी इति ॥ अन्तरिक्षम् । सूर्यः । आत्मा । जगतः । तस्थुषः च ॥

*Sâyana*:—देवानां दीव्यन्तीतिदेवारश्मयः तेषांदेवजनानामेववा अनीकंतेजःसमूहरूपंचित्रंआश्चर्यकरं सूर्यमण्डलं उदगात् उदयाचलंप्राप्तमासीत् कीदृशं मित्रस्यवरुणस्याग्नेश्चउपलक्षणमेतत् एतदुपलक्षितानांजगतांचक्षुःप्रकाशकं चक्षुरिन्द्रियस्थानीयंचउदयंप्राप्यचद्यावापृथिवी दिवंपृथिवींअन्तरिक्षंचआप्राः स्वकीयेनतेजसाआसमन्तादपूरयत् ईदृग्भूतमण्डलान्तर्वर्ती सूर्यः अन्तर्यामितयासर्वस्यप्रेरकः परमात्मा जगतोजङ्गमस्यतस्थुषः स्थावरस्यचआत्मास्वरूपभूतः सहिसर्वस्य स्थावरजङ्गमात्मकस्यकार्यवर्गस्यकारणं कारणाच्चकार्यंनातिरिच्यते तथाचपारमर्षसूत्रम्—तदनन्यत्वमारंभणशब्दादिभ्यइति यद्वा स्थावरजङ्गमात्मकस्यसर्वस्यप्राणिजातस्यजीवात्मा उदितेहिसूर्येमृतप्रायंसर्वजगत्पुनश्चेतनयुक्तंसदुपलभ्यते तथाचश्रूयते—योसौतपन्नुदेतिसससर्वेषांभूतानां प्राणानादायोदेतीति ॥ आप्राः प्रापूरणे लङिपुरुषव्यत्ययः अदादित्वाच्छपोलुक् । जगतः गमेर्द्वेचेतिक्विप् द्विर्वचनम् गमःक्वावित्यनुनासिकलोपः । तस्थुषः तिष्ठतेर्लिटःक्वसुः द्विर्व-

चनेशर्पूर्वाःखयः षष्ठ्येकवचने वसोःसंप्रसारणमितिसंप्रसारणं आतोलोपइटिचेत्याकारलोपः शासिवसिघसीनांचेतिषत्वम् ॥ १ ॥

*Word-meaning and Commentary* :—चित्रं = chitram, bright, wonderful, or brilliantly. According to Uvaṭa it is an adverb qualifying the verb "ud-agât." According to Sâyaṇa it is an adjective qualifying "anîkaṃ," "the solar orb," and it means "the wonderful orb of the sun." Another meaning of "chitra" is "chayanîyam, or pûjanîyam" (worshipful, adorable).

देवानां = of the Devas or of the rays. उत् अगात् = has arisen, अनीकं = the train or the face, चक्षुः = the eye, the revealer, मित्रस्य वरुणस्य अग्नेः = of Mitra, Varuṇa and Agni, आप्राः = thou hast pervaded, द्यावा पृथिवी अन्तरिक्षं = the Heaven, the Earth and the Intermediate region, सूर्यः = the Sûrya, आत्मा = the cause, the self, जगतः = of that which moves, च = and, तस्थुषः = of what is stable.

*Translation* :—The beautiful sphere of rays (or the beautiful face of Devas) has risen up—the eye of Mitra, Varuṇa and Agni, Sûrya, the cause of all that moves and is immoveable, thou hast pervaded the Heaven, the earth and the regions between.

*Grammatical notes* :—आप्राः is the imperfect ( लङ् ) of आ पूरणे This root belongs to the Adâdi class, hence takes no Vikaraṇa. The verb is 2nd person, singular. (2). जगतः is from the root गम् with the affix क्विप् there is reduplication. See vârtika under p. III, 2. 178, of my edition of the Aṣṭâdhyâyî, p. 479. The nasal म् is elided by P. VI, 4, 40. See also Unadi II. 84. (3) तस्थुषः is genitive singular of तस्थस्. It is derived from the root स्था by adding the affix क्वसु (P. III. 2. 107). There is reduplication, because this affix is a participial affix, being a substitute of लिट्. The व of वस् is vocalised before the Genitive affix (P. VI. 4. 131.) The Nom. sing. will be तस्थिवान् (P. VI. 4. 66). Thus स्था + क्वसु + अस = स्था + स्था + वस् + अस = तस्था + वस् + अस = तस्था + उस् + अस (P. VII. 4. 61.) = तस्थ् + उस + अस (P. VI. 4. 131.) = तस्थुष + अस (P. VIII. 3. 60.)

*Note* :—The word अनीक also means face and has been so interpreted by Sâyaṇa himself in a previous ṛik माता देवानामदितेरनीक (R. V. I. 113. 19). Here अदितेरनीकं is explained as मुखमेमुख = as the face reveals the man, so Uṣâ reveals or manifests Aditi. I do not see why this meaning should not be taken here. देवानां चित्रं अनीकम् would then mean "that most wonderful *face* of Devas—that is the revealer or manifester of all Devas." This will also be found more appropriate, as taken with the next word "chakṣus" = the eye of Mitra, etc.

The brilliant presence of the gods hath risen, the eye of Mitra, Varuṇa and Agni, The soul of all that moveth not or moveth, the Sun hath filled the air, earth and heaven.

*Further Grammatical Notes* :—The word आप्राः, âprâ, is compounded of 'â'+aprâh'. According to Whitney the form "aprâh" is aorist, third person, singular of the √प्रा prâ. See para 888 and 889 of Whitney's Grammar :—"The principal peculiarity of the older language in regard to inflection is the frequent absence of i in the endings of 2nd and 3rd sing. act., and the consequent loss of the consonant-ending, and sometimes of the root-finals........................If the root ends in a vowel, only the consonant of the ending is necessarily lost : thus, *aprás* (for both *aprás-s* and *aprás-t*) from √*prá*.

*Translation* :—The brilliant front (van-guard) of the gods hath arisen, the eye of Mitra, Varuṇa, and Agni : Sûrya, the soul of the movable and immovable, hath filled the heaven and the earth and the air, Hail ! (Eggeling).

The bright face of the gods is gone up the sky, the eye of Mitra, of Varuṇa, of Agni : Sûrya has filled heaven, earth, and the mid sky, soul of the moving and standing world. (Peterson).

The wondrous front of the gods hath arisen, the eye of Mitra, of Varuṇa, of Agni ; he hath filled heaven and earth, the atmosphere ; the sun is the Soul of the moving creation (jagat) and of the stationary (tasthivâmsa). (Whitney).

## Mantra I. 115. 2.

सूर्यो देवीमुषसं रोचमानां मर्यो न योषामभ्येति पश्चात् ।
यत्रा नरो देवयन्तो युगानि वितन्वते प्रति भद्राय भद्रम् ॥ २ ॥

सूर्यः । देवीम् । उषसम् । रोचमानाम् । मर्यः । न । योषाम् । अभि । एति ।
पश्चात् । यत्र । नरः । देवऽयन्तः । युगानि । विऽतन्वते । प्रति । भद्राय । भद्रम् ।

*Sâyaṇa* :—(योऽयं) सूर्यः (अस्ति सोऽयं) रोचमानां (दीप्यमानाम्) उषसम् (उषोभिमानिनीं) देवीम् (अभिलक्ष्य) पश्चादेति (पृष्ठभागे गच्छति) । (तत्र दृष्टान्तो) मर्यो न योषा (यथा मर्त्यो योषां अभिलक्ष्य पृष्ठतो गच्छति तद्वत्) । (उषा देवी प्रथमं प्रभातं करोति पश्चात्सूर्य उदेतीत्यर्थः) । यत्र (यस्यामुषसि प्रवृत्तायां) नरो (मनुष्या यजमाना) देवयन्तो (देवानात्मार्थमिच्छन्तो) युगानि (दम्पतिरूपाणि युग्मानि भूत्वा) भद्राय (कल्याणाय) भद्रं वितन्वते (कल्याणं कर्मानुतिष्ठन्ति) । (यस्यामुषसि कर्मानुष्ठानप्रवृत्तिस्तामुषसमभ्येति इति पूर्वत्रान्वयः) ।

*Word-meaning* :—सूर्यः , sûrya, the sun ; रोचमानां , rochamânâm, the shining, the refulgent ; उषसम् , uṣasam, the Dawn ; देवीम् , Devîm, the goddess, the Divine ; अभि, abhi, towards ; पश्चात् एति, paśchât eti, goes after. The sun goes after towards the goddess, the brilliant Uṣâ. मर्यः , maryaḥ, mortal, a man ; न , na, like ; योषाम्, yoṣâm, the maiden ; यत्र, yatra, where (at the time of the dawn) ; नरः , naraḥ, the men, the sacrificers ; देवयन्तः , Devayantaḥ, desirous of propitiating the Devas ; युगानि, yugâni, in couples, husband and wife ; भद्राय, bhadrâya, for the sake of auspiciousness ; भद्रम् वितन्वते, bhadram vitanvate, perform auspicious sacrifices.

*Translation* :—The sun follows after the brilliant goddess Uṣâ like unto a young man following a maiden, at that time when men accompanied by their wives in couple propitiate the Devas and perform auspicious sacrifices for the sake of auspiciousness.

*Note* :—Sâyaṇa gives another meaning of the word "devayanta," viz., "desirous of sacrificing to the deva Sun." "Yugâni," he explains "as sacrifices performed at that *time* of dawn." "Yuga" means "time." Another meaning of "devayanta" is "desirous of getting wealth to sacrifice to the Devas." In that case "Yugâni" would mean "yokes for ploughs," and then "vitanvate" would mean "ploughing," and the second sentence would then mean "for at this season, men seeking to propitiate the gods by the profit which agriculture yields equipped their ploughs."

*Translation* :—Like as a young man followeth a maiden, so doth the Sun the Dawn, refulgent Goddess : Where pious men extend their generations, before the Auspicious One for happy fortune. (Griffith).

"The exact meaning of the second line is somewhat uncertain. As I have rendered it, in accordance with Ludwig, it reminds one of Shelley's, 'Man, the imperial shape, then multiplied His generations under the pavilion of the Sun's throne.' Wilson, following Sâyaṇa, paraphrases,

At which season pious men perform (the ceremonies established for) ages." " (Griffith).

*Note* :—" In the first line the " Sun follows after the shining Dawn as a man follows after the maiden he loves." It is a natural supposition that the next clause, introduced as it is by यत्र, indicates the goal of their common wandering. They go, he pursuing and she pursued, " there where pious men add life to life, each new one happier than the one before," that is, to highest heaven, where the righteous enjoy eternal happiness." Benfey, Orient and Occident, iii. p. 158, refers यत्र to the house of the sacrificer in which this hymn is being sung. The sun hastens there (to shine on that house), " where god-fearing heroes continue their generations, one glorious after the other." Grassman takes युगानि वितन्वते to mean unyoke, outspan. In his dictionary (1873) he asks if we are to supply सूर्याय to भद्राय. In his translation (1877) he accepts Roth's explanation of that phrase. Ludwig translates " where pious men stretch out their generations happily (भद्राय) under the eye of the auspicious sun." " (Peterson).

*Grammatical Notes* :—मर्यः, maryaḥ, comes from the √मृङ् mṛiṅ, 'to die.' It is irregularly formed by the affix यत्, 'yat' under Pâṇini, III. 1.123. It has Udâtta accent on the first syllable by Pâṇini, VI. 1, 213. युगानि, yugâni, is derived from the √युज्, yuj, with the affix घञ्, ghañ, with the force of an accusative. It has acute accent on the last syllable, as it belongs to the उञ्छादि, uñchhâdi class (See Pâṇinî, VI. 1,107.)

वितन्वते vitanvate, is derived from the √तनु, tanu, to spread. तन्वते, tanvate, with the उपसर्ग वि, vi, is compounded under Pâṇinî, II. 1. 4. See my Aṣṭâdhyâyi, p. 217. The Sûtra सह सुपा, saha supâ, is divided into two, and so there is compounding of a verb with an उपसर्ग Therefore, the word वितन्वते "vitanvate" has the acute accent on the final by Pâṇini VI. 1. 223.

MANTRA I. 115. 3

भ॒द्रा अश्वा॑ ह॒रित॒ः सूर्य॑स्य चि॒त्रा एत॑ग्वा अनु॒माद्या॑सः ।
न॒म॒स्यन्तो॑ दि॒व आ पृ॒ष्ठम॑स्थुः परि॒ द्यावा॑पृथि॒वी य॑न्ति स॒द्यः ॥

*Pada pâṭha* :—भ॒द्राः । अश्वा॑ः । ह॒रित॑ः । सूर्य॑स्य । चि॒त्राः । एत॑ऽग्वाः । अ॒नु॒ऽमाद्या॑सः । न॒म॒स्यन्त॑ः । दि॒वः । आ । पृ॒ष्ठम् । अ॒स्थु॒ः । परि॑ । द्यावा॑पृथि॒वी इति॑ । य॒न्ति॒ । स॒द्यः ।

*Sâyaṇa* :—भद्रा (कल्याणा) अश्वा एतग्वा (इत्येतदुभयमश्वनाम तत्रैकं क्रिया परयोजनीयं) अश्वाः (तुरगाः) व्यापनशीला वा हरितः (हर्त्तारः) चित्राः (विचित्रावयवाः) अनुमाद्यासः (अनुक्रमेण सर्वे स्तुत्या मादनीयाः) एवंभूताः सूर्यस्य एतग्वा अश्वाः । नमस्यन्तः (अस्माभिर्नमस्यमानाः सन्तः) दिवो (अन्तरिक्षस्य) पृष्टं (उपरि प्रदेशं पूर्वभागलक्षणं) आ अस्थुः (अतिष्ठन्ति प्राप्नुवन्ति) द्यावापृथिवी (द्यावापृथिव्यौ) सद्यः (तदानीमेव एकेनाह्ना) परियन्ति (परितो गच्छन्तिव्याप्नुवन्ति इत्यर्थः)

*Word-meaning* :—भद्राः bhadrâḥ, auspicious; अश्वाः aśvâḥ, horses; हरितः haritaḥ, baycoloured, yellow; सूर्यस्य sûryasya, of the sun; चित्राः variegated forms, of wonderful limbs; एतग्वाः etagvâḥ, swift-moving, chitrâh, bright, of going on the road to be traversed; अनु-माद्यासः anu-mâdyâsaḥ, to be praised duly, or worthy of praise; नमस्यन्तः namasyantaḥ, saluted by us, or bending; दिवः divaḥ, of heaven, पृष्ठं pristham, back, the upper portion, the steep; आ-अस्थुः â-asthuḥ, attain, reach, climb; द्यावा-पृथिवी = dyâvâ-prithivî, the heaven and earth; परि-यन्ति pari-yanti, pervade, go over; सद्यः sadyaḥ, at once.

*Grammatical Notes, &c.*—हरितः may mean "the drier up (haruṇa-śîlâ) of waters." The rays of the sun dry up waters. Therefore His horses or rays are called haritaḥ or "drier up." अश्वाः horses, is derived from the √अश् to pervade, with the affix क्वन् एत. From √इण् to go, with the affix तन् by असि हसि etc. ग्वः From √गम् to go, with the Uṇâdi affix ड्‌ That whose going (gva) is towards the path to be traversed (eta) is called etagva. It is a Bahuvrîhi and the first member therefore retains its accent अनुमाद्यासः. From √मद्, to praise: with the affix यत् added to the causative. The accent is on the first syllable by यतोऽनाव नमस्यन्तः pl. of pre. part. namasyat. Formed by क्यच् under sûtra नमोवरिव with the sense of respect. The affix शतृ is added irregularly. अस्थुः. Is Aorist pl. The सिच् is elided by गातिस्थ The झि is changed to जुस् by आतः.

According to Peterson the word namasyantaḥ does not mean "adored by us" as Sâyaṇa explains it. But it means "bending" and is an epithet of "horses."

**Translation** :—Bringing us blessing, the yellow horses of the Sun, bright, swift, worthy to be praised, bend, and climb the steep of the sky; in a moment they go over heaven and earth. (Peterson).

**MANTRA I. 115. 4.**

तत् मूर्यस्य देवत्वम् तन्महित्वं मध्याकर्त्तोर्विततं संजभार।
यदेद युंक्त हरितः सधस्था दाद्रात्री वासस्तनुते सिमस्मै ॥ ४ ॥

*Pada Pâtha* :—तत्। सूर्यस्य। देवत्वम्। तत्। महित्वम्। मध्या। कर्तोः। विततम्। सम्। जभार। यदा। इत्। अयुंक्त। हरितः। सधस्थात्। आत्। रात्री। वासः। तनुते सिमस्मै ॥ ४ ॥

*Sâyaṇa* :—सूर्यस्य ( सर्वप्रेरकादित्यस्य ) तद्देवत्वम् (ईश्वरत्वम् स्वतन्त्र्यमितियावत्) महित्वम्(महत्वम् महात्म्यंच) यत्कर्तोः ( कर्मनामैवत् प्रारब्धापरिसमाप्तस्य कृष्यादि लक्षणस्य कर्मणो ) संजभार अस्माल्लोकात्स्वात्मनि उपसंहरति कर्मकरश्च प्रवृत्तं अपरि समाप्त मेव विसृजति ) हरितो ( रसहरणशीलान् स्वरश्मीन् हरितवर्णान् अश्वान् वा ) सधस्थात् ( सहस्थानादस्मात्पार्थिवाल्लोकादाकाश्य) अयुक्त ( अन्यत्र संयुक्तान्करोति ) आत् ( अनन्तर-

मेव ) रात्री ( निशावासः अच्छादयित् तमः ) सिमस्मै ( सर्वस्मिन् लोके ) वनुते ( विस्तारयति )

*Word-meaning.*—सूर्यस्य Sûryasya, of the Sun ; तत् देवत्वं tat devatvam, that the God-head ; तत् महित्वं tat mahitvam, that the greatness ; कर्तोः kartoḥ, of work (like weaving, tilling) ; मध्या madhyâ, in the midst of (yet unfinished) ; विततम् vitatam, spread out, out-stretched : labour ; सञ्जभार saṁ jabhâra, rolled away : rolled together ; यदा yadâ, when, इत् it, even, alone ; अयुक्त ayuktaḥ, yoked (Peterson), loosens ; हरितः haritaḥ, the yellow (horses), the rays ; सधस्थात् sadhasthât, from the stall, from the world or chariot ; आत् ât, then ; रात्री râtrî, the Night ; वासः vâsaḥ, garment, the darkness ; or the day ; तनुते tanute, spreads ; सिमस्मै simasmai, from all, one's self.

*Translation :*—This is the divine strength, the might of Sûrya ; labour, though only half done, comes to an end, as soon as he loosens his horses from his car, and night covers all with her veil. (Siebenzig Lieder).

This is Sûrya's god-head, this his greatness : but that widespread greatness he has, after bringing it into our midst, again rolled together &c. (Ludwig).

That is the god-head, that the might of Sûrya ; in the midst of her work she rolled up the spread out web, so soon as he yoked the bays from the stall. And the Night works the veil for herself. (Geldner).

This is the god-head, this the greatness of the sun ; while yet it was forming he has rolled the web of darkness away ; for, when he yoked his horses from their stall, Night was spreading her garment over all. (Peterson).

MANTRA I. 115. 5.

तन्मित्रस्य वरुणस्याभिचक्षे सूर्यो रूपंकृणुतेद्योरुपस्थे ॥
अनन्तमन्य द्रुशंदस्य पाजः कृष्णमन्यद्धरितः संभरन्ति ॥ ५ ॥

*Pada pâṭha* :—तत् । मित्रस्य । वरुणस्य । अभिचक्षे । सूर्यः । रूपम् । कृणुते । द्योः । उपस्थे अनन्तम् । अन्यत् । रुशत् । अस्य । पाजः । कृष्णम् । अन्यत् हरितः सम । भरन्ति ।

*Sâyana* :—तत्तदानींउदयसमये मित्रस्य वरुणस्य एतदुभयोपलक्षितस्य सर्वस्यजगतः अभिचक्षे आभिमुख्येन द्योर्नभसउपस्थे उपस्थानेमध्ये सूर्यःसर्वस्यप्रेरकः सवितारूपं सर्वस्यप्रभावा अनन्तं निरूपकंप्रकाशकं तेजः कृणुतेकरोति अपिचास्यसूर्यस्य हरितोरसहरणशीलारश्मयः हरिद्वर्णाअवसानरहितं कृत्स्नस्य जगतोव्यापकं रुशद्दीप्यमानंश्वेतवर्णम् पाजः बलनामैतत् अतिबलस्याधिनैशस्यतमसोनिवारणेसमर्थं अन्यत्तमसोविचक्षणंतेजःसंभरन्ति अहनि स्वकीयगमनेननिष्पादयन्ति तथाकृष्णं कृष्णवर्णं अन्यत्तमः स्वकीयापगमनेन रात्रौअस्यरश्मयोऽप्येवंकुर्वन्ति किमुवक्तव्यं तस्यमाहात्म्यमितिसूर्यस्यस्तुतिः ॥ अभिचक्षे संपदादिलक्षणोभावेक्विप् कृदुत्तरपदप्रकृतिस्वरत्वम् । द्योः ङसिङसोश्चेतिपूर्वरूपता । उपस्थे घञर्थेकविधानमितिकप्रत्ययः मरुद्वृधादित्वात्पूर्वपदान्तोदात्तत्वम् । पाजः पातिरक्षतीतिपाजोबलम् पातेर्बलेजुट् चेत्यसुन जुडागमश्च छान्दसोमत्वर्थीयस्यविनोलोपः ॥ ५ ॥

*Word-meaning* :—तत् tat, that, then (at the time of rising); मित्रस्य mitrasya, of Mitra; वरुणस्य varuṇasya, of Varuṇ a' अभि चक्षे abhi-chakṣe, to see; सूर्यः sûryaḥ, the Sun; रूपम् rûpam, form, the light, the glory; कृणुते Kṛiṇute, does; द्योः dyoḥ, of heaven; उपस्थे upasthe, in the bosom, in the midst; अनन्तम् anantam, end-less, untiring; अन्यत् anyat, another (*i.e.*, light); रुशत् ruśat, brilliant, white; अस्य asya, his, of the sun; पाजः pâjaḥ, strength, power; कृष्णम् Krisṇam, dark; अन्यत् anvat, another (*i.e.*, darkness); हरितः haritaḥ, yellow or bay (horses), or rays; सम् भरन्ति sam-bharanti, bring.

*Translation* :—Then the Sun put his glory in the bosom of heaven, to be a light to Mitra and to Varuṇa; in endless succession his horses bring, now the clear day-light, now the darkness. (Peterson).

MANTRA I. 115. 6.

अद्यादेवा उदिता सूर्यस्य निरंहसः पिपृतानिरवद्यात् ।
तन्नो मित्रो वरुणो मामहन्ता मदितिः सिन्धुः पृथिवी उत द्यौः ॥ ६ ॥ ॥७॥

*Pada pâtha* :—

अद्य । देवाः । उत्ऽइता । सूर्यस्य । निः । अंहसः । पिपृत । निः । अवद्यात् । तत् नः । मित्रः । वरुणः । ममहन्ताम् । अदितिः सिन्धुः । पृथिवी । उत । द्यौः ॥६॥ ॥७॥

*Sâyana* :—हेदेवाः द्योतमानाःसूर्यरश्मयः अद्यास्मिन्काले सूर्यस्यआदित्यस्यउदिता-उदितौउदये सतिइतस्ततःप्रसरन्तोयूयंअस्मात्अंहसःपापात्निष्पिपृत निष्कृष्यपालयत यदिद-मस्माभिरुक्तंनोस्मदीयंतन्मित्राद्यःषड्देवताःममहन्तांपूजयन्तुअनुमन्यन्तां रक्षन्त्वितियावत्-मित्रःप्रमीते त्रायकःअहरभिमानीदेवः वरुणोनिष्टानांनिवारयितारात्र्यभिमानी अदितिर-खण्डनीयाअदीनावादेवमाता सिन्धुःस्यन्दनशीलोदकाभिमानिनीदेवता पृथिवीभूलोकस्या-धिष्ठात्री द्यौःद्युलोकस्य उतशब्दःसमुच्चये ॥ अद्य निपातस्यचेतिसंहितायांदीर्घत्वम् । उदिता इत्पूर्वादेतेर्भावे क्तिन् सुपांसुलुगितिडादेशः तादौचेतिगतेःप्रकृतिस्वरत्वम् । पिपृत पृपालनपू-रणयोः पृइत्येके लोटिजुहोत्यादित्वाच्छपःश्लुः द्विर्वचनेारदत्वहलादिशेषाः अर्तिपिपर्त्योश्चे त्य-भ्यासस्येत्वम् सार्वधातुकमपिदितितशब्दस्यङित्त्वेसतिविश्चितुनुघेत्यादिनासंहितायांदीर्घः ॥६॥

*Word-meaning* :—अद्य adyâ, to-day, at this time; देवाः devâh, O Devas, O rays of the Sun; उदिता uditâ = उदितौ uditau, having risen; सूर्यस्य sûryasya, of the Sun; अंहसः aṁhasaḥ, from sin, from danger; निः nir, to be joined with the following verb; पिपृत piprita = निष्पिपृत nis-pipṛita = पालयत protect; free (us), ferry (us) across; निः nir, to be joined with the following verb; अवद्यात् avadyât, from shame; तत् that; नः naḥ, our, us; मामहन्ताम् mâmahantâm, may (they) grant the boon, may protect; मित्रः mitraḥ, Mitra, the Lord of Day; वरुणः varuṇaḥ, Varuṇa, the Lord of Night; अदितिः aditiḥ, Aditi, the Undivided, the Infinite; सिन्धुः sindhuḥ, Sindhu, the Lord of Waters; पृथिवी prithivî, the Goddess of Earth; द्यौः dyauḥ, the Heaven—Lord; उत uta, and.

*Translation* :—To day O Gods, at the rising of the Sun free us from trouble, free u from sin: this boon may Mitra, Varuṇa, Aditi, Sindhu, Pṛithivi and Heaven, fulfil to us (Peterson)

### COMMENTARY ON NAMASKARA MANTRAS.

**Page 64.**

RIGVEDA III. 59, 6.

मित्रस्य चर्षणी धृतोऽवो देवस्य सानसि ।
द्युम्नचित्रश्रवस्तमम् ॥ ६ ॥

*Pada-pâṭha* :—मित्रस्य चर्षणीऽधृतः अवः देवस्य सानसि । द्युम्नम् चित्रश्रवः तमम् ॥ ६ ॥

*Sayana* :—चर्षणी धृतः मनुष्याणां वृष्टिप्रदानेन धारकस्य मित्रस्य देवस्य सम्बन्धि अवः अन्नं सानसि सर्वैः सम्भजनीयं द्युम्नं तदीयं धनञ्च चित्रश्रवस्तममतिशयेन चायनीय कीर्त्तियुक्तम् । सानसि । सनोतः सानसिपर्णसीत्यादिना सिच् प्रत्ययान्तत्वेन निपातनादुपधावृद्धिः । चित्त्वादन्तोदात्तः । स्वमेरिति स्वमोलुक् ।

*Word-meaning* :—चर्षणि-धृतः Charṣaṇi-dhṛitaḥ, of the protector of men, (by giving them rain) of the supporter of the race of men, the sustainer of the tribes of men. मित्रस्य Mitrasya, of Mitra. देवस्य Devasya, of the God. अवः Avaḥ, Protection, food, help, grace. सानसि Sânasi, "Is the procurer of." The word is an adjective in the nominative, agreeing with अवः and governing द्युम्नं in the accusative. "Bringing again, winning, making booty victorious."—(Roth. Gold.) द्युम्नम् Dyumnam, Splendour, riches, booty. चित्र-श्रवस-तमम् Chitra-Śravas-tamam, glorious fame, to be heard by all.

*Grammatical Notes.*—The word सानसि sânasi is formed from the √सन् by the affix असिच् asich, and the penultimate is vriddhied by nipâtana as given, in the Uṇâdi sûtra. It has accent on the final, because it has an indicatory च *cha* of the affix असिच् The word being a neuter noun, the case affix is elided by VII. 1, 23. See Uṇâdi "sânasi, varṇasi" No. 546. सन् असिच = सान् = असिच् (vriddhi by Nipâtana as the word is so exhibited in the Uṇâdi.

*Translation* :—Mitra sustains the tribes of men; the help this God gives us shall win us fame that all shall hear of. (Peterson .

Mantra.

अभि यो महिना दिवं मित्रो बभूव सप्रथाः । अभि श्रवोभिः पृथिवीम् ॥७॥

Rigveda III 59. 7.

*Pada-pâṭha* :—

अभि यः महिना दिवम् मित्रः बभूव सऽप्रथाः । अभिश्रवःऽभिः पृथिवीम् ॥७॥

*Sâyana* :—योमित्रो महिना स्वकीयेन महिम्ना दिवमन्तरिक्षमभि बभूव अभिभवति समित्रः सप्रथाः । प्रथः प्रसिद्धः कीर्त्तिः । तत्सहितः श्रवोभिः वृष्टिद्वारोपादितैरन्नैः पृथिवीमभि अभिभवति बह्वन्नयुक्तां करोतीत्यर्थः ।

*Word-meaning* :—यः, Yaḥ, Who ; मित्रः, Mitraḥ, Mitra ; महिना ; Mahinâ, by His glory, In ordinary Sanskrit, the form would have been Mahimnâ, महिम्ना; दिवम्, Divam, Heaven, the sky ; अभि-बभूव, Abhi-babhûva, Overpowered, surpassed, encompassed; स-प्रथः, Saprathaḥ, with glory ; Prathas means 'glory,' and स, sa means 'with.' The whole word, therefore, means "He who is glorious." श्रवोभिः, Śravobhiḥ, with food, with glory, according to Roth the word श्रवस्, śravas, here means "stream, flow" and he translates it "in his flight." पृथिवीम्, Pṛithivîm, the earth ; अभि, Abhi, the word babbhûva, बभूव, is understood here. Surpasses.

*Grammatical Notes.*—The word sa-prathas, सप्रथस्, is a compound of saha, सह, and prathas, प्रथस्. Saha, सह, becomes sa, स, by VI. 3. 82. Prathas, प्रथस्, is derived from the √pratha "to be famous" (Bhu-âdi, 765), with the affix असुन्, asun.

*Translation.*—The universal God, who encompasses heaven with his greatness, and earth with his glory. (Peterson).

Mantra.

मित्राय पञ्च येमिरे जना अभिष्टिशवसे । स देवान्विश्वान्बिभर्ति ॥ ८ ॥

Rigveda III. 59. 8.

*Pada-pâtha.*—

मित्राय पञ्च येमिरे जनाः अभिष्टिशवसे । सः देवान् विश्वान् बिभर्त्ति ॥८॥

*Sâyana* :—पञ्चजनाः निषादपञ्चमा श्चत्वारो वर्णाः अभिष्टि शवसे शत्रूणामभिगन्तृ बलयुक्ताय मित्राय येमिरे हवींष्युद्य गच्छन्ति । सः तादृशो मित्रः विश्वान् सर्वान् बिभर्ति स्वस्वरूप तया धारयति । अभिष्टि शवसे । इषेर्मन्त्रे वृषेत्यादिना क्तिन् । तादौ च नितीत्यभेरन्तोदात्तत्वम् शकन्ध्वादित्वात्पररूपत्वम् । बहुव्रीहौ पूर्वपदस्वरः ॥

*Word-meaning* :—पञ्च-जनाः, Pañcha-janâh, the five tribes, the five castes, *viz.* : the four well-known castes, together with Niṣâda as the fifth ; अभिष्टि-शवसे, Abhiṣṭiśavase, the Giver of help to conquer enemies. The word Abhiṣṭi, अभिष्टि, is a compound of Abhi and Asti, अस्ति, and means 'help.' Or it may be considered as derived from the √iṣ, इष, with the affix ktin, क्तिन्, by III. 3. 96. मित्राय, Mitrâya, to Mitra ; येमिरे, Yemire, went, repaired, offered oblations ; सः, Sah, He; देवान्, Devân, gods; विश्वान्, Viśvân, all; बिभर्ति, Bibharti, supports, sustains.

*Grammatical Notes.*—The word Abhiṣṭi, अभिष्टि, has accent on the final of Abhi, अभि, by VI. 2. 50. There is Pararûpa of abhi and iṣṭi as the word belongs to Śakandhvâdi Gaṇa by VI. 1. 94. Therefore Abhi + iṣṭi = Abhiṣṭi (no lengthening). As the word is a Bahuvrihi compound, the first member retains its original accent.

*Translation.*—To Mitra our five tribes go for help ; and He sustains all the gods. (Peterson).

Mantra.

मित्रो देवेष्वायुषु जनाय वृक्तबर्हिषे । इष इष्टव्रता अकः ॥ ९ ॥

Rigveda III 59. 9.

*Padapâṭha.*—

मित्रः देवेषु आयुषु जनाय वृक्त बर्हिषे । इषः इष्ट व्रताः अकरित्यकः ॥ ८ ॥

*Sâyana* :—मित्रः ( भगवानादित्यः ), देवेषु ( द्योतमप्नादिगुणायुक्तेषु ) आयुषु ( मनुष्येषु ) मध्ये यः ( जनः ) वृक्तबर्हिः । वृक्तं लूनं बर्हिर्येनसः । ( बर्हिलवनासादनपूर्वहविषो दाता ऋत्विगित्यर्थः ) तस्मैवृक्तबर्हिषे जनाय इष्टव्रताः इष्टाश कल्याणानि व्रतानि-कर्माणि याभिः सिध्यन्ति ता इषः तादृशान्यन्नानि अकः करोति तस्मै ददातीत्यर्थः वृक्तबर्हिषे । ओ व्रश्चू छेदने । कर्मणि निष्ठायां यस्य विभाषे तेाट् प्रतिषेधः । वहुव्रीहै पूर्वपदस्वरः । अकः । करोतेर्लुङि च्लेर्मन्त्रे घसेत्यादिना लुक् सिपो हल्ङ्यादिलोपः । निघातः ॥

*Word-meaning.*—Mitraḥ, the adorable Âditya, the friend; Deveṣu, among the Devas or gods; Âyuṣu, among living men; Janâya, to the man, to the person; Vṛikta-barhiṣe, to Him who has cut or trimmed (vrikta), the sacrificial grass called Barhis. Thus the word Vṛikta-barhis is generally a name of the priest, so called because he has to trim the sacrificial grass. 'The Sacred Kuśa grass (Poa cynosuriodes) after having had the roots cut off, is spread on the Vedi or altar, and upon it the libation of Soma-juice, or oblation of clarified butter, is poured out. In other places, a tuft of it in a similar position is supposed to form a fitting seat for the deity or deities invoked to the sacrifice. According to Mr. Stevenson it is also strewn over the floor of the chamber in which the worship is performed. (Max Muller). Iṣaḥ, desired objects; Iṣṭa-bratah, obeying the wish, fulfilling the wish, or the sacred law; Akar, He did. It is third person singular of the aorist of √kṛi "to do."

*Grammatical Notes.*—Vṛikta is past participole of the √o-vraśchñ, "to cut." The इट् 'it' is prohibited by VII. 2. 15. As a member of a bahuvrihi compound it retains its accent. Akar is from the √kri. The sign of the aorist is elided by P. II. 4. 80. The tense afflx sip सिप् is elided by VI. 1. 68. it is accentless.

*Translation.*—A friend indeed to gods and to men, to those that worship him, Mitra fulfils their hearts' desires. (Peterson).

## COMMENTARY ON ATMA-RAKSÂ MANTRAS.

**Page 64.**

MANTRA.

ओं । जातवेदसे सुनवाम सोममरातीयतो निदहाति वेदः ।

स नः पर्षदति दुर्गाणि विश्वा नावेव सिन्धुं दुरितात्यग्निः ॥

Rig Veda I. 99. 7.

*Pada-pátha* :—जातऽवेदसे । सुनवाम । सोमम् । अरातीऽयतः । नि । दहाति । वेदः ॥ सः । नः । पर्षत् । अति । दुःऽर्गानि । विश्वा । नावाऽइव । सिन्धुम् । दुःइता । अति । अग्निः ॥

*Sáyana* :—जातवेदसे जातानां उत्पत्तिमतांसर्वेषांवेदित्रे यद्वा जातैःसर्वैः प्राणिभिः ज्ञायमानाय जातधनायजातप्रज्ञायवाग्नये लतारूपं सोमंसुनवामअभिषुणवाम जातवेदोगुणकमग्नियष्टुंसोमाभिषवंकरवामेत्यर्थः सोग्निः अरातीयतः अरातिंशत्रुमिवास्मानाचरतः शत्रोर्वेदोधनंनिदहाति नितरां दहतुभस्मीकरोतु अपिचसोग्निर्नोस्मान् विश्वाविश्वानि-सर्वाणिदुर्गाणिदुर्गमनानि भोक्तुमशक्यानिदुःखानिअत्तिपर्षत् अतिपारयतु अतिक्रमय्यदुःखरहितंसुखंप्रापयतु तत्रदृष्टान्तः—नावेवसिन्धुं यथाकश्चित्कर्णधारः ग्राहादिभिर्दुष्टसत्त्वैराकुलितांनदीं नावातारयति तद्वत् तथादुरितादुरितानि दुःखहेतुभूतानिपापानि अस्मानग्निरतिपारयतु दुःखनिमित्तात्पापादप्यस्मानुत्तारयत्वित्यर्थः । अत्रनिरुक्तम्—जातवेदाःकस्माज्जातानिवेदजातानिवैनंविदुर्जातेजातेविद्यतइतिवाजवित्तोवाजातधनोजातविद्योवाज़ातप्रज्ञानोयत्तज्जातःपशून्नविन्दतेतितज्जातवेदसोजातवेदस्त्वमितिहिब्राह्मणमित्यादि[1] ॥ जातवेदसे जातानिवेत्तीतिजातवेदाः गतिकारकयोरपि पूर्वपदप्रकृतिस्वरत्वंचेतिवचनात्कारकपूर्वाद्वेत्तेरसुन् पूर्वपदप्रकृतिस्वरत्वम् । अरातीयतः नविद्य तेरातिर्दानमस्मिन्नित्यरातिःशत्रुः तमिवास्मानाचरति उपमानादाचारेइत्युपमानभूतात् कर्मणःक्यच् क्यजन्ताल्लटःशतृ शतुरनुमइतिशसउदात्तत्वम् । दहाति दहभस्मीकरणे लेट्याडागमः । वेदः विद्यतेलभ्यतेइतिवेदोधनं विद्लृलाभे औणादिकःकर्मण्यसुन् । पर्षत् पॄपालनपूरणयोः अस्मादन्तर्भावितण्यर्थाल्लेट्यडागमः सिब्बहुलंलेटीतिसिप् । दुर्गाणि दुःखेन गम्यतेएष्विति सुदु रोरधिकरणेइतिगमेर्डः ॥ १ ॥

*Word meaning* :—**जातवेदस** for the Jâtavedas, to the knower of all that live ; **सुनवाम** we prepare the juice or press out ; **सोमम्** the Soma, the pleasant ; **अरातीयतः** of the enemy ; of the ungenerous (**न विद्यते राति दानमस्मिन्**) ; **निदहाति** consumes, purifies ; **वेदः** wealth, thought ; **सः** that (agni) ; **नः** our ; **अति-पर्षत्** may take across ; **दुर्गाणि** difficulties ; **विश्वा** all ; **नावा** by a boat ; **इव** as ; **सिन्धुम्** river, sea ; **दुरिता** pains, sins ; **अति** ati-pârayatu, take across : **अग्निः** Agni.

*Translation* :—We prepare the pleasant for the Omniscient, may He purify the evil thoughts of the ungenerous. May He take us across all difficulties. As by a boat the river, so may Agni enable us (to) surmount all our sins.

*Grammatical Notes* :—Jâtavedas is so called because "He knows (veda) all that are born (jâtâni)" or because "all who are born know Him,"

१ नि० ७. १६. ।

or because "He exists (vidyate) in all and every living being," or because "He is the Fount of all wealth (vedas=wealth)," or because "He is the Source of all knowledge." Dahâti is the लेट् or Vedic subjunctive of दह् "to burn." Vedas meaning "wealth" comes from the √विद् विद्यते लभ्यते "that which is obtained, that which exists, the possessions and acquisitions." It is formed by adding the affix असुन् ( अस् ) to विद् लृ "to acquire, to gain." Parṣat is derived from √पृ "to nourish, to protect, to fill." It is also a Vedic subjunctive.

*Translation* :—For Jâtavedas let us press the Soma; may he consume the wealth of the malignant.

May Agni carry us through all our troubles, through grief as in a boat across the river. (Griffith).

Mantra.

पिशंगभृष्टि मंभृणं पिशाचिं मिन्द्र सं मृण । सर्वं रक्षो नि बर्हय ॥ ५ ॥

Rig Veda I. 133. 5.

*Pada-pâtha* :- पिशंगऽभृष्टिं । अंभृणं । पिशाचिं । इंद्र । सं । मृण । सर्वं । रक्षः । नि । बर्हय

*Sâyana*.:—हे राजन्नीश्वर वरुण त्वदीयं मृन्मयं मृदादिभिर्निर्मितं गृहं मो मा उमैव अहंगमं गतो ऽस्मि अपितु सुशोभनं सुवर्णमयमेव त्वदीयं गृहं प्राप्नवानि । सत्वं मां मृल सुखय हे सुचत्र शोभनधनवरुण मृलय उपदयां च कुरु ॥

*Word-meaning* :—पिशंगभृष्टिं Piśaṁga-bhriṣṭim, A little reddish in color, brown, fiery-weaponed; अंभृणं Aṁbhṛiṇam, roaring fearfully, terrible; पिशाचिं Piśâchim, the eater of raw flesh, fiend, carnivorous savage; इंद्र Indra, O Indra; संमृण Sam mṛiṇa, kill totally, annihilate; सर्वं Sarvam, All; रक्षः Rakṣaḥ, Goblin, demon, Râkṣasa. निबर्हय Ni-barhaya, strike to ground, destroy.

*Grammatical Notes* :— 1) The word Aṃbhṛiṇam, अम्भृणम् comes from the √bhraṇ "to make noise." It is yan luk intensive form with the affix अच 'ach' of the Pachâdi class. The Bha भ is elided as a Vedic irregularity. Or the whole word Aṃbhṛiṇam अम्भृणम् may mean "great," "very powerful." (2) The pisâchi mentioned in the text is explained by some as meaning 'old age.' (3) The word "barhaya" बर्हय is derived from the Churâdi √bṛih 'to kill.'

*Translation*.—O Indra! Annihilate the brown, howling, carnivorous, savage and destroy entirely every Râkṣasa brood.

COMMENTARY ON MIDDAY SANDHYÂ MANTRAS.

Page 68.

*Sûryopasthânam*.

Rig Veda I. 50. 1 to 13.

Mr. Griffith translates these Mantras thus :—

1. His bright rays bear him up aloft, the God who knoweth all that lives,

Sûrya, that all may look on him.

2. The constellations pass away, like thieves, together with their beams,
Before the all-beholding Sun.

3. His herald rays are seen afar refulgent o'er the world of men,
Like flames of fire that burn and blaze.

4. Swift and all beautiful art thou, O Sûrya, maker of the light
Illuming all the radiant realm.

5. Thou goest to the hosts of Gods, thou comest hither to mankind
Hither all light to be beheld.

6. With that same eye of thine wherewith thou lookest, brilliant Varuna,
Upon the busy race of men,

7. Traversing sky and wide mid-air, thou metest with thy beams our days,
Sun, seeing all things that have birth.

8. Seven Bay Steeds harnessed to thy car bear thee, O thou far-seeig One,
God, Sûrya with the radiant hair.

9. Sûrya hath yoked the pure bright Seven, the daughters of car; with these,

10. Looking upon the loftier light above the darkness we have oome
To Sûrya, God among the Gods, the light that is most excellent.

11. Rising this day, O rich in friends, ascending to the loftier heaven,
Sûrya, remove my heart's disease, take from me this my yellow hue.

12. To parrots and to starlings let us give away my yellowness,
Or this my yellowness let us transfer to Haritala trees.

13. With all his conquering vigour this Âditya hath gone up on high,
Giving my foe into mine hand: let me not be my foeman's prey.

MANTRA.

ओम् उदुत्यं जातवेदसं देवं वहन्ति केतवः । दृशे विश्वाय सूर्य्यम् ।

Rig Veda I. 50. 1.

*Pada-pâṭha* :—उत् । ऊं इति । त्यं । जातऽवेदसं । देवं । वहन्ति । केतवः
दृशे । विश्वाय । सूर्यं ॥ १ ॥

*Sâyaṇa* :—केतवः प्रज्ञापकाः सूर्याः यद्वा सूर्यरश्मयः सूर्यसर्वस्यप्रेरकमादित्यं उदुवह-
न्ति ऊर्ध्वंवहन्ति उइति पदपूरणःउक्तश्च—मिताक्षरेष्वनर्थकाःकमीमिद्धितोति किमर्थविश्वाय-

विश्वस्मैभुवनायदृशेद्रष्टुं यथासर्वेजनाः सूर्यपश्यन्तितथोर्ध्वंवहन्तीत्यर्थः कीदृशंसूर्यं त्यंप्रसिद्धं-जातवेदसं जातानांप्राणिनांवेदितारंजातप्रज्ञंजातधनंवा देवंद्योतमानम् अत्रनिरुक्तम्—उद्वहन्ति तंजातवेदसंदेवम श्वाः केतवोरश्मयो वा सर्वेषांभूतानांसंदर्शनायसूर्यमिति¹ ॥ जातवेदसं जाता-निवेत्तीतिजातवेदाः गतिकारकयोरपि पूर्वपदप्रकृतिस्वरत्वम्चेत्यसुन् पूर्वपदप्रकृतिस्वरत्वंच । दृशे दृशेविख्येचेतितुमर्थे निपातितः । सूर्यं राजसूयसूर्येत्यादिना षूप्रेरणे इत्यस्मात्क्यपरुडा-गमसहितोनिपातितः अतःप्रत्ययस्यपित्त्वादनुदात्तत्वेधातुस्वरेणाद्युदात्तत्वम् ॥ १ ॥

*Word-meaning* :—(1) केतवः, Ketavaḥ, the heralds, the rays of the sun, the horses of the sun, the lights; (2) उत्वहन्ति, Ud-vahanti, carry up, draw up ; (3) त्यं, Tyam, Him ; (4) ऊं, Um, a mere expletive ; (5) जातवेदसं, Jâta-vedasam, the knower of every thing that is born, the omniscient ; (6) देवं, Devam, The God, the heavenly ; (7) दृशे, Dṛiśe, To see, to be seen ; (8) विश्वाय, Viśvâya, by all ; (9) सूर्यं, Sûryam, The sun.

*Grammatical Notes* :—(1) The word जातवेदसं Jâta-vedasam being a kṛit-formed word (Jâtâni vetti जातानि वेत्ति ) would be governed by Unâdi IV. 226 for its accent The first member retains its accent. It is formed with the affix asun असुन्. (2) The word dṛiśe is formed by III. 4. 11., with the sense of infinitive and has the same meaning as Drasṭum द्रष्टुम्. (3) The word Sûrya सूर्यं is so exhibited in sûyra III. 1. 114. It is formed by the affix क्यप् kyap added to the √sû "to send," with the augment ruṭ The affix kyap being पित् is anudâtta. Therefore, the word has accent on the first syllable, retaining the root accent.

*Translation* :—His bright rays bear him up aloft, the God who knoweth all that lives. Sûrya, that all may look on him.

MANTRA.

अप॒ त्ये ता॒यवो॑ यथा॒ नक्ष॑त्रा यन्त्य॒क्तुभिः॑ । सूरा॑य वि॒श्वच॑क्षसे ॥ २ ॥

Ṛig Veda I. 50, 2.

*Pada-pâtha* :—अप॑ । त्ये । ता॒यवः॑ । य॒था॒ । नक्ष॑त्रा । य॒न्ति॒ । अ॒क्तुभिः॑ । सूरा॑य । वि॒श्वऽच॑क्षसे ॥ २ ॥

*Sâyana* :—त्येतायवोयथाप्रसिद्धास्तस्कराइवनक्षत्रानक्षत्राणिदेवगृहरूपाणि देवगृ-हावैनक्षत्राणीति श्रुत्यन्तरात्² । यद्वा इहलोकेकर्मानुष्ठानाय येस्वर्गंप्राप्नुवन्ति तेनक्षत्ररूपे-णदृश्यन्ते तथाचश्रूयते योवाइहयजते अमुंलोकंनक्षते तन्नक्षत्राणांनक्षत्रत्वमिति³ । यद्वातेषां-सुकृतानांज्योतींषिनक्षत्राण्युच्यन्ते सुकृतांवाएतानिज्योतींषियन्नक्षत्राणीत्याम्नानात्⁴ । यास्क-स्त्वाह—नक्षत्राणिनक्षतेर्गतिकर्मणोनेमानिक्षत्राणीतिचब्राह्मणमिति⁵ । तथाविधानिनक्षत्राणि-अक्तुभिः रात्रिभिःसहअपयन्तिअपगच्छन्तिविश्वचक्षसेविश्वस्यसर्वस्यप्रकाशकस्यसूरायसूर्यस्य आगमनंदृष्ट्वेतिशेषः तस्करानक्षत्राणिचरात्रिभिःसहसूर्यआगमिष्यतीतिभीत्यापलायन्तइत्यर्थः

१ नि० १२· १५. । २ तै० ब्रा० १. ५. २. । ३ तै० ब्रा० १. ५. २. ।
४ तै० सं. ५. ४. १. । ५ नि० ३. २०. ।

तायुरितिस्तेननाम तायुस्तस्करइतितन्नामसुपाठात् अक्तुरितिरात्रिनाम शर्वरीअक्तुरितितत्रपाठात् ॥ यथा यथेतिपादा न्तेइतिसर्वानुदात्तत्वम् । नक्षत्रा नक्षगतौ अमिनक्षियजिबन्धिपतिभ्योत्रन्नित्यत्रन्प्रत्ययः नित्वादाद्युदात्तत्वम् नभ्राण्नपादित्यत्रवृत्तौत्वेवमुक्तम् नक्षरतिनक्षीयतइतिवानक्षत्रम् क्षीयतेःक्षरतेर्वा नक्षत्रमितिनिपात्यतइति शेश्छन्दसिबहुलमितिशेर्लोपः । यन्ति इण्गतौ इणोयणितियणादेशः । सूरायविश्वचक्षसे विश्वंचष्टेप्रकाशयतीतिविश्वचक्षाः चक्षेर्बहुलंशित्वंत्यसुन्प्रत्ययः शित्त्वेनसार्वधातुकत्वात् ख्याञादेशाभावः उभत्रषष्ठ्यर्थेचतुर्थीवक्तव्येतिचतुर्थी ॥ २ ॥

*Word-meaning* :—(1) त्ये, Tye, these ; (2) तायवः, Tâyavaḥ, Thieves ; (3) यथा, Yathâ, as, like ; (4) नक्षत्रा, Nakṣatrâ, the stars, asterisms, constellations ; (5) अपयंति, Apāyanti, go away ; (6) अक्तुभिः, Aktubhiḥ, with the nights, with their rays, or beams ; (7) विश्वचक्षसे, Viśva-chakṣase, the illuminer of all, the all-beholding ; (8) सूराय, Sûrâya, of the sun, of the hero. The dative has the force of Genetive here.

*Grammatical Notes* :—(1) नक्षत्र Nakṣatra is derived from the √nakṣa 'to go' by the affix Atran ( अत्रन् ) under Unâdi III. 105. It has accent on the first syllable, because it is formed by an affix having an indicatory न् ॥ (2) Chakṣas is formed by the affix asun असुन् under Unâdi IV. 232. The affix being treated as शित् and therefore sárvadhâtuka, the root चक्ष is not replaced by ख्या ॥

*Translation* :—The constellations pass away, like thieves, together with their beams, Before the all-beholding Sun.

MANTRA.

अदृश्रमस्य केतवो वि रश्मयो जनाँ अनु भ्राजन्तो अग्नयो यथा ॥ ३ ॥

Rig Veda I. 50. 3.

*Pada-pâtha* :— अदृश्रं । अस्य । केतवः । वि । रश्मयः जनान् । अनु । भ्राजन्तः । अग्नयः । यथा ॥ ३ ॥

*Sâyana* :—अस्यसूर्यस्यकेतवःप्रज्ञापकाः रश्मयोदीप्तयः जनाँअनुव्यदृश्रंजातान्सर्वान्अनुक्रमेणप्रेक्षन्ते सर्वंजगत्प्रकाशयन्तीत्यर्थः तत्रदृष्टान्तः—भ्राजन्तोदीप्यमानाः अग्नयोयथाअग्नयइव ॥ अदृश्रं दृशिर्प्रेक्षणे वर्तमानेलुङि इरितोवेतिच्लेरङादेशःऋदित्यनुवृत्तौ बहुलंछन्दसीतिरुडागमः अतएवबहुलवचनात् ऋदृशोङिगुणइतिगुणाभावइत्युक्तं तिङ्ङतिङोभवन्तीतिप्रथमपुरुषबहुवचनस्य उत्तमपुरुषैकवचनादेशः प्रथमापुरुषएवशाखान्तरेश्रूयते—अदृश्रन्नस्यकेतवइति । जनानित्यस्यनकारस्यसंहितायांमुत्वयत्वादिपूर्ववत् । भ्राजन्तः शपःपित्त्वादनुदात्तत्वम् शतुरप्यलसार्वधातुकस्वरेणधातुस्वरएवशिष्यते ॥ ३ ॥

*Word Meaning* :—(1) अदृश्रं Adṛiśram, are seen. It is aorist of the √dṛiśir दृशिर "to see :" the an अङ् is added by III. 1. 57. The augment ruṭ is added by VII. 1. 8. It is in the first person singular with the force of the third person plural. In fact this very Hymn occurs in the Athara Veda XIII. 2. 18., where the form is Adṛiśran ; (2) अस्य Asya, His, sun's ; (3) केतवः Ketavaḥ, the heralds, the lights ; (4) वि Vi, an Upasarga which is to be added to the Verb Adṛiśram, which would then become Vyadṛiśram, meaning "are seen abroad" ; (5) जनान् Janân, men ; (6) अनु Anu, after, among; (7) भ्राजंतः Bhrâjantaḥ, shining, burning, blazing; (8) अग्नयः Agnayaḥ, fires ; (9) यथा Yathâ, As, like,

*Translation* :—His herald rays are seen afar refulgent o'er the world of men, Like flames of fire that burn and blaze. (Griffith).

MANTRA.

तुरणिर्विश्वदर्शतो ज्योतिष्कृदसि सूर्य । विश्वमाभासि रोचनं ॥ ४ ॥

Ṛig Veda I. 50. 4.

*Pada-pâṭha* :—तुरणिः । विश्वऽदर्शतः । ज्योतिःऽकृत् । असि । सूर्य । विश्वं । आ भासि । रोचनं ॥ ४ ॥

*Sâyaṇa* :—हेसूर्य त्वंतरणिःतरिताअन्येनगन्तुमशक्यस्यमहतोध्वनोगन्तासितथाचस्मर्यते—योजनानांसहस्रे द्वेद्वेशतेद्वे चयोजने । एकेननिमिषार्धेनक्रममाणनमोस्तुतइति । यद्वा उपासकानांरोगात्तारयितासि आरोग्यंभास्करादिच्छेदितिस्मरणात् । तथाविश्वदर्शतः विश्वैः-सर्वैःप्राणिभिर्दर्शनीयः आदित्यदर्शनस्यचाण्डालादिदर्शनजनितपापनिर्हरणहेतुत्वात् तथाचापस्तम्बः—दर्शने ज्योतिषांदर्शनमिति । यद्वा विश्वंसकलंभूवजातंदर्शतंद्रष्टव्यंप्रकाश्यंयेनसतथोक्तः तथाज्योतिष्कृत् ज्योतिषःप्रकाशस्यकर्तासर्वस्यवस्तुनःप्रकाशयितेत्यर्थः यद्वा चन्द्रादीनां-रात्रौप्रकाशयिता रात्रौहिअम्मयेषुचन्द्रादिबिंबेषुसूर्यकिरणाःप्रतिफलिताःसन्तोन्धकारंनिवारयन्ति यथा द्वारस्थदर्पणोपरिनिपातिताःसूर्यरश्मयोगृहान्तर्गतंतमोनिवारयन्तितद्वदित्यर्थः यस्मादेवंतस्मात् विश्वंव्याप्तं रोचनंरोचमानमन्तरिक्षमासमन्ताद्भासिप्रकाशयसि यद्वा हेसूर्यअन्तर्यामितयासर्वस्य प्रेरकपरमात्मन्तरणिःसंसाराब्धेस्तारकोसि यस्मात्त्वंविश्वदर्शतः विश्वैःसर्वैर्मुमुक्षुभिर्दर्शतो द्रष्टव्यः साक्षात्कर्तव्यइत्यर्थः अधिष्ठानसाक्षात्कारेह्यारोपितंनिवर्तते ॥ ज्योतिष्कृत् ज्योषतिः सूर्यादेःकर्ता तथाचाम्नायते—चन्द्रमामनसोजातश्चक्षोःसूर्योअजायतेति । ईदृशस्त्वं-चिद्रूपतयाविश्वंसर्वंदृश्यजातंरोचनंरोचमानंदीप्यमानंयथाभवतितथाआभासिप्रकाशयसि चैतन्यस्फुरणेहिसर्वंजगद्दृश्यते तथाचाम्नायते—तमेवभान्तमनुभातिसर्वंतस्यभासासर्वमिदंविभातीति । तरणिः तॄप्लवनतरणयोः अस्मादन्तर्भावितण्यर्थात् अर्तिसृधृधम्यश्यवितृभ्योनिरित्य-निप्रत्ययः प्रत्ययाद्युदात्तत्वम् । ज्योतिःकरोतीतिज्योतिष्कृत् क्विप्चेतिक्विप्नित्यंसमासेनुत्तरपदस्थस्येतिविसर्जनीयस्यषत्वम् । भासि भादीप्तौ अन्तर्भावितण्यर्थाल्लटिअदादित्वाच्छपोलुक् ॥ ४ ॥

*Word-meaning* :—(1) तरणिः Taraṇiḥ, swift, saviour, He who makes men to *cross* the Ocean of the world ; (2) विश्वदर्शतः Viśva-darśataḥ, seen by all, whose sight purifies all sins. Conspicous to all. Who is to be seen by all who desire salvation ; (3) ज्योतिष्कृतः Jyotiṣ-kṛit, The maker of the light ; (4) असि Asi, thou art ; (5) सूर्य Sûrya, O Sun, O Supreme-Self, O Impeller ; (6) विश्वं Viśvam, All, the all-pervading ; (7) रोचनं Rochanam, the sky, the radiant realm, bright space, the illumined heart ; (8) आभासि Âbhâsi, Thou illuminest.

*Grammatical Notes* :—(1). Taraṇiḥ from the √tri 'to cross.' The affix Ani अनि is added to it by Uṇâdi I. 259. It means a saviour, a ship, any thing that goes swiftly. The accent is on the first syllable of the affix Ani.

(2). Jyotiṣ-kṛit, formed by the affix kvip क्विप् ॥ The Visarga is changed to ष by VIII. 3. 45.

(3). Bhâsi, from the Adâdi √bhâ "to illumine."

*Translation* :—Swift and all beautiful art thou, O Sûrya, maker of the light, Illuming all the radiant realm. (Griffith).

O Supreme Self thou art the Saviour whom all must realise.

Thou art the giver of light (to all these luminaries like the Sun, Moon, etc.) Thou illuminest the hearts of all, (with Thy light of self-consciousness).

Rig Veda I. 50 5.

*Mantra.*—प्रत्यङ् देवानां विशः प्रत्यङ्ङुदेषि मानुषान् । प्रत्यङ्विश्वं स्वर्दृशे ॥ ५ ॥

*Pada-pâtha.*—प्रत्यङ् । देवानां । विशः । प्रत्यङ् । उत् । एषि । मानुषान् । प्रत्यङ् विश्वं । स्वः । दृशे ॥ ५ ॥

*Sâyana* :—हेसूर्य त्वं देवानांविशःमरुन्नामकान्देवान् मरुतोवैदेवानांविशइतिश्रुत्यन्तरात्[1] । तान्मरुत्संज्ञकान्देवान्प्रत्यङ्ङुदेषिप्रतिगच्छस्युदयंप्राप्नोषितेषामभिमुखंयथाभवतितथेत्यर्थः तथामानुषान्मनुष्यान्प्रत्यङ्ङुदेषितेपियथाअस्मदभिमुखएवसूर्यउदेतीतिमन्यन्तेतथाविश्वंव्याप्तं स्वःस्वर्लोकंदृशेद्रष्टुंप्रत्यङ्ङुदेषि यथास्वर्लोकवासिनोजनाः स्वस्वाभिमुख्येनपश्यन्तितथाउदेषीत्यर्थः एतदुक्तंभवति—लोकत्रयवर्तिनोजनाः सर्वेपिस्वस्वाभिमुख्येनसूर्यंपश्यन्तीतितथाचाम्नायतेतस्मात्सर्वएवमन्यतेमांप्रत्युदगादिति[2] । प्रत्यङ् प्रत्यञ्चतीतिप्रत्यङ् अञ्चुगतिपूजनयोः ऋत्विगित्यादिना क्विन् अनिदितामितिनलोपः उगिदचामितिनुम् हल्ङ्यादिसंयोगान्तलोपौ संयोगान्तलोपस्यासिद्धत्वात् उपधादीर्घनलोपयोरभावः क्विन्प्रत्ययस्यकुरितिकुत्वं अनिगन्तोञ्चतावप्रत्ययइति पर्युदासात्पूर्वपदप्रकृतिस्वराभावेकृदुत्तरपदप्रकृतिस्वरत्वम् । एषि इणगतौ सिपि अदादित्वाच्छपोलुक् आदेशप्रत्यययोरितिषत्वम् । स्वः सुपूर्वादर्तेर्विच् गुणेयणादेशः न्यङ्स्वरौस्वरितौचेतिस्वरितत्वम् । दृशेदृशिर्प्रेक्षणेइत्यस्मात्दृशेविख्येचेतितुमर्थेनिपातितः ॥ ५ ॥

*Word Meaning.*—प्रत्यङ् Pratyaṅ, In front of, going towards, देवान

[1] तै० सं० २. २. ५. ।   [2] तै० सं० ६. ५. ४. ।

Devânâm, Of gods. विशः Viṣaḥ, Hosts, clans, the devas called Maruts are the Viṣas of gods. प्रत्यङ् Pratyan̆, In front of. उत् एषि Ut-eṣi, Thou risest, thou goest. मानुषान् Mânuṣân, Men. प्रत्यङ् Pratyan̆, In front of. विश्वं Viśvam All स्वः Svaḥ, Heaven-world. दृशे Dṛiśe, To be seen.

*Garammaticrl Notes.*

(1). प्रत्यङ् Pratyan̆ from the √añchu 'to go' 'to worship,' with the affix kvin, Under Sûtra III. 2. 59. The न् is elided by VI. 4. 24. The augment नुम् is added by VII. 1. 70. The final consonants are elided by VI. 1. 68. and by VIII. 2. 23. Since this last rule VIII. 2. 23 is considered as non effective, consequently there is absence of the vowel-lengthening of the penultimate, and there is absence of the elision of न्. The च is changed to guttural by VIII. 2. 62. The accent is governed by VI. 2. 52.

(2) Eṣi, from the Adâdi √in 'to go' the स of सिप् is changed to ष by VIII. 3. 59.

(3) Svar, from the √ṛi ऋ 'to go,' preceded by the word see सु with the affix vich विच्. The accent is governed by the Phiṭ Sûtra 74 (See Siddhânta Kaumudi).

*Translation* :—Thou goest to the hosts of Gods, thou comest higher to mankind, Hither all light to be beheld. (Griffith).

Thou goest to the Shining Ones of the middle region (called the Viṣas of the Devas), thou goet to men (who dwell on earth). Thou goost to the dwellers of the heaven-world to be seen by all.

Mantra.

येना पावक चक्षसा भुरण्यन्तं जनाँ अनु। त्वं वरुण पश्यसि ॥ ६ ॥

.Rig Veda I. 50. 6.

*Pada-pâṭha* :—येन। पावक। चक्षसा। भुरण्यन्तं। जनान्। अनु। त्वं। वरुण पश्यसि ॥ ६ ॥

*Sâyana* :—हेपावक सर्वस्यशोधकवरुणअनिष्टनिवारकसूर्य त्वंजनान्जातान्प्राणिनः भुरण्यन्तंधारयन्तंपोषयन्तंवाइमंलोकंयेनचक्षसाप्रकाशेनानुपश्यसि अनुक्रमेणप्रकाशयसि तंप्रकाशंस्तुमइतिशेषः यद्वा उत्तरस्यामृचिसम्बन्धः तेनचक्षसाव्येषीति तथाचयास्केनोक्तं— तत्तेवयंस्तुमइतिवाक्यशेषोपिवोत्तरस्यामन्वयस्तेनव्येषीति[१] ॥ भुरण्यन्तं भुरणधारणपोषणयोः कण्ड्वादित्वाद्यक् ततःशतरिकर्तरिशप् अदुपदेशाल्लसार्वधातुकानुदात्तत्वेयकएवस्वरःशिष्यते । वरुण वृञ्वरणे अस्मादन्तर्भावितण्यर्थात् कृवृदारिभ्यउनन्निति उनन्प्रत्ययः अत्रवरुणशब्देन- आदित्यएवोच्यते तथाचान्यत्राम्नातम्—तस्यैवमित्रश्चवरुणश्चाजायेतामिति । मित्रश्चवरुणश्च- धाताचार्यमाचेति[२] ॥ ६ ॥

*Word Meaning* :—(1). येना Yenâ, with whom, by which. (2). पावक Pâvaka, O purifying one: O brilliant. (3). वरुण Varuṇa, Averter of evil, O Varuṇa. It is an appellation of Sûrya here. (4). त्वं Tvam, Thou. (5).

१ नि १२. २२. । २ तै० ब्रा० १. १. ४. ।

जनान् Janân, Men : living beings. (6). भुरण्यंतं Bhûranyantam, Upholding, Nourishing, (this world); the busy man. (7). येनाचक्षसा (Yenâ) chakṣasâ, By which light, by what eye. (8). अनुपश्यसि Anu paśyasi, Thou seest, or thou illumest in due order. The phrase " that light we praise" should be supplied here to complete the sentence. Or this stanza should be read with the next verse to complete its meaning. Then it would mean "by what light thou seest, by the same light thou pervadest or traversest' Or अनु may govern the janân in the accusative, and then the meaning be "amongst men (thou seest the busy man).

*Grammatical Notes.*

(1). Bhuraṇyentam is formed from the ✓ bhuraṇa "to support to nourish'. It belongs to the Kaṇḍvâdi class, and takes the affix yak यक It is present participle of that verb. The accent is governed by the affix yak (VI. 1. 186) makes the Sârvadhâtuka affix śatri &c. accentless, because it comes after a root which has an indicatory ष. Thus the accent of yak यक remains. (2). Varuna Derived from the ✓ vṛiñ 'to cover' to choose with the Uṇâdi affix Unan उनन् ॥ (Unâdi III. 53.)

*Translation* :—O (Sûrya) purifier of all and averter of evil, (we praise that light) with which thou illuminest all living beings and supportest this world.

Or,

With that same eye of thine wherewith thou lookest brilliant Varuṇa.
Upon the busy race of men. (Griffith).

Mantra :

वि द्यामेषि रजस्पृथ्वहा मिमानो अक्तुभिः । पश्यञ्जन्मानि सूर्य ॥ ७ ॥

Rig Veda I. 50 7.

*Pada-pâtha* :—वि । द्यां । एषि । रजः । पृथुः । अहा । मिमानः । अक्तुऽभिः । पश्यन् । जन्मानि । सूर्य ॥ ७ ॥

*Sâyana*:—हेसूर्य त्वंपृथुविस्तीर्णरजोलोकं लोकारजांस्युच्यन्तइतियास्कः । कंलोकंद्यामन्तरिक्षलोकंव्येषिविशेषेणगच्छसि किंकुर्वन्अहाअहानिअक्तुभीरात्रिभिःसहमिमानः उत्पादयन् आदित्यगत्यधीनत्वादहोरात्रविभागस्य तथाजन्मानिजननवन्तिभूतजातानिपश्यन्प्रकाशयन् ॥ रजस्पृथ्वित्यत्र छन्दसिवाप्राम्रेडितयोरितिविसर्जनीयस्यसत्वम् । अहाशेश्छन्दसिबहुलमितिशेर्लोपः । मिमानः माङ् माने जौहोत्यादिकः शानच्श्लौद्विर्भावेभृञामिदित्यभ्यासस्येत्वम् आभ्यस्तयोरातइत्याकारलोपः अभ्यस्तानामादिरित्यभ्यस्तस्याद्युदात्तत्वम् । जन्मानि जनीप्रादुर्भावे अन्येभ्योपिदृश्यन्तइतिमनिन् नित्त्वादाद्युदात्तत्वन् ॥ ७ ॥

*Word Meaning* :—(1). पृथु Pṛithu, Broad, wide, (2). रजः Rajas, World, mid-air, welkin, (3). द्यां Dyâm, Sky, intermediate region, (4) वि एषि Vi-eṣi, Thou goest through, thou traversest. Or वि "through" may govern dyâm sky, in the accusative, (5). अहा Ahâ, Days, (6). अक्तुभिः Aktubhiḥ, with the nights : with (thy) rays, (7). मिमानः Mimânaḥ, Measuring out, creating fashioning, (8). जन्मानि Janmâni, Lives, living creatures, generations, (9). पश्यन् Paśyan, Seeing, giving light, (10). सूर्य Sûrya, O Sun.

*Grammatical Notes* :—

1. Rajas-prithu. The visarga is changed into स् by VIII. 3. 49.

2. Ahâ, The affix शि is elided by VI. 1. 70.

3. Mimânaḥ. From the Juhotyâdi √ mâṅ 'to measure,' with the affixes śânach and ślu, with re-duplication, and the changing आ into इ by VII. 4. 76. The long आ is elided by VI. 1. 189.

4. Janmâni, From the √ jani 'to be born,' with the affix मनिन् Manin III. 2. 75. The accent is governed by the indicatory न VI. 1. 197.

***Translation*** **:—Traversing sky and wide mid-air' thou metest with thy beams our days,**
**Sun, seeing all things that have birth. (Griffith).**

Mantra :

सुप्त त्वां हरितो रथे वहन्ति देव सूर्य । शोचिष्केशं विचक्षण ॥८॥

Rig Veda I. 50 8.

*Pada-pâṭha* :—सप्त । त्वा । हरितः । रथे । वहंति । देव । सूर्य । शोचिःऽकेशं । विऽचक्षण ॥ ८ ॥

*Sâyana*:—हेसूर्यसर्वस्यद्योतमानविचक्षणसर्वस्यप्रकाशयितः सप्त सप्तसंख्याकाः हरितोश्वाः रसहरणशीलारश्मयोवात्वात्वांवहन्तिप्रापयन्ति कीदृशं रथे अवस्थितमितिशेषः तथाशोचिष्केशंशोचींषितेजांस्येवयस्मिन् केशाइवदृश्यन्तेसवथोक्तः तम्। हरितइत्यादित्याश्वानांसंज्ञा हरितआदित्यस्येतिनिघण्टावुक्तत्वात् ॥ शोचिष्केशं शुचदीप्तौ अर्चिशुचिहुसृपीत्यादिनाइसिप्रत्ययान्तोदात्तः सएवबहुव्रीहौपूर्वपदप्रकृतिस्वरत्वेनशिष्यते नित्यंसमासेनुत्तरपदस्थस्येतिविसर्जनीयस्यषत्वम् ॥ ८ ॥

*Word Meaning* :—(1). सूर्य Sûrya, O Sun, (2). देव Deva, O God, O shining One. (3). विचक्षण Vi-chakṣaṇa, O who sees through, O far-seeing, O who gives light to all. (4). सप्त Sapta, Seven. (5). हरितः Haritaḥ, Bay-coloured horses, rays. (6). त्वा Tvâ, Thee, (7). वहंति Vahanti, Draw, bear. (8). रथे Rathe, In the chariot, (9). शोचिष्केशं Śochiṣ-keśam, Flame-haired. Radiant haired.

*Grammatical Notes* :—1. Śochiṣ-keśam, From the √ śuch 'to shine' with the Uṇâdi affix इसि. (Siddhânta Uṇdâi 265.) The accent is on the final इ of śochis. This accent is retained even when compounded with the word 'keśa' as a Bahuvrihi. The visarga is changed into ष by VIII. 3. 45.

***Translation*** **:—Seven Bay Steeds harnessed to thy car bear thee, O thou far-seeing One,**
**God, Sûrya, with the radiant hair (Griffith).**

Mantra.

अयुक्त सप्तशुन्ध्युवः सूरो रथस्य नप्त्यः । ताभिर्याति स्वयुक्तिभिः ॥ ९ ॥

Rig. Veda I. 50. 9.

*Pada-pâṭha*.—अयुक्त । सप्त । शुन्ध्युवः । सूरः । रथस्य । नप्त्यः । ताभिः । याति । स्वयुक्तिऽभिः ॥९॥

*Sáyana*:— सूरः सर्वस्य प्रेरकः सूर्यः शुन्ध्युवः शोधिकाः अश्वस्त्रियः तादृशीः सप्तसप्तसंख्याकाः अयुक्त स्वरथे योजितवान् कीदृश्यः रथस्य नप्त्यः नपातयित्र्यः याभिर्युक्ताभिः रथो यातिन पतति वा तादृशीरित्यर्थः एवंभूताभिस्ताभिरश्वस्त्रीभिः स्वयुक्तिभिः स्वकीययोजनेन रथे सम्बद्धाभिर्याति यज्ञगृहं प्रत्यागच्छति अतस्तस्मै हविर्दातव्यमिति वाक्यशेषः ॥ अयुक्त युजिर् योगे स्वरितत्वात्कर्त्रभिप्राये आत्मनेपदम् लुङि च्लेः सिच् एकाच इतीट्प्रतिषेधः लिङ्सिचावात्मनेपदेष्विति सिचः कित्वाल्लघूपधगुणाभावः झलो झलीति सिचः सकारलोपः चोः कुरिति कुत्वम् । शुन्ध्युवः शुन्ध शुद्धौ यजिमनिशुन्धिदसिजनिभ्यो युरिति युप्रत्ययः शसि तन्वादीनां छन्दसि बहुलमुपसंख्यानमिति उवङादेशः । सूरः षू प्रेरणे सुसूधागृधिभ्यः क्रन्निति क्रन्प्रत्ययः नित्त्वादाद्युदात्तत्वम् । नप्त्यः नपातयतीत्यर्थे नप्तृनेष्टृ इत्यादिना उणादिषु नप्तृशब्दस्तृजन्तो निपातितः ऋन्नेभ्यो ङीबिति ङीप् यणादेशे उदात्तयणो हल्पूर्वादिति ङीप उदात्तत्वम् सुपां सुपो भवन्तीति शसो जसादेशः ततो यणादेशे उदात्तस्वरितयोर्यण इति स्वरितत्वम् रेफलोपश्छान्दसः उक्तं च द्वौ चापरौ वर्णविकारनाशाविति । शाखान्तरे तु नप्त्र्य इत्येव पठ्यते । स्वयुक्तिभिः स्वकीयाः सूर्यसम्बन्धिन्यः युक्तयो योजना नियासां बहुव्रीहौ पूर्वपदप्रकृतिस्वरत्वम् ॥ ९ ॥

*Word-meaning.*—1. सूरः, Sûrah, ° the impeller of all, the sun. 2. शुंध्युवः, Sundhyuvah, the pure, the neat, the wives of the horses, the mares. 3. सप्त, Sapta, the seven. 4. अयुक्त, Ayukta, has yoked. 5. रथस्य; Rathasya, of the chariot. 6. नप्त्यः Naptyaḥ, the daughters: the supporters of the chariot. which do not (न) allow the chariot to fall (पत्)
7. ताभिः, Tâbhiḥ, by them, by these mares. 8. स्वयुक्तिभिः, Sva-yuktibhiḥ, harnessed to his own (chariot). With his own dear team, self-yoked. 9. याति Yâti, He goes.

*Grammatical Notes.*—1. Ayukta, is the aorist of √yujir 'to yoke;' it is Âtmanepada and the affix is treated as having an indicatory ङ by I. 2. 11., and so there is no Guṇa of the penultimate short vowel. The स् of सिच् is elided by VIII. 2. 26. The च is changed to क by VIII. 2. 30. 2. Śundhyuvaḥ, is plural of the feminine noun Śundhyû. It is derived from the √śundha 'to be pure.' The Uṇâdi affix यु is added by III. 20. The augment Uvañ is added by VI. 4. 77. 3. Sûraḥ from the √षू su 'to impel' with the Uṇâdi affix Kran (II. 24.) The word has accent on the first syllable because the affix has an indicatory न (VI. 1. 197.) 4. Naptyaḥ; the word Naptṛi is formed by the affix Tṛich. Under Uṇâdi II. 96. The feminine affix ṅîp is added by IV. 1. 5. So we get Naptṛî. The affix Ṅîp is Udâtta when it is changed into य before the accusative plural Sas by VI. 1. 174. The affix Sas is replaced by jas by VII. 1. 39. The ई is changed to य which takes Svarit accent by VIII. 2. 4. Thus the accusative plural of the feminine Naptṛî is Naptryaḥ. But in the text here the R is elided as a Vedic anomaly. But in the Atharva Veda XIII. 2. 24., the reading is Naptryaḥ. 5. Sva-yuktibhiḥ, is a

Bahuvrîhi compound meaning "those mares whose harnesses (yukti) belonged to Him (the Sun)." It is accented on the first syllable because in a Bahuvrîhi compound, the first word retains its accent by VI. 2. 1.

*Translation.*—Sûrya hath yoked the pure bright Seven, the daughters of the car; with these, His own dear team, he goeth forth. (Griffith.)

Mantra.

उद्वयं तमसस्परि ज्योतिष्पश्यंत उत्तरं । देवं देवत्रा सूर्यमगन्म ज्योतिरुत्तमम् ॥ १० ॥

Rig Veda 1. 50. 10.

*Pada-pâtha*—उत् । वयं । तमसः । परि । ज्योतिः । पश्यन्तः । उत्ऽतरं । देवं । देवत्रा । सूर्यं । अगन्म । ज्योतिः । उत्ऽतमम् ॥ १० ॥

*Sâyana*:—वयमनुष्ठातारःतमसस्परितमसउपरिरात्रेरूर्ध्वंवर्तमानंतमसःपापात्परिउपरिवर्तमानंवापापरहितमित्यर्थःतथाचाम्नायते-उद्वयंतमसस्परीत्याह पाप्मावैतमः पाप्मानमेवास्मादपहन्तीति । ज्योतिस्तेजस्विनंउत्तरं उद्गततरंउत्कृष्टतरंवादेवत्रादेवेषुमध्येदेवंदानादिगुणयुक्तंसूर्यंपश्यन्तः स्तुतिभिर्हविर्भिश्चउपासीनाःसन्तःउत्तमंउत्कृष्टतमंज्योतिः सूर्यरूपं अगन्मप्राप्नुवाम तथाचश्रूयते--अगन्मज्योतिरुत्तममित्याह असौवाआदित्योज्योतिरुत्तममादित्यस्यैवसायुज्यंगच्छतीति । युक्तंचैतत् तं यथायथोपासतेतदेवभवन्तीतिश्रुत्यन्तरात् ॥ तमसस्परि पञ्चम्याःपरावध्यर्थेइतिविसर्जनीयस्य सत्वं । ज्योतिष्पश्यन्तःइसुसोःसामर्थ्येइतिविसर्जनीयस्यषत्वं व्यपेक्षालक्षणंसामर्थ्यंतत्राङ्गीक्रियते । देवत्रा देवमनुष्यपुरुषपुरुषमर्त्येभ्योद्वितीयासप्तम्योर्बहुलमितिसप्तम्यर्थेत्राप्रत्ययःप्रत्ययस्वरः । अगन्म छन्दसिलुङ् लङ् लिटइतिप्रार्थनायांलङ्बहुलंछन्दसीतिशपोलुक् म्वोश्चेतिधातोर्मकारस्यनकारः अडागमउदात्तः पादादित्वान्निघाताभावः । उत्तमंतमपःपित्त्वानुदात्तत्वेप्राप्तेउत्तमशश्वत्तमौसर्वत्रेत्युञ्छादिषुपाठात्अन्तोदात्तत्वम् ॥१०॥

*Word-meaning.*—1. वयं, Vayam, we, the sacrificers. 2. तमसः, Tamasas, of the darkness. 3. परि Pari, beyond, above. That is "beyond the darkness," or "after the night." Or "above the sin;" for the Sun is sinless and destroys the sins of His worshippers, as mentioned in Tait. Sam. V. 1. 8. 6. 4. ज्योतिः, Jyotir, Light, the illuminous. 5. उत्तरं, Uttaram, the loftier, the Superior. 6. देवत्रा, Devatrâ, among the Devas. 7. देवं, Devam, the God. 8. सूर्यं, Sûryam, the Sun. 9. पश्यंत, Paśyantaḥ, seeing, praising (with hymns and oblations). 10. उत्तमं, Uttamam, the highest, the most excellent. 11. ज्योतिः, Joytir, the light, the form of the Sun. 12. अगन्म, Aganma, we have obtained, we have come. 13. उत्, Ut, Out of, above.

*Grammatical Notes.*—1. Tamasas-pari, the Visarga is changed to स by VIII. 3. 51. 2. Jyotis-paśyantaḥ, the Visarga is changed to ष by VIII. 3. 44. 3. Devatrâ. The affix Trâ is added by V. 4. 56., in the sense of locative. The affix retains its accent. 4. Aganma, is the aorist of the √गम्, gam, by III. 4. 6. And the म is changed to न by VIII 2. 65. The augment अ is then added, and it has the Udâtta accent; and the verb Aganma does not become accentless, because it stands at the beginning of a Pâda.

5. Uttamam. It is formed with the Tamap, which having an indicatory प would have been accentless, but it being read in the Unchâdi class, it has accent of the final by VI. 1. 160.

*Translation.*—Looking upon the loftier light above the darkness, we have come To Sûrya, God among the Gods, the light that is most excellent. (Griffith).

Mantra.

उद्यन्नद्य मित्रमह आरोहन्नुत्तरां दिवं । हृद्रोगं मम सूर्य हरिमाणं च नाशय ॥ ११ ॥

Ṛig. Veda I. 50. 11.

*Pada-pâṭha.*—उत्ऽयन् । अद्य । मित्रऽमहः । आरोहन् । उत्ऽतरां । दिवं । हृत्ऽरोगं । मम । सूर्य । हरिमाणं । च । नाशय ॥ ११ ॥

*Sâyaṇa:*—हेसूर्यसर्वस्यप्रेरकमित्रमहः सर्वेषामनुकूलदीप्तियुक्त अद्यास्मिन्कालेउद्यन् उदयंगच्छन्उत्तरां उद्गततरांदिवमन्तरिक्षंआरोहन्आभिमुख्येनप्राप्नुवन् यद्वा दिवमन्तरिक्षं-उत्तरामारोहन्उत्कर्षेणप्राप्नुवन् एवंविधस्त्वंममहृद्रोगंहृदयगतंअन्तरंरोगंहरिमाणंशरीरगतकान्तिहरणशीलं बाह्यंरोगं यद्वाशरीरगतंहरिद्वर्णरोगप्राप्तंवैवर्ण्यमित्यर्थः तदुभयमपिनाशय मांस्तोतारंउभयविधाद्रोगान्मोचयेत्यर्थः ॥ मित्रमहः मित्रमनुकूलंमहस्तेजोयस्यासौ आमन्त्रितनिघातः। उत्तरां उदित्यनेनोपसर्गेणस्वसंसृष्टधात्वर्थोलक्ष्यतेतस्मादातिशायनिकस्तरप् प्रथमपक्षे अन्तरिक्ष-विशेषणत्वेनद्रव्यप्रकर्षप्रतीतेराम् न भवति द्वितीयेत्वारोहणक्रियायाःप्रकर्षोगम्यतइतिकिमेत्तक्व्ययघादाम्वद्रव्यप्रकर्षेइत्याम् प्रथमपक्षे शप्तरपोःपित्त्वादनुदात्तत्वेउपसर्गस्वरएवशिष्यते द्वितीयेतुआम्प्रत्ययस्यसतिशिष्टत्वात्तस्यैवस्वरेप्राप्ते व्यत्ययेनाद्युदात्तत्वम् वृषादिर्वाद्रष्टव्यः सह्याकृतिगणः। हृद्रोगम् वाशोकष्यञ्रोगेष्वितिहृदयशब्दस्यहृदादेशः। मम युष्मदस्मदोर्ङसीत्याद्युदात्तत्वं। हरिमाणं हृञ्हरणे जनिहृभ्यामिमनिन्नित्यौणादिकइमनिन्प्रत्ययः व्यत्ययेनान्तोदात्तत्वं यद्वा हरिच्छब्दस्यवर्णवाचित्वात् वर्णदृढादिभ्यःष्यञ्चेतिचकारादिमनिन्प्रत्ययः इष्ठेमेयः-स्वित्यनुवृत्तौटेरितिटिलोपः ॥११॥

*Word meaning.*—1. सूर्य, Sûrya, O Sun, O Impeller of all. 2. मित्रमहः, Mitra-mahas, O rich in friends, O endowed with light, which is friendly to all. 3. अद्य, Adya, to-day. 4. उद्यन्, Udayan, rising. 5. उत्तरां, Uttarâm, loftier. 6. दिवं, Divam, heaven, sky. 7. आरोहन्, Ârohan, ascending. 8. मम, Mama, my. 9. हृद्रोगं, Hṛid-rogam, heart's disease, mental disease. 10. हरिमाणं, Harimâṇam, yellowness, external or bodily disease, which makes the body look yellow. 11. नाशय, Nâśaya, destroy.

*Grammatical Notes.*—1. Mitra-mahas: means "he whose light (mahas) is friendly (Mitra):" being in the Vocative case, the word has no accent. 2. Uttarâm, it is either an adjective qualifying the noun Divam, "loftier heaven," or it is an adverb qualifying the verb Ârohan "Rising more high." In the first case, the affix Âm is not added, because it is used as an adjective, and so rule V. 4. 11. is prohibited. In the second case, Âm is added by that rule, because it is used as an adverb. In the first case, when it is taken as an adjective, then the accent is governed by the indicatory प of the affixes Ṭâp and Tarap, and so they are accentless. The Upasarga Ut, therefore, retains its accent : thus the word Uttarâ has accent on the first syllable and Uttarâm is accusative singular. In the second case, when it is taken as an adverb, the âm of Uttarâm is the affix Âmu of V. 4. 11., and the accent ought to have fallen on this Âm, and the word Uttarâm ought have been end-accute. It is however not so; as an anomaly. Or it is considered as a word belonging to the Vṛiṣâdi class of VI. 1. 203. 3. Hṛid-rogam, the word Hṛidaya is changed to Hṛid by VI. 3. 51. 4. Mama, has accent on the first syllable by VI. 1. 211. 5. Harimâṇam, from the √hṛiñ 'to steal.' It is formed by the Uṇâdi affix Imanin, under Sûtra IV. 148. It ought to have accent on the first syllable by VI. 1. 197., but it is not so, the accent is on the third syllable. Or it is formed from the word Harit, with the affix imanich under Sûtra V. 1. 123. The final syllable is elided by VI. 4. 155.

*Translation.*—Rising this day, O rich in friends, ascending to the loftier heaven, Sûrya, remove my heart's disease, take from me this my yellow hue. (Griffith).

Mantra.

शुकेषु मे हरिमाणं रोपणाकासु दध्मसि ।
अथोहारिद्रवेषुमे हरिमाणं नि दध्मसि ॥१२॥

Ṛig. Veda I. 50. 12.

*Pada-pâṭha.*—शुकेषु । मे । हरिमाणं । रोपणाकासु । दध्मसि ।
अथो । इति । हारिद्रवेषु । मे । हरिमाणं । नि। दध्मसि ॥ १२ ॥

*Sâyaṇa:*—मेमदीयंहरिमाणं शरीरगतंहरिद्वर्णस्यभावंकेषुताद्दशंवर्णकामयमानेषुपच्चिषु-तथारोपणाकासुशारिकासुपच्चिविशेषेपुदध्मसिस्थापयामः अथोअपिचहारिद्रवेषुहरितालद्रुमेषु-ताद्दग्वर्णवत्सुमेमदीयंहरिमाणंनिदध्मसिनिदधीमहि सचहरिमातत्रैवसुखेनास्तांअस्मान्माबा-धिष्टेत्यर्थः ॥ दध्मसिइदन्तौमसिरितिमसइकारागमः ॥ १२ ॥

*Word meaning.*—1. मे, Me, my. 2. हरिमाणं, Harimâṇam, yellowness. 3. शुकेषु, Śukeṣu, in the parrots. 4. रोपणाकासु, Ropaṇâkasu, in the bird called ropanaka or śârikâ, in the starlings. 5. दध्मसि, Dadhmasi, let us place, let us give. 6. अथो, Atho, also. 7. हारिद्रवेषु, Hâridraveṣu, in the trees called harital, in yellow birds. 8. नि-दध्मसि, Ni-dadhmasi, let us place, let us transfer.

*Grammatical Notes.*—1. Dadhmasi, first person plural. The classical form would be Dadhîmahi. The इ is added to the affix मस by VII. 1. 46.

*Translation.*—To parrots and to starlings let us give away my yellowness, Or this yellowness let us transfer to Haritala trees.

Mantra.

उदगादय मादित्यो विश्वेन सहसा सह । द्विषंतं मह्यं रन्धयन्मो
अहं द्विषते रधम् ॥ १३ ॥

Rig Veda I. 50. 13.

*Pada-pâṭha.*—उत् । अगात् । अयं । आदित्यः । विश्वेन । सहसा । सह ।
द्विषंतं । मह्यं । रन्धयन् । मोइति अहं । द्विषते । रधं ॥ १३ ॥

*Sâyaṇa:*—अयंपुरोवर्तीआदित्यःअदितेःपुत्रःसूर्यःविश्वेनसहसासर्वेणबलेनसहउदगात्-
उदयंप्राप्तवान् किंकुर्वन्मह्यद्विषन्तंह्यंन्धयन्ममोपद्रवकारिणंरोगहिंसन् अपिचअहंद्विषतेअ-
निष्टकारिणेरोगायमोरधंमैवहिंसांकरोमि सूर्य एवअस्मदनिष्टकारिणंरोगंविनाशयत्वित्यर्थः ॥
आगात्एतेर्लुङिइणोगालुङीतिगादेशःगातिस्थेतिसिचोलुक् । आदित्यः दित्यदित्यादित्येत्यापत्या-
र्थेप्राग्दीव्यतीयोण्यप्रत्ययः । रन्धयरन्धहिंसासंराध्योः ण्यन्तालटःशतृ रधिजभोरचीतिणौ-
धातोर्नुमागमः । मो मा उ निपातद्वयसमुदायोमैवेत्यस्यार्थे ओदितिप्रगृह्यत्वेप्लुतप्रगृह्याअचीति-
प्रकृतिभावः । द्विषते शतुरनुमइव विभक्तेरुदात्तत्वम् । रधम् रधेर्लुङ्क्पुषादित्वात् च्लेरङादेशः-
रधिजभोरचीतिधातोर्नुम् अनिदितामित्यनुषङ्गलोपः नमाङ्योगे इत्यडभागोव: ॥ १३ ॥

*Word meaning.*—1. अयं, Ayam, this, in front of us. 2. आदित्यः, Âdityaḥ, Sûrya, the son of Aditi. 3. विश्वेन, Viśvena, with all. 4. सहसा Sahasâ, with power. 5. सह, Saha, with. 6. उत्अगात्, Ud-agât, has arisen. 7. मह्यं, Mahyam, my. 8. द्विषंतं, Dviṣantam, enemy, the hater. 9. रंधयन्, Randhayan, obstructing, injuring, warding of. 10. मो, Mo, it is a compound particle made up of मा + उ meaning "Not at all." 11. अहं, Aham, I. 12. द्विषते, Dviṣate, towards the hater, towards my enemy. 13. रधं Radham, I injure.

*Grammatical Notes.*—1. Agât, is from the √in 'to go' of the Adâdi class. In the aorist gâ is substituted for √इ by II. 4. 45. The Sich is elided by II. 4. 77. 2. Adityaḥ, is formed by the affix Nya added to the word Aditi under VI. 1. 85.3. Randhayan, from the √रध, radh 'to injure.' The form is of the Causative present participle. The augment num is added by VII. 1. 61. 4. Mo, is a compound of माउ : The O of Mo is not changed by Sandhi before Aham, because it is treated as a pragṛihya by I. 1. 15. read with VI. 1. 125. 5. Dviṣate, the accent is on the case-affix by VI. 1. 173, in the present participle. 6. Radham, is the first person singular aorist of radh. The न is added to the root by VII. 1. 61., but it is again elided by VI. 4. 24. The augment अ of the aorist is not added after the negative particle Mâ by VI. 4. 74.

**Translation :—With all his conquering vigour this Âditya hath gone up on high Giving my foe into mine hand ; let me not be my foeman's prey. (Griffith,)**

**Or**

**This son of Infinity has arisen with all his might, destroying all who bear hatred towards me : but let me not injure those who hate me.**

NOTE.—The second translation is according to Sâyana, who holds that the Sun is asked to destroy all those diseases which injure a man. The verse, however, plainly means to affirm :—" O God judge Thou my enemies, let me not judge them." It leaves the punishment of one's enemies to God. These last three verses are meant as a special prayer to God to cure all illness.

Mantra.

गौरीर्मिमाय सलिलानि तक्षत्येकपदी द्विपदी सा चतुष्पदी ।
अष्टापदी नवपदी बभूवुषी सहस्राक्षरा परमे व्योमन् ॥ ४१ ॥

Rig Veda I. 164. 41.

*Pada-pâṭha*—गौरीः । मिमाय । सलिलानि । तक्षती । एकऽपदी । द्विऽपदी । सा । चतुःऽपदी । अष्टाऽपदी । नवऽपदी । बभूवुषी । सहस्रऽअक्षरा । परमे । विऽओमन् ॥ ४१ ॥

*Sâyana* :—गौरीः गरणशीलामाध्यमिकावाक् सुलोपाभावश्छान्दसः मिमायशब्दयति किंकुर्वती सलिलानि वृष्ट्युदकानि तक्षती संपादयित्री एकपदीएकपादोपेता एकाधिष्ठानामेघे-वर्तमाना गमनसाधनेनवायुना एकपदीवा द्विपदी मेघान्तरिक्षाख्ये द्वयधिष्ठाना आदित्योवा द्वितीयः तथा सा चतुष्पदी पादचतुष्टयोपेता दिक्चतुष्टयाधिष्ठाना अथाष्टापदी अवान्तरदिग-पेक्षयाष्टपादोपेता अष्टाधिष्ठाना नवपदी उपरिदिगपेक्षयासूर्येणवा नवदिगधिष्ठानाबभूवुषी एवं-भूता भवतेश्छान्दसःक्वसुः वलोकोपिवसोःसंप्रसारणं किमनयापरिगणनया सहस्राक्षरा अपरि-मितवचनोयं अपरिमितव्याप्तियुक्ता बहुव्यापनशीलोदकवतीत्यर्थः कुत्रेतितदुच्यते—परमे-व्योमन् उदकाश्रयत्वोत्कृष्टेन्तरिक्षे केचिदेवमाहुः गौरीः गरणशीलाशब्दब्रह्मात्मिकावाक् मिमाय मिमतिःप्रतिष्ठार्थे धातुः प्रतिष्ठितानि घटादिद्रव्याणि तक्षती तत्तद्वाचकत्वेननिष्पादयन्ती एकपदी अव्याकृतत्वेनैकप्रतिष्ठाना एकरूपावा प्रणवात्मनाद्विपदी सुप्तिङ्भेदेन पादद्वयवती चतुष्पदी नामाख्यातोपसर्गनिपातभेदेन । अष्टापदी आमन्त्रितसहिताष्टविभक्तिभेदेनाष्टापदी नवपदी बभूवुषी साव्ययैरुक्तै रष्टभिर्नवपदी अथवा सनाभिकेयूरःकण्ठादीषुनवसुपदेषुभवन्ती पश्चाद्बहुविधाभिव्यक्तिमुपेयुषी परमेव्योमन् उत्कृष्टहृदयाकाशेमूलाधारेवासहस्राक्षरा अनेका-कारेण व्याप्ता अनेकध्वनिप्रकाराभवतीत्यर्थः । अयंमन्त्रः आचार्येणैवं व्याख्यातः—गौरी र्मिमायसलिलानितक्षतीकुर्वत्येकपदीमध्यमेनद्विपदीमध्यमेनचादित्येनचचतुष्पदीदिग्भिरष्टापदी दिग्भिश्चावान्तरदिग्भिश्चनवपदीदिग्भिश्चावान्तरदिग्भिश्चादित्येनसहस्राक्षराबहूदकाप-रक्षेव्यवनेइति ॥४१॥

*Word-meaning*—1. गौरीः, Gaurîḥ, (The white, the Mâdhyamikâ vâk). The buffalo, the voice of heaven or thunder is called Vâk and is represented as a buffalo. 2. मिमाय, Mimâya, Lowed, has made noise. 3. सलिलानि, salilâni, waters, rain waters. 4. तक्षती, Takṣati, the accomplisher of all, the fashioner. 5. एकपदी, Eka-padî, one-footed, as sounding from the cloud and moved by the wind : thus having only *one* foot, as it were.

6. द्विपदि, Dvi-padî, two-footed, that is from cloud and sky, or from cloud and sun. 7. सा, Sâ, she, the vâk 8. चतुष्पदि, Chatuṣ-padî, four-footed, *viz.* from the four cardinal points. 9. अष्टापदि, Aṣṭâpadî, eight-footed, from the four cardinal points and the four intermediate points. 10. नवपदि, Nava-padî, nine-footed, the above-mentioned eight points and Zenith, the ninth point. 11. बभूवुषी, Babhûvuṣî, became. 12. सहस्रा-क्षरा, Sahasra-âkṣarâ, thousand-syllabled. 13. परमे, Parame, in the sublimest, highest. 14. व्योमन्, Vyoman, Heaven.

Sâyaṇa gives an alternative explanation of this verse. The speech or vâk is eka-padî when it merely denotes substances like pots, &c., or words in general. The speech becomes two-footed, when these words are divided into substantives and verbs. It becomes four-footed when it is divided into nouns (nâma), verbs (âkhyâta) prepositions (upasarga), and particles (nipâta). It is eight-footed having regard to the eight cases or vibhaktis including the vocative case. It is nine-footed, when to the same eight cases is added the caseless noun called the Avyaya or indeclinable. Or, the various feet of Vâk represent the nine organs of pronunciation such as chest, throat, palate, teeth, lips etc.

It becomes thousand-fold in the highest heaven *viz.*, in the ether of the heart which is the root basis of all speech, and of diverse sounds.

The first explanation has the approval of Yâska (Nirukta XI. 40).

*Grammatical Notes.*—1. Gaurîḥ, means Garaṇa-śîlâ. The case-affix is not elided as a vedic irregularity. 2. Babhûvuṣî, is formed by the affix kvasu, added to the √bhu. To this is added the feminine affix ṅîp, and then there is the vocalisation of the V व into U उ ॥

**Translation.**—Forming the water-floods, the buffalo hath lowed, one-footed or two-footed or four-footed, she, Who hath become eight-footed or hath got nine feet, the thousand-syllabled in the sublimest heaven. (Griffith).

### COMMENTARY ON EVENING SANDHYÂ.

*Sûryopasthânam.*

Page 73.

Ṛig Veda VII. 89. 1.

Mantra.

मोषु वरुण मृन्मयं गृहं राजन्नहं गमम् । मृळा सुक्षत्र मृळय ॥१॥

*Sâyaṇa* :—हे राजन्नीश्वर वरुण त्वदीयं मृन्मयं मृदादिभिर्निर्मितं गृहं मो मा च नैव अहं गमं गतोऽस्मि । अपि तु सुशोभनं सुवर्णमयमेव त्वदीयं गृहं प्राप्नुयानि। स त्वं मां मृळ सुखय हे सुक्षत्र शोभनधन वरुण मृळय उपदयां च कुरु ॥

*Word meaning.*—1. राजन्, Râjan, O King, O God. 2. वरुण, Varuṇa, O Varuṇa. 3. मृन्मयम्, Mṛiṇmayam, earthly, made of earth. 4. गृहम्, Gṛiham, house, "The earthy house"—the grave. 5. मो, Mo, never, it is compound of मा + उ. 6. अहम्, Aham, I. 7. गमम्, Gamam, may go. 8. सु, Su, Good.

9. मृळ, Mṛiḷa, have mercy. 10. सुक्षत्र, Su-kṣatra, possessing beautiful riches, O powerful one. 11. मृळय, Mṛiḷaya, Have mercy.

*Translation.*—Let me not, O King Varuṇa, go down to the earthy house: have mercy, O Lord, have mercy. (Peterson.)

*Note.*—Mṛiṇmayam-gṛiham, 'the grave.' The dead body was either consigned to the flames or laid away to gentle rest in the mother Cf. R. V. X. 18 10 12 and 13 "May he not become a dweller in the house of earth" is uttered over a sick person (A. V. 5, 30, 14.)

Mantra.

यदेमि प्रस्फुरन्निव दृतिर्न ध्मातो अद्रिवः । मृळा सुक्षत्र मृळय ॥२॥

Ṛig Veda VII. 89. 2.

*Sâyana*:—हे अद्रिवः आयुधवन्वरुण यद्यदा प्रस्फुरन्निव शैत्येन प्रविचलन्निव त्वद्भयाद्वेपमानो दृतिर्नदृतिरिव ध्मातो वायुना पूर्णः सन् त्वया बद्धो ऽहं एमि गच्छामि तदानीं मृळ सुखय हे सुक्षत्र सुधन मृळय उपदयां कुरु ॥

*Word meaning.*—1. अद्रिवः, Adri-vaḥ, O Wielder of thunder-bolt: O Caster of the Stone. 2. यत्, Yat, when, for. 3. प्रस्फुरन्, Prasphuran, tottering, tremulous through cold, trembling on account of fear of Thee. 4. इव, Iva, like. 5. दृतिः, Dṛitiḥ, bellow, skin. 6. न, Na, like. 7. ध्मातः, Dhmâtaḥ, blown up. Filled with air (and bound by Thee). 8. एमि, Emi, I go.

*Translation.*—For I go tottering, O Thunderer, like a blown-up skin: have mercy, O Lord have mercy. (Peterson.)

Mantra.

क्रत्वः समह दीनता प्रतीपं जगमा शुचे । मृळा सुक्षत्र मृळय ॥३॥

Ṛig Veda VII. 89. 3.

*Sâyana*:—हे समह सधन शुचे स्वभावतो निर्मल वरुण दीनता दीनतया अशक्ततयाक्रत्वः कर्मणः कर्त्तव्यत्वेन विहितस्य श्रौतस्मार्तादिलक्षणस्य प्रतीपं प्रतिकूलं अननुष्ठानं जगम प्राप्तवानस्मि अतएव त्वया बद्धः तादृशं मां मृळ सुखय अन्यद्गतम् ॥

*Word meaning.*—समह, Samaha, O Rich, O Powerful; शुचे, Śuche, O Pure, O Bright Varuṇa; दीनता, Dînata, through poverty (of power), through weakness; क्रत्वः, Kratvaḥ, of duty, of strength; प्रतीपम्, Pratîpam, improper, wrong, astray; जगम, Jagama, I went.

*Translation.*—O Rich and Pure Varuṇa, (whenever) I have gone wrong through weakness (of power to fulfil) my duty, (forgive all that and) have mercy, O Powerful One, have mercy.

Or. My strength was very weakness, and I went wrong, O pure God: have mercy O Lord, have mercy. (Peterson.)

Mantra.

अपां मध्ये तस्थिवांसं तृष्णाविदज्जरितारम् । मृळा सुक्षत्र मृळय ॥ ४ ॥

Rig Veda VII. 89. 4.

*Sayana*:—अपां समुद्राणा मुदकानां मध्ये तस्थिवांसं स्थितवतमपि जरितारं तव स्तोतारं मां तृष्णा पिपासा अविदत् प्राप्तवती। लवणोत्कटस्य समुद्रजलस्य पानानर्हत्वात। अतस्तादृशं मां मृल सुखय ॥

*Word meaning.*—अपाम्, Apâm, of waters; मध्ये, Madhye, in the midst of; तस्थिवांसम्, Tasthi-vâṁsam, staying, stood; तृष्णा, Triṣṇâ, thirst; अविदत्, Avidat, found; जरितारम्, Jaritâram, worshipper.

*Translation.*—Thirst found thy worshipper, as he stood in the midst of waters; have mercy, O Lord have Mercy. (Paterson).

*Note.*—Thirst: avarice. In the midst of water-floods: when surrounded by abundant wealth. According to the Commentator, the allusion is to Vasiṣtha's sea-voyage; or perhaps the perpetual thirst of dropsy may be intended.—Griffith.)

Mantra.

यत्किं चेदं वरुण दैव्ये जनेऽभिद्रोहं मनुष्यां श्चरामसि ।
अचित्ती यत्तव धर्मा युयोपिम मा नस्तस्मा देनसो देव रीरिषः ॥ ५ ॥

Rig Veda VII 89 5.

*Sâyana*:—देवसुवां हविःषु वारुणस्य हविषः यत्किं चेदमिति याज्या। सूत्रितंच। यत्किंचेदं वरुण दैव्ये जन उपते स्तोमान्पशुपा इवाकरमिति द्वे इति ॥

हे वरुण दैव्ये देवसमूहरूपे जने यदिदं किंचन अभिद्रोहं अपकारजातं मनुष्या वयं चरामसि चरामः निर्वर्तयामः तथा अचित्ती अचित्त्या अज्ञानेन तव त्वदीयं यद्धर्म धारकं कर्म युयोपिम वयं विमोहितवन्तः हे देव तस्मादेनसः पापात् नोऽस्मान् मा रीरिषः मा हिंसीः ॥

*Word meaning*—वरुण, Varuṇa, O Varuṇa; दैव्ये, Daivye, regarding the (hosts of) devas; जने, Jane, regarding the people; यत्, Yat, what; इदम्, Idam, this; किं, Kim, what; च, Cha, and; अभिद्रोहम्, Abhi-droham, offence, evil; मनुष्याः, Manuṣyâḥ, men; चरामसि, Charâmasi, we commit; अचित्ती, Achitti, through thoughtlessness, यत्, Yat, what; तव, Tava, thy; धर्म, Dharma, law, command; युयोपिम, Yuyopima, violate; मा, Mâ, not; नः, Naḥ, us; तस्मात्, Tasmât, for that; एनसः, Enasaḥ, sin. देवः, Deva, O God. रीरिषः Ririṣaḥ, Punish.

*Translation.*—Whatever be the evil, O Varuna, we men do against the folk of the gods, however in thoughtlessness we transgress Thy laws—do not, O God, punish us for that sin.—(Peterson).

The end